Jerusalem Crucified, Jerusalem Risen

Jerusalem Crucified, Jerusalem Risen

The Resurrected Messiah,
the Jewish People, and the Land of Promise

Mark S. Kinzer

JERUSALEM CRUCIFIED, JERUSALEM RISEN
The Resurrected Messiah, the Jewish People, and the Land of Promise

Cascade Books
An Imprint of Wipf and Stock Publishers
199 W. 8th Ave., Suite 3
Eugene, OR 97401

www.wipfandstock.com

PAPERBACK ISBN: 978-1-5326-5337-7
HARDCOVER ISBN: 978-1-5326-5338-4
EBOOK ISBN: 978-1-5326-5339-1

Cataloguing-in-Publication data:

Names: Kinzer, Mark S., author.

Title: Jerusalem crucified, Jerusalem risen : the resurrected Messiah, the Jewish people, and the land of promise / Mark S. Kinzer.

Description: Eugene, OR : Cascade Books, 2018 | Includes bibliographical references and index.

Identifiers: ISBN 978-1-5326-5337-7 (paperback) | ISBN 978-1-5326-5338-4 (hardcover) | ISBN 978-1-5326-5339-1 (ebook)

Subjects: LCSH: Bible. Luke—Criticism, interpretation, etc. | Bible. Acts—Criticism, interpretation, etc. | Israel (Christian theology)—Biblical teaching. | Jerusalem. | Eschatology. | Jews—Restoration. | Temple of Jerusalem (Jerusalem)—In the Bible. | Messianic Judaism. | Zionism.

Classification: BR158 K56 2018 (print) | BR158 (ebook)

Manufactured in the U.S.A.

The author and publisher gratefully acknowledge permission to include in chapters 1 and 3 paragraphs drawn from Mark S. Kinzer's "Zionism in Luke-Acts: Do the People of Israel and the Land of Israel Persist as Abiding Concerns in Luke's Two Volumes?" which appeared in The New Christian Zionism: Fresh Perspectives on Israel & the Land, edited by Gerald R. McDermott (InterVarsity Press, P.O. Box 1400, Downers Grove, IL 60515, USA. www.ivpress.com).

For Roslyn

My beloved partner, friend, and fellow-lover of Jerusalem

Table of Contents

Acknowledgements

The writing of this book was a painfully difficult task. I began the project in 2011, and am making these overdue acknowledgements seven long years later. While the essential thesis has remained unchanged throughout, I have wrestled over those years with the best way to convey my message and demonstrate its force. At each step along the way I have learned new things, and, I hope, the text has matured along with its author.

I am grateful to Markus Bockmuehl, Gerald McDermott, Isaac Oliver, Ray Pickett, David Rudolph, Kendall Soulen, Fr. Justin Taylor, and Joel Willitts, who all read an early draft of this work, and offered wise counsel directed to its improvement. Their advice helped me greatly—though I assume that each will find much that still could be stated better.

I am also grateful to Gavin D'Costa who read a later draft, and provided much needed guidance and encouragement.

I am most thankful to my editor, Robin Parry, and all the dedicated staff at Wipf and Stock. Publishing for them is a calling and a mission, and not merely a business. They are trusted colleagues, and also faithful friends.

I am most indebted to my wife Roslyn, and her mother Helen, who bring me back to earth each day. Because of them (along with Rivka, our Boston Terrier) there is no place I would rather be than my own home . . . except, of course, Jerusalem. To Roz, the love of my life, I dedicate this book.

Introduction: Jesus, Israel, and the Prophetic *Euangelion*

A De-Judaized *Euangelion*

> Now I would remind you . . . of the good news [*euangelion*] that I proclaimed to you . . . that Christ died for our sins in accordance with the scriptures, and that he was buried, and that he was raised on the third day in accordance with the scriptures, and that he appeared to Cephas [i.e., Peter], then to the twelve. (1 Cor 15:1, 3–5)

> . . . the gospel [*euangelion*] of God, which he promised beforehand through his prophets in the holy scriptures, the gospel concerning his Son, who was descended from David according to the flesh and was declared to be Son of God with power according to the spirit of holiness by resurrection from the dead, Jesus Christ our Lord . . . . (Rom 1:1–4)

The *euangelion* ("good news" or "gospel") which Paul and his fellow apostles proclaimed transformed the ancient world. It reshaped the personal lives of individuals as well as the corporate life of the societies in which they resided. While some found its message neither believable nor salutary, those who embraced the *euangelion* celebrated it as "the power of God for salvation" (Rom 1:16).

The message itself spoke of a particular Jewish man, who was heralded as the "Christ"—the royal Messiah "descended from David" whom the Jewish people had long awaited. The message had been "promised beforehand . . . in the holy scriptures"—the sacred writings composed, preserved, and studied by generations of Jews. All of the apostolic witnesses to his resurrection were Jews, as were the first recipients of their message, and the movement they launched had its worldwide center in Jerusalem, the capital city of the Jewish people.

Nevertheless, within a century the community born from this *euangelion* was largely gentile in composition. More significantly, the way these gentiles interpreted the apostolic message resembled nothing that a Jew would call "good news." They rejoiced at the destruction of the city of Jerusalem, and understood that event as the definitive termination of the Jewish people's priestly role among the nations. Some expected an eschatological restoration of Jerusalem, while others rejected such a crass material hope, but few of these gentile heirs of the *euangelion* thought that Jews would have any distinctive identity or positive function in the age to come. When individual Jews somehow managed to overcome these impediments and sought baptism, they were discouraged or forbidden from observing Jewish practices or participating in Jewish communal life. If a multitude of Jews had taken that course, the Jewish people would have been decimated as a historical community. The "good news" as now proclaimed by the *ekklēsia* could hardly be recognized as "the power of God for salvation" for the Jewish people, or as in any sense "good" from a Jewish perspective.

Few twenty-first century Christians would condone the virulent anti-Jewish rhetoric of that contentious ecclesial era. Most respect their Jewish neighbors and the Jewish tradition. Taking seriously the Pauline assertion that "the gifts and the calling of God are irrevocable" (Rom 11:29), many Christians today even believe that the Jews remain special to God. But this belief in the enduring character of God's choice of the Jewish people has no discernible connection to the "gospel" these Christians affirm and proclaim, which in its Jewish implications differs little from that announced in the second century. The death and resurrection of Jesus still have no positive bearing on the historical life or eschatological destiny of Jews as a priestly nation. These redemptive events may no longer be "bad" news for the Jewish people, but they are hardly "news" at all.

A Jewish and Prophetic *Euangelion*

In the present volume, I argue that it was not always so, and that it should no longer be so. I propose an interpretation of the *euangelion* in which the death and resurrection of Jesus are inseparable from the historical journey and eschatological destiny of the Jewish people. The message received from the apostles is thus inherently *prophetic* in character, pointing to an accomplished redemptive act by Israel's Messiah but also to that act's future outworking in the life of the Messiah's Israel. Moreover, the Messiah and his people "according to the flesh" retain a special bond with the land of Israel and the city of Jerusalem, and the death and resurrection of the Messiah are as inseparably tied to the destiny of that place as they are to the life of that people.

The first steps in such an argument have been taken in the seminal writings of N. T. Wright. With compelling force Wright rejects the notion that the *euangelion* is "an abstract and timeless system of theology" that addresses individual souls and promises them the reward of a beatific afterlife in heaven.[1] For Wright, the "good news" always has the restoration of Israel in view. In his study of the Synoptic Gospels Wright examines the "good news of the kingdom of God" (Mark 1:14–15; Luke 16:16), and identifies Isaiah 52 as "thematic for the whole work of Jesus."[2] These are the verses he has in mind:

> 7 How beautiful upon the mountains
> are the feet of the messenger who announces peace,
> who brings good news,
> who announces salvation,
> who says to Zion, "Your God reigns."
> 8 Listen! Your sentinels lift up their voices,
> together they sing for joy;
> for in plain sight they see
> the return of the Lord to Zion.
> 9 Break forth together into singing,
> you ruins of Jerusalem;
> for the LORD has comforted his people,
> he has redeemed Jerusalem.
> 10 The LORD has bared his holy arm
> before the eyes of all the nations
> and all the ends of the earth shall see
> the salvation of our God.

Wright suggests that Jesus read these verses concerning the "good news" of Israel's return from exile in light of the chapter that follows

1. Wright, *Jesus and the Victory of God*, 603–4; Wright, *Surprised by Hope*.
2. Wright, *Jesus and the Victory of God*, 601–2.

(Isaiah 53) which describes the suffering servant: "[I]f, then, we ask how the message of Isaiah 52.7–12 was to be put into effect, the prophecy as Jesus must have read it had a clear answer. The arm of YHWH . . . was revealed, according to Isaiah 53.1, in and through the work of the servant of YHWH."[3] While Wright's reconstruction of the reading strategy of the historical Jesus may be open to debate, it is clear that the authors of the Synoptic Gospels read Isaiah 52–53 in this manner. According to Mark, Matthew, and Luke, the *euangelion* deals with the restoration of Israel, and it is put into effect through the suffering and death of the "servant of the LORD."

Wright's exposition of the Pauline letters reaches the same conclusion. He first highlights the role of Jesus as Israel's Messiah, who embodies the entire nation in his own person. Commenting on Romans 1:1–4, Wright notes that "[w]hen Paul says 'the gospel,' then, he does not mean 'justification by faith,' though of course justification is the immediate result of the gospel. The 'good news' Paul has in mind is the proclamation of Jesus, the Davidic Messiah of Israel, as the risen lord of the world."[4] Wright offers a similar reflection on the use of *Christos* in 1 Corinthians 15:3: "It is important, first, that Jesus is designated in this formula as 'Messiah,' *Christos*. Precisely because this is such an early formulation there is no chance that this word could have been a proper name without connotation, and every reason to suppose that the early Christians intended it to have its royal designation."[5]

Wright proceeds to explain the phrase "in accordance with the scriptures," which Paul attaches to each of the *euangelion*'s core assertions—that Jesus died for sins, and rose from the dead on the third day (1 Cor 15:3–4). Wright argues that this phrase refers not to "one or two, or even half a dozen, isolated passages" employed artificially as "proof-texts." Instead, Paul "is referring to the entire biblical narrative as the story that has reached its climax in the Messiah, and has now given rise to the new phase of the same story, the phase in which the age to come has broken in, with its central characteristic being (seen from one point of view) rescue from sins, and (from another point of view) rescue from death, i.e., resurrection."[6] The story in view deals with Israel's national restoration, which could be described equally well as "rescue from sin"

3. Wright, *Jesus and the Victory of God*, 601–2.
4. Wright, *The Resurrection of the Son of God*, 242.
5. Wright, *The Resurrection of the Son of God*, 319.
6. Wright, *The Resurrection of the Son of God*, 320.

(i.e., "the Messiah died for our sins") or "rescue from death" (i.e., "the Messiah was raised on the third day"). Jesus achieves that rescue as Israel's royal Messiah, who sums up his people in himself.

At the same time, Wright acknowledges that a few biblical texts stand out as particularly relevant to the formulation of the *euangelion* in 1 Corinthians 15. In relation to the death of Jesus, he singles out Isaiah 40–55.[7] In relation to the resurrection of Jesus, he points to Ezekiel 37 (the revival of Israel's exilic dry bones) and Hosea 6:1–2. The latter text reads:

> Come, let us return to the LORD;
> for it is he who has torn, and he will heal us;
> he has struck down, and he will bind us up.
> After two days he will revive us;
> on the third day he will raise us up,
> that we may live before him.[8]

What all of these texts have in common is their primary reference to Israel as a people. While the so-called servant songs of Isaiah 40–55 combine reference to an individual and corporate expression of "Israel," Ezekiel 37 and Hosea 6 speak only about the resurrection of the *nation*. According to Wright, the *euangelion* applies these national texts to Jesus because he is the royal Messiah, who sums up the life of the people in himself. "[T]he earliest Christians believed both that Jesus had been bodily raised and that this event fulfilled the scriptural stories. These were perceived as stories not simply about a Messiah, emerging out of the blue, but about Israel, about the doing away with Israel's time of desolation, about the coming of the new age that would reverse the effects of the present evil age."[9]

Wright has reframed the *euangelion* as good news *for* Israel and *about* Israel. But who and what *is* this redeemed Israel? Does it refer to, or at least include, the Jewish people as an identifiable nation? And to what land and city does this Israel return from exile? At this point Wright reverts to the traditional ecclesial rendering of the *euangelion*. The Israel in view includes Jews, but only such as become disciples of Jesus, who, as Messiah, redefines the identity of Israel around himself. Moreover, these Jewish members of the redefined Israel no longer have any particular

7. Wright, *The Resurrection of the Son of God*, 320–21.

8. Wright, *The Resurrection of the Son of God*, 321–22.

9. Wright, *The Resurrection of the Son of God*, 322.

vocation or role as Jews. And, of course, the restoration of the people that the Messiah's resurrection effects has nothing to do with the city of Jerusalem or the land of Israel.

Since the concepts intrinsic to Wright's interpretation of the *euangelion* are so thoroughly Jewish in character, he acknowledges that this sudden departure from a Jewish perspective requires explanation: "the historian must account for the fact that, with early Christianity thus being so clearly a 'resurrection' movement in the Jewish sense, the well-established metaphorical meaning of 'resurrection'—the restoration of Israel in a concrete socio-political sense—is almost entirely absent, and a different set of metaphorical meanings emerge instead."[10] In the present volume, I will argue that no such explanation is required, for the *euangelion* suffers no such radical disjunction with Judaism. The *euangelion* includes the promise of Jewish national redemption in Israel's ancestral land and holy city—but, of course, it also includes much more.

N. T. Wright has taken the first steps in rethinking the *euangelion* in Jewish terms, but we must continue along the path from which he eventually retreats. Accordingly, in the chapters that follow I propose that the apostolic message concerning the death and resurrection of Jesus possesses a prophetic dimension that binds those events in the life of Israel's Messiah to the future history of the Jewish people. By his suffering and death Jesus anticipates and shares in the destruction of Jerusalem of 70 CE and the Jewish exile that follows, and imparts to those later events a redemptive character that becomes manifest in the course of Jewish history. By his resurrection Jesus anticipates and ultimately will accomplish the glorification of Jerusalem through "the return of the LORD to Zion" (Isa 52:8). Thus, the good news concerning the death and resurrection of Jesus is simultaneously the good news of God's coming reign in Jerusalem. This is not only good news about what God *has* done, but also good news about what God *is* doing and *will* do. This is a *prophetic euangelion that tells of God's past, present, and future saving deeds in the life of the people of Israel through Israel's resurrected Messiah.*

My aim in this volume is to recapture a fundamental feature of the *euangelion* that was obscured in the second century and has never been fully recovered. Accordingly, the scope of what follows is narrowly circumscribed. I will offer no comprehensive exposition of the death and resurrection of Jesus. However, if I accomplish what I set out to do,

10. Wright, *The Resurrection of the Son of God*, 210.

this focused discussion will facilitate a richer treatment of the universal import of those redemptive events in light of their particular prophetic meaning for the Jewish people.

A Theological Reading of Scripture

The method which I employ in pursuing my aim involves a theological reading of scripture. While it is unnecessary in this context to defend such a method, a brief explanation of its contours are in order.

The "scripture" in view is primarily the New Testament. Since the question being addressed concerns the content of the apostolic *euangelion*, the textual boundaries for our discussion are determined from the outset. At the same time, the New Testament—as Israel's disputed scripture—cannot be isolated from Israel's undisputed scripture, the *Tanakh*.[11] This is evident from Paul's inclusion of the phrase "according to the scriptures" in his summary account of the *euangelion* (1 Cor 15:3–4), and from N. T. Wright's commentary on that phrase.

My manner of reading scripture is avowedly *theological*.[12] What I mean by this term can best be conveyed by four adjectives. First, a theological mode of reading, as I practice it, is *compositional*. This means that I take seriously the role of the final author or editor of a biblical book as an active theological interpreter of the material contained in the book. The author or editor is never to be viewed as a passive collector of traditions or a mechanical recorder of events. Likewise, we cannot assume that the words, phrases, or ideas used in one biblical book will mean the same thing when they appear in another book. Each book and each author or editor is assumed to have a distinctive set of theological concerns and objectives, and each is to be heard on its/his own terms. This first aspect of a theological reading of scripture overlaps with historical critical methodology, and benefits especially from the results of redaction and literary criticism.

11. A traditional Jewish acronym referring to the Torah, the Prophets (i.e., *Nevi'im*), and the Writings (i.e., *Ketuvim*).

12. Much discussion of this notion has occurred over the past decade, and a concerted attempt to practice such a mode of reading is evident especially in the impressive Brazos Theological Commentary on the Bible, a series whose general editor is R. R. Reno. The initial volume to appear was Jaroslav Pelikan's commentary on Acts (2005).

Second, a theological mode of reading scripture is *canonical*. While the voice of each biblical book and author or editor is taken seriously on its/his own account, Jewish and ecclesial readers seeking theological wisdom hear each voice only in the context of the multi-vocal chorus that is the biblical canon. We do not expect the books to say exactly the same thing in the same way, but we do expect them to form a coherent whole. Moreover, a canonical reading of scripture pays attention to the shape of the canon, that is, the order in which the books appear. Just as the ordering of material within a particular book reflects the theological concerns and convictions of the author or editor, so the arrangement of books within the canon carries its own message, and sheds light on how each book is to be read.

Third, a theological mode of reading scripture is *covenantal/communal*. This means that Jewish and ecclesial readers seeking theological wisdom from the biblical text encounter that text as members of a historical community in covenant with God. The biblical books and their canonical arrangement only exist because of that community, and we are able to read them only because the community has passed them on to us. As Paul Van Buren put it, the Bible is always a *carried book*: "we have to realize that we have this book in our hands not directly from its original authors or even from the communities for which and in the context of which they were written, but from those who immediately preceded us in the Way, and through the whole long line of those who have walked before them."[13] Scripture grows out of the life of the people of God, and is to be understood within the framework of that life.

An important implication of this covenantal/communal dimension of reading scripture is the role tradition plays in the process. We read scripture in the midst of the community in covenant with God, and within the context established by the wisdom the community has received through scripture in the past. While this implies that we should pay respectful attention to traditional interpretations of particular biblical texts, it suggests even more that our reading should be guided by the fundamental truths that have defined the essence and existence of the people of God throughout its history.

At this point in my introduction a careful reader might be puzzled. How can I advocate and practice a mode of reading scripture that respects theological tradition, and argue from that same scripture for a

13. Van Buren, *A Theology of the Jewish-Christian Reality*, 121.

revision of the traditional understanding of the *euangelion* which lies at the core of ecclesial identity? The answer to this question derives from my particular ecclesial location as a Messianic Jew. That location entails identification with *both* the Jewish people and the *ekklēsia*. For me, and for my theological mode of reading scripture, *both* traditions are authoritative. The people of God has suffered a schism, and a Messianic Jew like myself views these historical communities as estranged covenantal partners, each of which needs the other to be whole.[14]

So, my critical disposition toward the traditional ecclesial interpretation of the *euangelion* is inspired by its denial of the fundamental truths that define the essence and existence of the Jewish people. While such a theological orientation admittedly precedes and influences my exegetical decisions, the reading of scripture that results needs to be convincing on its own terms. In other words, I am here explaining my theological approach to exegesis as a frank admission of my starting point, not as a reason for accepting that exegesis. It is the end point that matters. Either my reading of the text makes sense, or it does not.[15]

Fourth and finally, a theological mode of reading (as I practice it) is *world-historical*. This means that I assume that the ultimate author of the biblical text, who reveals divine truth through the mediation of human agents, is also the lord of history whose activity in relation to the people of God in the post-biblical period will be consistent with what is found in scripture. A world-historical approach to reading scripture requires that we first do our best to interpret the ambiguous events of history in light of scripture, and then return to the text and re-read scripture in light of those later events. In the present volume, I will undertake this task in relation to second-century developments in the *ekklēsia* and Judaism, and in relation to the modern movements of Zionism and Messianic Judaism.[16]

In summary, my theological approach to scripture is compositional, canonical, covenantal/communal, and world-historical. General awareness of the components of this approach will enable the reader to better

14. I explain and illustrate this Messianic Jewish hermeneutical approach in "Finding Our Way through Nicaea," an article included as an appendix to Kinzer, *Searching Her Own Mystery*.

15. Of course, the theological presuppositions of the reader will also play a role in assessing the success or failure of my exegesis.

16. For further discussion of the world-historical component of a theological reading of scripture, see Kinzer, *Postmissionary Messianic Judaism*, 38–46.

understand the questions I ask of the text, and the textual details that I find most relevant to answering those questions.

Acts of the Apostles in Light of the Gospel of Luke

In my quest to recover the Jewish character of the *euangelion* as good news for Israel, I will focus on Acts of the Apostles and its relationship to the Gospel of Luke. Only in Acts do we find accounts of the apostolic announcement of the *euangelion* to predominantly Jewish audiences. Critical biblical scholars may question the historicity of those accounts, but such questions are irrelevant for my purpose. My theological mode of reading takes as its starting point the canonical authority of the biblical text, and I am only concerned with what its human (and divine) authors are trying to say through it.

I will attempt to show that Acts of the Apostles (read in light of the Gospel of Luke) presents an *euangelion* that is directed especially to the Jewish people, and whose content relates to the consummation of Jewish history. That consummation involves the exile and return of the Jewish people to its land and its capital city. The Jewish people remain in covenant with God and in relation to the risen Messiah, even in exile, and the Torah remains the constitutional expression of that covenant. Moreover, the apostolic *ekklēsia* of the Messiah has Torah-faithful Jews at its heart, to whom others from the nations are joined in order to be linked in fellowship with the Jewish people. As such, the *ekklēsia* of Acts represents a prophetic anticipation of the eschatological content of the *euangelion*, in which Israel and the nations are joined through the resurrected Messiah.

While concentrating on Acts of the Apostles, I will also pay close attention to the Gospel of Luke. It is evident from their prologues addressed to the same Theophilus (Acts 1:1; Luke 1:3) that the final form of these two volumes derives from a common author. For most of the last century scholars went beyond the inference of common authorship, asserting a literary unity between the two books. Luke and Acts were thus not separate works composed by the same person, but two parts of a single unified narrative that scholars called "Luke-Acts."[17] This latter thesis has been challenged in recent years.[18] Some have even called into

17. This thesis of literary unity is traced back to Henry J. Cadbury and his 1927 volume *The Making of Luke-Acts*.

18. See Parsons and Pervo, *Rethinking the Unity of Luke and Acts*; Gregory and

question the assumption of common authorship, but most agree that at least the final form of the Gospel of Luke is to be attributed to the author of Acts.[19]

I will reflect further on authorship and dating questions for Luke and Acts in chapter 5, but at this point I need only note the operating assumptions that govern my exegesis. While I remain impressed by the exegetical results obtained by those adopting the scholarly construct of "Luke-Acts," in the following chapters I will assume only that the final edition of Luke is composed by the author of Acts, and that the Gospel contains numerous consciously crafted literary anticipations of material that will appear in the later book. For my purposes it is irrelevant whether those anticipations are original to the Gospel or added by a subsequent editor, or whether Luke was written with Acts already in mind or Acts was conceived later and composed with Lukan themes, concepts, and terms as building blocks.

The significance of Acts of the Apostles for my work becomes especially clear when the book is considered in relation to the theological mode of reading articulated above—an approach to scripture that is compositional, canonical, covenantal/communal, and world-historical. First, the *compositional* perspective on Acts (and Luke) focuses attention on the theological concerns and convictions of the author rather than the traditions he employs or the underlying historical events he recounts.[20] While critical exegetes of the last century have often reflected on Lukan theology, rarely have such studies guided the thinking of theologians. In the ecclesial and normative context of theology, Luke and Acts are usually viewed independently of one another, with Luke (like Mark) living in the shadows of Matthew and John, and Acts treated as a historical sourcebook for the early *ekklēsia* and the writings of Paul. As a result, neither Luke nor Acts have played a major role in theological discourse. I see this as a deficiency that the following chapters seek to rectify. When it comes to interpreting the meaning of the *euangelion* in relation to the Jewish people, Acts (read in light of Luke) provides essential theological insight.

Rowe (eds.), *Rethinking the Unity and Reception of Luke and Acts.*

19. The most radical position has been advocated by Walters, *The Assumed Authorial Unity of Luke and Acts.* See also Pervo, *Dating Acts*; Tyson, *Marcion and Luke-Acts*; and Smith and Tyson (eds.), *Acts and Christian Beginnings.*

20. I have no reservations in using the third person masculine pronoun for the author of Acts or the author/editor of Luke, for I think it highly unlikely that the author was female.

Second, the *canonical* perspective underlines the unique importance of Acts within the New Testament. Considered together, Acts and Luke "dominate the landscape of the New Testament," comprising "almost one-fourth of its total verses."[21] But their unique significance in the canon derives as much from their content as from their bulk. Acts provides an integrated and coherent vision of the life and teaching of the apostolic *ekklēsia* as a fitting sequel to the Lukan account of the life and teaching of Jesus. In this way, these books knit the diverse strands of the New Testament canon into a unified whole.[22]

David Trobisch argues that Acts of the Apostles performs an especially crucial function within the canon. According to Trobisch, the main concern of the final redaction of the New Testament is to minimize the conflict between Paul and the leaders of the Jerusalem *ekklēsia* (i.e., Peter, representing the Twelve, and James, representing the family of Jesus). Trobisch places Acts in this context: "Of all N.T. writings, it is the Book of Acts that most explicitly displays this harmonizing tendency."[23] He goes so far as to suggest that the account of the Council of Jerusalem in Acts 15 "might even form the heart of the NT [New Testament]."[24] Robert Wall agrees with Trobisch in his assessment of the canonical significance of Acts, though he emphasizes the *compatibility* of diverse apostolic viewpoints rather than their strict "harmonization": "The relations between James and Paul or between Peter and James as depicted at strategic moments in the plotline of Acts are generally collaborative rather than adversarial and frame the interpreter's approach to their biblical writings as essentially complementary (even though certainly not uniform and sometimes in conflict) in both meaning and function."[25]

Moreover, the canonical placement of Acts before the letters of Paul implies that the framers of the canon intended the former to guide the

21. Juel, *Luke-Acts*, 1.

22. "No other writing connects the . . . units of the NT as well as Acts. It continues the narrative of Luke, which is part of the Four-Gospel Book. It also serves as an introduction to the General Letters, introducing in its first part the authors of these writings—James, Peter, and John. In its second part, Acts provides biographical information concerning Paul that helps readers better understand the background of the individual letters" (Trobisch, *The First Edition of the New Testament*, 84).

23. Trobisch, *The First Edition of the New Testament*, 80.

24. Trobisch, *The First Edition of the New Testament*, 82.

25. Wall, "A Canonical Approach to the Unity of Acts and Luke's Gospel," 182.

interpretation of the latter. That is the reasonable conclusion reached by Brevard Childs:

> [T]he canon has retained the Pauline letters, but within the framework of Acts which provides hermeneutical guidelines for their interpretation. The content of the letters of Paul and the portrayal of Acts are certainly not to be simply identified, nor can one be allowed to destroy the witness of the other. However, Acts instructs the community of faith in one direction in which to move by translating the significance of Paul's original life and message for a different generation of readers who did not share in Paul's historical ministry.[26]

Scholars disagree about whether the author of Acts knew Paul personally and whether his portrait of the apostle to the gentiles is historically accurate. Regardless, the structure of the canon suggests that its framers wanted readers of the Pauline letters to take Acts into account when interpreting Paul's life, teaching, and purposes. Given the role Paul has played historically in shaping ecclesial attitudes toward Judaism, this hermeneutical function further emphasizes the importance of Acts for our concerns.

Third, the *covenantal/communal* dimension of theological exegesis is exemplified by the author/editor of Luke and Acts in his own approach to the traditional materials at his disposal. The two prologues demonstrate his posture as member of a community that is heir and product of the apostolic tradition.

> Since many have undertaken to set down an orderly account of the events that have been fulfilled among us, just as they were handed on [*paredosan*] to us by those who from the beginning were eyewitnesses and servants of the word, I too decided, after investigating everything carefully [*akribōs*] from the very first, to write an orderly account for you, most excellent Theophilus, so that you may know the truth concerning the things about which you have been instructed [*katēchēthēs*]. (Luke 1:1–4)

> In the first book, Theophilus, I wrote about all that Jesus did and taught from the beginning until the day when he was taken up to heaven, after giving instructions [*enteilamenos*] through the Holy Spirit to the apostles whom he had chosen. After his suffering he presented himself alive to them by many convincing

26. Childs, *The New Testament as Canon*, 240.

> proofs, appearing to them during forty days and speaking about the kingdom of God. (Acts 1:1–3)

The author of the Lukan prologue presents himself as the recipient of the apostolic tradition (*paradosis*) who has sought to be as careful (*akribōs*) and precise in its transmission and interpretation as the Pharisees are in handling their tradition (Acts 22:3; 26:5). He knows that his reader has already been "instructed" (i.e., "catechized") by other members of the community, but he seeks to deepen the reader's understanding of the truth of that instruction. The prologue to Acts shows a similar concern, emphasizing the role of the apostles as the chosen companions and disciples of Jesus both before and after his resurrection, and stressing the authoritative instruction (*enteilamenos*) they had received from their master. The author writes the story of the *ekklēsia* from the perspective of one of its loyal members, and writes to an audience who are similarly situated.

Furthermore, the author of Acts identifies intimately with the figure of Paul. This is evident from the fact that chapters 13–28 of Acts are devoted to his story. It is also evident from the narrator's frequent use of the first-person plural (see Acts 16:10–17; 20:5–15; 21:1–18; 27:1–28:16) when telling Paul's story—whether taken as historical fact or literary device. The narrator presents himself as a member of Paul's company, and so as one sharing the Pauline perspective. When Paul speaks about himself in Acts, he consistently identifies himself as a loyal member of the Jewish people and a faithful adherent of the Jewish tradition (e.g., Acts 23:6; 24:14–21; 25:8; 26:5–7; 28:17). As will be seen in chapter 3, almost all the speeches of Acts adopt a similar standpoint. Therefore, I would suggest that the author views such a social location as paradigmatic, and approaches scripture from that perspective.[27] This means that the covenantal/communal perspective of Acts is *Jewish* as well as *ecclesial.*

Fourth and finally, Acts (and Luke) provide the strongest support possible for interpreting *world-historical* events in the light of scripture, and for reading scripture in the light of those same events.[28] Both books

27. In chapter 5, I will address the question of whether the author/editor of Acts and Luke is a gentile or a Jew. Here I am merely suggesting that the author views identification with the Jewish people and the Jewish tradition as part of the narrator's—and Paul's—rhetorical standpoint.

28. I will amplify this point in chapter 5, where it will provide the exegetical basis for my theological assessment of post-70 developments in the *ekklēsia* and the rabbinic movement.

do this in relation to the destruction of Jerusalem in 70 CE, and Acts appears to reflect on the subsequent rise of the Pharisees and demise of the Sadducees. Within the narrative itself, Acts presents the Jerusalem Council (Acts 15) as an attempt to interpret theologically a set of historical events (i.e., the turning of gentiles to the God of Israel through the resurrected Messiah) in the life of the *ekklēsia*. Acts and Luke assert that the God of Israel raised Jesus from the dead and thereby demonstrated ultimate sovereignty over the affairs of human beings. This means that the history of the people of God, however puzzling, contains a meaning that is potentially discernible with the help of the Holy Spirit. The theological approach taken by Acts and Luke to the events of their day, as well as the substance of their historical reflection, will guide my discussion as I reflect theologically on the post-biblical history of the Jewish people and the *ekklēsia*.

Given both the central issue addressed in the following chapters (i.e., the relationship between the *euangelion* and the ongoing life of the Jewish people) and the contours of my theological method, my reasons for choosing Acts and Luke as primary texts should now be clear. I may now proceed to introduce the chapters of this volume, and the logic of their arrangement.

Chapter Preview

Chapter 1 takes up the question of the *euangelion* in relation to the land of Israel by examining the role played by the city of Jerusalem in the Gospel of Luke and Acts of the Apostles. The Gospel of Luke depicts Jesus as a prophet who foresees the coming destruction of the holy city, and who superimposes the image of that judgment over the events of his own suffering and death. In this way, the atoning death of Jesus is linked to the future suffering of the Jewish people. I argue that the structure and content of Luke and Acts likewise points to a future redemption for the holy city. Since the destruction of the city is connected to the death of Jesus, we may infer that the redemption of the city is likewise connected to his resurrection. Thus, the first chapter lays out our basic thesis: *the euangelion of the Messiah, crucified and risen, is also the euangelion of Jerusalem, crucified and risen.*

The opening chapter will set this vision of Jerusalem and the Jewish people in the context of the complicated history of ecclesial attitudes toward the city. While the post-apostolic gentile *ekklēsia* belatedly came to honor Jerusalem as central to its own identity, the Jerusalem it honored was the city of Jesus rather than the capital of the Jewish people, the site of accomplished redemption rather than eschatological hope. Just as the people of God and the *euangelion* both suffered fracture, so the integral ecclesial vision of Jerusalem was now broken into pieces.

Chapter 2 examines a question raised by the results of the first chapter: does the New Testament orientation to the destruction and presumed obsolescence of the Jerusalem temple undermine hope for the city's ultimate redemption? This is the only chapter in which I consider New Testament material outside Luke and Acts. I will first reflect on the function of the temple in the Bible as a whole, arguing that the institution displays unique features that distinguish it from the city, the land, and the people. Thus, a conclusion reached concerning the temple cannot automatically be applied to the latter realities. I will then study the teaching concerning the temple found in the Pauline writings, the letter to the Hebrews, the Revelation of John, and the Gospel of John. These texts, in keeping with other Jewish writings of the period and the biblical tradition as a whole, view the temple as a symbolic institution pointing to realities beyond and greater than itself. They deepen our understanding of the cosmic implications of the *euangelion*, but they cohere well with a view of its message that also emphasizes the enduring significance of Jerusalem, the land, and the Jewish people. Finally, the chapter will return to the study of Acts and Luke, showing that these books stress the continuing importance of the Temple Mount as the center of the world and the final destination of the Messiah when he returns. The eschatological coming of Jesus enacts "the return of the LORD to Zion" (Isa 52:8), which was prefigured prophetically by the triumphal entry on Palm Sunday (Luke 19:28–44).

The thesis of this volume focuses upon the relationship between the *euangelion* of Jesus' death and resurrection, the Jewish people, and the land of promise. Chapter 1 addresses this topic directly, whereas chapter 2 considers a possible objection to the conclusions of chapter 1. Chapter 3 resumes exposition of the basic thesis by examining the perspective on the Jewish people found in Acts and Luke. It begins by reflecting on the speeches of Acts, demonstrating that their rhetorical form and prophetic content confirm the view that the death and resurrection of the Messiah have redemptive consequences for the Jewish people. I will then take up two sets of texts in Acts that are often treated as incompatible with this view, and show that in fact they count as evidence in its favor.

Just as chapter 2 on the temple supports and elaborates the results of chapter 1 on Jerusalem, so chapter 4 performs a similar function in relation to chapter 3. The new chapter studies the teaching of Acts and Luke concerning the Torah as the national constitution of the Jewish people. If the Jewish people remain a distinctive covenantal reality in Acts and Luke and are inseparable from the *euangelion* of the death and resurrection of the Messiah, then we would expect these books to affirm the enduring role of the Torah as a defining mark of Jewish national identity. As chapter 4 demonstrates, that is exactly what we find in these volumes. Moreover, their main concern in relation to the Torah deals with Jewish identity *within* the *ekklēsia*. If the Torah continues to govern the life of Jews *within* the *ekklēsia*, it certainly fulfills that same role for all Jews throughout the world. Moreover, the exemplary character of Torah-faithful ecclesial Jews and Torah-honoring ecclesial gentiles suggests that the *ekklēsia* as presented in Acts functions as a prophetic paradigm of the eschatological reconciliation of Israel and the nations.

Chapter 5 provides a transition from strictly exegetical analysis to broader theological reflection on the basis of that analysis. The chapter begins by examining the view of Luke and Acts regarding divine action in history. These volumes portray the God of Israel as overseeing the chaotic drama of human life in the world in such a way that evil deeds perpetrated by free human actors become means through which divine redemption is accomplished. For the author of Acts, the story of Joseph in Genesis serves as a template for this pattern of divine action, and the crucifixion of Jesus is its primary expression.

I then consider the historical context in which the author/editor of Acts and Luke completes his volumes, and suggest that he encountered two post-70 movements that stimulated his special concern and interest. On the one hand, he sought to counter a school of Pauline enthusiasts who interpreted the letters in a manner that was hostile to Jews and Judaism. On the other hand, he recognized the positive potential of the Pharisaic-influenced proto-rabbinic school of thought that was emerging in the wake of a ruined temple and priesthood. As it turned out, the anti-Jewish Pauline enthusiasts succeeded in fracturing the Lukan *euangelion*. The message proclaimed by the gentile *ekklēsia* of the second century severed the death and resurrection of Jesus from the life of the Jewish people in the land of Israel. Providentially, the portion of the *euangelion* lost by the *ekklēsia* was preserved by the successors of the very Jewish movement that stirred our author/editor's grudging admiration. When these historical developments are assessed theologically in light of the principles enunciated and embodied by Acts and Luke, we may conclude that God has acted to preserve the fractured *euangelion* by showing covenant faithfulness to both halves of the fractured people of God.

Chapter 6 draws upon the conclusions of the previous chapters in order to assess theologically two modern movements that seem connected in some way with the Lukan *euangelion*, and with one another. The main focus of the chapter is Zionism as a movement committed to the establishment and preservation of a Jewish national home in the land of Israel. While political Zionism took shape as a secular project, it was rooted in the central themes of traditional Jewish religious life that constituted the portion of the *euangelion* carried through history by the Jewish people. I propose in this chapter that disciples of Jesus should acknowledge the action of God in the re-establishment of Jewish national life in Jerusalem and the land. At the same time, I also distinguish between that national life and the state that orders its affairs, and propose that the state be viewed as a necessary instrument rather than an ultimate end. Moreover, current conditions should not be construed as the redemptive goal, or even as its first phase, but instead as a prophetic anticipation of something far greater that is yet to come.

Chapter 6 will also consider the Messianic Jewish movement, and its relationship to both Zionism and the prophetic *euangelion*. In its ideals if not in its concrete reality, the Messianic Jewish movement represents an attempt to recover the integral wholeness of both the people of God and the apostolic message. The dissolution of the Jewish center of the *ekklēsia* with the destruction of Jerusalem in 70 CE threatened ecclesial ties to the land of Israel, the Jewish people, and the Jewish way of life. The fraying of those ties was expressed internally in the suppression of the Jewish national life within the *ekklēsia*. In a strikingly co-incidental development, a new movement of Jewish disciples of Jesus seeking to live a visibly Jewish way of life arose at the same time as the re-establishment of a Jewish national presence in the land of Israel, and at the same time as ecclesial attempts to forge a constructive theological and practical connection to that national presence. I propose in this chapter that gentile disciples of Jesus should acknowledge the action of God in the recovery of Jewish life within the *ekklēsia* just as they acknowledge divine action in the restoration of Jewish life in the land of Israel. Once again, such acknowledgement need not be uncritical. Like the State of Israel, the Messianic Jewish movement has many glaring deficiencies. But one approaches such defects differently if one begins by affirming the essential reality as a historical work of the Holy Spirit.

Chapter 7 will conclude this volume by considering the integrative force of this construal of the prophetic *euangelion*. Most obviously, my proposal unifies ecclesial teaching concerning the Jewish people and the land of promise by centering it in the apostolic message that brought the *ekklēsia* into being. In this chapter, I will show how the prophetic *euangelion* also unlocks new and intertwined insights in biblical interpretation, soteriology, eschatology, ethics, and missiology. Finally, I will point to its impact on ecclesiology, and the unity of the entire people of God.

Jerusalem Crucified and Christian Zionism

At the outset many readers might assume that the present volume advocates political and theological positions characteristic of the movement that has come to be called "Christian Zionism." A large percentage of those who identify as Christian Zionists endorse the ideology of the religious settlers on the West Bank, and oppose on theological (rather than prudential) grounds any Israeli territorial concessions. They sometimes espouse a dispensationalist theology, and their Zionist political convictions accordingly correspond to well-defined expectations regarding the tribulation, rapture, second coming, and millennium. Christian Zionist readers of such vintage may appreciate and learn from *Jerusalem Crucified, Jerusalem Risen*, but they will not find in it an argument for the expansive ideology that has come to be associated with their movement.

My own political and theological convictions on these matters are not at all what one would expect from such a "Christian Zionist." In terms of Israeli politics, I am left of center, and have little enthusiasm for the settlement project. Theologically, I have never been a dispensationalist, and even hold an agnostic position regarding the millennium. On the other hand, I share N. T. Wright's view that the eschatological order will involve real bodies and a real place. In that context, I believe that genealogical-Israel will retain its distinct identity and priestly vocation in the coming age, and will inhabit an earthly Jerusalem of some sort.

While these are my personal convictions, I do not argue for them in *Jerusalem Crucified*. One might disagree with much in the above paragraph, and assent to everything contained in the following chapters. I mention my personal views only to alert readers to the character of the book they are reading, and to caution them against making assumptions about the author's opinions beyond what is asserted in the text.

Terminology

A concluding note regarding terminology: as is already evident, in some cases I use anglicized forms of Greek words in place of their customary English translations ("*ekklēsia*" in place of the noun "church"; "ecclesial" in place of the adjective "church" or the adjective "Christian"; "*euangelion*" in place of "gospel"; "*boulē*" in place of "plan" or "counsel" or "providence"). In the case of *ekklēsia* and *euangelion* I do so because the usual English translations (like the adjective "Christian") carry connotations that already imply the fractured understanding of the people of God and the apostolic message which I am seeking to combat. (This is also true of the noun "Christian.") Sometimes it is necessary to make familiar terms unfamiliar in order to challenge unconscious assumptions regarding their meaning.

The case of *boulē* is somewhat different. Here I could not find any single English word that adequately captured its meaning in the Lukan corpus. The richness of the term will become clear as we look at the texts in Acts and Luke where it is employed.

I will follow the convention of biblical scholars in using the name "Luke" to speak of the author of Acts of the Apostles and the author or final editor of the Gospel bearing his name. Accordingly, I will also use the adjective "Lukan" to speak of that which both books share in common. These terms should not be taken to imply a commitment to any particular theory regarding the identity of the author/editor.

We are now ready to begin our journey through what hitherto has been largely unexplored territory: the prophetic *euangelion* of Israel's crucified and risen Messiah.

Chapter 1

The Resurrected Messiah and Jerusalem

How is the prophetic *euangelion* of the crucified and risen Messiah related to the Jewish people and the land bestowed on its ancestors? Does Jesus' salvific act in offering himself to God, and God's salvific response in raising him from the dead, have redemptive consequences for the life of the people of Israel and its promised inheritance?

These questions focus on the linkage between Jesus and his people. However, they also *assume* a linkage between that people and its land. Beginning with the call of Abraham (Gen 12:1, 7), and continuing throughout the biblical narrative, the land of Israel constitutes the essential blessing appointed for the people of Israel. While the covenantal status of Jews has never been contingent on their inhabiting the land, Jewish religious identity has always included a passionate hope for the land's future possession. As Jewish liturgy amply demonstrates, the eschatology of Judaism centers on the expectation of the re-gathering of the people to the land promised to Abraham, Isaac, and Jacob.

I am proposing in this volume that Jesus died and was raised as the messianic representative of the Jewish people, and that these events in his life foreshadow and order the course of Jewish history. Jesus' suffering and death constitute a proleptic participation in the intensified exile of the Jewish people that will begin a generation later when the Romans destroy Jerusalem. This advance participation by the Messiah imparts to the coming exile a redemptive character, so that the dissolution of Jewish national existence centered in Jerusalem functions not only as punishment but also as a source of purification and corporate renewal. In corresponding fashion, Jesus' resurrection serves as the pledge and efficient cause of Jerusalem's ultimate redemption. Since the issue of exile and restoration is so central to my thesis, I will begin exposition of that thesis by considering the topic of the land.

As the previous paragraph indicates, the intensified exile of the Jewish people commences with the destruction of Jerusalem. The capital city stood at the center of the land, and symbolized the land in its entirety. Already in the book of Deuteronomy the blessing of the land was concentrated in one particular site where the Lord would "choose to set his name" (e.g., 12:5, 11, 14, 18, 21, 26). Once David established Jerusalem as his capital and Solomon built the temple on its summit, the city represented the land as a whole, and the messianic promise to David became inseparable from the promise to Zion (e.g., Ps 132:11–18). As Robert Louis Wilken writes, "Isaiah, like Ezekiel, reorients the blessing of Abraham so that it comes to center almost exclusively on Jerusalem, on Mount Zion. . . . What had formerly been attributed to the land as a whole is now transferred to the city and the holy mountain. . . . Like Ezekiel, Zechariah uses the traditional formulas associated with the promise of the land, but he has centered them solely on Jerusalem and Judah . . . ."[1]

In this chapter, I will examine the role of the city of Jerusalem in the Gospel of Luke and Acts of the Apostles. I will argue that these books view the holy city as the fulcrum of God's action in human history, and as indissolubly bound to the crucified and risen Messiah. Since the capital city represents the land as a whole, demonstration of the ongoing theological significance of the city in the New Testament is sufficient grounds for affirming the theological significance of the land. If Jesus identifies himself with Jerusalem, he thereby identifies himself with the land in its entirety, and with the Jewish people to whom that land was promised.

But first I will present a brief history of ecclesial attitudes toward Jerusalem. That will provide a context for understanding why Luke and Acts have not traditionally been read in the manner I am proposing. It will also show how key elements of the picture I am painting are already present in past ecclesial attitudes, albeit in a fragmented and confused state whose disorder can be attributed in large part to anti-Jewish presuppositions.

1. Wilken, *The Land Called Holy*, 15–16, 18.

Jerusalem and the *Ekklēsia* of the First Millennium

N. T. Wright asserts that "in a good deal of Christian theology the fall of Jerusalem has had no theological significance."[2] That may be true for theology in the modern era, but it fails to accurately describe ecclesial thought of the first millennium. For members of the *ekklēsia* in that era the fall of Jerusalem in 70 CE carried enormous theological weight. A visceral bond with the city was forged after Constantine transformed it into an ecclesial center, and after the *ekklēsia* experienced the conquests of the city by the Persians in 614 and the Arabs in 637. But there was never a period in the first millennium when the fall of Jerusalem was theologically insignificant for believers in Jesus.

Some Jewish disciples of Jesus in the second century seem to have shared the grief of their fellow Jews in response to that event. We infer this from the account of Hegesippus preserved for us by the fourth-century historian and bishop Eusebius. Hegesippus—who, according to Eusebius, was himself a Jewish believer in Jesus—tells of James the Just, the brother of the Messiah and the preeminent apostle for the scrupulously Torah-observant branch of the early Jesus movement. Hegesippus presents James as a Nazirite maintaining a strict code of ritual purity, who, like the high priest on the Day of Atonement, devoted himself to prayer in the Jerusalem temple, "asking forgiveness for the people" (*Ecclesiastical History* 2.23.5–6). The author also informs us that James was called "Oblias," meaning "Rampart of the people" (*EH* 2.23.7). Richard Bauckham sees this title for James as referring to his role as "the powerful and indefatigable intercessor whose prayers protected the city."[3] Hegesippus proceeds to recount the martyrdom of James, in which the leader of the Jerusalem *ekklēsia* follows his brother's example by praying for the forgiveness of those who are putting him to death (*EH* 2.23.16). Hegesippus concludes his narrative by noting that the Roman siege of Jerusalem begins not long after the death of James (*EH* 2.23.18). For Eusebius, this means that God is judging the Jews of Jerusalem for killing not only the Lord but also the Lord's brother (*EH* 2.23.19). For Hegesippus, however, the message appears to be more subtle: the intercessory prayers of this righteous man, who loved his people and his city, had preserved them from evil: "the protective wall removed, the city fell prey to God's judgment."[4] Regardless

2. Wright, *Jesus and the Victory of God*, 343.
3. Bauckham, "James and the Jerusalem Community," 69.
4. Bauckham, "James and the Jerusalem Community," 69.

of its historical value as an accurate depiction of James, this narrative demonstrates that there were disciples of Jesus in the second century who, like the ideal figure sketched by Hegesippus, loved Jerusalem and its Jewish inhabitants, and grieved over its destruction by the Romans.

Most of our records from the second century reveal a far different attitude toward Jerusalem within the *ekklēsia*. Like the James of Hegesippus, ecclesial writers such as Justin Martyr and Irenaeus loved and longed for the city; but, unlike James, the Jerusalem they loved and longed for was not a Jewish city rooted in Jewish corporate memory and symbolizing the Jewish people as a whole. Instead, they looked exclusively to an eschatological Jerusalem, anticipating a restored and glorified messianic kingdom centered in an earthly Zion but inhabited and ruled only by members of the *ekklēsia*.[5] Jewish Jerusalem had been judged and brought to a decisive end; but the Christ would return, and a glorious "Christian" Jerusalem would rise from its ashes.

The contrast between this attitude toward Jewish Jerusalem and that seen in Hegesippus comes to vivid expression in the opposing orientations taken to the desolate Temple Mount in the second and third centuries. After the rebuilding of Jerusalem (now renamed Aelia Capitolina) following the suppression of the Bar Kokhba revolt in 135 CE, Jews were forbidden to live in the city. They were, however, permitted to gather on the Mount of Olives opposite the Temple Mount to mourn for the destruction of the temple and the Jewish city and to pray for their restoration. As a result, a new type of pilgrimage emerged among Jews in which the main focus was lamentation and eschatological longing.

In the same period, gentile believers in Jesus also developed a form of pilgrimage to Jerusalem whose destination was the Mount of Olives and whose object of meditation was the Temple Mount and its ruins. Unlike their Jewish counterparts, they came not to mourn but to exult. They considered the destruction of the temple and the Jewish city—and the exile of its Jewish inhabitants—to be an act of divine vindication of Jesus. For them, the sight of the temple ruins was "profoundly satisfying."[6] Although this particular form of gentile pilgrimage began as early as the second century, it endured into the Byzantine period when holy sites

5. "The best-documented and most persistent eschatology in the first two Christian centuries was chiliasm, the belief that God would establish a future kingdom on earth centered in Jerusalem" (Wilken, *Land Called Holy*, 56).

6. Armstrong, *Jerusalem*, 172.

associated with the passion, death, and resurrection of Jesus had become the primary focus for pious pilgrims.

> For centuries Christians had appealed to the visible evidence of the ruins of the Jewish temple as certain proof that *Christianity had triumphed over Judaism*. One reason Christians went on pilgrimage to Jerusalem was to see with their own eyes the place where the famous Jewish temple had once stood. . . . Only by actually visiting Jerusalem could one see that *the city of the Jews was no more. This sight comforted and reassured Christians*. . . . A generation after Jerome . . . Theodoret from Cyrus, traveled to Jerusalem to "see the desolation with my own eyes." Standing before the ruins, he recalled the ancient prophecies about the city (Matt 24 and Dan 9) and his "*heart exulted*." The Jews have been deprived of their famous house, he writes, "as those who visit can see."[7]

For these gentile believers in Jesus the fall of Jerusalem had enormous theological significance: it meant that "Christianity had triumphed over Judaism." The stones of the Temple Mount bore witness that the Jews had been rejected by God, and that the *ekklēsia* now constituted God's beloved people.

In the second century, Justin Martyr and Irenaeus combined this orientation to *Jewish* Jerusalem with a vivid hope for an eschatological transformation of the earthly city at the second coming of Jesus. Origen attacked this notion in the early third century, arguing that the Jerusalem of ecclesial hope was a strictly spiritual and heavenly destination. The non-territorial theology of Origen flourished in the *ekklēsia* of the third century, so that by the beginning of the fourth century most believers in Jesus longed for neither the earthly Jerusalem of the Jewish past nor the earthly Jerusalem of the "Christian" future. The theological significance of *earthly* Jerusalem resided exclusively in its ruins.

This changed dramatically with the conversion of Constantine. Always alert to the power of symbols, the emperor sanctioned an excavation at the Jerusalem site that generations of local Jesus-believers had identified as the place of his execution and burial. Apparently this local tradition was reliable, for in 327 the excavation resulted in the discovery of a tomb that was assumed to be the place at which the Son of God was raised from the dead. This discovery sent shock waves through the worldwide *ekklēsia*, and ultimately produced a dramatic change in

7. Wilken, *Land Called Holy*, 143. Emphasis added.

attitude toward the earthly Jerusalem. Fourth-century believers in Jesus focused not on the Jerusalem of eschatological expectation, as did Justin and Irenaeus; nor did they care about the Jerusalem of Jewish memory, as did Hegesippus; the city that captured their imagination in this era was *the Jerusalem of Jesus*.[8]

Constantine built a church at the site of the tomb which soon became the earthly center of the ecclesial universe and the primary destination for pilgrims from throughout the world. Churches were also constructed at other sites associated with events in the life of Jesus, such as the Last Supper and the ascension. Jerusalem was now a "Christian" holy city, whose earthly stones had the sacramental power to connect members of the *ekklēsia* to both the redemptive events of the past and the heavenly realities to which they pointed. By the early eighth century, John of Damascus can call these holy places "receptacles of divine energy." As Wilken comments, "By this he means that they were not simply historical sites that mark the place where something had happened long ago, but palpable signs of God's continuing presence on earth."[9]

The stature of the Jerusalem Church was similarly transformed. Before Constantine the bishop of Caesarea had taken precedence over the bishop of Jerusalem. Now Jerusalemites started to speak of their city as the "mother of the churches," and argued that their bishop should have greater dignity and authority than the bishop of Caesarea.[10] Their claim was confirmed in 451 when the episcopal see of Jerusalem became a patriarchate, joining the ranks of Alexandria, Antioch, Constantinople, and Rome as the pre-eminent churches of the ecclesial world. The Jerusalem Church of the fifth and sixth centuries was gradually attaining the sort of ecclesial prestige that had been enjoyed by the Jewish Jesus-community of Jerusalem under the leadership of James the Just. Wilken speculates that "Had the Muslims not conquered Jerusalem in the seventh century Jerusalem might one day have challenged the authority of the church of Rome."[11]

8. There is, however, a correspondence between the exegetical treatment of Jerusalem by Eusebius and by the second-century Christian millenarians. As Wilken points out, Eusebius treats the Jerusalem of the Church of the Anastasis (Resurrection) much the way the earlier millenarian tradition had treated the earthly Jerusalem of the eschaton (*Land Called Holy*, 96).

9. Wilken, *Land Called Holy*, 253.

10. Armstrong, *Jerusalem*, 176.

11. Wilken, *Land Called* Holy, 172.

It thus came as an enormous shock when the Persian armies trampled Jerusalem in 614, and Arab invaders took the city in 637. At this time gentiles who had once mocked Jews for grieving over the fall of Jerusalem took up the language of lament which they had formerly derided.[12] It was now Jews who rejoiced at the humiliation and mourning of the Jesus-believers. These gentiles had come to share a love for the earthly city comparable to that which animated the Jewish people, and as a result they now experienced a similar pain in her loss. Yet, this new commonality did nothing to heal the relationship between the Jewish people and the *ekklēsia*, but only intensified their mutual hostility. The bitter fruit of that animosity would ripen four and half centuries later, when Crusaders from the West recaptured the holy city in an attempt to restore its "Christian" glory.

Ecclesial history thus testifies to the enduring power of Jerusalem to inspire passionate devotion as a sacramental sign of the saving work of God in the world. Gentile believers in Jesus came to see the earthly Jerusalem as central to their faith; but the Jerusalem they loved was the city of Jesus, the Jerusalem of an already-accomplished redemption—not the Jerusalem of the Jewish people, the city of an as-yet-unrealized eschatological restoration. Just as Jesus himself had been torn from the people who were his own flesh-and-blood, so the city of Jewish hope had likewise become exclusively "Christian" (i.e., non-Jewish) property. We are now ready to see how this picture compares with the vision of Jerusalem conveyed by the New Testament.

The Judgment and Redemption of Jerusalem

Drawing upon a common way of describing the Gospel of Mark, N. T. Wright characterizes the *Jewish War* by Josephus as "a passion narrative (the war itself) with an extended introduction."[13] Wright thus implies a

12. "The Christians had sharply differentiated their experience in Jerusalem from that of the Jews. Now as they went into exile in their turn, they turned naturally to the gestures and psalms of their predecessors in the Holy City, and like the Jews they spoke of God and Zion in the same breath" (Armstrong, *Jerusalem*, 214). See Wilken, *Land Called Holy*, 216–32, for a powerful summary of the grief expressed after the Persian invasion.

13. Wright, *The New Testament and the People of God*, 373. The saying concerning the Gospel of Mark apparently derives from the nineteenth-century German theologian Martin Kähler.

parallel between the way Mark presents the suffering and death of Jesus and the way Josephus depicts the suffering and destruction of Jerusalem. Wright then proposes that this parallel between the passion of Jesus and the passion of Jerusalem already exists within the New Testament itself—not in Mark, but in the Gospel of Luke: "Luke's narrative has, in this sense, a double climax to Josephus' single one, and that (I think) is part of the point: the fall of the Temple, seen as future from within Luke's narrative world, is set in close parallel with the death of Jesus. The distinction between Luke and Josephus at this point is a powerful clue to the theological point that Luke is making."[14] Wright's assessment is astute, though he slightly misstates Luke's concern; this gospel shows a unique preoccupation not only with the *fall of the temple* but also with the *fall of the entire city*. Luke juxtaposes the death of Jesus and the fall of Jerusalem in such a way as to make each an interpretation of the other. What precisely is "the theological point that Luke is making" through this juxtaposition?

"Jerusalem, Jerusalem" (Luke 13:31–35)

To answer that question, I will begin by examining four passages in the Gospel of Luke (13:31–35; 19:41–44; 21:20–24; 23:27–31) which anticipate the events of 70 CE. The last three of these texts are unique to Luke's Gospel, and display lucidly the author's particular theological emphasis. The first, Luke 13:31–35, appears also in Matthew, but its distinctive Lukan context and form manifest the same perspective as that of the latter three passages. This passage falls within Luke's lengthy narrative of Jesus' departure from Galilee and journey to Jerusalem.

> 31 At that very hour some Pharisees came and said to him, "Get
> away from here, for Herod wants to kill you." 32 He said to them,
> "Go and tell that fox for me, 'Listen, I am casting out demons
> and performing cures today and tomorrow, and on the third
> day I finish my work. 33 Yet today, tomorrow, and the next day
> I must be on my way, because it is impossible for a prophet to
> be killed away from Jerusalem.' 34 Jerusalem, Jerusalem, the city
> that kills the prophets and stones those who are sent to it! How
> often have I desired to gather your children together as a hen
> gathers her brood under her wings, and you were not willing! 35
> See, your house is left to you. And I tell you, you will not see

14. Wright, *New Testament and the People of God*, 374.

me until the time comes when you say, 'Blessed is the one who comes in the name of the Lord.'"

Verses 31–33 are found only in Luke. The Pharisees of verse 31 warn Jesus of Herod's murderous intentions, and as a group they are thereby distinguished from the Jerusalem authorities of the following verses who will implement Herod's wish.[15] This reflects Luke's moderate portrayal of the Pharisees in both his gospel and Acts, and likewise reflects his depiction of the chief priests as the primary actors initiating the arrest and conviction of Jesus and the subsequent persecution of his disciples in Jerusalem. Verse 33 highlights the special role of the city of Jerusalem in Luke as the object of both judgment and redemption. The final two verses (34–35) appear also in Matthew 23 (vv. 37–39), where they function as the climax of Jesus' lengthy denunciation of the scribes and Pharisees. In contrast to Luke, however, Matthew's placement of these verses stresses the Pharisees' shared-responsibility for the crucifixion. The broader context in Matthew of harsh rebuke also qualifies the tone of intense grief which these words convey in their Lukan setting.

In Matthew 23, Jesus' address to Jerusalem occurs *after* his triumphal entry into the city when the accompanying crowds shouted, "Blessed is the one who comes in the name of the Lord!" (Matt 21:9). Matthew's version of the promise "you will not see me" contains the added word "again" (Matt 23:39), which suggests that the triumphal entry was a prophetic symbolic act anticipating Jesus' future coming to the city in glory and victory. Jesus' address to Jerusalem in Matthew 23 also occurs *after* his arguments with various Jerusalem authorities (Matt 21:10–22:46), and the reference to Jerusalem's unwilling response to his overtures points back to those disputes. Luke's version, however, occurs *before* Jesus has arrived in Jerusalem, and *before* he has tested Jerusalem's "willingness" to be gathered under his wings. How then does Luke understand Jesus' sadness at Jerusalem's past rebuff, and his claim that the city "will not see" him? Luke here likely presents Jesus as a prophet speaking in the name of God. As Robert Tannehill argues, the words "how often have I desired to gather you" (Luke 13:34) refer to "the long history of God's dealing with Jerusalem," and the words "you will not see me" likewise refer not to Jesus, but to God: "verse 35 is speaking of the departure of

15. Luke's passion narrative is the only witness to Jesus' appearance before Herod after his arrest (Luke 23:6–12). Herod's contemptuous treatment of Jesus justifies the concern expressed by the Pharisees in 13:31.

Jerusalem's divine protector, who will not return to Jerusalem until it is willing to welcome its Messiah, 'the one who comes in the name of the Lord.'"[16] This interpretation makes sense of what is otherwise a difficult text. Luke here alludes to the theme of the return of the LORD to Zion, which N. T. Wright underscores as a central element in both first-century Jewish eschatological hopes and the aims of Jesus.[17]

In summary, Luke 13:31–35 focuses attention on the city of Jerusalem and its temple authorities as those who persecute the prophets and who will put to death the Messiah. The Pharisees are distinct from this persecuting body and in some measure opposed to it, as are the Galileans who accompany Jesus on his journey to the capital. The longing for a welcoming response from Jerusalem belongs not only to Jesus but even more to God, whose love for the city and whose grief at its wickedness is not a recent development but has extended through multiple generations. The predominant tone of this text, as of all four of the passages we are now considering, is one of lament.[18] Nevertheless, a more positive note emerges in the final words: "you will not see me until the time comes when you say, 'Blessed is the one who comes in the name of the Lord'" (Luke 13:35). There is reason to hope that the divine presence, whose departure renders the city vulnerable to its enemies ("See, your house is left to you"), will return once again, presumably to comfort and glorify Jerusalem. The condition for such a future return is clear: the city—apparently still in its character as the capital of the Jewish people—must offer the same welcome to the Messiah that he will receive from his Galilean disciples on Palm Sunday.[19]

16. Tannehill, *Luke*, 225. See also Caird, *Saint Luke*, 174, and Wright, *Jesus and the Victory of God*, 642. Tannehill also notes that the triumphal entry in Luke does not fulfill the condition of this promise, since it is not "Jerusalem" that utters the words "Blessed is the one who comes in the name of the Lord" but "the whole multitude of the disciples" who accompanied Jesus from Galilee (Luke 19:37).

17. See Wright, *Jesus and the Victory of God*, 612–53. See also my treatment of this theme in the next chapter.

18. "The four passages that address Jerusalem and prophesy its fate have an important role in the plot (see 13:33–35; 19:41–44; 21:20–24; 23:27–31). It is important to catch the dominant feeling tone of these passages. Jesus speaks words of anguished longing and lament (13:33–35; 19:42). . . . These four scenes, which build up to the crucifixion and help to set the tone for it, constitute one major reason for interpreting the story of Israel in Luke-Acts as tragic" (Tannehill, *The Shape of Luke's Story*, 134).

19. In a seminal article, Dale Allison demonstrates that Jesus depicts the words, "Blessed be he who comes," not as a response (joyful or mournful) which Israel will have to the Messiah after he comes, but instead as the catalyst that induces his coming:

Jesus Weeps for Jerusalem (Luke 19:41–44)

Luke 13 anticipates the inadequate response that Jerusalem will offer to Jesus, the divine representative. That inadequate response is then narrated in Luke 19. In comparison to the other gospels, the Lukan version of Jesus' entry to Jerusalem emphasizes the failure of the city to receive Jesus in a proper manner. As Steve Smith recognizes, "[I]t is only the followers of Jesus who welcome him, not the city . . . Far from being a triumphal entry, as the event is commonly understood, it is a non-triumphal entry . . . ."[20]

Jerusalem's failure sets the stage for a distinctive Lukan addition to the account:

> [41]As he came near and saw the city, he wept over it, [42]saying, "If you, even you, had only recognized [*egnōs*] on this day the things that make for peace [*eirēnē*]! But now they are hidden from your eyes. [43]Indeed, the days will come upon you, when your enemies [*echthroi*] will set up ramparts around you and surround you, and hem you in on every side. [44]They will crush you to the ground, you and your children within you, and they will not leave within you one stone upon another; because you did not recognize [*egnōs*] the time of your visitation [*epi-skopēs*] from God.' (Luke 19:41–44)

Here the tone of intense grief is unmistakable. Looking upon the city as he descends the Mount of Olives, Jesus weeps over it. He weeps because in one glance he beholds two prophetic pictures, one superimposed on the other: the first is his own suffering and death, which will reveal that Jerusalem has not "recognized . . . the things that make for peace" or the time of her "visitation"; the second is Jerusalem's destruction at the hands of the Romans in 70 CE.

"'Until you say' can be understood to signal a conditional sentence. The text then means not, when the Messiah comes, his people will bless him, but rather, when his people bless him, the Messiah will come. In other words, the date of the redemption is contingent upon Israel's acceptance of the person and work of Jesus" (Allison, "Matt. 23:39 = Luke 13:35b as a Conditional Prophecy," 77). Allison's argument reveals the weakness of the traditional Christian interpretation of these words, which portrays them as the Jewish people's coerced and mournful response when they behold the return of Jesus. Peter Walker is among those who continue to advocate the traditional view which Allison refutes (Walker, *Jesus and the Holy City*, 99).

20. Smith, *The Fate of the Jerusalem Temple in Luke-Acts*, 58.

One of the most striking features of these verses is their allusion to the Song of Zechariah in Luke 1:68–79. That song, uttered on the occasion of the circumcision of John the Baptist, is a celebration of God's saving power at work in the fulfillment of God's promises to Israel. The object of praise is "the Lord God of Israel" (v. 68), and his redeeming act is in accordance with his oath to Abraham (v. 73), his merciful covenant with all the patriarchs (v. 72), and the words spoken "through the mouth of his holy prophets from of old" (v. 70). Thus, the *tone* of the song is diametrically opposed to that of Luke 19:41–44. Even more, the *content* of Jesus' prophetic words as he approaches the city appears to be a direct negation of Zechariah's song. In the births of John the Baptist and Jesus, God has "visited [*epe-skepsato*] his people to redeem them" (1:68) and "to give knowledge [*gnōsin*] of salvation to his people" (1:77), but Jerusalem "did not know [*egnōs*] the time of its visitation [*epi-skopēs*]" (19:44). God has come to "give light to those who sit in darkness" and "to guide our feet into the way of peace [*eirēnē*]" (1:79), but now "the things that make for peace [*eirēnē*]" are "hidden from your eyes" (19:42). God's work through John and Jesus will result in Israel's being "saved" and "rescued" from its enemies [*echthroi*] (1:71; 73), but now Jesus foresees the coming siege of Jerusalem by Israel's "enemies" [*echthroi*] and the city's utter destruction at their hands [19:43–44]. We have here far more than a *non-fulfillment* of what was promised; the identical diction draws attention to the blatant *contradiction* between what was anticipated and what is actually taking place. Furthermore, the problem cannot be evaded by attempting to distinguish the "Israel" of Zechariah's Song from the "Jerusalem" that Jesus approaches, for the infancy narrative of Luke treats the "redemption [*lutrōsin*]" of Israel (1:68) as equivalent to "the redemption [*lutrōsin*] of Jerusalem" (2:38). If Jerusalem is judged rather than redeemed, then Israel is judged rather than redeemed.

Robert Tannehill has viewed this contradiction between the joyful expectation of Jerusalem's redemption in the infancy narrative and the actual events that occur in Jerusalem in both 30 and 70 CE as evidence that the Lukan narrative concerning Israel should be read as a tragedy.[21] Without denying the tragic element in the story, it is highly unlikely that Luke thinks the promises to Israel in his infancy narrative have been—or can be—definitively thwarted. To see God's dealings with Israel as ultimately tragic would mean that God's dealings with Jesus result in fail-

21. Tannehill has argued this point in virtually all his writings on Luke-Acts.

ure.[22] Jesus mourns over the coming suffering of Jerusalem just as many in Jerusalem mourn over *his* suffering (23:27–31). The suffering of Jesus and the grief it causes are swallowed up in the joy of his resurrection (Luke 24:41, 52); if Luke considers the promises to Israel cited in the Song of Zechariah as divine in origin, would he not expect Jerusalem's suffering and grief likewise to be swallowed up in joy?

Most commentators agree that Luke would never entertain the notion that God's dealings with Israel could fail. Many of them, however, propose that he radically reinterprets what those dealings entail: only those who believe in Jesus constitute the true Israel, and their communal life in the Spirit represents the redemption and restoration that the Lukan infancy narrative anticipates.[23] However, this view ignores the tone of lamentation that permeates the Lukan texts we are now considering. Furthermore, it misses the many indications in both Luke and Acts that the author/editor looks for a redemption of Israel that is yet to come.

While the Lukan infancy narrative resounds with the tone of joyful hope, an ominous hint of lamentation enters at one point, namely, when Simeon blesses Mary and Jesus: "Then Simeon blessed them and said to his mother Mary, 'This child is destined for *the falling and the rising of many in Israel*, and to be a sign that will be opposed so that the inner thoughts of many will be revealed—and a sword will pierce your own soul too'" (Luke 2:34–35). Many see this text as pointing to the division in Israel that will occur in response to the Messiah's words and actions. However, David Tiede argues persuasively that "the falling and rising of

22. To be fair, Tannehill also asserts that Luke *hopes for* Jerusalem's future redemption. However, Tannehill stops short of what we are asserting here: that the *certain* redemption of Jerusalem in the future is as essential to Luke's redemptive vision as is the resurrection of Jesus.

23. This view is well-represented by Fuller, *The Restoration of Israel*. For Fuller, the Jewish *ekklēsia* in Jerusalem, ruled by the twelve apostles, constitutes the fully restored Israel. "From heaven, Israel's messiah rules the world. The role of the restored Israel is to proclaim and interpret the significance of the messianic exaltation as the inauguration of Israel's (spiritual) rule over the occupied world" (268). Fuller regards as erroneous all attempts to interpret Luke 1–2 as referring to a redemption that will touch the Jewish people as a whole, whether those interpretations assume a future restoration of Israel or a tragic and unresolved failure in the accomplishment of the divine purpose: "A common error of scholars is to interpret these broadly construed hopes of restoration in Luke 1–2 as indications of Luke's retention of a pan-Israel salvation, either in terms of (future) Jewish conversions or even nationalistic liberation. Other scholars, while also seeing a pan-Israelite inclusion in these hopes of restoration contend they are ultimately unrealized over the course of the narrative due to widescale Jewish rejection" (206).

many in Israel" should be taken as a prophetic temporal sequence, with at first "many in Israel" falling and experiencing judgment, and afterward "many in Israel" rising to receive redemption.[24] This corresponds to the pattern of imminent judgment followed by future redemption that marks the prophecies of Isaiah, Jeremiah, and Ezekiel. This also fits the final verse of Luke 13:31–35, which anticipates a future welcome of the Messiah to be extended by the city of Jerusalem and a consequent return of the divine glory to Zion. If this is Luke's vision of Israel's future, then the allusion in Luke 19:41–44 to the Song of Zechariah is neither ironic nor contradictory, but instead a way of signaling that the sad events taking place in Jerusalem are not the end of Jerusalem's story. In fact, the judgment of Jerusalem—and Jesus' bearing of that judgment proleptically and representatively on the cross—will itself be instrumental in achieving her ultimate redemption.

Simeon's blessing points to the cross (the "sword" that will pierce Mary's heart) and to the coming judgment ("falling") of Israel. Entering Jerusalem, Jesus likewise ponders both events together. The disciples do not initially understand the role the cross will play in Jesus' work "to redeem Israel" (Luke 24:21). In order to "rise," Jesus himself had to "fall." It appears that Jerusalem must walk the same course.

The End of the Times of the Gentiles (Luke 21:20–24)

The third passage in Luke that anticipates the events of 70 CE (Luke 21:20–24) is found in Luke's version of Jesus' eschatological discourse (Luke 21:5–36). In Mark and Matthew this discourse combines and compresses references to the destruction of Jerusalem in 70 CE and the great distress at the end of the age in such a way that one event is superimposed on the other. The overlay effect is especially evident in Mark 13:14–20:

> [14] 'But when you see the desolating sacrilege [*to bdelygma tēs erēmōseōs*] set up where it ought not to be (let the reader understand), then those in Judea must flee to the mountains; [15] someone on the housetop must not go down or enter the house to take anything away; [16]someone in the field must not turn back to get a coat. [17] Woe to those who are pregnant and to those who are nursing infants in those days! [18] Pray that it may not be in winter. [19] For in those days there will be suffering, such as has

24. Tiede, "Glory to Thy People Israel," 27–28; see Kinzer, *Postmissionary Messianic Judaism*, 111.

> not been from the beginning of the creation that God created until now, no, and never will be. [20] And if the Lord had not cut short those days, no one would be saved; but for the sake of the elect, whom he chose, he has cut short those days.

The "desolating sacrilege"—or, more literally, "the detestable thing of desolation"—alludes to the apocalyptic prophecies of Daniel which had their preliminary realization in the desecration of the Jerusalem temple by Antiochus Epiphanes in 167 BCE (Dan 9:27; 11:31; 12:11; see also 1 Macc 1:54). The relationship between the eschatological message of Daniel and its partial historical enactment in the Syrian persecution of Antiochus is similar to the relationship between the eschatological message of Mark 13 and its partial enactment in the Roman destruction of Jerusalem. In each case, one event is telescoped typologically upon another in such a way that the two cannot be disentangled by means of a purely literary analysis.

In contrast, Luke's version of these verses distinguishes clearly between what will happen in Jerusalem in 70 CE and what will happen at the end of the age.

> [20] 'When you see Jerusalem surrounded by armies, then know that its desolation [*erēmōsis*] has come near. [21] Then those in Judea must flee to the mountains, and those inside the city must leave it, and those out in the country must not enter it; [22] for these are days of vengeance, as a fulfillment of all that is written. [23] Woe [*ouai*] to those who are pregnant and to those who are nursing infants in those days! For there will be great distress on the earth and wrath against this people [*laō*]; [24] they will fall by the edge of the sword and be taken away as captives among all nations; and Jerusalem will be trampled [*patoumenē*] on by the gentiles,[25] until the times [*kairoi*] of the gentiles are fulfilled. (Luke 21:20–24)

Luke transforms Mark's reference to the desecration of the temple (*to bdelygma tēs erēmōseōs*) so that it becomes a description of the "desolation" (*erēmōsis*) of the entire city. The sign itself becomes the armies surrounding Jerusalem rather than the erecting of an idolatrous altar. The Markan text implies a cosmic distress, whereas the Lukan version speaks of "wrath against *this people*" (i.e., the Jewish people who inhabit Jerusalem). Most significantly, the world in its unredeemed form—and the Jewish people—remain in existence after this event, for not all of the

25. I have uncapped the word "Gentiles" in Bible translations here and throughout.

inhabitants of Jerusalem are slain but some are "taken away as captives among all nations," and "Jerusalem will be trampled on by the gentiles, until the times of the gentiles are fulfilled." This concluding statement about Jerusalem implies that an extended period of time will elapse between the destruction of the city by the gentiles and the end of the age (which will occur only *after* "the times of the gentiles are fulfilled").[26]

While commentators generally assume that the period Jesus calls the "times of the gentiles" begins with their trampling of Jerusalem in 70 CE, the text permits another reading: the phrase may refer to the extended era of the four gentile empires described in Daniel 2 and 7, the fourth of which was understood by many first-century Jews to be Rome (4 Ezra 11:39–40). Such an interpretation is supported by Daniel's mention of the divine control of "times [*kairoi*] and seasons [*chronoi*]" (Dan 2:21 LXX), which may be alluded to by the resurrected Jesus when he responds to the disciples' question about the imminent restoration of the kingdom to Israel: "It is not for you to know the times [*chronoi*] or periods [*kairoi*] that the Father has set by his own authority" (Acts 1:7).[27] If that is correct, then the "times of the gentiles" begin with the Babylonian

26. Peter Walker proposes that the phrase "the times of the gentiles" refers only to the short period when the Romans are actually engaged in subjugating Jerusalem (*Jesus and the Holy City*, 100). If that is the case, what is the point of the statement? Given the climactic rhetorical context of the verse, one would expect that something significant is to occur after the "until." If only a short period is in view, and nothing is said about what is to follow that period, why even speak of the "fulfillment" of those "times"? Also, why the plural form of the word "times"? That seems to be an unusual way to refer to a short temporal span. Walker may sense the weakness of this proposal, for he immediately proceeds to an alternate interpretation: "even if the 'times of the Gentiles' does refer to a more extended period within the Church's history, there is nothing in the text to suggest that these times will be followed by the 'times of the Jews'" (pp. 100–101). In fact, the very use of the word "gentiles" itself implies something of the sort, for that word in Luke-Acts always means "non-Jews." Of course, it is possible, as Walker then suggests, that "the moment when the 'times of the Gentiles' are fulfilled will be the time of the 'coming' of the 'Son of Man'" (p. 101)—but it is also possible that his "coming" is expected to inaugurate an era of a restored Jerusalem that could be called the "times of the Jews." That Luke 21:24 refers in some way to a restored *Jewish* Jerusalem is confirmed by the tight interconnection between that verse, Acts 1:6–7, and 3:19–21 (see chapter 3, pp. 134–36, 156–58). Walker fails to note this interconnection, and so misinterprets each of the three passages.

27. "[T]he reference to 'times or periods (seasons)' in Acts 1:7 may lead the reader to recall the same phrase from Daniel 2, emphasizing divine control over kings and kingdoms within world history. It would, therefore, create expectations about the kingdom's restoration to Israel and the divine role in that." (Salmeier, *Restoring the Kingdom*, 25.)

conquest of 586 BCE rather than the Roman destruction of the city in 70 CE. Thus, according to this interpretation, Luke 21:24 implies that the exile continues—and is even intensified by a "trampling" of Jerusalem—after the death and resurrection of Jesus.

Luke 21:20–24 thus demonstrates once again this author's particular focus on the destruction of Jerusalem in 70 CE. However, verse 24 also confirms what we have already suggested in relation to Luke 13 and Luke 19—namely, Luke's anticipation of a future redemption for Jewish Jerusalem. Taking account of the literary traditions underlying this verse, Robert Tannehill offers the most cogent reading: "That Jerusalem or the sanctuary has been or will be 'trampled on' is a repeated theme in ancient Jewish writings. . . . This trampling of Jerusalem will last only 'until the times of the Gentiles are fulfilled.' We are not told explicitly what will happen then, but if we return to the other texts that speak of this trampling, we find the expectation that Jerusalem will be restored."[28]

Perhaps Luke expects the period in which the gentiles "trample" Jerusalem to end when the Jewish people corporately welcome Jesus as the Messiah with the words, "Blessed is the one who comes in the name of the Lord." If so, such "trampling" must be compatible with Jewish residence in the city, since Luke 13:35 appears to speak of a welcome extended to Jesus by the Jews *of Jerusalem*. On the other hand, perhaps the transition from the "times of the gentiles" to the fullness of the messianic age is an extended process rather than a singular event—a process that culminates in the corporate Jewish welcoming of the Messiah, but begins well before that greeting.

The Daughters of Jerusalem Weep (Luke 23:27–31)

The fourth and final Lukan passage concerning the destruction of Jerusalem brings that event once again into close proximity to the death of Jesus. The verses appear in the midst of Luke's passion narrative, as Jesus is being led to his place of crucifixion.

> [27] A great number of the people followed him, and among them were women who were beating their breasts and wailing for him. [28] But Jesus turned to them and said, "Daughters of Jerusalem, do not weep for me, but weep for yourselves and for your children. [29] For the days are surely coming when they will say,

28. Tannehill, *Luke*, 305–6.

> 'Blessed [*makariai*] are the barren, and the wombs that never bore, and the breasts that never nursed.' 30 Then they will begin to say to the mountains, 'Fall on us'; and to the hills, 'Cover us.' 31 For if they do this when the wood is green, what will happen when it is dry?" (Luke 23:27–31)

These verses, which appear only in Luke, contain a number of noteworthy features for our purposes. First, the women who beat their breasts and wail for Jesus' fate show that the city is divided in her response to Jesus, just as she will later be divided in her response to the twelve (Acts 5:33–39), Stephen (Acts 8:2), and Paul (Acts 23:6–10).[29] Nevertheless, in the final analysis, those who are sympathetic to Jesus and his disciples are unable to carry the day. Second, these women respond to what is happening to Jesus in the same way that he responded to what he envisioned of Jerusalem's fate as he anticipated his arrival in the city (Luke 13) and as he actually approached its gates (Luke 19). This gospel has already sounded the note of grief, and these women are but echoing a note that readers have heard before. Third, this echo means that readers have been prepared for the response that Jesus gives to the wailing women when he points them to what should be the true object of their grief. The passages being echoed—Luke 13 and 19—also enable us to understand the tone of Jesus' words to the women. He does not speak harshly or vindictively, but instead beckons the women to join him in his own grief for Jerusalem which is coming to a head as he reaches his place of execution. Fourth, Jesus' words concerning the happiness of barren women in that day allude to a verse from our previous passage: "Woe to those who are pregnant and to those who are nursing infants in those days!" (Luke 21:23). "Woe" (*ouai*) and "blessed" (*makariai*) are parallel and converse forms of speech, and Luke's literary preference for balancing one with the other is evidenced by Luke 6:20–26. Those who are "blessed" here in our fourth passage on the destruction of Jerusalem are those who are not subject to the "woe" of our third passage. Thus, the beginning of Luke's crucifixion narrative (Luke 23:27–31) echoes the three earlier grieving-for-Jerusalem texts (Luke 13:31–35; 19:41–44; and 21:20–24) as it sets the stage for their dramatic enactment. This echo confirms the bond connecting these four texts, and their special role in telegraphing an essential feature of the author's message.

29. In the case of the twelve and Paul, those sympathetic to the disciples of Jesus are Pharisees, just as we found Pharisees warning Jesus regarding Herod Antipas in Luke 13.

A fifth and final point concerns the closing words of this passage: "For if they do this when the wood is green, what will happen when it is dry?" (Luke 23:31). N. T. Wright describes this as one of Jesus' many "riddles" that reveal the meaning of what is happening in his crucifixion. Jesus is innocent of violent insurrection, yet he suffers the punishment reserved by the Romans for just such offenders. He is the green wood, which will be burned up in the "baptism of fire" that he must undergo. If one innocent of offense suffers in this way, what will be the fate of the city as a whole and its leaders—the dry wood—when the torch is tossed in their pile? In this way, Jesus takes his place as the innocent representative of his people, who bears in advance the judgment that they merit and will eventually receive. In interpreting this "riddle" Wright points readers in the proper direction:

> . . . what is happening to Jesus is a foretaste of what will happen to many more young Jews in the not too distant future. . . . It suggests, in its dark riddling way, that Jesus understood his death as being organically linked with the fate of the nation. He was dying as the rejected king, who had offered the way of peace which the city had rejected; as the representative king, taking Israel's suffering upon himself, though not here even with any hint that Israel would thereby escape. . . . Having announced the divine judgment upon Temple and nation alike, a judgment which would take the form of awful devastation at the hands of the pagan forces, Jesus was now going ahead of the nation, to undergo the punishment which, above all, symbolized the judgment of Rome on her rebel subjects. If they did this to the one revolutionary who was not advocating rebellion against Rome, what would they do to those who were, and those who followed them?[30]

Jesus here signals that his death is "organically linked with the fate of the nation." By inserting this fourth passage on the destruction of Jerusalem in the midst of the passion narrative, Luke underlines this organic linkage. In other words, rather than attempting to dissuade the daughters of Jerusalem from grieving at his death, Jesus urges them to recognize how his death—his "baptism of fire" (Luke 3:16; 12:49–50)—anticipates the national conflagration to come. He thus invites them to grieve *with* him rather than merely *for* him.

30. Wright, *Jesus and the Victory of God*, 570.

Jerusalem's Resurrection

These four passages confirm the assertion of N. T. Wright cited earlier concerning the shape of Luke's narrative. The author gives special attention to the future destruction of Jerusalem, and presents that catastrophe as intimately connected to the suffering and death of Jesus. In part, these passages imply that the events of 70 CE are a consequence of the events of 30 CE—or, more precisely, a consequence of the consistent behavior over several generations which comes to a head with Jerusalem's rejection of its divinely-appointed king. However, as implied by the riddle of the green wood and the dry, and by the grief of the soon-to-be-crucified Jesus, which has as its object not his own suffering but that which the city will undergo a generation later, the relationship between the two events is more complicated than such an exclusively unidirectional analysis would suggest. Indeed, Luke views the destruction of Jerusalem as judgment for the unjust execution of Jesus; but he also sees Jesus' death as a voluntary act in which Jerusalem's future king proleptically bears the judgment that will come upon his guilty but still beloved city.

Luke considers Jerusalem to be Jesus' rightful possession, though this Galilean has never resided there. This is evident already in the story of Jesus' visit to Jerusalem as a twelve-year old boy, accompanying his parents to celebrate the Passover.

> 43 When the festival was ended and they started to return, the boy [*pais*] Jesus stayed behind in Jerusalem, but his parents did not know it. . . . 45 When they did not find him, they returned to Jerusalem to search for him. 46 After three days they found him in the temple, sitting among the teachers, listening to them and asking them questions. . . . 49 He said to them, "Why were you searching for me? Did you not know that I must be in my Father's house?" (Luke 2:43–49)

The NRSV interprets Jesus' response as referring to the temple ("my Father's house"), but the Greek is less specific: *en tois tou patrou mou* means "in the things/places of my Father." Jesus may be speaking of the temple in particular, but he may also refer to the city as a whole. The use of *pais* ("boy") in verse 43 may also be significant. Elsewhere in the Lukan writings the word is used as a title for David and for Jesus as David's heir.[31] Jerusalem was the city of David and his dynasty, and therefore for

31. For *pais* in reference to King David, see Luke 1:69; Acts 4:25; for the same word in reference to Jesus as David's heir, see Acts 3:13, 26; 4:27, 30.

Luke it is also the city of Jesus. There may even be a play on words in the term *pater* in verse 49: the city of Jerusalem and its temple belong ultimately to God (Jesus' divine "Father"), but God has bestowed it as a heritage upon David (Jesus' human "father" or ancestor).

If Luke links the destruction of Jerusalem to the death of Jesus, and if in the very texts that establish that link he also anticipates a future restoration of Jerusalem as the capital of the Jewish people, it seems natural to ask a question that is rarely considered: does Luke assume the same sort of connection between Jesus' resurrection and the future "redemption of Jerusalem" (Luke 2:38) as exists between Jesus' death and the events of 70 CE?[32] Good reasons exist for answering that question in the affirmative. Prominent among them is Luke's pattern of associating the resurrection of Jesus with God's promises to David and his dynasty.[33] The author highlights this theme by featuring it prominently in the two most important speeches of Acts—Peter's first public proclamation of the apostolic message on the day of Pentecost, and Paul's speech in the synagogue of Pisidian Antioch on his first apostolic journey. Peter argues for the resurrection and ascension of Jesus by citing Psalms 16 and 110 and noting that their traditional author, David, spoke of events that he did not experience in his own life:

> [25] For David says concerning him . . . [27] "For you will not abandon my soul to Hades, or let your Holy One experience corruption . . . ." [29] Fellow Israelites, I may say to you confidently of our ancestor David that he both died and was buried, and his tomb is with us to this day. [30] Since he was a prophet, he knew that God had sworn with an oath to him that he would put one of his descendants on his throne. [31] Foreseeing this, David spoke of the resurrection of the Messiah . . . . [32] This Jesus God raised up, and of that all of us are witnesses. [33] Being therefore exalted

32. Peter Walker (*Jesus and the Holy City*, 78) succeeds in articulating this question forcefully: "the close connection between Jesus' death and Jerusalem's fate invites the question: would Luke have seen any parallel for Jerusalem comparable to Jesus' resurrection? One tragedy (Jesus' death) was followed by a divine reversal; would the same hold for the other tragedy (Jerusalem's destruction)?" However, because he is convinced that Luke-Acts—and the New Testament as a whole—anticipate no restoration of Jewish Jerusalem (and because that conviction governs his entire volume), the best he can offer in response is the suggestion that perhaps this is "precisely the point of contrast between the two." Given the emphasis in Luke-Acts on the "redemption of Jerusalem" (Luke 2:38), this is a weak response to a powerful question.

33. Jacob Jervell contends that Luke sees David, "father of the Messiah," as "the prophet par excellence, the central figure in Scripture" (*The Unknown Paul*, 126–31).

> at the right hand of God, and having received from the Father the promise of the Holy Spirit, he has poured out this that you both see and hear. [34] For David did not ascend into the heavens, but he himself says, "The Lord said to my Lord, 'Sit at my right hand, [35] until I make your enemies your footstool.'" [36] Therefore let the entire house of Israel know with certainty that God has made him both Lord and Messiah, this Jesus whom you crucified. (Acts 2:25–36)

The resurrection of Jesus constitutes his vindication and glorification as the promised Son of David, and his subsequent ascension represents his heavenly enthronement as "Lord and Messiah."

In Luke's description of Paul's opening speech we find the same exegetical logic displayed. He first underlines the importance of Jesus' lineage as David's descendant and heir (Acts 13:22–23). He then cites Psalm 2 as a Davidic prophecy of the resurrection (Acts 13:33) to accompany a reference to Psalm 16 (Acts 13:35) which he shares with Peter. He also adds an illuminating text from Isaiah 55:3: "As to his raising him from the dead, no more to return to corruption, he has spoken in this way, 'I will give you the holy promises made to David'" (Acts 13:34). The resurrection of Jesus thus stands at the heart of the "holy promises made to David." In other words, that momentous event is not merely the raising of a holy Galilean prophet in whom God was uniquely present, but also the glorification of Israel's Davidic king whose eternal reign could not be divorced from the city that was elected to be the place of his throne.[34] If the Son of David has been raised from the dead, and if the city of David is destined to likewise be raised from the dead, we have sufficient reason to see the former as a firm pledge, proleptic realization, and efficient cause of the latter.

This conclusion is reinforced by Paul's final speeches in Acts in which the resurrection of Jesus is presented as the source of hope for Israel's national resurrection.[35] When Paul appears before the Sanhedrin, he identifies himself as a Pharisee (i.e., as member of a party for whom

34. On the election of Jerusalem and its association with the election of David, see Psalm 132:11–18.

35. Peter Walker underlines this emphasis in the Pauline speeches of Acts. However, for Walker this only demonstrates that "for Luke the restoration had already been inaugurated through Jesus" (*Jesus and the Holy City*, 98). He acknowledges that "in a final sense Israel is 'restored' only at the Last Day" (99). However, he dismisses any notion that the final restoration might involve an earthly Jerusalem and a genealogical Israel. He thus misses a central Lukan theme.

Israel's future resurrection is a fundamental tenet of faith), and then makes the claim, "I am on trial concerning the hope of the resurrection of the dead" (Acts 23:6). The word "dead" here is plural ("resurrection of *those who are dead*"). Paul thus refers to the hope for Israel's future resurrection, a hope that he shares with his fellow Pharisees. While this claim was a shrewd political maneuver, setting the Pharisees in his audience against the Sadducees, it was also an entirely accurate statement. Paul was on trial for his proclamation of the risen Messiah of Israel, whose resurrection funded a firm and joyful hope in Israel's corporate destiny.

Paul restates this claim when he appears before Felix, the Roman governor (Acts 24:15, 21), but the fullest articulation of Paul's message of national hope and resurrection occurs when he appears before King Agrippa:

> [5] I have belonged to the strictest sect of our religion and lived as a Pharisee. [6] And now I stand here on trial on account of my hope in the promise made by God to our ancestors, [7] a promise that our twelve tribes hope to attain, as they earnestly worship day and night. It is for this hope, your Excellency, that I am accused by Jews! [8] Why is it thought incredible by any of you that God raises the dead [plural]? . . . [22] To this day I have had help from God, and so I stand here, testifying to both small and great, saying nothing but what the prophets and Moses said would take place: [23] that the Messiah must suffer, and that, by being the first to rise from the dead, he would proclaim light both to our people and to the gentiles. (Acts 26:5–8, 22–23)

Jesus is only "the first to rise from the dead," and Paul implies that his resurrection will be instrumental in effecting Israel's future resurrection, the "promise that our twelve tribes hope to attain." Paul does not here link Jesus' resurrection to the restoration of Jerusalem, since at this point in the narrative the city and its temple remained intact. Instead, he focuses more generally on Israel's national hope of future glory. In his final speech in Acts, this time to the Jewish leaders of Rome, Paul again reiterates his conviction that the message he proclaims concerns Israel's corporate destiny: "For this reason therefore I have asked to see you and speak with you, since it is for the sake of the hope of Israel that I am bound with this chain" (Acts 28:20). The "hope of Israel" to which Paul refers here is not Jesus himself, but the eschatological renewal of Israel that Jesus will accomplish. For readers at the end of the first century, aware that in the years immediately following Paul's proclamation Zion was not glorified but instead burned to the ground, these words would point to a future redemption of the city, which would be a true resurrection from the dead.[36]

This proposal regarding Luke's view of Jesus' resurrection coheres perfectly with Luke's portrayal of Jesus' death. Luke sets these two intertwined events within the context of a proleptic Israel-Christology, in which Jesus' death and resurrection are intrinsically and inseparably bound to Israel's eschatological destiny. For greater precision, one might characterize Luke's teaching as *Jerusalem-Christology*. But such a Jerusalem-Christology is but a particular expression of Israel-Christology. For Luke, as for Isaiah, Jeremiah, and Ezekiel, Jerusalem represents both the *people* of Israel and the *land* of Israel, fusing in one vivid image the corporate life of the Jewish people and the site apportioned as its promised inheritance.

Jerusalem and the Geographical Structure of Luke and Acts

The author/editor of Luke and Acts reinforces the thematic centrality of Jerusalem for his two volumes by structuring his narrative geographically, with Jerusalem as its pivot. No other books in the New Testament adhere to such a defined geographical pattern as a primary principle of organization. An examination of the geographical structure of Luke and Acts will provide clues regarding the message which the two volumes convey.

The Geographical Structure of the Gospel of Luke

Among the four Gospels, only Luke begins in Jerusalem—and not only in Jerusalem, but in the temple, with the future father of John the Baptist offering incense in the holy place and receiving there an angelic visitation. While both Matthew and Luke describe Jesus' birth near Jerusalem in Bethlehem, only Luke depicts the presentation of the infant Jesus in the Jerusalem temple, accompanied by the prophetic blessings of Simeon and

36. For a perceptive treatment of this theme in the Pauline speeches of Acts, see Tannehill, *The Narrative Unity of Luke-Acts, Volume 2*, 319–20. His conclusion concerning Acts 26:6–7 is especially apt: "Thus the hope and promise of which Paul speaks in 26:6–7 is not merely a hope for individual life after death but a hope for the Jewish people, to be realized through resurrection."

Anna. Only Luke among the canonical Gospels provides readers with a story of Jesus as a youth, and that story recounts his visit to Jerusalem for Passover and his lingering there in the courts of the temple. Thus, Luke's two-chapter introduction centers on the city of Jerusalem and its temple.

From the beginning of chapter 3 to the final paragraphs of chapter nine, Luke shifts focus to Galilee, following for the most part the order of events recorded in the Gospel of Mark. Then Luke begins a new section of his narrative which combines material from the double tradition (i.e., units shared by Luke and Matthew but not Mark) with material unique to Luke. The new section begins in this way: "When the days drew near for him to be taken up, he set his face to go to Jerusalem" (Luke 9:51). The next nine chapters of Luke's "Special Section" take the form of an extended travel narrative encompassing Jesus' final journey to Jerusalem (Luke 9:51—18:14). The material itself is only loosely geographical in character, consisting of parables and stories that for the most part lack an intrinsic connection to the journey and its destination. Nevertheless, Luke has chosen to organize the material around such a journey, with occasional editorial reminders of the geographical context (e.g., Luke 13:22; 17:11). In this way the central section of Luke's narrative, which occurs outside Jerusalem, employs the holy city as its point of orientation and source of structural unity.

As in all four Gospels, the events of Luke's passion narrative occur in Jerusalem and its immediate environs. However, only Luke restricts resurrection appearances to that location, and only Luke includes the dominical command that the disciples remain in the city (Luke 24:49). The Gospel ends as it began—in the Jerusalem temple, with a community of Jews worshipping the God of Israel (Luke 24:53).

Among the canonical Gospels only Luke begins *in* Jerusalem, ends *in* Jerusalem, and orients its central narrative around a journey *to* Jerusalem. Taken together with the particular Lukan material related to the destruction and redemption of Jerusalem considered above, this emphatic geographical structure underlines Luke's unique concern for the holy city and her enduring theological significance.

The Geographical Structure of Acts of the Apostles

Acts of the Apostles likewise features a narrative ordered according to a geographical pattern centered in Jerusalem, and that pattern finds explicit articulation in the verses that follow the book's preface:

> [6] So when they had come together, they asked him, "Lord, is this the time when you will restore the kingdom to Israel?" [7] He replied, "It is not for you to know the times or periods that the Father has set by his own authority. [8] But you will receive power when the Holy Spirit has come upon you; and you will be my witnesses in Jerusalem, in all Judea and Samaria, and to the ends of the earth." (Acts 1:6–8)

These are crucial verses for a proper interpretation of the entire book. Is Jesus attempting to correct the ethnocentric worldview of his disciples and urging them to adopt in its place a universal perspective in which Jerusalem and the Jewish people forfeit their role as the fulcrum and goal of the divine purpose? Only a reader holding such a belief as an established presupposition would interpret the verses in this way. In the text itself the only issue at hand is "the time"—will Israel's full eschatological restoration occur *now* (or *later*)? On even this point Jesus refrains from offering a negative answer but instead denies the appropriateness of the question. We will return to this topic momentarily. At this juncture we must attend to the substance of the response he does give: "'But you will receive power when the Holy Spirit has come upon you; and you will be my witnesses in Jerusalem, in all Judea and Samaria, and to the ends of the earth.'" As has been noted by generations of interpreters, this verse supplies us with a rough geographical outline of Acts.

Like the Gospel of Luke, Acts of the Apostles begins in Jerusalem, with a community centered on the temple (Acts 2:46; 3:1–10; 4:1–2; 5:12; 5:20–21; 5:42). The story develops as the message and power of Jesus radiate outwards—first to the towns of Judea and Samaria (Acts 8:1, 4–25), then with reference to Damascus (Acts 9:1–2, 10, 19). In Acts 10, Peter brings the message of Jesus to the gentile Cornelius and his household in the coastal city of Caesarea. Then in Acts 13 Paul begins his travels, wending his way through Asia Minor, and eventually crossing over to Europe and establishing Jesus-believing communities in Greece. The story concludes with Paul in Rome, capital of the Empire.

This narrative outline, like the condensed geographical summary of Acts 1:8, leaves out a particular detail that has profound implications for our interpretation of the geographical structure of Acts: while radiating steadily outwards, *the story continually reverts back to Jerusalem*.[37] Paul

37. Peter Walker notes this feature of the geographical structure of Acts, but minimizes its significance: "There are frequent returns to Jerusalem, but these become fewer, and give way to Paul's extended journey away from Jerusalem towards Rome. There

encounters Jesus on the road to Damascus, *and then returns to Jerusalem* (Acts 9:26–29). Peter proclaims Jesus to Cornelius in Caesarea, *and then returns to Jerusalem* (Acts 11:2). A congregation arises in Antioch, *and then sends aid to Jerusalem* in a time of famine (Acts 11:27–30). Paul and Barnabas journey from Antioch to Asia Minor, *and then return afterward to Jerusalem* for the central event in the book of Acts—the Jerusalem council (Acts 15:2). From Jerusalem Paul travels with Silas to Greece, *and then returns again to Jerusalem* (Acts 18:22).[38] Paul takes his final journey as a free man, *and then returns to Jerusalem*, where he is arrested (Acts 21:17—23:11). While this feature of the geographical structure of Acts is often ignored by commentators, Robert Brawley sees it clearly and notes its significance:

> Although Acts begins in Jerusalem and ends in Rome, it is inaccurate to conclude that Jerusalem falls out in favor of Rome. The narrative in Acts actually reciprocates between Jerusalem and the extended mission. . . . Even when Paul is in Rome, his memory reverts to Jerusalem to reiterate his fate there (28:17). Hence, Acts does not delineate a movement away from Jerusalem, but *a constant return to Jerusalem*. In the geography of Acts emphasis repeatedly falls on Jerusalem from beginning to end.[39]

If indeed Acts 1:8 is a geographical outline of the book, then its language supports this conclusion, for it characterizes Rome as being located at "the *ends* of the earth." Rome may be the capital of a gentile empire, holding political control over much of the earth, but for Luke and Acts it was neither the *center* nor the true capital of the world. That honor belonged to Jerusalem alone.

is a gradual severance from Jerusalem, with the city becoming increasingly 'dispensable'" (*Jesus and the Holy City*, 81–82). The "returns" do not, in fact, become "fewer," for every journey taken—except the last one—is concluded with such a "return." Since the entire point of Acts is to document the spread of the apostolic message and community from Jerusalem "to the ends of the earth," it is essential that Paul's journeys are of increasingly longer duration and take him farther away from Jerusalem. The fact that he always *returns* to the city after laboring at "the ends of the earth" shows that Jerusalem remains his *center*, that there is no "gradual severance" from the city, and that the notion of Jerusalem's "dispensability" is alien to Luke and Acts.

38. "When he goes on to say that *Paul went up and greeted the church*, this is usually understood as a reference to going up to Jerusalem and seeing the church there. . . . If this is a correct assumption, it means that each of Paul's missionary campaigns concluded with a visit to Jerusalem, so that Paul's work began from and ended in Jerusalem in each case" (Marshall, *Acts*, 301–2).

39. Brawley, *Luke-Acts and the Jews*, 35–36. Emphasis added.

This assessment finds further confirmation in the geographical structure of the list of Jews gathered for the holiday of Pentecost (Acts 2:5, 9–11). Richard Bauckham has analyzed this list, and his results deserve lengthy citation:

> Luke's list of the nations and countries from which the pilgrims attending the festival of Pentecost had come (Acts 2:9–11) provides a much more authentically *Jerusalem* perspective on the Diaspora. The order in which the names occur has perplexed interpreters. In fact, if we take the trouble to plot the names on a map of the world as an ancient reader would have perceived it, we can see that Luke's list is carefully designed to depict the Jewish Diaspora with Jerusalem at its centre. . . . The names in Acts 2:9–11 are listed in four groups corresponding to the four points of the compass, beginning in the east and moving counterclockwise. . . . The first group of names in the list . . . *begins in the far east and moves in towards Judaea*, which is then named. Recognizing that Judaea is in the list because it is the centre of the pattern described by the names is the key to understanding the list. The second group of names . . . is of places to the north of Judaea, and follows *an order which moves out from and back to Judaea*, ending at the point from which one might sail to Judaea. The third group of names . . . moves west from Judaea through Egypt . . . and Libya to Rome, *and then back to Judaea* by a sea route calling at Crete. Finally, a single name (Arabs) represents the movement south from Judaea, presumably indicating Nabataea, immediately due south of Judaea . . . .[40]

This list depicts Jerusalem as the center of the world. Moreover, it follows the same rhythm of outward and inward movement that characterizes the entire narrative of Acts. Reading Acts 1:8 in light of Acts 2:9–11 and in light of the overall narrative structure of Acts, we might say that the Pentecost list portrays the actual historical spread of the apostolic message in accordance with Acts 1:8, whereas the narrative of Acts focuses on one particular strand of that greater story—the strand associated with the figure of Paul. In both the greater story of the advance of the apostolic message and the more circumscribed story of Paul, the heart beats in an alternating diastolic and systolic rhythm, with Jerusalem as the perpetual center *to which all must eventually return*.

40. Bauckham, "James and the Jerusalem Church," 419. Emphasis added.

The Puzzling Conclusion to Acts of the Apostles

Yet, Acts ends in Rome rather than in Jerusalem. Moreover, it ends with Paul's rebuke of the Jewish leaders of Rome as those whose hearts had been dulled by a divine judgment, in accordance with the words of Isaiah 6. In many respects this is a puzzling conclusion to these two volumes. The second half of Acts deals exclusively with the work of Paul, who will die in Rome as a martyr not many years after the events described in Acts 28. Luke could have brought closure to his narrative of the early *ekklēsia* by recounting Paul's heroic death, yet he refrains from doing so. As we have seen above, the Gospel of Luke gives more attention to the destruction of Jerusalem than any other book in the New Testament, and both Luke and Acts were composed after this cataclysmic event. Luke could have brought closure to his narrative by concluding with a reference to the ruin of Jerusalem, yet he again refrains from doing so.

I propose that this lack of closure constitutes the essential message of Acts 28. The story that Luke is telling is not concluded, but has in fact only just begun. Ending with the death of Paul could signal that the proclamation of the kingdom of God and the earthly realization of its transforming power had come to a suitable narrative climax. Luke seeks to forestall such a false inference by concluding the book with the statement that Paul "lived there [i.e., in Rome] for two whole years at his own expense and welcomed all who came to him, proclaiming the kingdom of God and teaching about the Lord Jesus Christ with all boldness and without hindrance" (Acts 28:30–31). The work must continue, the kingdom to come must still be proclaimed, lived, and awaited. Similarly, ending with Jerusalem in ruins could signal that God had given up on the Jewish people and had made Rome the capital of not only a gentile empire but also of a reconstituted "Israel." Luke seeks to forestall such a false inference by avoiding explicit reference here to Jerusalem's destruction, only alluding to it cryptically through Paul's citation of Isaiah 6.

This reading of the end of Acts finds its most powerful support in the beginning of Acts. As we saw above, the first chapter of Acts begins with a question from the apostles to Jesus: "Lord, is this the time [*chronos*] when you will restore the kingdom to Israel?" (Acts 1:6.). They ask this question in Jerusalem, where the Messiah has just been raised from the dead. They clearly anticipate the imminent restoration of the Davidic kingdom in its ancestral capital.

The disciples appear to have forgotten Jesus' earlier teaching regarding the destruction of Jerusalem: "Jerusalem will be trampled on by the gentiles, until the times [*kairoi*] of the gentiles are fulfilled" (Luke 21:24). Jesus' response to their question about the Davidic kingdom reminds the disciples of his earlier words concerning the trampling of Jerusalem: "It is not for you to know the times [*chronoi*] or periods [*kairoi*] that the Father has set by his own authority" (Acts 1:7). The death and resurrection of the Messiah has begun the process that will lead to the overthrow of the final gentile empire, but Luke makes clear that much suffering still remains for the people of Israel and the city of Jerusalem. Since Jerusalem will soon be "trampled on by the gentiles," it is evident that the kingdom is now being restored to Israel in only a partial and imperfect fashion. Luke still awaits that day when "the times of the gentiles are fulfilled," which will also introduce the "time" when God will "restore the kingdom to Israel." Therefore, he rightly decides to leave his narrative without closure, for the narrative of God's dealings with Jerusalem, Israel, and the nations has not yet been closed.

Luke wants his readers to grasp the rhythmic geographical flow of his narrative, which streams out from Jerusalem always to return again, like waves that beat on the rocks and then return to their ocean home. He leaves his narrative in mid-flow, in anticipation of its future consummation that will occur at some point *after* the judgment of Jerusalem. Rome may be at the "ends of the earth," but it is not the end of the story. The story must end where it began—in Jerusalem.

The verses immediately following the opening dialogue between Jesus and his disciples in Acts 1 confirm this conclusion.

> 9 When he had said this, as they were watching, he was lifted up,
> and a cloud took him out of their sight. 10 While he was going
> and they were gazing up towards heaven, suddenly two men in
> white robes stood by them. 11 They said, "Men of Galilee, why
> do you stand looking up towards heaven? This Jesus, who has
> been taken up from you into heaven, will come in the same way
> as you saw him go into heaven." 12 Then they returned to Jerusalem from the mount called Olivet, which is near Jerusalem, a
> Sabbath day's journey away. (Acts 1:9–12)

What is meant by the revelation that Jesus "will come in the same way as you saw him go"? Verse 12 hints at the answer by telling us that the ascension occurred on the Mount of Olives. Luke's reference to the location alludes to the eschatological prophecy of Zechariah 14:

> For I will gather all the nations against Jerusalem to battle. . . . Then the Lord will go forth and fight against those nations as when he fights on a day of battle. On that day *his feet shall stand on the Mount of Olives*, which lies before Jerusalem on the east; and the Mount of Olives shall be split in two from east to west by a very wide valley. . . . *Then the* Lord *my God will come, and all the holy ones with him.* (Zech 14:2–5)

Given the almost certain allusion to Zechariah 14, and Luke's unequivocal Jerusalem-centered cartography, the phrase "in the same way" should be read as including the geographical site of the two events. Just as Jesus ascends now *from* the Mount of Olives, so he will descend at the end *to* the Mount of Olives. Just as the Mount of Olives serves now as his point of departure from Jerusalem, so that same site will mark his point of entry to the city when he returns. The angelic message calls the disciples to remember Jesus' "non-triumphal entry" on Palm Sunday, and to acknowledge that earlier event as a prophetic anticipation of the "triumphal entry" that is yet to come.

Acts 1:9–12 may also allude to the departure and return of the divine glory (*kavod*) as described in the prophet Ezekiel. When the *kavod* departs from the temple it first stops and rests on "the mountain east of the city" (Ezek 11:23)—that is, the Mount of Olives. When the *kavod* returns to the temple it comes "from the east" (Ezek 43:2)—that is, from the exiles in Mesopotamia. The prophet views the returning *kavod* from the vantage point of the Temple Mount, and so stands looking at the Mount of Olives. Thus, Ezekiel sees the *kavod* return "in the same way" as he saw it depart.[41]

Jerusalem will suffer many things, as the prophecies of Zechariah (12–14), Ezekiel, and Jesus (Luke 13, 19, 21, and 23) all foretell. But the city will be consoled when the Lord comes to defend her at the end, his feet standing on the Mount of Olives. "On that day" the Lord will be welcomed by Jerusalem in a fitting manner, reversing the failure of Palm Sunday. "On that day" the leaders and the people of the city will go out together to meet him, proclaiming with joy, "Blessed is the one who comes in the name of the Lord" (Luke 13:35; 19:38).[42]

41. Klaus Baltzer sees the relevance of these texts in Ezekiel for Luke and Acts, but he fails to draw the logical conclusion regarding the eschatological-geographical significance of Acts 1:9–12. See Baltzer, "The Meaning of the Temple in the Lukan Writings."

42. Peter Walker rightly underlines the importance of the Mount of Olives for

The narrative of the ascension in Acts 1:9–12 provides us with the strongest and clearest evidence for the Jerusalem-centered eschatology of Luke and Acts. This crucial scene set on the Mount of Olives casts a long shadow, encompassing the non-triumphal entry in Luke 19, the anticipation of that entry in Luke 13, and the disciples' question about the restoration of Israel's kingdom in the verses immediately preceding (Acts 1:6–8). Given the importance of this scene, it is surprising to see how little attention it receives from those who study Lukan eschatology. The present volume seeks to correct this error of negligence.

An eschatological reading of Acts 1:9–12 that highlights the allusion to Zechariah 14 enables us to perceive another signal of the incomplete character of Luke and Acts and their eschatological hope for "the redemption of Jerusalem"—namely, the approach taken by these two volumes to the pilgrimage festivals of Israel.[43] Early in Luke we read of Jesus and his family journeying to Jerusalem to celebrate the early-spring pilgrimage festival of Passover (Luke 2:41). As already noted, the central narrative of Luke is then structured around Jesus' journey to Jerusalem, again in order to celebrate the Passover (Luke 22:1, 7–8, 11, 13, 15). Acts of the Apostles has a similar orientation to the late-spring pilgrimage festival, Pentecost. The book begins with the giving of the Spirit on this day (Acts 2:1). Later the book describes Paul's final journey to Jerusalem in a way that makes it resemble Jesus' pilgrimage before his death.[44] But whereas Jesus went to Jerusalem to celebrate Passover, Paul goes for Pentecost (Acts 20:16). The narrative of Acts is thus focused on Pentecost in the same way as the narrative of Luke is focused on Passover. This covers the first two pilgrimage festivals of Israel—but what about the third, the autumn feast of Booths? The festival year is incomplete without this crucial

the narrative of Luke and Acts. However, he misses the allusion to Zechariah 14 and to Palm Sunday, and so misinterprets the text, claiming that the author *contrasts* the Mount and the city in favor of the Mount: "the Mount of Olives, not Jerusalem, is the geographical 'hinge' of Luke-Acts. . . . The Christian gospel has a close connection to Jerusalem, but its centre is fractionally, but significantly, different . . ." (*Jesus and the Holy City*, 81). In fact, the significance of the Mount of Olives in the narrative derives from its destined role as the first stage of the divine entrance *to the city*. Rather than detracting from the holiness and centrality of Jerusalem, the Lukan emphasis on the Mount of Olives serves to confirm those very characteristics.

43. I first proposed this interpretation of Luke's approach to the Jewish holidays in *Postmissionary Messianic Judaism*, 121.

44. "The parallels with Jesus' final journey to Jerusalem have often been noted and are considerable" (Witherington, *The Acts of the Apostles*, 627–28).

feast, which anticipates the final harvest and Israel's redeemed life (with the nations) in the world to come. It is likely that already in first-century Judaism, as in later Jewish tradition, a key reading from the prophets for this holiday was Zechariah 14. "And the LORD will become king over all the earth; on that day the LORD will be one and his name one. . . . Then all who survive of the nations that have come against Jerusalem shall go up year after year to worship the King, the LORD of hosts, and to keep the festival of booths" (Zech 14:9, 16). If the Gospel of Luke is related to Passover, and the Acts of the Apostles to Pentecost, then the as-yet-unwritten conclusion to this trilogy will be related to Booths. In the eschatological celebration that will fulfill the meaning of this holiday, the nations will join Israel in Jerusalem to glorify the One who is the "king over all the earth." Thus will be realized the "kingdom of God," which, according to the final verse of Acts, Paul proclaimed in Rome "with all boldness and without hindrance" (Acts 28:31). Only then will the story find its ultimate closure.

The conclusion of Acts, read in relation to the beginning of the book, supports our thesis. The geographical structure of Luke and Acts conveys the same message we discerned in their substantive message: the resurrection of Jesus is the pledge and power that ensures Jerusalem's future redemption. Only then will the "kingdom of God" reach its appointed goal.

Proleptic Joy in the Midst of Exile

Biblical scholarship is indebted to N. T. Wright for his identification of the theme of exile as central to the thinking of first-century Judaism and to the New Testament.[45] However, Wright's construal of that theme in the New Testament has problematic features. According to his reading, Jesus and the apostles assumed that the Babylonian exile continued even after the temple was rebuilt. In his death, Jesus endured the full power of that exile, and in his resurrection he overcame that power. When Jews rally to the resurrected Messiah, they become those who have already returned from exile. Paradoxically, the destruction of Jerusalem in 70 CE

45. Wright provides a succinct and nuanced explanation of his use of the term "exile" in Newman (ed.), *Jesus & the Restoration of Israel*, 257–61. In the same volume Craig Evans supports Wright's approach to exile ("Jesus & the Continuing Exile of Israel," 77–100). For more recent discussion, see Scott (ed.), *Exile: A Conversation with N.T. Wright*.

involves no intensification of exile but instead demonstrates its termination by confirming the prophetic words and actions of Jesus. Jerusalem had become the new Babylon, persecuting the servants of God, and her definitive judgment represented God's victory and the vindication of God's servants.[46]

Luke's reiterated lament at the fall of Jerusalem and expression of hope for Jerusalem's future redemption manifest a vision of Israel's restoration and exile that is far more complex than that offered by N. T. Wright. On the one hand, Luke would agree with Wright that the resurrection of Jesus constitutes the first-fruits and source of Israel's ultimate restoration. On the other hand, Luke also sees the destruction of Jerusalem as a new stage in Israel's enduring exile, which will not end until "the times of the gentiles are fulfilled." The exile endured by Jesus in his suffering and death was not primarily the exile that began in the distant past when the Babylonians destroyed Jerusalem and that continued to his own day, but the intensified exile that was coming upon his people in the near future at the hands of the Romans. Moreover, Luke portrays Jerusalem as both the capital of the Jewish people and the international center of the community of Jesus' disciples—and indeed of the world itself. The agony and humiliation of the city at the hands of the Romans inspired in his work a profound sense of grief rather than exultation.

We find this complex vision of exile and restoration not only in Luke but in the Synoptic tradition as a whole. No better witness to this complexity exists than the story of Jesus' teaching concerning feasting and fasting. All three Synoptic Gospels contain this pericope with little significant variation. Here is Luke's version:

> 33 Then they said to him, "John's disciples, like the disciples of the Pharisees, frequently fast and pray, but your disciples eat and drink." 34 Jesus said to them, "You cannot make wedding-guests fast while the bridegroom is with them, can you? 35 The days will come when the bridegroom will be taken away from them, and then they will fast in those days." (Luke 5:33–35)

N. T. Wright's comments on this unit are instructive: "Fasting in this period was not, for Jews, simply an ascetic discipline, part of the general practice of piety. It had to do with Israel's present condition: she was still in exile. More specifically, it had to do with commemorating the destruction

46. On the destruction of Jerusalem as divine vindication and victory, see Wright's exegesis of Mark 13 in *Jesus and the Victory of God*, 339–65.

of the Temple. Zechariah's promise that the fasts would turn into feasts could come true only when YHWH restored the fortunes of his people. That, of course, was precisely what Jesus' cryptic comments implied."[47] Wright helpfully characterizes the practice of fasting as a corporate Jewish response to exile. He also rightly sees Jesus' feasting rather than fasting as a sign that Jesus is the one who will bring the exile to an end. However, in order to fit this text into his unambiguous understanding of restoration, Wright must go beyond this useful insight. "This is . . . a claim about eschatology. The time is fulfilled; the exile is over; the bridegroom is at hand. Jesus' acted symbol, feasting rather than fasting, brings into public visibility his controversial claim, that in his work Israel's hope was being realized; more specifically, that in his work *the Temple was being rebuilt*."[48] Unfortunately, this reading only makes sense if we ignore the final verse of the unit: "The days will come when the bridegroom will be taken away from them, and *then they will fast in those days*" (Luke 5:35). This verse implies that Jesus' physical presence served as a proleptic sign of the coming restoration, but was *not the final restoration itself*. Fasting was not appropriate in his physical presence, but it would be appropriate *after his ascension*. The resurrection and ascension of Jesus may secure the ultimate end of exile, but the appropriateness of fasting in the era inaugurated by these messianic events suggests that the condition of exile in some sense endures.

The restoration had begun, and through faith in Jesus, the gift of the Spirit, and participation in the apostolic community one could receive an authentic foretaste of the final redemption. Nevertheless, for Luke the destruction of Jerusalem constituted a new stage in the exile rather than its conclusion. Still, this new stage also contained positive elements, even for Jews outside the apostolic community. First, the doors of the apostolic community remained open, and there the powers of the messianic age were available in proleptic form. Second, the Messiah had risen from the dead and ascended on high, and these events—and his continued presence in the world by his Spirit—stood as a sure pledge of Jerusalem's ultimate restoration and glorification. Third, Jesus took upon himself Jerusalem's suffering when he died upon the cross. This established a dynamic connection between his redemptive work and the suffering endured by the Jewish people as a consequence of the exile. As

47. Wright, *Jesus and the Victory of God*, 433.

48. Wright, *Jesus and the Victory of God*, 434. Emphasis original.

one aspect of this connection, I propose that Luke envisions the Jewish people in post-70 exile as benefiting corporately from the redemptive suffering of Jesus—even apart from explicit communal reception of Jesus as Israel's Messiah. At the very least, we may confidently assert that the radical identification of Jesus with the Jewish people in his suffering and death—and in his resurrection and ascension—solidified a bond that is thereafter unbreakable.

The Roman conclusion of Acts may be viewed as further evidence for the author's vision of exile as both enduring and potentially redemptive. Writing from a post-70 vantage point, Luke knows that Roman armies will demolish Jerusalem after Paul dies in Rome. He concludes his two volumes with Paul proclaiming Jesus and "the kingdom" in the very city that will be the agent of divine judgment upon the promised seat of that kingdom. Rome thus occupies the same position vis-à-vis Jerusalem as that previously held by Babylon in the sixth century BCE. The armies of Babylon had destroyed Jerusalem and taken many of its inhabitants into exile; but it was from the midst of that exile, and from the city that had brought it to pass, that the post-exilic renewal of Judaism and the Jewish people would originate. Ezra, "a scribe skilled in the law of Moses," comes to Jerusalem "from Babylonia" (Ezra 7:6). For Luke, as for 1 Peter 5:13, Rome is the new Babylon, the agent of judgment on Jerusalem which is destined also to become an incubator for her eschatological renewal.

Luke thus sees the saving work of Jesus in his death and resurrection as simultaneously deepening Israel's exile (through the judgment of Jerusalem in 70 CE), transforming it to realize its redemptive potential (through association with Jesus' suffering and death), and initiating the exile's ultimate demise (through his resurrection). The community of Jesus' disciples takes its place in the midst of Israel, and in the midst of Israel's exile, as a prophetic sign of the meaning of that exile and a pledge of the restoration to come. In fellowship with their Messiah, the disciples of Jesus mourn for the destruction of Jerusalem, which was the center of their communal life and the focal point of their eschatological hope. With Paul, the *ekklēsia* takes up her temporary residence in Rome, at the *ends* of the earth—but without losing her expectation of returning home to Zion, the true capital of the world. Indeed, this is a far more complex vision of exile and restoration than the one enunciated by N. T. Wright. Though we should be grateful to Wright for highlighting the importance of exile and restoration for the New Testament, we should also recognize the limitations of his manner of elucidating that theme.

Conclusion

In light of this initial study of the Lukan writings, it appears that the portrait of James the Just found in Hegessipus reflects a tradition concerning Jerusalem and the Jewish people that existed more broadly among some of the early disciples of Jesus. In this tradition, the followers of Jesus in the city pray passionately for her redemption and, through their prayer and presence, seek to forestall the judgment that looms over Zion. The love shown for Jerusalem by the disciples of Jesus is identical to that shared by all Jews, as is the grief at her suffering and destruction.

This attitude toward Jerusalem and the Jewish people soon faded among gentile disciples of Jesus. In the wake of the Bar Kochba revolt of 132–35 CE, many retained the eschatological hope for Jerusalem seen in Luke and Acts, but, in stark contrast to these books, divorced that hope from any connection to the Jewish people. This means they rejoiced without trace of ambivalence in the destruction of *Jewish* Jerusalem in 70 CE, while at the same time cherishing an expectation of a future "Christian" (i.e., Jesus-ruled but non-Jewish) Jerusalem.

In the third century, even this de-Judaized eschatological hope for Jerusalem fades away. At that point the *ekklēsia* comes perilously close to losing any awareness of the holiness of earthly Zion. Then Constantine arrives on the scene, and launches a stunning building program that establishes Jerusalem as the center of the ecclesial world. The Lukan vision of Jerusalem as an intrinsically Jewish city, symbolizing the Jewish people itself and its hopes (a vision shared by Hegessipus), has been forgotten. So has the Lukan vision of Jerusalem as the future capital of a restored creation (a vision shared by Justin Martyr and Irenaeus). But a new vision emerges of Jerusalem as a sacramental city, binding the followers of Jesus to the redemptive events in the life of their Master. This attitude to the holy city recaptures other aspects of the Lukan reverence for Jerusalem, especially those manifested in his infancy narrative.

As a result of Constantine's Christianization of Jerusalem, the holy city once again takes its place as a crucial component of the ecclesial imagination. When the city is conquered in the seventh century, first by Persians, then by Arabs, devout gentile believers in Jesus mourn with an intensity rivaling that of the Jews whose grief at the events of 70 CE had earlier stirred ecclesial mockery. Those who loved Jesus had once again learned to love Jerusalem, and to place her above their highest joys. But they had not yet learned to love their Jewish neighbors, or to see the ineradicable connection between the holy city and the flesh-and-blood children of Abraham and Sarah.

Luke and Acts portray Jerusalem as the city of David and the city of David's greater son, the city of the holy temple, the city that Jesus loved and the city in which he died and rose again from the dead. These two volumes present Jerusalem as the center of the land of Israel, the center of the Jewish people, the center of the messianic *ekklēsia*, and the center of the entire world. They depict the suffering and death of Jesus as a proleptic embodiment of and participation in the suffering and destruction of Jerusalem in 70 CE, and imply that his resurrection is the pledge and future catalyst of Jerusalem's eschatological restoration. The fragmentary insights of Hegessipus, Justin Martyr, Irenaeus, Cyril of Jerusalem, and Vatican II's *Nostra Aetate*, are all anticipated in Luke and Acts, but they appear there as part of a comprehensive vision of Jerusalem, the holy city.

That comprehensive vision concerned not only the city itself, but also that which the city represented—the land of Israel and the Jewish people. According to Luke and Acts, the death and resurrection of the Messiah are bound inextricably to both the land and the people. In the final analysis, his salvific work either includes them in its scope, or fails in its purpose.

Chapter 2

Jerusalem and the Temple

If the city of Jerusalem is joined indissolubly to the crucified and resurrected Messiah, what about the temple that dominated both her skyline and her day-to-day life? The temple played such an important role in the city that it could represent the whole of which it was the most prominent part. If the death of Jesus is a proleptic participation in the judgment of Jerusalem executed forty years later, then his death should likewise be closely related to the destruction of the temple.

The Gospels confirm that such a relationship exists. They report not only that Jesus prophesied the destruction of the temple (Mark 13:1–2; Matt 24:1–2; Luke 21:5–6) but also that his arrest and execution were precipitated by an audacious exercise of authority in that very place—a demonstration that may have been intended as a symbolic enactment of the prophecy (Mark 11:15–18; Matt 21:12–16; Luke 19:45–48).[1] John's account of the temple incident underlines the relationship between the death of Jesus and the destruction of the temple by reporting that Jesus said, "Destroy this temple, and in three days I will raise it up" (John 2:19). His hearers think he speaks of the architectural structure in which they stand (John 2:20). Jesus, of course, refers to his own body (John 2:21). But his hearers have not completely misunderstood him, for John here hints that the death of Jesus and the destruction of the Jerusalem temple are interconnected events.[2]

1. At least that is the common interpretation of the temple incident among contemporary New Testament scholars, following the lead of E. P. Sanders (see *Jesus and Judaism*, 69–76).

2. John returns to this theme later in the Gospel when recounting the decision of the council to arrest Jesus. The leaders fear that, if left unchecked, all of the people

In the previous chapter I argued that Jesus' death and resurrection are linked to the destiny of the holy city. In his death Jesus shares in the future suffering of Jerusalem, imparting to that suffering a redemptive character. In his resurrection he pledges the city's future restoration, and displays the power that will accomplish it. If his resurrection serves as a pledge and efficient cause of the city's ultimate restoration, may the same be said about the future of her temple?

This is where problems arise. Numerous New Testament texts seem to challenge the hope for a restored temple structure in the age following Jesus' return. They do so in both indirect and direct ways. The New Testament frequently employs temple imagery to interpret the significance of Jesus and the community of his followers. If Jesus is the true temple, and his followers become part of that temple by sharing in his life, then one could conclude that there is no longer need for a temple building constructed from inanimate stones. And indeed, some texts imply or baldly assert that there will no longer be a temple building after Jesus returns (e.g., Heb 9:6–10; Rev 21:22). These texts assume that the temple structure is itself a sign of life in the present age, when access to the Holy One is available but restricted. In the future age such access will be unimpeded.

If the temple is not only a symbol of Jerusalem but her equivalent, then the transformation of the temple from an inanimate to an organic structure implies a similar transformation in the character of the city. We see this logic in the thinking of N. T. Wright, who states: "Jesus would build the new [human] Temple; his people would be the real new Jerusalem."[3] Such a transformation of temple and city suggests an analogous transformation of Israel's land and people, in which the Jewish particular yields to the cosmic universal. According to this line of reasoning, the apparently provisional and transitional character of the Jerusalem temple contradicts our basic thesis regarding the prophetic *euangelion* and its message concerning the resurrected Messiah, the Jewish people, the city of Jerusalem, and the land of promise.

In order to address these questions, I will need to range far afield from the main subject of this volume. I will begin with the biblical

will follow after the Galilean wonder worker, with the result that "the Romans will come and destroy both our holy place and our nation" (John 11:48). In their supposed attempt to save their "place" (i.e., the temple) from the Romans, the council acts in a manner that assures its eventual destruction. Once again, the death of Jesus and the destruction of the temple are interconnected.

3. Wright, *Jesus and the Victory of God*, 338.

tradition as a whole, exploring the history and significance of the temple in relation to the land, the city, and the people. I aim to show the unique role played by the temple in the symbolic world of ancient Judaism, a role that both highlights the importance of this institution and distinguishes it in kind from land, city, and people. The temple differed from land, city, and people in its *complexity* (combining the ark, other tabernacle furnishings, and sacred site); its *instability* (owing to its complexity, but also to its inherent fragility as a particular structure made with human hands); and its *symbolic function* (as an institution whose purpose was to point to realities beyond itself). Thus, the temple reveals much about the purpose of the land, city, and people, but all of the characteristics of the former cannot be attributed to the latter.

I will then turn my attention to the New Testament perspective on the temple, and—in contrast to the rest of this volume—I will reflect on non-Lukan texts before returning to the study of Luke and Acts. This is necessary because non-Lukan traditions raise the most difficult questions for our thesis, and the argument of this volume would lack cogency at this point if we limited ourselves to the Lukan texts. Accordingly, I will take up the role of the temple in the Pauline tradition, the letter to the Hebrews, the Revelation of John, and the Gospel of John. The conceptual distinctions that emerge from our study of the biblical tradition as a whole will help us make sense of these New Testament texts in a way that acknowledges their diverse perspectives while revealing their canonical coherence. Finally, I will return to the Gospel of Luke and Acts of the Apostles to show how their treatment of the temple complements that of the rest of the New Testament, and fits with their view of Jerusalem and the land. If we are successful, our discussion of the temple will not only dispel objections to our general thesis but also enrich our understanding of the prophetic *euangelion* concerning the resurrected Messiah, the Jewish people, and the land of promise.

The Temple in Jewish Tradition before the New Testament

Hebrew Scripture: Temple as Complex and Unstable Symbol

In the history of Israel up to 70 CE the city of Jerusalem, the land of Israel, and the people of Israel were all relatively stable in their meaning and reference. Each had clear minimal boundaries that most Israelites could agree upon. Maximal boundaries varied over time and could be disputed by rival parties, but the core realities were understood and accepted by the community as a whole.

Jerusalem was a city in the mountainous spine of the land of Canaan, straddling the border that separated the northern from the southern tribes of Israel. The location of the city walls shifted over time, and in the exilic and immediate post-exilic eras even the existence of those walls could not be taken for granted. Like all cities, Jerusalem expanded and contracted. Buildings were constructed, then destroyed, only to be replaced by new ones. Yet, Jerusalem always remained Jerusalem. We speak of the First and Second Temples, divided in time by the Babylonian exile, but we do not speak of the First and the Second Jerusalems. The city which was ravaged by Nebuchadnezzar was the same city which was later restored under Cyrus.

What is true of Jerusalem is also true of the land of Israel, which had Jerusalem at its heart. The maximal boundaries of the land promised to the patriarchs and matriarchs were somewhat fluid, but all recognized that Judea, Samaria, Galilee, and the sea coast formed the core of that inheritance.

The definition of the people of Israel was a more contentious affair. The emergence of distinctive Jewish and Samaritan forms of Israelite identity resulted in a communal rupture that left a perpetual question mark on the outer boundaries of the covenant community. However, once we accept the canonical tradition that privileged the Jewish form (e.g., John 4:22), the minimal boundaries of the people become clear. Those who had two Jewish parents, worshipped the God of Israel, and participated in Jewish communities were members of the covenant community. Differences of opinion existed regarding marginal cases, such as the Samaritans; individuals with only one Jewish parent; those of Jewish parentage who separated themselves from the worship of Israel's God and/or Jewish communal life; or those with non-Jewish parentage who sought to worship Israel's God and participate in its communal life. But these disputed cases resemble the questions regarding the maximal boundaries of Jerusalem or the land of Israel. The core reality was identifiable and enjoyed a relatively stable existence through time.[4]

4. An exception to this generalization occurred in the late Second Temple period, with the development of Jewish sectarianism. At least one sectarian group—namely, the one attested by the Dead Sea Scrolls—may have restricted Israel's communal boundaries to encompass only the members of their own sect. However, that was a historical and geographical anomaly. In general, the basic internal boundaries of the

In stark contrast, Israel's central sanctuary was a multi-dimensional and fluid institution that experienced violent ruptures and dramatic transformations. According to all biblical sources, the ark of the covenant—constructed at Sinai—served as the earthly throne of Israel's God (1 Sam 4:4; 2 Sam 6:2; 2 Kgs 19:15). The priestly material of the Torah situates the ark in the holy of holies of the desert tabernacle. That sanctuary contained other sacred furniture (e.g., the table of the bread of the presence, and the altar of burnt offering), but all was ordered in relation to the ark. After Israel entered the land, the ark (and its tent) came to rest at Shiloh (Josh 18:1; 1 Sam 3:3[5]), a sanctuary overseen by the priestly family of Eli.[6] Threatened by the Philistines, the army of Israel took the ark with them as they went into battle, and the ark was captured by enemy forces (1 Sam 4). The Philistines soon regretted the taking of this booty (1 Sam 5), which brought them only affliction, and they returned it to Israel (1 Sam 6:1–11). It landed first in Beth Shemesh (1 Sam 6:12–20), and then was transferred to Kiriath Yearim where it remained for twenty years (1 Sam 6:21—7:2).

At the same time, the descendants of Eli operated a sanctuary at Nob without the ark, but with other sacred items such as the bread of the presence (1 Sam 21:1–9). After the priests of Nob were slaughtered by Saul (1 Sam 22:6–23), what became of this sanctuary? According to the Chronicler, the tabernacle and the altar of burnt offering were situated at Gibeon in the reign of David, even after the ark had been brought to Jerusalem (1 Chr 16:37–40; 21:29; 2 Chr 1:3–6). Thus, after the capture of the ark by the Philistines, the items that in the priestly tradition of the Torah are inextricably integrated (i.e., the ark, the altar, the bread of the presence, the tabernacle) were divided between at least two distinct sites.[7]

Having brought the ark to his newly established capital city, King David desired to build a house for Israel's most sacred object (2 Sam

---

Jewish people were clear to all. Thus, in the Hellenistic period, ancient sources (Jewish and non-Jewish) could speak of Jewish communities in various cities and assume that readers knew exactly what and whom they were referring to.

5. The text speaks of Samuel lying down in the presence of the ark, and the wider context makes it clear that this scene took place in Shiloh.

6. Judges 20:26–28 states that the ark was at Bethel in an earlier period, namely, during the priestly tenure of Phinehas, grandson of Aaron.

7. My aim here is not to reconstruct the historical events underlying these accounts, but to trace the outlines of the story told by the biblical text. For a possible reconstruction of the history behind the text, see Haran, *Temples and Temple Service in Ancient Israel*, 189–204.

7:1–2), but was told by the prophet Nathan that it was not he but his son who was to accomplish that task (2 Sam 7:12–13). Nevertheless, according to the Chronicler, God revealed to David precisely *where* in Jerusalem the "house of the LORD" was to be located (1 Chr 21:15—22:1). On that site King Solomon erected the temple, bringing together the sacred items that for many years had been divided. The structure erected by Solomon adhered to the same basic pattern as the desert sanctuary, though the dimensions of the two main chambers in Solomon's temple are much larger than those of the tabernacle. Some scholars believe that the tabernacle itself was set up in the holy of holies of Solomon's temple.[8]

These acts by David and Solomon introduce the third of the fundamental elements (along with the ark and the tabernacle furnishings) that combine to establish the Jerusalem temple as a site unique in holiness. That third element is the place itself. According to Genesis 22, Mount Moriah, where Abraham bound Isaac as a sacrifice, is "the mount of the LORD": "So Abraham called that place 'The LORD will provide' [lit. 'see']; as it is said to this day, 'On the mount of the LORD it [or 'he'] shall be provided' [lit. 'seen']" (v. 14). The identification of the site of the binding of Isaac as the place of the future sanctuary revealed to David is made explicit in 2 Chronicles 3:1: "Solomon began to build the house of the LORD in Jerusalem on Mount Moriah, where the LORD had appeared to his father David, at the place that David had designated, on the threshing floor of Ornan the Jebusite." Abraham's wholehearted devotion to the LORD is thus presented as the paradigm of Israel's true worship at the temple, and the promise is given that the LORD will be "seen" at that place.

In other words, Genesis 22—in canonical context—establishes Mount Zion as a holy site centuries before Moses is commanded to build the ark and the tabernacle. The Song of Moses, sung (again, in canonical context) *before* the construction of the ark and tabernacle, and before Israel entered the land, confirms this view: "You brought them in and planted them on the mountain of your own possession, the place, O LORD, that you made your abode, the sanctuary (*mikdash*), O LORD, that your hands have established" (Exod 15:17). Read in light of Genesis 22 and 2 Chronicles 3, this verse refers to Mount Zion, which is also Mount Moriah.

The holiness of the Temple Mount, even apart from the ark and the tabernacle furnishings, is evident in the prayer of Solomon at the

8. See Friedman, *Commentary on the Torah*, 262–63.

dedication of the temple. He asks that God would hear the prayers directed to that place even when the people of Israel are taken captive into exile—and, presumably, the temple service is no longer conducted (1 Kgs 8:46–53). The Book of Daniel testifies to precisely this practice of praying toward Jerusalem even when the ark has disappeared, the temple destroyed, and the people taken into exile (Dan 6:10). As Jon Levenson writes,

> In the exile (587–539 B.C.E.), when the Temple was in ruins, the Israelite could still direct his prayers to the place upon which it stood (and was destined to stand again) in the assurance that YHWH would still be available, that prayers could still ascend on that sacred mountain (1 Kgs 8:28–29). Thus, the legendary savant Daniel, even when an exile in Persia, prays in the direction of Jerusalem in the hope that his supplications will ascend from there into the heavenly court (Dan 6:11). In short, Jerusalem retains its sanctity regardless of whether the Temple happens to be standing in it and regardless of whether the supplicant can approach it physically. The sacred city is the conduit through which messages pass from earth to heaven, no matter where, in a geographical sense, they originated.[9]

Thus, the Temple Mount was holy before Israel crossed the Jordan with the ark and the tabernacle, and it remains holy after the ark and the tabernacle furnishings are destroyed and Israel is taken back across the Jordan into captivity.

In 586 BCE, the ark of the covenant disappeared from history. It may have been destroyed, or taken by the victors as a trophy to Babylon, or even hidden away, but the crucial point for our concern here is that it played *no further role* in the worship practices of the Jewish people. The holy of holies of the modest edifice known as the Second Temple, dedicated in 515 BCE, was an empty room. Sacrifices were once again presented on the bronze altar; the fragrance of incense rose once again from the golden altar; the menorah was once again lit; and the bread of the presence once again rested on the golden table; but the *central* article of the desert tabernacle and the First Temple, which represented the throne of the Lord, was nowhere to be found. As in the days of the sons of Eli who officiated at the sanctuary of Nob, and as in the time of David when the tabernacle was separated from the ark, now Israel's central place of worship was bereft of its most precious and sacred object.

9. Levenson, *Sinai and Zion*, 125.

For almost six centuries this ark-less temple served as Israel's most holy site. And then, in 70 CE, Jerusalem fell to Roman Legions, and the Second Temple experienced the same fate as the First. Nearly two millennia have passed since that day. The ark and the temple have both vanished from history—yet the Jewish people remain, with its worship still directed toward the Temple Mount, and now with an embattled Jewish national presence in the land. The temple still functions as a symbol of the Jewish worldview—as can be gauged from the ubiquitous image of the menorah within the State of Israel, and from the unrivalled devotion to the sanctity of the Western Wall. But it is a symbol fashioned by the Jewish imagination from ancient texts, artistic traditions, and liturgical practices rather than a visible structure or social institution.

This summary narrative shows that, even when the temple did exist as an actual structure and institution, it consisted of a fluctuating fusion of ark, tabernacle furnishings, and geographical site, and lacked the integral and stable coherence of the city, land, and people that it represented.

Hebrew Scripture: Temple as Symbol Pointing to Realities beyond Itself

In the context of the Hebrew Bible, Jerusalem, the land, and the covenant people are particular realities whose significance derives from the role each plays in the ongoing story of God's dealings with the world. The temple, on the other hand, always pointed (and gave access) to particular realities beyond itself, and its significance in the biblical narrative derives in large part from this pointing function. There are four such realities to which the Jerusalem temple pointed: the heavenly temple, the cosmic temple, the eschatological temple, and the human temple (i.e., the people of Israel).

The connection between the Jerusalem temple and the *heavenly temple* becomes evident in the vision given to Isaiah as he receives his prophetic calling. Isaiah beholds the Lord "sitting on a throne, high and lofty, and the hem of his robe filled the temple" (Isa 6:1). The prophet is worshipping the Lord in the Jerusalem temple, and suddenly finds himself transported to its heavenly correlate. Jon Levenson describes the significance of the scene:

> What happened to Isaiah in the year King Uzziah died is that glyptic representation became immediate spiritual experience.

> Art became the reality to which it pointed. The Temple mythos came alive. In Isaiah's ecstatic experience, he sees and hears a session of the divine council. . . . The earthly Temple is thus the vehicle that conveys the prophet into the supernal Temple, the real Temple, the Temple of YHWH and his retinue, and not merely the artifacts that suggest them. This Temple is an institution common to the heavenly and terrestrial realms; they share it.[10]

According to later tradition, this is also the meaning of the vision given to Moses on Mount Sinai when he receives instruction regarding the tabernacle. Levenson considers that tradition a faithful interpretation of the text itself:

> The Temple on Zion is the antitype to the cosmic archetype. The real Temple is the one to which it points, the one in "heaven," which cannot be distinguished sharply from its earthly manifestation. Thus, when Moses is to construct Israel's first sanctuary, the Tabernacle in the wilderness, he does so on the basis of a glimpse of the "blueprint" or "model" of the heavenly shrine which he was privileged to behold upon Mount Sinai (Exod 25:9, 40).[11]

The language of "antitype" and "archetype," appropriate to the relationship of the earthly and heavenly temples, shows that the Jerusalem temple could not be severed from another intimately connected reality without losing something essential to its own existence.

The second reality to which the Jerusalem temple pointed was the *cosmic temple*, i.e., the cosmos *as* temple.[12] Jon Levenson demonstrates that the priestly narrative of the construction of the tabernacle (Exod 35–40) corresponds in several ways to the priestly narrative of the creation of the world (Gen 1:1—2:3). He then shows that the biblical description of Solomon's building of the Jerusalem temple follows the same pattern.[13] These texts support his basic thesis: "in the Hebrew Bible . . . the

10. Levenson, *Sinai & Zion*, 123.

11. Levenson, *Sinai & Zion*, 140.

12. According to Jonathan Klawans (*Purity, Sacrifice, and the Temple*, 111), ancient Jewish sources (including the Hebrew Bible) saw the Jerusalem temple as corresponding to *either* the heavenly temple or the cosmic temple, but never to both simultaneously. His treatment of these two patterns of temple symbolism (111–44) illustrates well the way the temple always points beyond itself. His contention that these two patterns never overlap merits further discussion, but is not relevant to our concerns here.

13. Levenson, *Sinai & Zion*, 142–44.

Temple is the epitome of the world, a concentrated form of its essence, a miniature of the cosmos. . . . [T]he Temple (or mountain or city) is a microcosm of which the world itself is the macrocosm."[14] This means that acts of worship in the temple precincts both reflect cosmic processes, and in turn have an impact on those very processes. In Levenson's words, "the creative ordering of the world has become something that humanity can not only witness and celebrate, but something in which he can take part."[15]

The third reality to which the Jerusalem temple pointed was the *eschatological temple*. This connection first becomes explicit in Ezekiel's prophetic vision of a new temple (Ezek 40–48). According to the opening verse of that unit, the prophet receives his vision in the twenty-fifth year of his exile, that is, 573 BCE, thirteen years after the destruction of the First Temple. The temple he sees is not the one that will be constructed by Zerubbabel, nor its later expansion by Herod. In fact, the vision given to Ezekiel contains features that entail an extraordinary divine intervention that transforms the landscape of Jerusalem and its surrounding territory, and even the natural order. This becomes clear in Ezekiel 47:1–12, where the prophet describes "water flowing from below the threshold of the temple toward the east" (v. 1). Ezekiel proceeds along the stream a thousand cubits, and discovers that the water is only ankle-deep. However, only three-thousand cubits beyond that point the water has become "a river that I could not cross, . . . deep enough to swim in" (v. 5). Such a dramatic deepening of the water defies natural explanation, for there are no other streams flowing into the river that would augment its contents. Moreover, the water itself has life-giving qualities beyond anything known in the present order of the world:

> Wherever the water goes, every living creature that swarms will live. . . . On the banks, on both sides of the river, there will grow all kinds of trees for food. Their leaves will not wither nor their fruit fail, but they will bear fresh fruit every month, because the water for them flows from the sanctuary. Their fruit will be for food, and their leaves for healing. (Ezek 47:9, 12)

As a result of these life-giving waters, the land of Israel now resembles the Garden of Eden (Gen 2:8–10).

14. Levenson, *Sinai & Zion*, 138–39. See also Levenson, *Creation and the Persistence of Evil*, 78–99.

15. Levenson, *Creation and the Persistence of Evil*, 127.

In light of Ezekiel's vision, other prophetic texts are recognized as similarly anticipating an eschatological temple and a transformed natural order. According to Joel 3:18, "In that day the mountains will drip sweet wine, the hills shall flow with milk, and all the stream beds of Judah shall flow with water; a fountain shall come forth from the house of the LORD and water the Wadi Shittim." The opening of this temple fountain signifies a final and definitive establishment of the people of Israel, and the destruction of its enemies (vv. 19–20). This theme takes even more dramatic form in Zechariah 14. As in Ezekiel and Joel, we read that "On that day living waters shall flow out from Jerusalem" (v. 8)—presumably issuing from "the house of the LORD." This phenomenon occurs after the LORD appears on the Mount of Olives, causing an earthquake and an alteration in the terrain surrounding Jerusalem (vv. 4–5, 10), and fighting against the nations that have attacked the holy city (vv. 2–3). As a result of the LORD's victory over his enemies and subsequent universal reign (v. 9), not only do "living waters flow out from Jerusalem," but the order of nature is reconfigured so as to eliminate the darkness of night (v. 7) and the cold of winter (v. 6). Finally, the holiness that formerly characterized only the high priest and the Holy Place extends now to include all the city's domestic animals and cooking vessels: "On that day shall be inscribed on the bells of the horses, 'Holy to the LORD.' And the cooking pots in the house of the LORD shall be as holy as the bowls in front of the altar; and every cooking pot in Jerusalem and Judah shall be sacred to the LORD of hosts" (vv. 20–21).

While the connection between the Jerusalem temple and its heavenly and cosmic correlates is found in our earliest sources, the eschatological connection first emerges after the destruction of Solomon's temple. Ezekiel's vision represents the hope for a glorious temple in the midst of exile and the ruins of the First Temple. After the erection of the Second Temple this eschatological hope only grows, but it is now linked to the structure that stands as a proleptic pledge pointing to a glorious future that transcends the inglorious present. The temple had always pointed *upwards* (to the heavenly temple) and *outwards* (to the cosmic temple); now it also pointed *forwards* (to the eschatological temple).

Finally, the Jerusalem temple also pointed beyond itself to a *human* temple—namely, the people of Israel. The LORD's aim in commanding the construction of a tabernacle was not to dwell "in *it*" (*betocho*) but "among *them* (*betocham*)" (Exod 25:8). The tabernacle and temple were not ends in themselves but instruments of this greater purpose. Israel was not made for the temple, but the temple for Israel.

The implications of this fact only become clear at the time of the Babylonian exile. The prophet Ezekiel, taken into exile ten years before the destruction of Jerusalem, beholds in a vision the holy city and its temple in their current state (Ezek 8–11). He sees the "glory" (*kavod*), that is, the divine presence, departing from the temple because of the people's appalling sins (see 8:3–4, 6; 9:3; 10:1–22). The *kavod* first stops above the *east* gate of the temple (10:19), and then moves to "the mountain *east* of the city" (11:23), i.e., the Mount of Olives. Ezekiel's vision ends here—but he knows from an earlier vision that the *kavod* does not ascend from earth to heaven but instead journeys *further east* to join the exiles in Babylonia (Ezek 1:1–28). The connection between the two visions is underlined by explicit reference in the second back to the first (8:4; 10:20). The temporary relocation of the *kavod* from Jerusalem to Babylonia is also implied later in the book of Ezekiel, where the prophet sees Jerusalem's future temple and the return of the *kavod* to the city (Ezek 43:1–7): "the glory of the God of Israel was coming *from the east*" (Ezek 43:2)—i.e., from Babylonia. Just as the second vision was linked to the first by explicit references, so the third vision refers back to the first two: "The vision I saw was like the vision that I had seen when he came to destroy the city, and like the vision that I had seen by the river Chebar" (Ezek 43:3).

This "exile" of the *kavod* from Judea to Babylonia is expressed succinctly by the prophet in priestly terminology: "Thus says the Lord God: Though I removed them far away among the nations, and though I scattered them among the countries, yet I have been a sanctuary [*mikdash*] to them for a little while in the countries where they have gone" (Ezek 11:16). Elsewhere in the book, the prophet employs the word *mikdash* in reference to the Jerusalem temple (e.g., 5:11; 8:6; 9:6; 44:7–9). That which made the Jerusalem temple holy was the *kavod*, and the relocation of the *kavod* entails a temporary relocation of the *mikdash*. The Lord dwells among his servants, who are now in exile.

A similar message appears in Isaiah 40–55. These chapters speak of "the return of the Lord to Zion"—a theme highlighted in the work of N. T. Wright.[16] The meaning of this phrase becomes clear in Isaiah 52:

16. See especially Wright, *Jesus and the Victory of God*, 612–53.

> 7 How beautiful upon the mountains
> are the feet of the messenger who announces peace,
> who brings good news, who announces salvation,
> who says to Zion, "Your God reigns."
> 8 Listen! Your sentinels lift up their voices,
> together they sing for joy;
> for in plain sight they see *the return of the* LORD *to Zion* . . . .
> 11 Depart, depart, go out from there!
> Touch no unclean thing;
> Go out from the midst of it,
> purify yourselves, you who carry the vessels of the LORD.
> 12 For you shall not go out in haste,
> and you shall not go in flight;
> for the LORD will go before you,
> and the God of Israel will be your rear guard.
> (Isa 52:7–8, 11–12; emphasis added)

The Judeans leave Babylonia as the Israelites left Egypt, but this time their exodus is peaceful rather than in fear and haste. They must purify themselves for the journey, for the LORD goes in their midst. In other words, *the return of the* LORD *to Zion* is inseparable from the return to that place of *the people* of the LORD. This only makes sense if Isaiah assumes something similar to what Ezekiel states: the LORD *returns with* the exiles because the LORD had accompanied them *in* their exile.[17]

These exilic prophecies imply that the divine presence was bound to the *people* of Israel (and especially to the faithful among them) more closely than to the building that they had constructed as its residence. Just as the temple pointed away from itself to its heavenly, cosmic, and eschatological correlates, so it likewise pointed to its human correlate—the people chosen at the exodus to be "God's sanctuary (*kodesh*)" (Ps 114:2).

Early Jewish Extra-Biblical Writings: Temple as Complex and Unstable Symbol

After the rebuilding of the temple in modest form (and minus its chief article, the ark), the Judeans were governed by a priestly client regime under a succession of foreign empires (Persian, Greek, and Roman). For three-and-a-half centuries they experienced a relatively secure though

17. The programmatic verses of Isaiah 40 (especially 3–5, 9–11) articulate the same motif.

dependent existence, and their trust in the temple is displayed in texts such as Sirach 50:1–24. This confidence wilted in the face of a paganizing program of radical Hellenizers (167–164 BCE), when idolaters defiled the temple with foreign gods and impure sacrifices. The trauma of this period reminded all Judeans of the fragility of their holy place and its pattern of worship. For some dissidents, such as those in the Enochian tradition, these events proved that the Second Temple was problematic from its inception.[18] For those fiercely loyal to that institution, on the other hand, the crisis intensified their determination to achieve as much independence from foreign powers as possible. The latter party enjoyed some success for a century under the Hasmonean dynasty, but then in 63 BCE a foreign general (this time, a Roman) once again violated the sanctity of Jerusalem's holy place.[19] When the temple was finally destroyed by another Roman general in 70 CE, the tragedy exposed what Jews throughout the world had known and feared for generations: the vulnerability of their sanctuary in the midst of the hostile forces arrayed against them.

Second Temple Judaism also features the extraordinary expansion of the Jewish diaspora. From the western shores of the Roman Empire to the eastern provinces of the Parthian Empire, colonies of Jews lived their own distinctive way of life. They observed the Sabbath, read the Torah, and prayed daily in the direction of the holy land and its holy city. They received visiting emissaries, formal and informal, from Judea who reminded them of their connection to the land, and most of them paid the annual temple tax. Many of them even made pilgrimage to Jerusalem at least once in their lifetime. In this way the symbol of the temple played an important role in their view of themselves and the world.

At the same time, the temple as a social, cultural, economic, and architectural institution had little impact on their daily lives. It inhabited the sphere of their corporate imagination rather than their concrete experience. This did not detract from the temple's significance for them, but it did distinguish this institution from the reality of the Jewish people, and to some extent also from the reality of the land of Israel and the city of Jerusalem.[20] The temple continued to function as a potent Jewish

18. This is evident from 1 Enoch 89.73 (describing the Second Temple) viewed in relation to 89.36 (the Tabernacle) and 89.50 (the First Temple). See Boccaccini, *Middle Judaism*, 157–58, and *Beyond the Essene Hypothesis*, 82–83.

19. See Josephus, *Antiquities* 14:4.

20. A geographic location (such as the land of Israel, the city of Jerusalem, or the

symbol, even for those residing thousands of miles from its site, for it expressed the fundamental reality of the LORD's presence in the midst of Israel and Israel's responsibility to worship the LORD. But the structure itself was distant from their daily existence.

Thus, in early Jewish extra-biblical literature we see an intensification of the inversely-proportional relation between the symbolic power of the temple and its stable institutional existence. This fact becomes more evident when we take account of early Jewish perspectives on the four realities to which the temple pointed. The symbolic dimension of the temple assumes even greater prominence in the extra-biblical literature than it enjoyed in the biblical texts, as the vulnerability of the humanly-constructed edifice is sensed ever more acutely. Let us review the four symbolic correlates to the Jerusalem temple with extra-biblical Jewish literature in view.

First of all, the *heavenly temple* takes on great significance in these writings. Texts likely composed in the immediate aftermath of the destruction of the Second Temple (Liber antiquitatum biblicarum [L.A.B.] 11.15; 2 Baruch 4.2–6) interpret Exodus 25:9 to mean precisely what Jon Levenson thinks the original meant: God showed Moses the heavenly temple as a blue-print for the construction of the earthly tabernacle. However, the heavenly temple had emerged as a central theme at a much earlier period. Already in 1 Enoch a seer ascends to the heavenly house of God and beholds the divine throne and the "Great Glory" (1 Enoch 14.8–25). As the Enochian tradition developed, but even before it hardened into sectarian forms, the angelic worship in the heavenly temple became a central focal point (Jubilees 30.14; 31.14; *Songs of the Sabbath Sacrifice*).[21] This emphasis then pervaded the sectarian literature of Qumran, but also left its mark on later rabbinic midrash, synagogue liturgy, and mystical writings of the Talmudic and post-Talmudic eras.[22] While

Temple Mount) can become a matter of personal experience through the daily practice of facing in its direction during prayer. The place thus provides geographical orientation to the person who prays, establishing a central point in relation to which all other geographical locations may be plotted. A building, on the other hand, along with its furniture and the normal activities conducted within it, can only become a matter of personal experience through visiting its domain.

21. See Hayward, *The Jewish Temple*, 87–88, 99–100; Newsom, *Songs of the Sabbath Sacrifice*.

22. See Elior, *The Three Temples*. She interprets the word *yachad* ("oneness"), employed by the Qumran community as a term of self-designation, as a reference to the bond joining the worship of the earthly community to the worship of the angels in the

the idea of the heavenly angelic temple was rooted in priestly biblical materials concerned with the earthly human institution, that idea thrived later in settings that were separated from that institution due to sectarian exclusion or the building's demise.

Second, the *cosmic temple* becomes a theme of particular concern in Hellenistic Judaism. Both Philo and Josephus provide elaborate descriptions of the way various features of the Jerusalem temple symbolize the components of the universe.[23] While this particular symbolic construal of the temple has biblical precedents, these Hellenistic Jewish writers posit a greater distance between the symbol and its cosmic correlate than is found in earlier materials. The biblical text assumes an intimate nexus between the two, such that what is transacted in the microcosm has an impact on the macrocosm. Something different appears in a writer like Philo:

> The whole universe must be regarded as the highest and, in truth, the holy temple of God. . . . As for the temple made by hands—it was necessary that there be no driving back of the eagerness of men who pay their religious dues to piety, and who wish by sacrifices either to give thanks for the good things which happen, or to ask forgiveness and pardon for matters in which they have sinned. (*De specialibus legibus* I.66–67)[24]

Here there is only one true holy temple—namely, the cosmos. For Philo, the "temple made by hands" is diminished by comparison with the greater reality it points to, rather than magnified by reference to that with which it is organically united. The Jerusalem temple plays a "necessary" and beneficial role, but it should not be confused with what it symbolically represents.[25]

---

heavenly temple (36, 58, 105, 171). On later Jewish mystical tradition, see 232–65. It is worth noting that rabbinic thinking on the heavenly temple also includes the notion of *heavenly sacrifice*. As Klawans recognizes, "A few midrashic sources . . . say that what is offered on the heavenly altar are the souls of the righteous (*Num. Rabbah* 12:12)" – i.e., the martyrs (*Purity, Sacrifice, and the Temple*, 140).

23. See Hayward, *The Jewish Temple*, 108–53; Klawans, *Purity, Sacrifice, and the Temple*, 114–28.

24. Hayward, *The Jewish Temple*, 109.

25. In rabbinic tradition, the connection between the temple service (as microcosm) and the universe (as macrocosm) bears a closer resemblance to what is seen in the biblical texts. Thus, the daily sacrifices are linked to the creation narrative of Genesis 1 (*m. Taanit* 4:3) in a way that suggests that what occurs in the microcosm has ramifications for the macrocosm.

Third, the *eschatological temple* comes into much clearer focus in the post-biblical period. As belief in a future resurrection became common among those who cherished a messianic hope, so also did belief in a future temple of transcendent glory, built not by human hands but by the direct intervention of God. Anticipation of such a divinely constructed edifice is already found in the early Maccabean period (Jubilees 1.17—18.29). The Temple Scroll (roughly contemporaneous with Jubilees and related to it in provenance) describes an ideal pre-eschatological sanctuary with some resemblance to that envisioned by Ezekiel, but this edifice—already grander than any earlier temple—is distinguished decisively from the one that will come on that glorious day "when I Myself will create My Temple" (29.7–10).[26] Two centuries later, in the wake of the Roman destruction of Jerusalem, the ontological gap separating Herod's temple from its eschatological successor has become a yawning chasm as vast as the difference between mortality and incorruption (see L.A.B. 19.12–13; 4 Ezra 10.53–55; 2 Baruch 4.2–6).[27]

Two biblical texts appear to have informed this theological development in the post-biblical Jewish world. The first and most important was from the Song of the Sea sung by Moses and the people of Israel in celebration of their deliverance:

> You brought them in and planted them
> on the mountain of your own possession,
> the place [*machon*], O LORD,
> that you made your abode [*leshivtecha pa'alta*],
> the sanctuary [*mikdash*], O Lord,
> that your hands have established.
> The LORD will reign forever and ever. (Exod 15:17–18)

26. Boccaccini, *Beyond the Essene Hypothesis*, 101; Maier, *The Temple Scroll*, 86; Klawans, *Purity, Sacrifice, and the Temple*, 159. Later texts from Qumran describe the eschatological city and temple as exhibiting what Klawans calls "extraworldly characteristics." In his words, "A glorious new temple is also imagined in the *New Jerusalem* texts from Qumran . . . which imagine a city with a golden wall, . . . jewel-encrusted structures, . . . streets paved in white stone, alabaster, and onyx . . . and a temple whose construction is similarly radiant" (158–59).

27. In his discussion of L.A.B., C. T. R. Hayward concludes that "This writer clearly restricts the significance and efficacity of the Temple and its Service to what we might call 'ordinary history'. . . . Temple and sacrifice do not appear to belong to this future with its other world and other heaven" (Hayward, *The Jewish Temple*, 166). While Hayward is right to emphasize the ontological disjunction in L.A.B. between this world and the next, it is difficult to determine from L.A.B. the contours of Israel's worship in the new heaven and earth.

This text was read by many in the post-biblical period as referring not to the temple of Solomon but instead to the eschatological temple. In doing so, Jewish hopes drew a contrast between the humanly constructed temples of their experience (made by human hands) and the divinely constructed temple to come (made by divine hands). Lawrence Schiffman believes that this biblical text gave rise to the conviction expressed in the Temple Scroll that a divinely created temple would succeed the humanly fashioned edifice it was describing.[28] 4 Ezra alludes to Exodus 15:17 by stating that "no work of man's building could endure in a place where the city of the Most High was to be revealed" (4 Ezra 10:54).[29] This interpretation of Exodus 15:17–18 takes explicit form in later rabbinic midrash.[30]

The second biblical text that played some role in this interpretative tradition is Daniel 2. After describing a statue representing four successive empires that would rule over Israel before the eschaton, Daniel speaks of "a stone cut out, not by human hands" that strikes the statue and breaks it to pieces (v. 34). Subsequently the stone becomes "a great mountain, and filled the whole earth" (v. 35). Daniel then explains that the stone represents "a kingdom that shall never be destroyed" (vv. 44–45). In 4 Ezra this "mountain carved out without hands" is said to be Mount Zion (13.6–7, 35–36), that is, the Temple Mount. In other words, 4 Ezra reads Daniel 2 in light of Exodus 15, and finds in both texts reference to the divinely constructed eschatological temple that will far transcend in glory the humanly constructed temple that the Romans have destroyed.[31] In this way

28. Schiffman, "The Importance of the Temple for Ancient Jews," 87–88.

29. Stone and Henze, *4 Ezra and 2 Baruch*, 65.

30. See *Mekilta de-Rabbi Ishmael* 10.24–28, 38–43, and Rashi on Exodus 15:17–18. While Nicholas Perrin's analysis and categorization of Jewish counter-temple movements over-simplifies a complex reality, he rightly emphasizes the importance of Exodus 15:17 (*Jesus the Temple*, 10–11, 102).

31. Later rabbinic texts anticipate an eschatological temple complete with priests and sacrifice, but the character of that temple and its pattern of worship are obscure. Some texts portray the future temple as a divinely constructed edifice that "waits in heaven ready to descend to earth at the appointed time" (Klawans, *Purity, Sacrifice, and the Temple*, 139). The prayers of the Jewish liturgy suggest that the daily *tamid* offering and the special *musaf* sacrifices for holidays will be restored in the messianic age (Sacks [ed. and trans.], *Koren Siddur–Nusah Ashkenaz*, 542–45), yet a tradition ascribed to amoraic authorities claims that the only sacrifice that will remain in that age will be the thanksgiving offering (Klawans, *Purity, Sacrifice, and the Temple*, 200). The first chief rabbi of Israel, Rabbi Abraham Isaac Kook, who is acknowledged to be the pioneer and fountainhead of orthodox religious Zionism, taught that no animals

prominent streams of extra-biblical Judaism interpret these two biblical texts as demonstrating that the temples of Solomon and Herod were but hints of a reality to come of incomparable splendor.

Finally, extra-biblical Judaism manifests a widespread consciousness that Israel itself should be considered a *human temple*. This vision of the people as temple takes explicit form among the sectarians at Qumran, with the phrase *mikdash adam* ("a human sanctuary") employed as a communal self-designation (4Q *Florilegium*).[32] But a similar perspective appears also in Jewish circles that continued to support the Jerusalem temple. Recent archaeological work in Galilee demonstrates that temple imagery and rites had been extended to synagogue and communal contexts far beyond the borders of the holy city.[33] Pharisaic practice consisted largely of extending temple purity rules to non-sacrificial meals. Moreover, later rabbinic literature portrays Torah study, prayer, and deeds of loving-kindness as equal or superior to temple sacrifice, and asserts that the divine presence resides with communities of Jews who undertake such practices, wherever they may be located.[34]

As Klawans rightly contends, this extension of temple categories to non-temple facilities and activities should not be viewed as a "spiritualization" of the temple and its rites, but as a "templization" of synagogues (and thus of the Jewish communities that gathered there) and as a "sacrificialization" of non-sacrificial modes of worship.[35] The Jerusalem temple represented God's desire to dwell in a human temple, but it did so without diminishing its own structural particularity. In fact, this envisioning of Israel itself as a temple and its daily activities as sacrifice actually intensified devotion to the Jerusalem institution, even after its destruction. Dalia Marx articulates this fact vividly in her description of the rabbinic orientation to the temple:

> Paradoxically, the Temple's influence increased following its destruction and its absence is present in the tapestry of Jewish life. In the past, only those who made pilgrimage and entered its

would be offered or eaten in the age to come (*Olat Rayah* 1, 292). On the significance of Rav Kook, see Mirsky, *Rav Kook*.

32. Klawans disputes this interpretation of the phrase *mikdash adam* (*Purity, Sacrifice, and the Temple*, 163), yet acknowledges that "What cannot be denied is that the sect's own behaviors are described in sacrificial terms" (164).

33. Aviam, "Reverence for Jerusalem and the Temple in Galilean Society."

34. See Marx, "The Missing Temple."

35. Klawans, *Purity, Sacrifice, and the Temple*, 171–72.

> gates experienced the Temple. Yet only after its destruction can every Jew symbolically visit the Temple on a regular basis, by studying its laws, praying in its direction, observing the festivals of the Jewish calendar, and celebrating life cycle events.[36]

The reason that this is the case, however, is because the Herodian temple also pointed *backwards* to the desert tabernacle and Solomon's temple (containing the holy ark), *upwards* to the heavenly temple, *outwards* to the cosmic temple, and *forwards* to the eschatological temple. Israel as the *human* temple was thus linked not merely to the pre-70 institution, but even more to the transcendent realities to which it had pointed. As a result, the people of Israel obtained an extraordinary place in the universe and in the divine plan.

All four of these biblical patterns of temple symbolism are expanded and deepened in extra-biblical Jewish writings. In combination with Jerusalem's political vulnerability and the spread of the Jewish diaspora, *this intensified symbolism heightened the significance of the Jerusalem temple in the Jewish imagination while at the same time reinforcing the consciousness of its relativity and provisionality.*

This paradox distinguishes the post-exilic temple from the city of Jerusalem, the land of Israel, and the people of Israel. While the temple had always pointed to realities beyond itself, this was not the case for the city, the land, and the people. In some extra-biblical texts these do take on such symbolic meaning—the city and the land representing eschatological realities, and the people of Israel representing all those who "see God."[37] Nevertheless, the concrete realities of the city, the land, and the people are not thereby rendered relative or provisional, but instead are placed at the center of a more expansive canvas.

The temple thus occupies a unique symbolic position in ancient Judaism, both in biblical and extra-biblical literature. We must keep that fact in mind as we examine New Testament perspectives on the temple, and as we assess their theological significance for our understanding of the resurrected Messiah, the Jewish people, and the land of promise.

36. Marx, "The Missing Temple," 105–6.

37. On the land as the world, see Jubilees 22.14, 32.18–19; on Israel as "the man who sees God," see Philo, *On the Change of Names* 81.

The Temple in the Non-Lukan Writings of the New Testament

Paul & the Pauline Tradition

Unlike the author/editor of Luke and Acts, the apostle Paul writes before the Jerusalem temple was destroyed by the Romans. Therefore, his attitude toward this Jewish institution has special relevance for our understanding of the temple-theology of the early Jesus-movement.

Paul considered the communities he formed to be expressions of the human-temple to which the Jerusalem temple pointed (2 Cor 6:14–7:1; 1 Cor 6:19–20). He likewise viewed his own life and that of his followers as priestly in character, with the offering of apostolic and practical service and material support as analogous to temple sacrifice (Rom 12:1; 15:15–16, 27; Phil 2:17; 4:18). As we have seen, this extension of temple-concepts beyond the boundaries of the Jerusalem institution was a common feature of the Jewish world of his time, and amplified rather than diminished the honor bestowed on that institution. Employing the useful (if somewhat infelicitous) terminology of Klawans, the Pauline texts do not "spiritualize" the temple and its rites, but instead "templize" his communities and "sacrificialize" their non-sacrificial modes of worship.[38]

This conclusion finds support in the fact that the uncontested Pauline corpus contains no criticism, explicit or implicit, of the Jerusalem temple. But we need not rely solely on the absence of contrary evidence. In three texts, Paul displays unequivocally his esteem for the most important Jewish religious institution of his day. The first is Romans 9:4, where Paul enumerates the privileges bestowed on Israel:

> They are Israelites, and to them belong
> the adoption [*huiothesia*],
> the glory [*doxa*],
> the covenants [*diathēkai*],
> the giving of the law [*nomothesia*],
> the worship [*latreia*],
> and the promises [*epangeliai*] . . . (Rom 9:4)

The parallel forms of the six Greek words used to designate these privileges—the first (*huio-thesia*) corresponding closely to the fourth

38. On Paul's respect for the Jerusalem Temple, see Fredriksen, *Sin*, 38–39, and "Judaizing the Nations," 349; Klawans, *Purity, Sacrifice, and the Temple*, 219–21; and Eisenbaum, *Paul was not a Christian*, 156–57.

(*nomo-thesia*), and the third (*diathēk-ai*) to the sixth (*epangeli-ai*)—reinforce the connection between the second ("the glory" [*doxa*]) and the fifth ("the worship" [*latreia*]). As Paula Fredriksen notes, the RSV (and NRSV) translation of *doxa* and *latreia* fails to convey the temple connotations of the words: "The RSV's famously bloodless translation of Paul's Greek terms masks Paul's Temple imagery in 9:4, where *doxa/kavod* speaks precisely of God's glorious presence in Jerusalem's sanctuary, and *latreia/avodah* refers to the cult of offerings enacted there."[39] Paul thus sets the blessing of the temple within the context of the gifts given through Moses (i.e., the exodus from Egypt—referred to here as "the adoption" [see Exod 4:22–23]—and the revelation at Sinai), and the series of covenants and promises that originated before Moses (with the patriarchs) and were elaborated after him (with David and the prophets). Paul here leaves no doubt as to his favorable view of the temple and its sacrificial regimen.

1 Corinthians 10:14–21 is the second text in which Paul's attitude toward the Jerusalem temple becomes visible. In these verses, Paul aims to dissuade his hearers from participating in pagan sacrificial banquets. His argument depends on a set of assumptions that support Fredriksen's interpretation of *doxa* and *latreia* in Romans 9:4.

> . . . flee from the worship of idols. . . . The cup of blessing that we bless, is it not a sharing in the blood of Christ? The bread that we break, is it not a sharing in the body of Christ? Because there is one bread, we who are many are one body, for we all partake of the one bread. Consider the people of Israel [lit. Israel according to the flesh]; are not those who eat the sacrifices partners in the altar? What do I imply then? That food sacrificed to idols is anything, or that an idol is anything? No, I imply that what pagans sacrifice, they sacrifice to demons and not to God. I do not want you to be partners with demons. You cannot drink the cup of the Lord and the cup of demons. You cannot partake of the table of the Lord and the table of demons. (1 Cor 10:14–21)

Paul compares three ritual actions: (1) the Lord's Supper; (2) the partaking of meat sacrificed at the temple in Jerusalem; and (3) participation in a sacrificial meal at a pagan temple. Mention of the second ritual action is necessary to establish the meaning of the first, since it is not self-evident that the Lord's Supper is a sacrificial meal. Paul then uses the sacrificial character of the Lord's Supper as the basis for his argument

39. Fredriksen, "Judaizing the Nations," 349.

against partaking of pagan sacrifices. In short, he cites the example of Jewish temple sacrifice to explain the meaning of "sharing [*koinonia*] in the body of Christ," and then cites the Lord's Supper (understood as a sacrificial banquet) as a reason for avoiding pagan sacrificial banquets.

The cogency of this argument requires a positive view of the Jerusalem temple and its sacrificial service. To be "partners [*koinonoi*] in the altar [of the Jerusalem temple]" is to be partners of the God whom that altar represents.[40] Paul speaks of this partnership in the present rather than the past tense: those who eat the sacrifices offered at the Jerusalem temple—"Israel according to the flesh"—*are* (rather than "*were*") partners in the altar. Paul's conviction that Jews entered into communion with God when they worshipped at the Jerusalem temple provides the foundation for his assertion that disciples of Jesus likewise enter into communion with the Messiah through the Lord's Supper. 1 Corinthians 10 thus supports Paula Fredriksen's contention that "the Eucharist, for Paul, does not replace, displace or contest the sacrifices made to God by Jews in Jerusalem's temple. For Paul's gentiles-in-Christ in the Diaspora, however, the Eucharist replaces and in some sense annuls their former sacrifices to false gods."[41] In fact, 1 Corinthians 10 does more than this: it shows that Paul esteems highly "the sacrifices made to God by Jews in Jerusalem's temple," and in some sense even connects the Lord's Supper to those offerings.

The third key Pauline text, 1 Corinthians 9:13, follows a similar pattern as that found in 1 Corinthians 10. Once again Paul launches an argument whose premises assume a favorable assessment of the Jerusalem temple. In this case he seeks to prove that apostles have the right to receive material provision for their labor. He cites the example of the Jerusalem priests as evidence for this conclusion. "Do you not know that those who are employed in the temple service get their food from the temple, and those who serve at the altar share in what is sacrificed on the altar?" (1 Cor 9:13). As in Romans 15:16, Paul treats the apostolic office as involving a type of priestly service. But just as 1 Corinthians 10 assumes the enduring value of the worship conducted in the Jerusalem

40. N. T. Wright acknowledges this fact: "This 'sharing' in the Messiah's body and blood [in 1 Corinthians 10] is conceived . . . on the model of the 'sharing' which Israel, from the time of the exodus through to Paul's own day, believed was happening 'in the altar', a reverent periphrasis for the one God himself . . ." (*Paul and the Faithfulness of God*, 2:1345). Unfortunately, Wright draws no inferences from this text regarding Paul's view of the Jerusalem temple.

41. Fredriksen, *Sin*, 39.

temple in order to establish the sacrificial character of the Lord's Supper, so this text assumes the same in order to establish the priestly prerogatives of the apostolate. Paul's "priesthood" does not nullify the Aaronic order, but extends it in a new direction. Therefore, James Charlesworth is correct when he infers from this verse that "Paul, as a faithful Jew, seems to have a very positive view of the Holy Place, the Temple."[42]

These three texts derive from letters whose authorship is uncontested. Scholarly opinion concerning the authorship of a fourth text, 2 Thessalonians 2:3–4, is divided, but the letter certainly represents the Pauline tradition. As with the other passages already considered, this one displays a high view of the Jerusalem temple:

> Let no one deceive you in any way; for that day [i.e., the day of the *parousia* of the Lord Jesus] will not come unless the rebellion comes first and the lawless one is revealed, the one destined for destruction. He opposes and exalts himself above every so-called god or object of worship, so that he takes his seat in the temple of God, declaring himself to be God. (2 Thess 2:3–4)

The author speaks here of the antichrist, and interprets the "abomination that makes desolate" of Daniel (11:31; 12:11) as his enthronement in the Jerusalem temple (see Mark 13:14). That structure is here called "the temple of God," and is viewed as central to the final scenes of the eschatological drama. Once again, Charlesworth is justified when he claims that "The author [of 2 Thessalonians] celebrates the extreme importance of the Jerusalem Temple in the economy of salvation."[43]

In light of these texts, we have no reason to view Paul's temple-ecclesiology as entailing either a nullification or relativization of the significance of the Jerusalem temple. However, the Pauline tradition does include a letter whose temple-ecclesiology may suggest at least the superiority of the *ekklēsia* to the Jerusalem institution, which points in its direction. That letter is Ephesians, and its classic statement of temple-ecclesiology is found in chapter 2, verses 11–22.[44] The chapter concludes with an explicit statement of its theme: "In him [Messiah Jesus] the whole building is joined together and grows into a holy temple in the Lord; in whom you also are built together into a dwelling-place of God in the

42. Charlesworth, "The Temple and Jesus' Followers," 192.

43. Charlesworth, "The Temple and Jesus' Followers," 195.

44. For an extended exposition of Ephesians 1–3, see Kinzer, *Searching Her Own Mystery*, 65–82.

Spirit" (Eph 2:21–22).[45] Moreover, temple imagery pervades the unit as a whole. The imagery of distance and proximity (vv. 13, 17) alludes to the spatial relationship to the Jerusalem sanctuary and its altar that is signified in the Pentateuch by the Hebrew root *k-r-v* (meaning "to be near"). Similarly, the word "access" (*pros-agogē*; v. 18) is a nominal form of the verb (*pros-agō*) commonly employed in the Septuagint to translate the Hebrew word *hikriv* (the causative form of *k-r-v*) in the priestly writings of the Torah: thus, to have "access" is to be "brought near" to the holy place. The gentile recipients of this letter who had been "far off" have now been "brought near" by "the blood of the Messiah" (v. 13)—that is, by the Messiah's *korban* (i.e., the Hebrew word for sacrifice, which literally means "that which is brought near").

The central verse of Ephesians 2:11–22 tells of how the Messiah has united Jews and gentiles in himself, and "has broken down the dividing wall, nullifying in his flesh the hostility between us" (v. 14). Given the dominant role of temple imagery in the unit as a whole, this verse likely alludes to the balustrade in the courts of the Jerusalem temple, which prevented gentiles from drawing near to the sanctuary proper.[46] Ephesians thus asserts that the *korban* of the Messiah has effected a change in the status of gentiles who are united to him, so that they are now able to draw near to God in a way that was prohibited in the Jerusalem temple. While this challenges the Jewish conventions of the time, it does not in fact violate the Torah (which imposes no such barriers to gentile participation in Israel's worship). Moreover, the prophetic message of Isaiah (e.g., 56:6–8; 66:18–23) would lead one to expect just such an alteration in gentile status in the eschaton.[47]

45. All citations from Ephesians 2:11–22 are from my own translation.

46. Luke Timothy Johnson, *The Writings of the New Testament*, 415.

47. It is plausible that the author/editor of Luke and Acts is acquainted with Ephesians, and that he narrates the story of Paul's arrest in Jerusalem in a way that aims to remove misunderstandings that the letter might have generated. In Acts 21:27–30, Paul is seized in the temple by crowds who suspect him of bringing a gentile beyond the balustrade. It is almost as if they had heard something about the teaching of Ephesians 2:14, and concluded from it that Paul would disregard the words inscribed on the balustrade warning gentiles not to proceed further. Strikingly, those who stir up the crowds with this false accusation are "Jews from *Asia*" (Acts 21:27), that is, the province in which the city of Ephesus is located. Furthermore, the reason given for their suspicion is that they had seen Paul earlier with a gentile companion—Trophimus *the Ephesian* (Acts 21:29). In the various speeches that follow this incident, Paul takes pains to stress his willing conformity to Jewish customs, including those obtaining in the temple (e.g., Acts 24:12–13, 17–18; 26:4–5; 28:17). In this way, Acts makes clear

According to Ephesians, the *korban* of the Messiah brings blessing not only to gentiles (who had been "far off") but also to Jews (who were already "near"): "So he came and announced-good-news of peace to you who were far off and peace to those who were near; for through him we both have access in one Spirit to the Father" (vv. 17–18). The promise of a more intimate "access" to God, through the Messiah and in the Spirit, available to Jews and gentiles together, suggests that the temple balustrade was not the only barrier that had been removed by the Messiah's *korban*. Ephesians may here hint at what the letter to the Hebrews emphatically asserts—that the way is now open "to enter the sanctuary by the blood of Jesus" (Heb 10:19; see 6:19–20). The proximity to God that was formerly granted only to the high priest, and to him only one day per year, was now the constant privilege of all who are united to the Messiah.

In accord with the temple-ecclesiology of the uncontested Pauline letters, Ephesians presents the *ekklēsia* as a temple in which God resides. In contrast to the earlier letters, however, Ephesians appears to portray this temple as in some respects superior to the Jerusalem temple. While the earlier Pauline writings may only view the *ekklēsia* as an *extension* of the Jerusalem institution, Ephesians evidently considers the body of the Messiah to be the foretaste of its greater eschatological *archetype*. At the same time, there is nothing in Ephesians to suggest that the preliminary manifestation of the perfect *archetype* entails the *nullification* of the institution that served as its imperfect type.[48] As we will see below in our study of Hebrews, it is possible to hold type and archetype together in eschatological tension.

The Pauline tradition shows no interest in the heavenly, cosmic, or eschatological temples.[49] When drawing upon the rich symbolic field of realities to which the temple might point, it focuses exclusively on the human temple represented by the community of the Messiah.

that Paul's temple-ecclesiology would never lead him to violate the rules that governed conduct in the Jerusalem temple.

48. If Ephesians was written after the destruction of the temple in 70 CE, the coexistence of type and archetype would be a non-issue. In that case, the letter would offer consolation to those mourning the loss of the temple, assuring them that an even greater spiritual reality remained in their midst.

49. The Pauline tradition (i.e., Col 1:19; 2:9) does offer a passing allusion to temple-Christology (see Wright, *Paul and the Faithfulness of God*, 675). Temple-Christology and temple-ecclesiology are two distinct but related expressions of a view that sees the Jerusalem institution as pointing to the reality of the human-temple.

In doing so, the temple-ecclesiology of the Pauline writings poses no obstacle to the affirmation of an enduring bond between the resurrected Messiah and the Jewish people, the city of Jerusalem, and the land of Israel.

Hebrews

Scholars of the last century often featured the Letter to the Hebrews as the poster-child for an early "Christianity" that had left Judaism and the Jewish people behind. The following characterization of the text by Bruce Chilton and Jacob Neusner is typical:

> The Temple in Jerusalem has in Hebrews been replaced by a conception of the divine throne in heaven and the faithful congregation on earth. . . . The author understands Israel, literally, as a thing of the past, the husk of the first, now antiquated covenant. . . . The true high priest has entered once and for all (9:12) within the innermost recess of sanctity, so that no further sacrificial action is necessary or appropriate.[50]

As is evident, the letter's temple-theology has provided the main rationale for this post-Jewish reading of Hebrews. However, recent studies have challenged this scholarly consensus, and a fresh interpretation of the book has emerged that is powerful and compelling.[51]

Like Paul, the author of Hebrews has tunnel vision when reflecting on the field of realities to which the Jerusalem temple points. Whereas Paul focuses exclusively on the *human* temple, Hebrews concentrates on

50. Chilton and Neusner, *Judaism in the New Testament*, 182–83, 180. See also the view of Klawans: "The antitemple, antisacrificial, and antipriestly polemics here [in the book of Hebrews] are simply unmistakable. . . . This text is the basis of Christian supersessionist approaches to the temple" (*Purity, Sacrifice, and the Temple*, 243).

51. Already in an important 1989 article Charles Anderson argued that the frame of reference of Hebrews is entirely Jewish, with an intended audience composed exclusively of Jews and a continued upholding of all Torah provisions except those directly associated with the temple (Anderson, "Who are the Heirs of the New Age in the Epistle to the Hebrews?"). The arguments and conclusions of Anderson have been rehearsed and confirmed more recently by Richard Hays (Hays, "'Here We Have No Lasting City': New Covenantalism in Hebrews," 151–73). Anderson took the key step beyond a post-Jewish reading of Hebrews, but he still maintained the traditional interpretation of the temple-theology of Hebrews. That traditional interpretation has now likewise been challenged, and the substance of that challenge will be my focus in this section.

the *heavenly* temple. Chilton and Neusner are reading Paul into Hebrews when they assert that "The Temple in Jerusalem has in Hebrews been replaced by . . . the faithful congregation on earth." There is no temple-ecclesiology in Hebrews, and the significance of that fact will become clear as we proceed.[52]

In describing the heavenly temple and asserting its superiority over its earthly antitype, Hebrews follows the Jewish exegetical tradition in its reading of Exodus 15:17 and Daniel 2:34–35, 44–45:

> But when Christ came as a high priest of the good things that have come, then through the greater and perfect tent (not made with hands [*ou cheiro-poiētou*], that is, not of this creation) he entered once and for all into the Holy Place . . . . (Heb 9:11–12a)
>
> For Christ did not enter a sanctuary made by human hands [*ou gar eis cheiro-poiēta*], a mere copy [*anti-typa*] of the true one, but he entered into heaven itself, now to appear in the presence of God on our behalf. (Heb 9:24)
>
> . . . [Christ is] a minister [*leitourgos*] in the sanctuary and the true tent that the Lord, and not any mortal [*anthrōpos*], has set up. (Heb 8:2)

Traditional Jewish readings of Exodus 15:17–18 and Daniel 2:34–35 contrast the humanly fashioned temple ("made with hands") of this age with the divinely constructed eschatological temple. Hebrews instead emphasizes the *heavenly* temple.[53] In other words, Hebrews appears to posit a strictly vertical spatial duality between the earthly and heavenly temples rather than a horizontal temporal duality. However, this apparent distinction collapses when the eschatological horizon of the latter book is accounted for, as we will soon see.

This stress on the heavenly temple derives from Christological and soteriological concerns: the author focuses on heaven not as the place of angelic worship but as the site of the priestly office and atoning work of Jesus. In a recent volume, David Moffitt has underlined the importance of these points, and has drawn an inference from them that has escaped past

52. See Chance, *Jerusalem, the Temple, and the New Age in Luke-Acts*, 26: "[T]he author of Hebrews does not 'ecclesiologize' or 'christologize' the temple, for in Hebrews neither the church nor Jesus actually becomes the new eschatological temple."

53. On the use of Exodus 15:17–18 in Hebrews, and its similarity to later Jewish exegetical tradition, see Tomson, *'If this be from Heaven . . .'*, 369–70.

commentators.[54] First, Moffitt shows how the author of Hebrews carefully distinguishes the Davidic genealogy of Jesus from the Aaronic descent of the Jerusalem priesthood. Two texts are significant in this regard:

> 13 Now the one of whom these things are spoken belonged to another tribe, from which no one has ever served at the altar. 14 For it is evident that our Lord was descended from Judah, and in connection with that tribe Moses said nothing about priests. 15 It is even more obvious when another priest arises, resembling Melchizedek, 16 one who has become a priest, not through a legal requirement concerning physical descent, but through the power of an indestructible life. (Heb 7:13–16)

> Now if he were on earth, he would not be a priest at all, since there are priests who offer gifts according to the law. (Heb 8:4)

According to the proper order of worship in the earthly sanctuary in Jerusalem, priests descended from Aaron "offer gifts according to the law." As one descended from David rather than Aaron, Jesus is not qualified to serve as a priest in *that* venue. His qualification for priestly service derives instead from the "power of indestructible life," which he now possesses—i.e., from his resurrection and ascension (which God enacted in fulfillment of promises made to David and David's successors). By virtue of his resurrection power, Jesus enters into the heavenly sanctuary and there exercises his priestly vocation. His priesthood is *heavenly, not earthly*.[55]

Second, Moffitt argues convincingly that Hebrews views the sacrifice of Jesus as a heavenly act in which he presents his crucified and now glorified human body before the throne of God.[56] In other words, Hebrews does not focus on the crucifixion itself as a sacrifice, but on its heavenly aftermath. The heavenly setting of Jesus' atoning work is evident in numerous verses (1:3; 4:14; 6:19–20; 8:2; 9:11–14; 9:23–24; 10:12), and corresponds to the regimen of the Torah in which the death of the animal constitutes only a preliminary stage in the sacrificial process. According to the Torah, the sacrificial act culminates in the presentation of the blood on the altar and (in some cases) in the holy place. Moreover, a heavenly setting for Jesus' sacrifice is required by the letter's unambiguous assertion that Jesus could not function as an earthly priest. Since

54. Moffitt, *Atonement and the Logic of Resurrection in the Epistle to the Hebrews.*

55. Moffitt, *Atonement and the Logic of Resurrection*, 199.

56. Moffitt, *Atonement and the Logic of Resurrection*, 220–96.

Jesus is qualified to serve as priest *only* in the heavenly sanctuary (and not in its earthly antitype), the saving sacrifice which he offers must have its locus in that heavenly setting.

Moffitt infers from these two points a conclusion that challenges past readings of Hebrews:

> The author emphasizes Jesus' ascension and heavenly session in part because *he acknowledges the authority of the Law, at least on earth*. Jesus can serve as high priest only if he is in heaven. . . . *The authority of the Law remains valid on earth*, and on earth a lawfully appointed order of priests already exists. Therefore, Jesus, being from the tribe of Judah (7:14), cannot serve in that priesthood.[57]

Now we see the significant implications of the fact that Hebrews lacks any temple-ecclesiology, or even a trace of temple-Christology: such temple-theologies attend to *earthly* realities signified by the Jerusalem sanctuary or the desert tabernacle. In a literary work that stresses so forcefully the overwhelming superiority of Jesus' priesthood and sacrifice to the institutions of the Torah, which prefigure them, it would be difficult to interpret temple-ecclesiology or temple-Christology as merely *extensions* or *archetypes* of Torah institutions. If Jesus were an earthly priest and his sacrifice were an earthly sacrifice, then the logic of Hebrews would entail the obsolescence, abrogation, and *replacement* of these Torah institutions. But since his priesthood and his sacrifice are both heavenly, they may *coexist*—at least in the interim period between the resurrection of Jesus and his return—with the earthly institutions that prefigure them.

Because Jesus has entered into the heavenly sanctuary with his own body and blood, an atonement has been effected whose transformative power transcends that available through the priestly institutions ordained by the Torah: "For if the blood of goats and bulls, with the sprinkling of the ashes of a heifer, sanctifies those who have been defiled so that their flesh is purified, how much more will the blood of Christ, who through the eternal Spirit offered himself without blemish to God, purify our conscience from dead works to worship the living God!" (Heb 9:13–14). Moreover, his priestly mediation now gives his followers a preliminary access to the heavenly throne of God, to which the holy of holies of the temple corresponds (Heb 6:19–20; 10:19–22). But since Jesus has accomplished this as a resurrected embodied human being, the ultimate goal

57. Moffitt, *Atonement and the Logic of Resurrection*, 220; 199. Emphasis added.

for his "brothers" (Heb 2:5–18) is not heavenly existence as disembodied spirits but resurrection life in "the coming world" (*tēn oikoumenēn tēn mellousan*; Heb 2:5), the ultimate land of promise (Heb 4:1–11). Thus, the *vertical* spatial duality of Hebrews' temple-theology unfolds in a way that reveals its underlying *horizontal* temporal duality.

Recognition of the crucial role played by *unrealized* eschatology in Hebrews characterizes the fresh reading of Hebrews offered in recent scholarship. Richard Hays succinctly summarizes this fundamental insight: "Hebrews—despite its conviction that Jesus has in fact completed his atoning work in the heavenly sanctuary—retains a remarkably open-ended eschatology that continues to look to the future for the consummation of salvation."[58] The book's temple-theology does not merely coexist with this "open-ended eschatology," but is formulated for the purpose of expressing it. This becomes most evident in Hebrews 9:6–10:

> [6] Such preparations having been made, the priests go continually into the first tent to carry out their ritual duties; [7] but only the high priest goes into the second, and he but once a year, and not without taking the blood that he offers for himself and for the sins committed unintentionally by the people. [8] By this the Holy Spirit indicates that the way into the sanctuary has not yet been disclosed as long as the first tent is still standing. [9] This is a symbol of the present time [*hētis parabolē eis ton kairon ton enestēkota*], during which gifts and sacrifices are offered that cannot perfect the conscience of the worshiper, [10] but deal only with food and drink and various baptisms, regulations for the body imposed until the time comes to set things right [*mechri kairou diorthōseōs epikeimena*].

As Jesper Svartvik has argued, the distinction between the first and second tent symbolizes the distinction between the present world subject to the power of death (Heb 2:14) and the coming world of the resurrection (Heb 7:16).[59] The first tent—the world subject to death—is "still standing," and so "the way into the sanctuary has not yet been [fully] disclosed" (Heb 9:8).

> What is so important to the author—and, hence, also to the reader—is that *the outer tent is still standing.* In other words, in the ninth chapter there is a contrast between the present and the

58. Hays, "New Covenantalism," 166.

59. Svartvik, "Reading the Epistle to the Hebrews without Presupposing Supersessionism."

> future. The author states that he is living in the present time (9:9: *eis ton kairon ton enestēkota*), but that he longs for "the time of a better order" (9:10: *mechri kairou diorthōseōs epikeimena*).[60]

Our "hope" enters even now into the "inner shrine behind the curtain" (Heb 6:19), but hope is not yet full possession (Heb 11:1). The followers of Jesus already partake of an appetizer consisting of the "powers of the age to come" (*dynameis te mellontos aiōnos*; Heb 6:5), but they are not yet able to recline at table and enjoy the full feast.

The eschatological temple-theology of Hebrews also provides the rationale for the book's interpretation of the "new covenant" of Jeremiah 31. The "first tent" (Heb 9:2) corresponds to the "first covenant" (Heb 9:1), and the "second tent" represents both the "new covenant" and the world to come. This straightforward correlation leads to a surprising conclusion: in the words of Svartvik, "the time of the new covenant *has not been realized*, not yet."[61] Svartvik here follows the reading of Hebrews proposed by Peter Tomson:

> While the author is clear on the superbness of the worship of the "new" covenant, he speaks of the "old" as something that still continues and that is symbolized in the temple service in the present time. The work of Christ consists, then, not so much in disbanding the worship prescribed by the old covenant, but in fulfilling its true significance while "the first tent still stands." . . . *The "new covenant," if we may thus accentuate it, is valid only in heaven, not yet upon earth.* The "good things," of which Christ is the direct image, are yet to come. In fact, the whole Platonizing allegory remains within the eschatological framework supposed in the original text from Jeremiah . . . .[62]

Svartvik reinforces Tomson's reading by attending to the use of the verb *palaioō* ("to grow old") in Hebrews 8:13: "By speaking of a new covenant, he implies that the first one is old [*pe-palaiōken*]. And anything old [*to de palaioumnenon*] and ageing is ready to disappear [*engus a-phanismou*]."[63] As Svartvik points out, this verb appears only twice in

60. Svartvik, "Reading the Epistle to the Hebrews," 86. Emphasis original.

61. Svartvik, "Reading the Epistle to the Hebrews," 86. Emphasis added.

62. Tomson, *"If this be from Heaven,"* 361–62. Emphasis added.

63. New Jerusalem Bible. Like many other versions, the NRSV here translates *palaioō* as "made obsolete." Richard Hays ("Here We Have No Lasting City," 160–61) notes that the Greek word need not have such a radical connotation: "Our author's concluding comment in [Hebrews 8] v. 13 is perhaps less negative than suggested by

Hebrews. We find it first in the opening chapter of the book in a citation from Psalm 102:25–26, where it refers to the transitory nature of the present order of the world: "In the beginning, Lord, you founded the earth, and the heavens are the work of your hands; they will perish, but you remain; they will all wear out [*palaiōthēsontai*] like clothing . . ." (Heb 1:10–11).[64] Thus, what is "ready to disappear" is not "Judaism" in favor of "Christianity," but a world subjected to the power of death in favor of a world renewed by the power of indestructible life.

The conviction expressed in Hebrews that the first covenant is growing "old" and is "ready to disappear" cannot be separated from the book's claim that the risen and ascended priestly-Messiah will soon return and transform the present order of the world:

> [36] For you need endurance, so that when you have done the will of God, you may receive what was promised. [37] For yet "in a very little while, the one who is coming will come and will not delay; [38] but my righteous one will live by faith. My soul takes no pleasure in anyone who shrinks back." [39] But we are not among those who shrink back and so are lost, but among those who have faith and so are saved. (Heb 10:36–39)

Like the apostle Paul, the writer of Hebrews possesses a vivid anticipation of the coming reign of the Messiah, and this anticipation shapes the contours of his theology of the temple and the covenant.

The eschatological tension of Hebrews explains the apparent contradiction posed by the author's writing an urgent letter of instruction and exhortation to those who, as partakers of the "new covenant," supposedly no longer need such instruction (Jer 31:33–34). The comments of Mark Nanos are apropos:

> The author and the addressees know that such a *new* covenant has not in fact been experienced—witnessed by no less than the need to write this letter to 'teach' people who are not obeying the covenant as if the 'teaching' (= Torah) was now written on their hearts or minds. . . . Those who experience Jer. 31 do not need to have their 'faculties trained by practice to distinguish good from evil' (Heb. 5:14). . . . Jer. 31 cannot be accurately used to describe the experience of any community—yet.[65]

the NRSV, which uses the world "obsolete" to describe the first covenant. What Hebrew actually says is that God has "made old" the first covenant (*pepalaiōken*)."

64. Svartvik, "Reading the Epistle to the Hebrews," 80n14, 87–88.

65. Nanos, "*New* or *Re*newed Covenantalism?" 186, 188.

Svartvik draws the same conclusion about the proper understanding of the new covenant of Jeremiah 31, and states his position in a series of rhetorical questions: "Have all hearts of stone disappeared? Is it true that Christians need not teach each other? Do all Christians know the Lord—from the smallest to the greatest?"[66] For Hebrews, the new covenant is in the process of being realized, just as the first covenant is in the process of growing "old." But neither process has yet been completed.

As David Moffitt points out, the eschatological tension of Hebrews also reveals the purpose for which the book was written: "Whether or not the audience is presently experiencing persecution, the recognition of this eschatological metanarrative suggests that the question of the community's falling back into some kind of Judaism they had already left behind is simply not the point at hand. The eschatological time clock is the issue."[67] In the face of suffering and unexpected delay, the hearers are in danger of losing their hope in the coming of the Messiah. The author writes to give them courage to persevere.

The two interconnected dualities of Hebrews—one vertical and spatial, the other horizontal and temporal—support the book's contention that the laws of the Torah for Israel's sanctuary are prophetic or typological, and thus transitional or temporary. However, until "the one who is coming will come" (Heb 12:37), the order of the earthly sanctuary remains in effect. It is not replaced by a superior earthly reality, that is, the *ekklēsia*. If Hebrews originates in the pre-70 period, this would mean that the author acknowledges the legitimacy of the Jerusalem temple in the period before the Coming One comes. If, on the other hand, Hebrews derives from the period after 70, then the author treats the destruction of the Jerusalem temple as an eschatological sign that the current order of the world will soon pass away. In that case, Hebrews begins to look much like other Jewish texts of the same era, such as L.A.B., 4 Ezra, and 2 Baruch, all of which express hope in the establishment of a new order of worship transcending that experienced by Israel in the past.

These three Jewish texts from the period immediately following the destruction of the Jerusalem temple also raise the possibility that the heavenly temple of Hebrews, "not made with hands," is envisioned by the author as ultimately *becoming* the eschatological temple.[68] In 4 Ezra and

66. Svartvik, "Reading the Epistle to the Hebrews," 90.

67. Moffitt, *Atonement and the Logic of Resurrection*, 301.

68. Klawans describes this widespread motif in Second Temple literature: "By combination of the accounts concerning Moses' vision of the tabernacle's patterns with

2 Baruch, in particular, the heavenly temple is inextricably connected to the heavenly city and land, and all three images together comprise Israel's future hope.[69] The eschatological imagery of Hebrews depicts the world to come as *land* (Heb 3:7–4:11; 11:14–16) and *city* (Heb 11:10, 16; 12:22; 13:14), but not explicitly as *temple*. However, the eschatological *city* is called Mount Zion (Heb 12:22)—i.e., the Temple Mount—and is associated with angels and heavenly worship (Heb 12:23–24). In context, the immediate contrast is between the eschatological city (i.e., the new covenant) and Mount Sinai (i.e., the first covenant), but readers cannot help seeing the connection between Mount Sinai and the tabernacle first constructed there. In coming to the heavenly Mount Zion, the followers of Jesus also come to the "sprinkled blood that speaks a better word than the blood of Abel" (Heb 12:24), and readers know that this atoning blood is found now in the heavenly sanctuary. In the final analysis, it appears that the two dualities of Hebrews coalesce, and the heavenly temple "not made with hands" becomes the eschatological temple. More precisely, we might say that the heavenly *holy of holies* becomes the eschatological temple/city, for the temporal and ontological duality symbolized by the spatial separation of the holy of holies from the holy place shall itself be abrogated.

I would underline the observation that Hebrews speaks explicitly of an eschatological city and land but not of an eschatological temple. In a sense, there is no temple in the eschatological vision of this book, for the city and the land are themselves equivalent to the heavenly holy of holies. Yet, as Moffitt stresses, that city and that land are "physical" realities, just as the resurrected form of Jesus is truly a "physical" body. Moreover, while the city and the land of the future age are distinguished from the city and land of the present age, the two ontological orders must

Ezekiel's vision of the future temple, a set of traditions emerged that imagined that a glorious new temple was in heaven, ready and waiting to descend to earth at the end of days, and able to be seen by those visionaries who ascend to heaven (e.g., 1 Enoch 90.28–37; 2 Baruch 4.1–6; 2 Esdras 10.25–28; cf. the *Temple Scroll* XXIX:9–10 and The New Jerusalem texts from Qumran) . . ." (Klawans, *Purity, Sacrifice, and the Temple*, 128–29).

69. Carla Sulzbach argues persuasively that these heavenly realities in 4 Ezra and 2 Baruch are not entirely discontinuous with their earthly correlates, but indicate glorious and transformed versions of what Israel had known before ("The Fate of Jerusalem in *2 Baruch* and *4 Ezra*: From Earth to Heaven and Back?"). David Moffitt takes a similar approach to these Jewish texts, and comments extensively and with insight on the parallels between the eschatology of Hebrews and that of L.A.B., 4 Ezra, and 2 Baruch (*Atonement and the Logic of Resurrection*, 96–119).

have some relation to one another—just as the future world as a whole is distinct from the present world and yet related to it.

Hebrews does not delegitimize the traditional Jewish order of worship in the age before the coming of the Coming One, nor does it negate the significance of the city of Jerusalem, the land of Israel, or the Jewish people. The traditional scholarly view that the author viewed Israel as "a thing of the past, the husk of the first, now antiquated covenant" should be discarded.[70]

Revelation

Like the book of Hebrews, the Revelation of John focuses attention on the heavenly temple—but, unlike Hebrews, without any polemical intent. Revelation offers no comment on the imperfection of the earthly temple, but instead looks exclusively to its heavenly archetype as the site from which the universe is governed and all reality is rooted.

Revelation describes the heavenly sanctuary and its activities in terms that display its detailed correspondence to the earthly sanctuary ordained in the Torah and embodied in the Jerusalem temple. The heavenly temple includes a seven-branched menorah (4:5), a golden incense-altar (8:3–4; 9:13; 14:17–18), an altar for burnt-offering (6:9; 16:7), the ark of the covenant (11:19), a laver (4:6; 15:2), and the tent of witness (15:5). Heavenly beings are robed in priestly attire (15:6), and offer incense to the One who sits upon the throne (5:8; 8:3–4). The heavenly temple is situated on a heavenly Mount Zion (14:1), and all who reside there participate in a song of praise resembling the levitical music of the Jerusalem sanctuary (14:2–3; 4:9–11; 5:9–14; 7:11–12; 11:16–18; 15:2–4).

Revelation also shares with Hebrews the soteriological conviction that Jesus consummates his sacrifice in heaven rather than on earth. That is the meaning of the extraordinary scene in which the lamb appears in heaven ("standing as if it had been slaughtered [*esphagmenon*]"), takes the scroll from the one seated on the throne, and receives the worship of the four living creatures, the twenty-four elders, myriads of angels, and all creation (5:6–14). The Davidic Messiah conquers through the sacrificial shedding of his blood, and his sacrifice takes effect only after he presents his resurrected martyred body before the heavenly throne.

70. Chilton and Neusner, *Judaism in the New Testament*, 183.

This reading of Revelation 5 is confirmed by the chapter that follows, when the seer beholds "the souls of those who had been slaughtered [*esphagmenōn*] for the word of God and for the testimony [*martyrian*] they had given" (6:9). John tells us that these "souls" are placed "under the altar"—that is, at the base of the altar of burnt offering, where the priests pour out the blood of Israel's sacrifices.[71] Whereas the heavenly altar of incense is the site where the *prayers* of the saints are presented before God (5:8; 8:3–4), the heavenly altar of burnt offering receives the gift of their *souls*, i.e., their life. But the sacrifice of these martyrs has effect only because they participate in the sacrifice of the lamb. Revelation 12:11 says this of the martyrs: "They have conquered him [Satan] by the blood of the Lamb and by the word of their testimony, for they did not cling to life even in the face of death." Richard Bauckham draws the necessary inference from Revelation 12:11:

> The whole verse requires that the reference to "the blood of the Lamb" is not purely to Christ's death but to the deaths of the Christian martyrs, who, following Christ's example, bear witness even at the cost of their lives. But this witness even as far as death does not have an independent value of its own. Its value depends on its being a continuation of his witness. So it is by the Lamb's blood that they conquer. Their deaths defeat Satan only by participating in the victory the Lamb won over Satan by his death.[72]

If the sacrifice of the martyrs is a *continuation* of the sacrifice of the lamb, and if their sacrifice is consummated at the heavenly altar, then we may conclude that the lamb's sacrifice is likewise consummated in heaven, and that Revelation 5 portrays the scene in which this takes place.

While Revelation shares the heavenly view of Jesus' sacrifice found in Hebrews, just as it shares Hebrews' focus on the heavenly sanctuary, we see that once again this motif in Revelation has no polemical function. Undoubtedly the heavenly sacrifice of the martyrs is superior to Israel's earthly sacrifice of animals, but Revelation shows no interest in making that point.[73]

---

71. Later rabbinic texts (e.g., *Numbers Rabbah* 12.12) likewise depict the blood of the martyrs as offered on a heavenly altar. See Klawans, *Purity, Sacrifice, and the Temple*, 140.

72. Bauckham, *The Theology of the Book of Revelation*, 75–76.

73. The superior efficacy of martyr-sacrifice to animal-sacrifice would not, in any case, be controversial in Jewish circles, ancient or modern. See Wyschogrod, *The Body of Faith*, 17–29.

For Hebrews, attention to the heavenly temple and sacrifice coincides with an absence of temple-ecclesiology or temple-Christology. The earthly sanctuary ordained in the Torah and its sacrifices are deficient in comparison to their heavenly archetypes, but no superior earthly forms replace them in the present age. Is this also true for Revelation? For the most part, this appears to be the case. The followers of the lamb are given access to the heavenly temple, as in Hebrews, but that access is not mediated through an earthly body or institution conceived of as a temple.[74] Thus, in the letters to the seven *ekklēsiai* (Rev 1–3) the seven are represented by golden lamp stands in the midst of which appears "one like the Son of Man"—but, rather than earthly fixtures, these lamps are parts of the heavenly menorah in which burn "the seven spirits of God" of Revelation 4:5. Here the *ekklēsiai* do not constitute the temple itself but only one of the important pieces of temple furniture, and while these human communities exist on earth their true life is a heavenly one in the presence of the risen Messiah.

Many commentators see Revelation 11:1–2 as the exception to this pattern, or as a basis for interpreting the pattern differently: "Then I was given a measuring rod like a staff, and I was told, 'Come and measure the temple of God and the altar and those who worship there, but do not measure the court outside the temple; leave that out, for it is given over to the nations, and they will trample over the holy city for forty-two months.'" In keeping with a tradition transmitted by Irenaeus, scholars generally hold that Revelation was written in 95 or 96, two and half decades after the Roman destruction of Jerusalem. If that is correct, then it is unlikely that 11:1–2 refers to the Jerusalem temple.[75] However, there have been many dissenting voices over the past three centuries who have contended that the book was written in the 60s, and that these verses refer to the Jewish war with Rome.[76] Among modern commentators who accept the later date of composition, some have seen 11:1–2 as speaking figuratively of Jerusalem, others as referring to the Jewish people, and

74. "In line with his use of the temple image the author of Rev. also does not see in the interim time any liturgy on earth, but locates it only in heaven" (Fiorenza, *The Book of Revelation*, 99).

75. Of course, it is possible that the text speaks *only* of a distant future, and anticipates that the Jerusalem temple will be rebuilt in that future. However, that view is dubious, for the book as a whole speaks to its immediate hearers with great urgency, as would not be the case if its message were relevant only for a future generation.

76. See Wainwright, *Mysterious Apocalypse*, 118–19.

still others to the heavenly temple.[77] But the majority view claims that these verses refer to the disciples of Jesus, considered as equivalent to the earthly temple.[78] The fact that such diverse opinions are conceivable suggests that temple-ecclesiology, even if present in Revelation 11:1–2, plays at best a marginal role in the book as a whole.

Throughout most of the book of Revelation the only temple in view is the heavenly one. This changes in the final chapters, when the Jerusalem on high descends to earth. At that climactic moment a voice issues from the throne, saying, "See, the tent [*skēnē*] of God is among human beings, and he will dwell (i.e., pitch-his-tent [*skēnōsei*]) among them" (21:3).[79] Thus is fulfilled the purpose first enunciated to Moses at Sinai: "And have them make me a sanctuary, so that I may dwell among them" (Exod 25:8). Thus is also fulfilled the promise concerning the martyrs of Revelation 7, who shall always stand "before the throne of God, and worship him day and night within his temple" (7:15; see also 3:12).

It appears that Israel's deepest hopes are now to be realized. Yet, as John proceeds to describe this new Jerusalem, we are surprised to learn that the city *contains no temple* (21:22). We should be hesitant to consider this an instance of "antitemple polemic," as Klawans asserts, for the book shows no such polemical tendencies in dealing with Jewish symbols in general and the temple in particular.[80] But then how are we to interpret the absence of a temple? The answer comes from the dimensions of the city, which John recounts just before stating "I saw no temple in the city" (21:22): "its length and width and height are equal" (21:16). This makes the city equivalent to a massive "holy of holies," which was likewise a perfect cube, and implies that the new creation, centered in this new Jerusalem, has become a universal cosmic temple. As James Charlesworth recognizes, "The author of Revelation does portray the New Jerusalem without a Temple, but that is not because the Temple is obsolete. It is because of the fulfillment of prophecy: God now is living among his faithful ones in an unprecedented imminence [*sic*]."[81]

77. For the first view, see Tomson, "'*If this be from Heaven*,'" 377; for the second, see Ladd, *The Revelation of John*, 152; for the third, see Perrin, *Jesus the Temple*, 52.

78. See, for example, Bauckham, *Theology of the Book of Revelation*, 127.

79. Translation mine.

80. Klawans, *Purity, Sacrifice, and the Temple*, 242–43.

81. Charlesworth, "The Temple and Jesus' Followers," 211. See also Bauckham, *Theology of the Book of Revelation*, 136, and Wright, *Paul and the Faithfulness of God*, 102.

Rather than "antitemple polemic," what we have here is a unique coalescing of typical Jewish motifs—the expansive holiness of the eschatological temple blended with the universality of the cosmic temple—to form a powerful vision of a transcendent future world filled with the presence of God.

This eschatological vision resembles what we found in the Letter to the Hebrews. The *structure* of the sanctuary ordained in the Torah fits and represents only the present age, where access to the divine presence is available but restricted. But the fundamental *reality* to which the temple pointed—the reality of God dwelling on earth in intimate communion with human beings—is attained perfectly only in the future age.

In sum, the book of Revelation displays many of the same perspectives on the temple as are found in Hebrews, but without any polemical overtones. We again find an emphasis on the heavenly temple and, in a fashion, the eschatological temple, but little attention given to temple-ecclesiology. There is nothing in either book that undermines the validity of temple worship in the present age, and there is certainly nothing in either book that challenges the enduring significance of the city of Jerusalem, the land of Israel, or the Jewish people.

Temple and City in Paul, Hebrews, and Revelation

All of the above New Testament traditions share a motif that deserves comment before proceeding further. They all speak of a "Jerusalem" that is "above" (Gal 4:26), "heavenly" (Heb 12:22), or "coming down out of heaven" (Rev 21:10). Has the earthly city of Jerusalem become a transitory and provisional symbol, like the temple "made with hands" stationed in her midst? Is the distinction between city and temple utterly dissolved, so that the former goes the way of the latter?

Hebrews and Revelation underline the provisional and transitional character of the temple by depicting an eschatological scenario in which the temple is no more. In contrast, both books present the *heavenly* city as that which endures. Far from threatening the distinction between city and temple, both books provide further support for the significance of that distinction.

The Pauline material differs from Hebrews and Revelation in lacking any reference to the heavenly temple or to a temple-free eschaton, and in treating the existing Jerusalem temple with unqualified respect. Galatians offers a biting critique of the earthly city of Jerusalem and no such critique of her temple. As the context of the letter shows, this emphasis derives from Paul's struggle against political forces within the *ekklēsia* (Gal 1:11—2:14), and perhaps also in the wider Jewish world (Gal 1:13–14).[82] Thus, the motif common to Galatians, Hebrews, and Revelation serves a different purpose for Paul than for the authors of the other two texts.

Furthermore, it is not evident that any of these references involve a heavenly (i.e., non-earthly) eschatology that dismisses the enduring significance of Jerusalem as a geographical site. Robert Louis Wilken asserts that Origen was the source of such a spiritualizing interpretation of Jerusalem in Hebrews and Galatians, and that earlier ecclesial tradition read these texts in concrete and earthly terms:

> Origen appeals to two texts [Gal 4:26; Heb 12:22] in the Christian Scriptures that seem to divest Jerusalem of its historical and hence political significance. . . . These texts show that when the Scriptures speak of Jerusalem they do not have in mind the city in Judea that was once the capital of the Jewish nation; Jerusalem, according to Origen, does not designate a future political center but a spiritual vision of heavenly bliss. In his use of Galatians 4 and Hebrews 12 Origen breaks with earlier Christian tradition. Irenaeus and Tertullian had cited Galatians 4 to support a belief in a future Jerusalem on earth.[83]

Wilken considers the earlier reading of these texts credible. Like David Moffitt, he notes the parallel between the view of Jerusalem found in Hebrews and that seen in the contemporaneous Jewish texts 2 Baruch and 4 Ezra, and suggests that "it is possible that the author [of Hebrews] has in mind a city that had been prepared beforehand by God, a city that one day would be unveiled and would majestically come down from the heavens to its resting place in the promised land."[84] This may be why Paul contrasts "the Jerusalem above" with "the *present* Jerusalem [*tē nun Ierousalēm*] rather than with "the earthly Jerusalem" (Gal 4:25); as in Hebrews, the vertical-spatial imagery is pressed into the service of a horizontal-temporal (i.e., eschatological) assertion. Such a reading of

82. Mark Nanos argues that the "influencers" whom Paul opposes in Galatians include leaders of the Jewish community who seek to normalize the Israelite status of his gentile adherents by facilitating their full conversion to Judaism. See Nanos, *The Irony of Galatians.*

83. Wilken, *The Land Called Holy*, 70.

84. Wilken, *Land Called Holy*, 54–55.

Galatians and Hebrews also fits the imagery of Revelation, where "the holy city Jerusalem" is seen "*coming down* out of heaven from God" (Rev 21:10). Heaven (i.e., God) is its architect and builder, but the city does not remain *in* heaven (i.e., a realm transcending embodied human existence) but descends to earth.

In sum, there is nothing in Galatians, Hebrews, or Revelation concerning the city of Jerusalem that undermines our thesis regarding her distinction from the temple, her relationship to the Jewish people, or her enduring bond with the resurrected Messiah.

The Gospel of John

The temple-theology of the Gospel of John enters territory previously uncharted in the New Testament or in Jewish literature in general. For the first time we encounter a full-orbed temple-Christology that honors the Jerusalem temple while asserting that the institution's purpose has been realized in a greater way through the incarnation of the Logos.[85] As Richard Hays recognizes, "For John, Jesus becomes, in effect, the Temple."[86]

Unlike Hebrews and Revelation, John shows little interest in the heavenly temple or the temple of the age to come.[87] Unlike the Pauline tradition, John never depicts the community established by Jesus as a temple. For John, the Jerusalem temple points exclusively to one supreme reality that is both earthly *and* heavenly: the flesh-and-blood person of Jesus the Messiah, the embodied Logos, now risen from the dead.

It is crucial to recognize from the outset that John's temple-Christology entails no criticism of the Jerusalem temple in itself. For John, the temple was a divinely-ordained and consecrated institution. The Johannine Jesus refers to the building as "my Father's house" (John 2:16). His behavior in the temple leads his disciples to recall the biblical verse, "Zeal for your house will consume [*kata-phagetai*] me" (John 2:17). The verb in this psalm citation has been shifted from the past (LXX Ps 68:10: *kat-ephagen*) to the future tense (*kata-phagetai*) in order to indicate that

85. See Kinzer, "Temple-Christology in the Gospel of John."

86. Hays, *Reading Backwards*, 82. Hays entitles his chapter on John, "The Temple Transfigured" (75).

87. John 14:2 may be an exception to this generalization, but its temple imagery is implicit and undeveloped, and the futurist dimension of its eschatology may be subordinated to what has already been realized Christologically. See Kinzer, "Temple-Christology," 450–51.

Jesus' aggressive act in devotion to the temple will provoke the priestly authorities to initiate his execution. The Johannine Jesus is motivated by his "zeal" for the Jerusalem temple, an institution that he considers to be "his Father's house." He shows displeasure with how its affairs are being conducted, but that displeasure derives from his reverent regard for its intrinsic significance.

This reverent regard is expressed concretely in the chapters that follow by accounts that consistently place Jesus in the temple precincts. Unlike the Synoptic Gospels, the vast majority of the Johannine narrative occurs in Judea rather than Galilee. Most of the Judean scenes are set in Jerusalem, and most of those take place in the temple during various festivals. Jesus appears there for an unspecified holiday (John 5:14; see 5:1), but also for Passover (2:14–15), Booths (7:14, 28; 8:20, 59), and Hannukah (10:23). While attendance at the temple during Passover and Booths was officially mandated by the Torah, those who lived in remote regions were not expected to make the annual pilgrimage for both holidays, and the journey for Hanukkah was meritorious but voluntary. Through his frequent presence at the site the Johannine Jesus displays an exceptional devotion to the Jerusalem temple which demonstrates the "zeal" for his Father's house noted at the beginning of the story.

A final example of Jesus' reverent regard for the Jerusalem temple in John is found in a text where we would least expect it: Jesus' exchange with the Samaritan woman, in which he announces the coming of a new era in which the unique holiness of the Jerusalem temple will be transcended (John 4:20–23). I will discuss this text further below, but at this point we should notice Jesus' affirmation of the unique dignity of the Jerusalem temple in the historical outworking of the divine purpose. The Samaritan woman mentions the contentious dispute between Samaritans and Judeans over the site that the Torah refers to as "the place that the LORD your God will choose out of all your tribes as his habitation to put his name there" (Deut 12:5). The Samaritans had identified the site as Mount Gerizim, whereas Judeans thought it to be Mount Zion. Jesus answers her implied question without equivocation: "You worship what you do not know; we worship what we know, for salvation is from the Jews [i.e., Judeans]" (4:22). In other words, the site that God chose "to put his name" is Jerusalem, and salvation for all the world will come from that place and from the people who have been devoted to it.

Despite these expressions of respect for the Jerusalem temple, John's central message concerns not that edifice, nor the tent of meeting that preceded it, but the person of Jesus to whom both institutions pointed. John makes this clear in his prologue: "And the Word became flesh and pitched-his-tent [*eskēnōsen*] among us" (John 1:14).[88] The verb here is the same as that found in Revelation 21:3, and both verses allude to the tent of meeting in the wilderness. The Word/Name/Glory of God, which God placed first in the tent of meeting and later in the Jerusalem temple, now resides permanently in the consecrated flesh of Jesus, the Messiah. John reiterates this theme in the next chapter when telling of Jesus' zeal for the Jerusalem temple. When asked for a sign to justify his action, Jesus responds "Destroy this temple, and in three days I will raise it up" (2:19). His interlocutors interpret this as referring to the edifice in whose midst they are standing, but the author tells us that "he was speaking of the temple of his body" (2:21). In this way, John, like Luke, establishes a connection between the death of Jesus and the destruction of Jerusalem in 70; but whereas Luke thinks of the city as a whole, John focuses on the temple that was its heart. In this way, John, like Luke, also establishes a connection between the resurrection of Jesus and Israel's eschatological restoration. However, John focuses not on the ultimate destiny of Israel and all creation, but on the preliminary eschatological realization that has already occurred through the death and resurrection of the incarnate Logos. According to John, *the risen Jesus is himself the eschatological temple*, accessible now to all who put their faith in him.[89]

The temple-Christology expressed boldly in John 1:14 and 2:19–21 takes a more subtle form elsewhere in the Gospel, but its impact can be felt throughout the work. One vivid example appears in chapter 10, where the author depicts Jesus as walking in Solomon's portico during the festival of Dedication (i.e., Hanukkah) (vv. 22–23). This holiday celebrates the recapture and re-consecration of the Jerusalem temple after it had been defiled by idolatrous practices during the reign of Emperor Antiochus Epiphanes. On this occasion, Jesus audaciously proclaims, "I and the Father are one" (v. 30). At these words Jesus' opponents prepare to stone him, accusing him of making himself to be God (vv. 31–33). In their minds, his claim shows him to be as blasphemous as the self-deifying Emperor Antiochus. Jesus responds by clarifying his assertion of unity with the Father, asserting not that he is God but that he is the *Son*

88. Translation mine.

89. The centrality of temple-Christology to John's message probably explains why he has placed the temple incident at the beginning of his account rather than in the week of Jesus' arrest and execution.

of God (v. 36). In the same verse, he identifies himself as "the one whom the Father has sanctified [*hēgiasen*] and sent into the world." John here employs the verb used in the Septuagint in reference to the initial consecration of the tent of meeting and its furnishings (e.g., LXX Exod 30:29; 40:9–10). Jesus is not "making himself" to be anything—the initiative comes entirely from his Father, who has consecrated and sent him to be a human temple in the world. The holiday that Jesus and his opponents are celebrating, and the holy building whose consecration is the theme of that holiday and in whose courts they stand—both point to and find fulfillment in *him*.[90]

A second subtle example of temple-Christology in John is found in chapter 7, which is set at the autumn festival of Booths. On that occasion Jesus proclaims, "If anyone is thirsty, let him come to me, and let the one who believes in me drink. Just as the scripture says, 'From within him will flow rivers of living water'" (NEB vv. 37b–38).[91] Which biblical text is cited here? Almost certainly John has in mind those prophetic passages that speak of waters flowing from the eschatological temple (e.g., Ezek 47:1; Zech 14:8). For John, these "rivers of living water" refer to the Spirit, which Jesus will give to his followers after his resurrection (v. 39). Once again, temple-Christology provides the framework for John's interpretation of the meaning of Jesus' person and work.

An understanding of John's temple-Christology helps us appreciate the significance of Jesus' encounter with the Samaritan woman. As noted above, in this conversation Jesus emphatically upholds the sanctity of Jerusalem and its temple in opposition to the Samaritan claims for Mount Gerizim. In keeping with a prominent strand of Jewish tradition, Jesus considered the Judean temple to be but an anticipatory sign of an eschatological reality that would far transcend it in scope. But the Johannine Jesus takes a step beyond Jewish precedents in asserting that this eschatological reality was already unfolding in his own person: "Jesus said to her, 'Believe me, woman, a time is coming when you will worship the Father neither on this mountain nor in Jerusalem. . . . But a time is coming—and now is here—when the true worshipers will worship the Father in spirit

90. See Kinzer, "Temple Christology," 450.

91. The Greek text is ambiguous as to the antecedent of the pronoun "him" in verse 38. Most translations interpret the verse as speaking of the heart of "the believer" (see NRSV), but the NEB wisely identifies the pronoun as referring to Jesus himself. This allows us to locate the biblical verses to which these words allude, which are otherwise untraceable.

and truth, for the Father seeks such people to be his worshipers'" (John 4:21, 23). In keeping with John 7:39, where the water that flows from the eschatological temple is identified as the Holy Spirit, we should understand the phrase "spirit and truth" as equivalent to the term "the Spirit *of* Truth" (14:17; 16:13). Jesus does not here advocate an abstract, disembodied form of worship in contrast to the traditional earthy practices of the Jerusalem temple, but instead indicates that the divine presence has now "pitched-its-tent among us" in his own human flesh (1:14) so that the living water of the Spirit might flow from his crucified side (19:34).

The point of John 4:21 is not to deny the enduring value of worshiping God on either Mount Zion or Mount Gerizim. In keeping with biblical and post-biblical eschatological tradition, John aims not to *constrict* the realm of holiness and worship but to *expand* it. The resurrected Jesus is now accessible in *every* place *through the gift of his Spirit*, enabling his followers—wherever they may find themselves—to taste the richness of the eschatological temple of the age to come.

When reading John 4:21 we should also recall a fact duly noted by Richard Hays: "John writes his Gospel ten or twenty years after the great Temple in Jerusalem has been destroyed by the Romans. But in place of Herod's once-impressive building, now in ruins, John declares that Jesus' *body* is now the place where God dwells . . . ."[92] In other words, John develops his temple-Christology in a priestly vacuum rather than in opposition to an existing priestly institution. Just as Hebrews and Revelation (assuming a post-70 date for each text) offer access to the heavenly temple as consolation for those who struggle with the loss of the Jerusalem temple, so John in the same circumstances offers proleptic access to the earthly eschatological temple.

While recent commentators, such as Hays, devote ample attention to John's *temple*-Christology, they less frequently take note of his *Israel*-Christology, and of the intimate connection established in the narrative between these two patterns of christological reflection. John's Israel-Christology becomes most clearly manifest through his explicit messianic terminology. The Gospel of John provides the only instances in the New Testament in which the Aramaic term "Messiah" appears in transliterated form (1:41; 4:25). Moreover, John employs the Greek translation of this title ("*Christos*") more often than any other of the evangelists, and includes it in the book's most important confessional statements (e.g.,

92. Hays, *Reading Backwards*, 82.

1:41; 4:25–26; 11:27; 20:31). One might have thought that John used this terminology in a merely "spiritual" and universalistic manner if he had not also exceeded the other evangelists in references to Jesus as "the king of Israel" (1:49; 12:13) and "the king of the Jews" (18:33, 37, 39; 19:1–3, 12, 14–16, 19–22). While John insists that Jesus' kingship is "not from this world" (18:36), he stresses just as strongly its particular association with the people of Israel.[93]

Secondly, John's Israel-Christology becomes manifest in his use of the Servant Songs of Second Isaiah. Richard Bauckham has showed that the Gospel of John draws from Isaiah 52:13 in its two main ways of speaking of the cross as Jesus' "coming destiny": (1) at the cross Jesus will be "lifted up" (*hypsoō*); and (2) at the cross Jesus will be "glorified" (*doxazō*).[94] The Septuagint of Isaiah 52:13 contains both of these words in its summary description of the servant who will bear the sins of the people: "Behold, my servant . . . shall be exalted [*hypsōthēsetai*] and shall be glorified [*doxasthēsetai*] greatly." But John also draws upon another verse from the Servant Songs that deals with "glorification," namely Isaiah 49:3 (LXX): "And he said to me, 'you are my servant, Israel, and in you I will be glorified [*doxasthēsomai*].'"[95] The Johannine Jesus alludes to this verse after symbolically representing his coming death through serving his disciples by washing their feet: "Now the Son of Man has been glorified, and God has been glorified in him. If God has been glorified in him, God will also glorify him in himself and will glorify him at once" (13:31–32; see also 14:13; 17:1, 4; 21:19). In both Isaiah 49 and 52–53, the servant is simultaneously a corporate figure and an individual, the people of Israel and its representative. This fits well with John's Israel-Christology, which acclaims Jesus as the "king of Israel" who will "die for the nation" (11:48–52).

We find a third example of Israel-Christology in the Johannine farewell discourse. Here Jesus identifies himself as the "true vine" (15:1–11). As commentators generally recognize, this alludes to a wide array of biblical texts in which Israel is compared to a vine.[96] This image had special resonance in the immediate post-70 era, as Raymond Brown recognizes:

93. See Bauckham, "Jewish Messianism according to the Gospel of John."

94. Bauckham, *Jesus and the God of Israel*, 46–50.

95. Bauckham does not mention John's use of Isaiah 49:3 in *Jesus and the God of Israel*, for Israel-Christology is not directly relevant to the questions he there addresses.

96. Hos 10:1, 14:8(7); Jer 6:9; Ezek 15:1–6; 17:5–10; 19:10–14; Ps 80:9(8). See Brown, *The Gospel according to John XIII-XXI*, 670.

"One of the notable ornaments of the Jerusalem Temple was a golden vine with clusters as tall as a man . . . and on the coins of the First Jewish Revolt (A.D. 66–70), struck to honor Jerusalem the holy, there was an outline of a vine and branches. After the fall of the Temple the regroupment of rabbinical disciples at Jamnia under Rabbi Johannan ben Zakkai was known as a vineyard (Mishnah *Kethuboth* 4:6)."[97] The image of the vine thus represents the people of Israel and its capital city, but is also associated with its temple. These associations find vivid expression in L.A.B.—a document likely composed in this same post-70 period—where the vine's roots reach down into the deep and its shoots stretch to the heights of heaven (12:8–9; see also 28:4).[98] In identifying himself as the true vine, Jesus thus presents himself as the individual embodiment of the people of Israel, and, as such, also as the one in whom the divine presence has pitched his tent.

In light of the above, we should pay special attention to the two Johannine texts that refer or allude to the biblical figure of Jacob/Israel. Strikingly, they both have implications not only for John's Israel-Christology but also for the book's temple-Christology. This is especially evident in John 4, where Jesus speaks with the Samaritan woman about the relative status of Mount Zion and Mount Gerizim. John introduces their encounter in this way: "So he came to a Samaritan city called Sychar, near the plot of ground that Jacob had given to his son Joseph. Jacob's well was there, and Jesus, tired out by his journey, was sitting by the well" (John 4:5–6). The conversation begins with Jesus asking the woman for water from Jacob's well (v. 7), and then telling her that he is able to give her *living* water (v. 10). The Samaritan responds with the question, "Are you greater than our ancestor [father] Jacob?" (v. 12). She intends the question to be taken rhetorically, with a presumed negative answer, but the author thinks otherwise. Indeed, Jesus *is* greater than Jacob, for the water that Jesus will give is that which the prophets said would flow from the midst of the eschatological temple. Yet, Jesus is also *like* Jacob, who as father of the people represented all his descendants, for he is the servant-Messiah who similarly embodies the entire people in his particular individual identity.

The close connection between Israel-Christology and temple-Christology appears likewise in Jesus' conversation with Nathaniel, which John

97. Brown, *Gospel according to John XIII–XXI*, 674.

98. On this image in L.A.B. see Hayward, *The Jewish Temple*, 159–61.

recounts at the conclusion of the book's opening chapter. As Nathaniel approaches Jesus, the latter greets him as "an Israelite in whom there is no deceit" (1:47). The word "deceit" evokes the Jacob story of Genesis (27:35; 34:13), especially when attached to the national moniker "Israelite." Nathaniel responds by hailing Jesus as "the king of Israel" (1:49). He thus proves that he is a true Israelite by acknowledging Israel's appointed Messiah. Jesus then tells Nathaniel of the great things he will behold in the coming days: "Very truly, I tell you, you will see heaven opened, and the angels of God ascending and descending upon the Son of Man" (1:51). These words refer to Jacob's dream of a ladder whose base was set on the earth but whose top reached to heaven, "and the angels of God were ascending and descending on it" (Gen 28:12). Jesus thus presents himself as the ladder which Jacob beholds, joining earth to heaven. This resembles the image of the vine as employed in L.A.B., for that vine had its roots in the depths of the earth and its uppermost branches in the heavens.

As rabbinic tradition notes (Genesis Rabbah 68:12), the Hebrew of Genesis 28:12 may also be translated as "the angels of God were ascending and descending on *him* [i.e., Jacob]." According to that reading, *Jacob himself* is the ladder that joins earth to heaven. Given the other examples of Israel-Christology cited above, it is reasonable to suppose that John here follows the Hebrew text of Genesis 28:12, and presents Jesus as the eschatological Jacob/Israel who unites heaven and earth in himself.[99] At the same time, John here presents Jesus as the "fearful place" of Genesis 28:17—the one who embodies in himself "the house of God" (*beth-el*). When one approaches Jesus one finds oneself at the "gate of heaven" (Gen 28:17). Thus, Jesus is both Israel and Bethel, and he is Bethel *because he is Israel.*

Peder Borgen has suggested that John 1:47–51 also builds upon a traditional Jewish etymology that understands the name "Israel" to mean

99. This would mean that John here utilized the Hebrew text of Genesis 28:12 over against the Septuagint, which employs a feminine pronoun (*ep' autes*—"on *it*") and thus unequivocally refers to the ladder rather than to Jacob. This is not implausible, for, while John normally uses the Septuagint, "he was capable of going direct to the Hebrew, and on occasion did so" (Barrett, *The Gospel according to St. John*, 28). Raymond Brown dismisses this interpretation of John 1:51 on the grounds that "it is Nathaniel in John who is the equivalent of Israel, not Jesus" (Brown, *The Gospel according to John I–XII*, 90). However, John presents Nathaniel as a true "Israelite," i.e., one descended from Jacob and sharing his best characteristics, rather than as the "equivalent of Israel." And, as in John 4:12, John here presents Jesus as similar to but *greater than* Jacob (not as his "equivalent"). Nathaniel demonstrates his status as an "Israelite" by hailing Jesus as "the king of Israel," i.e., the representative and perfect embodiment of Israel.

"the man who sees God" (*ish roeh el*).[100] This etymology was employed by some ancient sources to speak of a heavenly figure bearing this name who dwelt in the presence of God and beheld God's face.[101] As Borgen recognizes, John speaks of Jesus in just this way: he is the only one who has ever seen God (John 6:46; 3:11, 32; 8:38), and as such his mission entails revealing to others the God he has seen (1:18). Jesus does this by embodying the character of God so fully that all who see him are in fact seeing God (14:8–9). In this way Jesus, the true heavenly Israel, will enable his disciples—true Israelites—to see "heaven opened" (1:51).

Thus, John's temple-Christology shows multiple connections to his Israel-Christology. Given the fact that the temple itself signified the reality of God's presence in the midst of the people of Israel—the human temple—these connections reflect the logic of the temple-theology of the biblical and post-biblical periods. As the divine presence dwelt among the people of Israel, even in the absence of the ark, the tent of meeting, or the Jerusalem temple itself—even in exile from the land of promise—so all the more the divine presence now rested upon the king of Israel, who was with God before the foundation of the world (17:5) and who summed up the people as a whole in his person.

John's concentrated focus on temple-Christology is unique in the New Testament, and in the world of first-century Judaism. But its basis in temple-*Israelology*—i.e., the temple as pointing to the reality of the divine presence in the midst of the people of Israel—demonstrates its potential compatibility with the teaching of Luke and Acts discerned in our previous chapter. As the king of Israel and the individual embodiment of his people, the resurrected Messiah who fulfills the purpose of the temple may also sustain God's enduring earthly promises to the land, the city, and his own family.

Having surveyed the history and significance of the temple in Hebrew scripture and ancient Jewish literature, and the temple theology of several crucial strands of New Testament tradition, we are now prepared to examine the perspective on the temple found in Luke and Acts.

100. Borgen, "God's Agent in the Fourth Gospel," 77n33. See also 73–74.

101. Philo, *On the Confusion of Tongues*, 146, and *On Flight and Finding*, 205; *The Prayer of Joseph*; *On the Origin of the World* 105:20–30. See also Kugel, *The Bible as It Was*, 227–29.

The Temple in Luke and Acts

Jerusalem and the Temple

Our study of the geographical structure of Luke and Acts demonstrated the enduring importance of the city of Jerusalem for the author of these volumes. The narrative of Luke begins and ends in Jerusalem, while the story told in Acts involves a series of expanding outward movements each followed by a return to the holy city. This geographical structure has implications for our interpretation of Luke's view of the temple, for not only the city but also its most important edifice anchors the movement of the narrative.

The first scene in the Gospel of Luke takes place in the temple, and its first dialogue occurs not only in the temple precincts but in the Holy Place itself (Luke 1:8–22). The final words of the book again focus on Israel's central place of worship: "and they were continually in the temple blessing God" (Luke 24:53). The first scene of Acts of the Apostles is set on the Mount of Olives, across from and above the Temple Mount (Acts 1:6–12), and the opening chapters refer time and again to the frequent gathering of the disciples of Jesus in the temple courts (Acts 2:46; 3:1; 5:12, 42).

Acts 8 introduces the figure of Saul (later referred to as Paul), and from chapter 13 to the conclusion of the book this disciple dominates the narrative. He embarks on three apostolic journeys, each of which extends further west; but, as noted in chapter 1, each of those journeys also concludes with a return to Jerusalem. Of these visits to Jerusalem, the third and final one plays an especially significant role in the narrative of Acts, and the temple figures prominently in that visit.

Paul designs the itinerary for this third return to Jerusalem in order to arrive in time for the pilgrim feast of Pentecost (Acts 20:16).[102] This enables him to participate in the temple rites ordained for the holiday. Paul explains later that this was indeed his intention: "Now after some years I came to bring alms to my nation and to offer sacrifices" (Acts 24:17). After entering the city and meeting with James, Paul seeks to demonstrate his loyalty to the Torah and the Jewish people by engaging in a public temple rite (Acts 21:17–25). As he nears its completion (Acts 21:26–27), Paul

102. In this way, Paul's journey recalls Jesus' final march to the city for the pilgrim feast of Passover; the parallel is reinforced by portentous warnings of what will befall Paul upon his arrival (Acts 21:4, 10–14).

is accused falsely of bringing a gentile into the sacred space restricted to Jews, and is arrested (Acts 21:26–28). His accusers believe Paul to be an apostate who has contempt for the Jewish people, the Torah, and the temple: "This is the man who is teaching everyone everywhere against our people, our law, and this place" (Acts 21:28). In the scenes that follow Paul defends himself against both the specific charge related to his conduct in the temple, and the general accusation of his apostasy: "I have in no way committed an offense against the law of the Jews, or against the temple" (Acts 25:8; see also 24:11–13).[103] Speaking in the courts of the temple immediately after his arrest, Paul further underlines his devotion to the sanctuary by describing an experience he had while praying in that place. Just as God appeared to Isaiah when the prophet worshiped in the temple (Isa 6), so Jesus appeared to Paul (Acts 22:17). Apparently, the temple is especially suited to a revelation of the risen Lord.[104]

Like first-century Jews in general, the author/editor of Luke and Acts associates Jerusalem with the temple that was its heart and soul. Did he expect a future restoration of the temple along with the city? At the very least, we may infer from this intimate association of city and temple, and from our study of the rhythmic structure of Luke and Acts, that the outward momentum of the book *cannot* be taken to imply the opposite conclusion—namely, that Luke and Acts view the temple as but a sacred memory relegated to the past.[105]

103. In case one might think that there is some significance to Paul's mentioning here the Torah and the temple but not the people, see Acts 28:17: "Brothers, though I had done nothing against our people or the customs of our ancestors, yet I was arrested in Jerusalem." Here the people and the Torah are mentioned, and the temple is left out.

104. In a brief comment, Craig R. Koester (*The Dwelling of God*, 88) appears to interpret this vision as implying the superseding of the temple, since the verbal content conveyed by the vision expresses both a critique of the Jerusalemite response to the apostolic message (v. 18), and a command directing Paul to go to the gentiles (v. 21). In Acts, the hostility of the rulers of the temple to the apostles does contribute to the spread of the good news among the nations of the world (see also Acts 8:4). However, this is but part and parcel of a basic theme of the book embodied in its structure: the Messiah who was rejected by temple authorities is to be proclaimed throughout the world; those temple authorities (and the temple itself) will come under divine judgment, but in the end Jesus will return to Jerusalem and restore the kingdom to Israel. In the final analysis, Paul's temple vision is not that different in substance from Isaiah's temple vision (Isa 6): each involves a negative assessment of Israel's spiritual condition, each involves a "sending," and each assumes a reverent regard for the Jerusalem temple as a place of access to the divine presence.

105. This mistaken view is espoused by James H. Charlesworth: "In Luke-Acts,

The *Tamid* and Temple-Ecclesiology

The daily temple liturgy, known as the *tamid* (i.e., the continual offering), features prominently in Luke and Acts.[106] The *tamid* sacrifice was presented twice daily—once in the morning, and once in the late afternoon (Exod 29:38–42; Num 28:1–8). The community as a whole could participate in this liturgy by praying at the time of the sacrifice, either in the temple courts, or toward the temple structure (if at a distance from it). The Gospel of Luke begins with Zechariah the priest offering incense in the temple as part of the *tamid* liturgy (Luke 1:8–9), accompanied by the prayers of the people "outside" (Luke 1:10). Early in Acts of the Apostles, Peter and John ascend the Temple Mount to join other Jews "at the hour of prayer, at three o'clock in the afternoon" (Acts 3:1)—in other words, at the hour of the afternoon *tamid*. Residing in the coastal city of Caesarea, Cornelius the centurion prays to the God of Israel at the time of the afternoon *tamid* (Acts 10:2), and four days later he and his household receive the Holy Spirit at that same hour (Acts 10:30).[107]

I will examine these texts further in a later chapter, and argue that the Pentecost narrative of Acts 2 is likewise to be read in the context of the *tamid*. What is crucial for us to note here is that Luke does not portray daily prayer as a *substitute* for temple sacrifice, but instead as its essential *accompaniment*. Peter, John, and the people pray in the temple courts as the priests offer the *tamid*; the disciples and family of Jesus pray in an upper room in Jerusalem as the priests offer the *tamid*; Cornelius prays in his own house in Caesarea as the priests offer the *tamid*. All of them participate in the temple liturgy through prayer.

---

one-and-the-same author begins by emphasizing Jerusalem as the Holy City and then concludes his narrative with Paul in Rome. The rhetoric seems to move the 'Good News' from the Holy Land to the world stage. In the process, the Temple is portrayed not only as the place of worship for Jesus, Peter, John, and Paul but also the source of opposition to this new messianic movement. Eventually, any focus on the Temple is lost as Luke portrays the Palestinian Movement moving away from its motherland. . . . The Temple remains a remnant of previous history . . ." ("The Temple and Jesus' Followers," 204–5).

106. See Kinzer, "Sacrifice, Prayer, and the Holy Spirit: The Daily Tamid Offering in Luke-Acts," and Hamm, "The Tamid Service in Luke-Acts."

107. Hamm points to several other texts in Luke that may allude to the *tamid*: the parable of the Pharisee and the Tax Collector who pray in the temple (18:9–14); the death of Jesus at 3:00 p.m. (23:44–46); and the "priestly" blessing offered by Jesus as he ascends, (24:50–53).

At the same time, it is just as crucial to note the connection established in Acts 2 and Acts 10 between the *tamid*, the prayers of the *ekklēsia.* and the gift of the Holy Spirit. This linkage points to the temple-like character of the *ekklēsia.* Just as fire falls from heaven to consecrate the altar of the wilderness tabernacle and Solomon's temple, tongues of fire now rest on each of the disciples of Jesus gathered in prayer. After the day of Pentecost the *ekklēsia* no longer gathers in the upper room, but in the temple itself. Just as their prayer complements rather than replaces the temple sacrifices, so their corporate presence perfects the Temple Mount and structure by bringing the foretaste of the eschatological human-temple into the precincts of the temple made with human hands.

Stephen's Speech: A Fly in the Ointment?

Many commentators believe that Luke undercuts this positive orientation to the temple by highlighting a fierce attack on that very institution: Stephen's speech, which leads to his martyrdom (Acts 7).[108] Even a New Testament scholar such as James Dunn, who otherwise acknowledges Luke's high regard for the temple, asserts that Acts 7 breaks with this pattern: "Stephen marks the beginning of a radical critique of the Temple on the part of the infant Christian movement."[109]

This reading of Acts 7 fails to do justice either to the particular passage in question or to the coherent message of Luke and Acts. The burden of proof falls on those who would claim that the author here features material that contradicts what is consistently upheld elsewhere in his writings. The hermeneutical principle of charity, which expects non-contradiction in a text until proven otherwise, is a commendable reading practice in general. Within the framework of a theological reading of scripture, such a principle is essential.[110]

108. For example, see Fuller, *The Restoration of Israel*, 266: "His [Stephen's] condemnation of Israel's idolatry at Sinai leads him to denounce Israel's next great sin of idolatry, *the Temple itself*. . . . [T]he first Temple is rejected as an idol and illegitimate structure . . ." (emphasis original).

109. Dunn, *The Partings of the Ways*, 67. Dunn believes that this inconsistency in perspective arises because Luke draws upon a source for his account of Stephen's speech and martyrdom, and refuses to alter the source in order to make it consistent with his own viewpoint.

110. On reading scripture theologically, see the Introduction, pp. 7-9.

The first thing to note about Stephen's speech is the description of the accusations against him:

> [11] Then they secretly instigated some men to say, "We have heard him speak blasphemous words against Moses and God." . . . [13] They set up false witnesses who said, "This man never stops saying things against this holy place [*kata tou topou tou hagiou*] and the law; [14] for we have heard him say that this Jesus of Nazareth will destroy this place [*ton topon touton*] and will change the customs that Moses handed on to us [*ta ethē ha paredōken hēmin Mōusēs*]." (Acts 6:11, 13–14)

Luke tells us from the outset that the accusers are "false witnesses" whose contrived testimony is solicited by Stephen's adversaries. Given the devotion to the temple shown by the apostles in the previous chapters, this detail suggests that Stephen's views regarding the temple have been distorted by those who seek his conviction. I thus share the astonishment of Ben Witherington III when he states: "Now it is quite amazing in the face of the whole way that Luke presents the material in 6:11–14 that many scholars have concluded that though Luke tells us that the witnesses were false and the whole process rigged . . . nonetheless we should *believe these charges.*"[111] Moreover, the charges against Stephen are identical to the ones later leveled against Paul (Acts 21:28), and Luke's primary aim in the final chapters of Acts is to exculpate Paul in the face of such accusations (e.g., Acts 28:17).[112] With these considerations in mind, we should read the ensuing speech with the assumption that, at least in the view of the author/editor of the text, nothing in its contents will confirm the charges of Stephen's accusers.

The witnesses charge Stephen with speaking against Moses (i.e., the "customs" commanded by Moses in the Torah) and against the temple (described as "this holy place" and "this place"). His defense against these charges consists largely of a narrative drawn from the Torah, concentrating on the story of Moses (vv. 17–44). Stephen's aim in doing so is to present Jesus as the prophet *like* Moses, whom Moses himself anticipated (v. 37; see Deut 18:15–19), and to portray those Israelites who opposed Moses as the forerunners of those Jews who now oppose Jesus (and his

111. Witherington, *The Acts of the Apostles*, 258; emphasis original.

112. Even the language used in the two cases is nearly identical: *kata tou topou* (Acts 6:13) and *kata . . . tou topou toutou* (Acts 21:28); *ta ethē ha paredōken hēmin Mōusēs* (Acts 6:14) and *tois ethesi tois patrōois* (Acts 28:17).

disciples). In speaking of the Torah itself and its "customs," Stephen displays the veneration one would expect of a faithful Jew. After recounting the promises made to Abraham, he notes that God then "gave him the covenant of circumcision. And so Abraham became the father of Isaac and circumcised him on the eighth day . . ." (v. 8).[113] The revelation at Sinai receives similar treatment: Moses "was in the congregation in the wilderness with the angel who spoke to him at Mount Sinai, and with our ancestors; and he received living oracles to give to us" (v. 38). Those "living oracles" contained instructions for the building of a sanctuary, and Stephen honors that institution: "Our ancestors had the tent of testimony in the wilderness, as God directed when he spoke to Moses, ordering him to make it according to the pattern he had seen" (v. 44).

Thus, in his speech, Stephen refutes the charge that he spoke "blasphemous words against Moses," or against the "law" of Moses and its "customs." He turns the tables on his accusers, claiming that *they* are the ones who are disobeying Moses and the Torah by failing to honor the prophet whom Moses spoke of. They are not following the way of Moses but the way of those Israelites who rebelled against Moses. As the final sentence of the speech states, "You are the ones that received the law as ordained by angels, and yet you have not kept it" (v. 53). If Stephen unequivocally denies the first charge leveled at him by his opponents, the reader expects him to do the same with the second charge—namely, that he spoke against "this holy place [*topos*]."

Such an expectation is indeed satisfied, but only if the reader pays close attention to Stephen's use of the word *topos* ("place"). Stephen provides a summary of the revelation given to Abraham in Genesis 15:13–14, which foretells Israel's Egyptian bondage and deliverance. That summary concludes in this way: "'But I will judge the nation that they serve,' said God, 'and after that *they shall come out and worship me in this place* [*en tō topō touto*]'" (v. 7; emphasis added). The italicized words in this citation derive not from Genesis but from Exodus 3:12, where they refer to Mount Sinai. In Stephen's speech these words refer instead to the Temple Mount, and likely allude to the frequent appearance of the word *topos* ("place") in the Septuagint's account of the binding of Isaac (LXX Gen 22:3, 4, 9, 14)—that "place" being Mount Moriah. Just as Israel worshiped God at Mount Sinai after the exodus from Egypt, where God had first appeared to Moses, so Israel then entered the land and attained

113. For an illuminating assessment of the significance of this reference to circumcision in Stephen's speech, see Thiessen, *Contesting Conversion*, 116–19.

the goal of redemption by worshipping on Mount Zion ("in *this* place"), where Abraham had offered up his beloved son. As Robert Tannehill states, "The promise in 7:7 anticipates a specific place of worship within the land, and that place will be the temple."[114]

We already have an abundance of reasons for assuming that Stephen's speech offers no criticism of the temple itself. With this in mind, let us now consider the verses that, in the eyes of many commentators, prove the contrary. As noted above, Stephen speaks of the "tent of testimony" with profound respect. God commanded its construction, and showed Moses its heavenly archetype (v. 44). Joshua brings the tent into the land, and David—"who found favor with God"—asks "that he might find a dwelling place for the house of Jacob" (vv. 45–46). The NRSV renders the next verse in this way: "But [*de*] it was Solomon who built a house for him" (v. 47). By translating *de* as "but" rather than as "then" (which is just as reasonable a rendering on lexical grounds), the NRSV interprets verse 47 as a negative contrast of Solomon with his father David. While this rendering is possible, the reasons already cited for viewing the speech in a temple-positive manner would militate against it. Stephen does not attack Solomon here, any more than he attacks David, Joshua, or Moses. He finds fault neither with these biblical figures, nor with the institutions they established, but with the infidelity of the people of Israel who failed to understand or relate to these institutions properly.

As Ben Witherington III argues, the negative contrast comes not at verse 47—with the ambiguous particle *de*—but in verse 48 with the unambiguous adversative *alla* ("but," "yet").[115]

> 48 Yet [*alla*] the Most High does not dwell in houses made with human hands [*ouch ho hupsistos en cheiropoiētois katoikei*]; as the prophet says, 49 "Heaven is my throne, and the earth is my footstool. What kind of house will you build for me, says the Lord, or what is the place of my rest [*tis topos tēs katapauseōs mou*]? 50 Did not my hand make all these things [*ouchi hē cheir mou epoiēsen tauta panta*]?"

114. See Tannehill, *Narrative Unity*, 2:92–93; Witherington, *Acts of the Apostles*, 266; Salmeier, *Restoring the Kingdom*, 112. Koester acknowledges the importance of Acts 7:7, and cites it as evidence that Stephen's reservations about the temple do not concern its *immobility* (and thus its localization) but instead its *construction* as a building rather than as a tent (Koester, *Dwelling of God*, 85). This still gives too much credibility to the accusations that Luke (and/or Luke's source) insistently rejects.

115. Witherington, *Acts of the Apostles*, 263.

The issue here is neither the building of the First Temple by Solomon (or the Second by Zerubbabel), nor the validity of worshiping God at this site, but instead a distorted perception of the temple as the exclusive locus of the divine presence. While the NRSV renders verse 48 as "the Most High does not dwell in *houses* made with human hands"—as if the contrast were between *houses* and *tents*—the Greek text says only that "the Most High does not dwell in *things* made with human hands." This assertion applies as much to the "tent of testimony" (which Moses was commanded to build) as to the temple of Solomon. Indeed, Stephen sees the infidelity of his fellow-Jews as following the pattern set by the Israelites in the wilderness, who had the tent of testimony yet consistently fell into idolatry (vv. 39–43).[116] God is as accessible at the temple as he was in the tent of testimony, but the presence of God may not be confined to either place.

The quote from Isaiah 66 refers to "heaven" and "earth" as products "made" (*poieō*) by God's "hand" (*cheir*), in contrast to the tent and the temple, which were both "made with [human] hands" (*cheiro-poiētois*). In this way, Stephen, like Philo of Alexandria, hints that the true temple in which God seeks to dwell is the entire cosmos, to which the Jerusalem temple points. When this pointing function of the Jerusalem temple is forgotten and the structure is treated as an end in itself, it ceases to fulfill its intended purpose and—like any sacred object so treated—the temple then becomes an obstacle to the worship of God

At this point we should recall the role played by Exodus 15:17 and Daniel 2:34–35, 44–45 in Jewish writings antecedent to and contemporaneous with Luke and Acts. These texts speak of a sanctuary constructed by divine hands, and a messianic stone cut "not by human hands." In their light, we may detect in these words of Stephen the hope for an *eschatological* temple "not made with human hands." Such an interpretation draws support from the overall content of Stephen's speech, in which emphasis falls on the "land" promised to the patriarchs (vv. 3, 4–5, 15–16, 43, 45) and the "place" where redeemed Israel was to worship God (vv. 7, 17). The land of Israel was made by God's hand, as was Mount Zion, and—as we saw in chapter 1—Luke considers the city and the land to be the

116. This is one reason why verse 48 employs the provocative word *cheiropoiētos* ("made with hands"), which had connotations of idolatry. The author aims to connect the distorted approach to the temple in Stephen's generation with the distorted approach to the tent of testimony at the time of Moses. Of course, the term also alludes to the traditional Jewish interpretation of Exodus 15:17.

future capital of a redeemed cosmos. We may have in Stephen's speech a hint that an eschatological temple, made through divine rather than human agency, would be established in the midst of a transformed Mount Zion. On the other hand, the speech may suggest that the city as a whole would become that temple or its holy of holies. We cannot be certain, for Luke-Acts displays as much reticence as L.A.B., 4 Ezra, and 2 Baruch in delineating the character of that eschatological structure and the worship that would be conducted in its precincts. Regardless, it is clear that this text retains as much reverence for the "place" of the Temple Mount as any other Jewish writings of the period, and anticipates an eschatological fulfillment of the land-promise made to Abraham.

Finally, in assessing Stephen's speech we should also take account of the post-70 perspective in which Luke and Acts (along with L.A.B., 4 Ezra, and 2 Baruch) are written. The author/editor of these books knows that the temple and city have been destroyed, and—as seen in chapter 1—this event has profoundly shaped the narrative of Luke-Acts. Stephen has been accused of speaking "against this holy place," proclaiming that "Jesus of Nazareth will destroy this place" (Acts 6:13–14). He responds to that charge by turning it back on his accusers, claiming that in fact *they* will be responsible for the coming destruction—for it is their hostility to Jesus and his disciples that will provoke divine judgment (Acts 7:51–52). Thus, Stephen's answer to the charge of speaking against the temple is identical to that concerning Moses and the Torah: in both cases, Stephen asserts that his accusers are the ones guilty of the very charges they unjustly level at him.

In conclusion, we see that Stephen's speech coheres well with the overall message of Luke and Acts in regards to the temple, the city of Jerusalem, the land of Israel, and the Jewish people. The building "made by human hands" may be destroyed, but its "place" maintains a unique status in God's redemptive plan for Israel and the nations. The temple itself may be judged because of the sins of its custodians, but the Temple Mount will endure as the center of the city, the land, and the visible cosmos.

The Return of the Lord to Zion

In what has been examined so far, the perspective of Luke and Acts on the temple diverges from other Jewish writings of the same period only in its implicit temple-ecclesiology. Do these two books offer any distinctive interpretation of the temple *in relation to the person and work of Jesus* that would make sense of this temple-ecclesiology? The analysis of the Gospels offered by N. T. Wright proves helpful at this point—though it requires modification in light of what has been presented in the present and previous chapters.

Wright identifies three basic features of Jewish expectation regarding the coming of the messianic kingdom: the kingdom would involve the defeat of evil, the return of Israel from exile, and the return of Israel's God to Zion.[117] Wright is most known for his treatment of the second of these themes, but his view of the third is no less noteworthy. As seen in our history of the theme of Israel as the *human-temple*, the return of Israel to Zion and the return of Israel's God are inextricably intertwined. Wright is thus amply justified in bringing the two together. Just as Wright portrays Jesus as embodying Israel's exile and restoration in his death and resurrection, so he depicts Jesus' final journey to Jerusalem and the events that transpire there as the embodiment of the return of Israel's God to Zion. While Wright contends that this way of understanding Jesus' journey to Jerusalem is present in each of the Synoptic Gospels, it is highlighted most emphatically in Luke where Jesus' journey to Jerusalem provides the structure for much of the narrative.

This interpretation of Jesus' final journey explains his lament over Jerusalem in Luke 13:34–35. In the first of these verses, Jesus cries out, "Jerusalem, Jerusalem, the city that kills the prophets and stones those who are sent to it! How often have I desired to gather your children together as a hen gathers her brood under her wings, and you were not willing!" As discussed in the previous chapter, Jesus here speaks in the name of God.[118] Otherwise the saying remains obscure, for in Luke's narrative the adult Jesus has not yet exercised his prophetic office in Jerusalem. Later, the Lukan Jesus adopts the same perspective as he prepares to enter the city: he weeps over it, bemoaning the fact that it does not recognize the time of its divine "visitation" (Luke 19:44). The entry of Jesus to the city is thus equivalent to the entry of Jesus' God.

117. "Israel would 'really' return from exile; YHWH would finally return to Zion. But if these were to happen there would have to be a third element as well: evil, usually in the form of Israel's enemies, must be defeated. Together these three themes form the metanarrative implicit in the language of the kingdom" (Wright, *Jesus and the Victory of God*, 206).

118. Wright understands Luke 13:34–35 in this way, and cites it as evidence for his interpretation of Jesus' final journey (*Jesus and the Victory of God*, 642).

These Lukan texts also reinforce Wright's construal of the subversive manner in which Jesus embodies the return of the LORD to Zion. In Isaiah, this divine return brings glory to Zion and joy to Israel. In Luke, however, the LORD's appearance in Zion results in judgment and lamentation: "The Isaianic messenger who appears on the Mount of Olives has a message of woe, not of joy, for Zion."[119] There will be joy and victory, but it will only be tasted by those who welcome the visitation of Jesus as the visitation of God.[120] Wright reconfigures Israel and Israel's story so that the destruction of Jerusalem and its temple signifies not Israel's defeat but its vindication.

As demonstrated in the previous chapter, Wright misses a fundamental feature of the Lukan story. Jerusalem and its temple will indeed suffer divine judgment, but a day will come when the "times of the gentiles are fulfilled" (Luke 21:24) and the returning Messiah will "restore the kingdom to Israel" (Acts 1:6). How does this expected consummation of the story recontextualize Wright's construal of "the return of the LORD to Zion," and illuminate Luke's view of Jesus and the temple?

To answer these questions, let us return to Jesus' lament over Jerusalem in Luke 13:34–35. The lament concludes with these words: "See, your house is left to you. And I tell you, you will not see me until the time comes when you say, 'Blessed is the one who comes in the name of the Lord.'" The "house" which will be deserted may be the temple, or the city as a whole—in this context, the two are virtually indistinguishable. The image of the deserted house likely alludes to Ezekiel's depiction of the departure of the divine presence from the First Temple (Ezek 10:18; 11:22–23), which made the temple and city vulnerable to foreign armies.[121] Because of Israel's persistent rebellion expressed in its rejection of God's prophetic messengers, Israel will no longer "see me"—that is, they will no longer experience the joy of encountering God in the Jerusalem temple.[122] As argued above, Jesus here speaks prophetically in the name of the God whom Jerusalem has time and again resisted. However, the lamentation

119. Wright, *Jesus and the Victory of God*, 639.

120. "Israel's hopes of national victory would be set aside; the only people vindicated when their god returned, to act in fulfillment of his promise, would be those who responded to the divine summons now being issued in Jesus' kingdom-announcement" (Wright, *Jesus and the Victory of God*, 637).

121. Tannehill, *Luke*, 225.

122. The language of visual perception in relation to God is common in psalms that speak of the temple (e.g., Pss 27:4; 63:2; 84:7). See Levenson, "The Jerusalem Temple in Devotional and Visionary Experience."

does not end on this note, but with a glimmer of hope conveyed by the word "until" (*heōs*): Jerusalem will once again "see God" (i.e., worship in an eschatologically renewed temple) when it welcomes the Messiah "who comes in the name of the Lord." These words are drawn from Psalm 118:26a, where they are followed by the parallel line, "We bless you from the house of the LORD" (Ps 118:26b).

This reference to Psalm 118:26 anticipates the conclusion of Jesus' journey to Jerusalem, when he enters the city from the Mount of Olives riding on a colt (Luke 19:28–36). Jesus is then hailed by those who shout, "Blessed is the king who comes in the name of the Lord!" (Luke 19:38). The other Synoptic Gospels describe the speakers as "many people" or "crowds" who go before and follow after Jesus (Mark 11:9; Matt 21:8–9,11); the reader assumes that they are fellow pilgrims rather than Jerusalem residents. Luke is more specific in defining their identity: he calls them "the whole multitude of the disciples" (Luke 19:37). They are neither Jerusalem residents, nor a mixed multitude of pilgrims who happen to be on the scene, but those people who already adhere to Jesus as their master. Luke thus removes any uncertainty about how Jesus' entry into the city relates to the lament and promise of Luke 13:34–35. Only the disciples of Jesus who accompany him on his journey shout the welcome of Psalm 118:26. The city of Jerusalem itself remains silent, for it does not recognize "the time" of its "visitation from God" (Luke 19:44). As noted in the previous chapter, Luke 19 depicts a "non-triumphal entry."

Palm Sunday does indeed represent in symbolic form the "return of the LORD to Zion" in the person of Israel's Messiah. That is evident from the twofold reference to the Mount of Olives (Luke 19:29, 37), recalling the prophecy of the LORD's descent to that place in Zechariah 14:4, and from Jesus' decision to ride into the city on a colt to fulfill the messianic promise of Zechariah 9:9. This is a symbolic act, but what does it symbolize? For Wright, the action presents in dramatic form the events that will take place in the days that immediately follow. The LORD has come to Jerusalem in the person of Jesus, and those who rule (and thus represent) Jerusalem contend with him, arrest him, and crucify him. Only Jesus' disciples hail him with the words of Psalm 118:26, and only they will be consoled by his resurrection and the gift of the Holy Spirit. Together with him they become the Zion to whom the LORD has returned in victory. As for the city itself and its temple, their destruction forty years later will complete this "return of the LORD to Zion" by manifesting God's wrath on God's enemies.

The poverty of this interpretation of Jesus' entry into Jerusalem becomes clear in light of our exposition of the ascension of Jesus in Acts 1:11.[123] Jesus *ascends* from the Mount of Olives, and will again *return* to that same location. This implies that Jesus' entry into Jerusalem—and his entire journey to the city which is completed in that scene—symbolize the future coming of Israel's king, when the entire city of Jerusalem will welcome him in the same way his disciples did on Palm Sunday. In that day Jerusalem will "repent . . . and turn to God" so that her sins are "wiped out" and "times of refreshing . . . come from the presence of the Lord" (Acts 3:19–20). In that day, the glory of God, whose departure from the temple and city was demonstrated by the Roman victory in 70 CE, shall return to the Temple Mount, just as Ezekiel promised (Ezek 43:1–7).

What does this Lukan motif tell us about Jesus and the temple? We have seen how Stephen's speech expresses the traditional biblical and post-biblical theme that the temple points to realities beyond itself—in this case, primarily to the *eschatological* temple. We have also seen how the community of Jesus' followers after Pentecost becomes the preliminary human form of this eschatological temple. The Lukan portrayal of Jesus' journey to Jerusalem suggests that *Jesus the Messiah is the embodiment of the divine glory* (i.e., the *kavod* or *shekhinah*), whose resurrected presence establishes the proleptic temple-identity of the *ekklēsia*.[124] Luke and Acts thus resemble John in employing temple imagery to convey Jesus' divine identity, but they depart from John when they use this imagery to fund temple-ecclesiology rather than temple-Christology. They also depart from John in emphasizing the partial and proleptic (rather than realized) character of this temple-ecclesiology, and its ultimate consummation in a future age.

In the case of the Gospel of Luke, Wright is on the mark when he asserts that "the return of YHWH to Zion, and the Temple-theology which it brings into focus, are the deepest keys and clues to gospel christology."[125]

However, Wright's conception of that "temple-theology" must be modified in light of the future-oriented Jerusalem-centered eschatological

123. See chapter 1, pp. 50–53.

124. This was the central thesis of Klaus Baltzer's seminal article, "The Meaning of the Temple in the Lukan Writings." Baltzer discerned an allusion to Ezekiel 11 and 43 in Luke's emphasis on the Mount of Olives in his narratives of Jesus' entry to Jerusalem and ascension from Jerusalem. Nevertheless, like most commentators, Baltzer neglected the prophetic and eschatological implications of these events.

125. Wright, *Jesus and the Victory of God*, 653.

context that we have proposed as a way of understanding the symbolism of Jesus' journey and grand entry to the city. The three aspects of the "return to Zion" theme in both Isaiah and Ezekiel here come together: (1) the exile and return of *the divine presence*; (2) the intimate connection between the exile and return of the divine presence and the exile and return of *the people of Israel*, among whom the divine presence resides; (3) *the place* from which the divine presence and the people went into exile, and to which they together return. As argued in the previous chapter, Luke and Acts assume that the exile continues after the destruction of the temple and city in 70 CE. The "return to Zion" that Jesus symbolically enacts on Palm Sunday points forward to a future day of consummation, when that exile will be definitively ended. In that day, Jerusalem will no longer be "trampled by the gentiles," but will again be a Jewish city. In that day, Jesus, embodying the divine presence, will stand on the Mount of Olives, and will enter the city, which will welcome him with the words "Blessed is the one who comes in the name of the LORD" (Ps 118:26a). Given the prominence assigned to the *place* of the Temple Mount in Stephen's speech, and the location of the Mount of Olives directly overlooking the Temple Mount, we may assume that Luke and Acts expect that this return will reach its climax on Mount Moriah/Zion, as the people of Jerusalem shout "We bless you from *the house of the* LORD" (Ps 118:26b; emphasis added).

In this scenario, the future temple is not Jesus himself, but his disciples and the redeemed people of Israel, in the *place* where Abraham had offered up Isaac and where David had been inspired to set the ark of the covenant. This is a type of temple-ecclesiology which posits Jesus (and his Spirit) as the *kavod*; which refuses to separate the *ekklēsia* from the Jewish people; and which refuses to separate Jesus, the *ekklēsia*, and the Jewish people from the land of Israel, the city of Jerusalem, and the Temple Mount. Here the temple structure points to a reality beyond itself—that is, to the *human*-temple at the heart of the *eschatological*-temple—but without losing its own specificity as a particular *place*. In this way, the symbolic function of the temple *undergirds* rather than undermines the central importance of the city of Jerusalem.

The resurrection of Jesus constitutes both the pledge that the "return of the LORD to Zion" will be fulfilled and the power that will fulfill it. Moreover, the resurrection of Jesus likewise intensifies the reality of Israel as the *human-temple*, and extends that reality to the nations of the world. The intensification becomes evident on the day of Pentecost, as the

Messiah pours out the Holy Spirit on his Jewish disciples in Jerusalem at the time of the morning *tamid* offering and prayer. The extension of that intensified reality becomes just as evident when the gentile Cornelius in the gentile city of Caesarea receives the same Spirit at the time of the afternoon *tamid* offering and prayer. While temple-ecclesiology is intensified and extended in the present age through the work of Jesus and the gift of the Spirit, the present age remains an ambiguous time involving *both* restoration *and* exile. The *ekklēsia* points prophetically to Israel's destined future, but represents only a partial and preliminary sketch of the glorious "return of the LORD to Zion" that is yet to come.

Excursus: When Does the *Kavod* Abandon the Temple?

As seen above, Luke shares with Matthew a prophecy of Jesus regarding the departure of the divine presence from the second temple: "See, your house is left to you" (Luke 13:35; Matt 23:38). This alludes to Ezekiel's vision of the departure of the *kavod* from the first temple (Ezek 11:22–23). An important question then arises whose answer will affect our reading of Acts of the Apostles: from Luke's perspective, at what time does this divine departure occur?

Two recent volumes have argued that Luke sees the rending of the temple veil at the hour of Jesus' death (Luke 23:45) as a sign of the divine abandonment of the Jerusalem temple.[126] This incident is not a distinctively Lukan narrative detail, but is found also in Mark (15:38) and Matthew (27:51). While Luke slightly modifies the Markan sequence of events, he does not thereby heighten the significance attributed to this particular feature of the crucifixion story. Nevertheless, the rending of the veil is a vivid symbol which links the death of Jesus to the temple and its system of worship, and suggests that his death has a decisive impact on Israel's relationship with God. It is therefore reasonable to ask whether the death of Jesus is the point at which the divine departure prophesied in Luke 13:35 occurs.

There is one obvious objection to this thesis that arises in the case of Luke but not Matthew: we have a second Lukan volume, and the temple features prominently in its narrative as the center of ecclesial life. Peter Rice answers this objection as follows:

126. Rice, *Behold, Your House is Left to You*; Steve Smith, *The Fate of the Jerusalem Temple in Luke-Acts.*

> The rending of the veil is the most climactic, most significant, and probably culminating moment of God's abandoning the Temple for Luke, despite the fact that God's people continue to frequent and even to worship within the Temple thereafter (Luke 24; Acts 1–5). This latter worship is after all not qualitatively different from the kind of worship offered in Christian homes in Acts or indeed different from the kind of worship offered in synagogues, and the Temple's somewhat central placement in the early third of Acts is explainable in light of Jerusalem's role as launching pad for the Christian mission.[127]

Steve Smith offers a similar assessment of the temple narratives in Acts:

> [T]he torn temple veil in Lk. 23.45 represented the abandonment of the temple. The continued use of the temple by the disciples in the early chapters of Acts is not evidence that they thought otherwise: it shows that they regarded it as an appropriate place for prayer and revelatory teaching; the eschatological life they experienced in the temple was a life they brought with them through Jesus by the power of the Spirit, not something in the temple itself.[128]

These arguments make sense in the overall context of their books, for neither author views the Temple Mount as of enduring importance for Luke, and neither discerns any eschatological significance in the city, the land, or the Jewish people. Like most commentators, they ignore the eschatological import of Jesus' ascension from the Mount of Olives, and minimize the eschatological dimension of Luke's overall theological vision. Their interpretation of the temple narratives in Acts loses all persuasive power once we understand Stephen's speech as an affirmation of the centrality of the Temple Mount; see the geographical structure of Luke and Acts and the eschatological character of the ascension as indicating the abiding significance of Jerusalem; and connect not only the death of Jesus to Israel's judgment, but also his resurrection to Israel's redemption.

But even apart from Acts of the Apostles, there are two reasons for doubting the theory that the divine presence departs from the temple when Jesus dies. First, Ezekiel's vision of the departure of the *kavod* from Solomon's temple occurs immediately before its destruction. The first event explains the second: once Israel's God has departed, the city is defenseless—in effect, its walls have collapsed. Jerusalem's downfall is

127. Rice, *Your House is Left to You*, 115n93.

128. Smith, *Fate of the Jerusalem Temple*, 177.

not only assured but immediately accomplished. One would expect the same to be true of Herod's temple. Second, the identical linkage between the departure of the divine presence and the destruction of the city is inherent in the prophecy of Jesus in Luke 13. While the imminent judgment of Jerusalem is only implicit in that chapter, it takes explicit form in Luke 19, 21, and 23. The divine abandonment of the city is manifested immediately in the city's destruction. In light of the temporal nexus binding divine departure to military disaster, the former along with the latter should be situated in 70 CE rather than forty years previous.

The rending of the temple veil signals that a new dimension has opened in Israel's covenantal relationship with God. The death and resurrection of Jesus—who is himself the individual personal embodiment of the *kavod*—must have a transformative effect on Israel's place and pattern of worship. But Luke and Acts offer scant evidence for the view that this transformation entails the abandonment of the temple—and thus also of Israel—by the divine presence.

Conclusion

As we draw this chapter to a close, I would offer two negative conclusions that remove obstacles from our path, and two positive conclusions that strengthen our case and augment its momentum.

On the negative side, we have demonstrated the difference between the temple and the city, land, and people, and thereby undercut attempts to diminish the enduring character of the latter through a false equation with the transitory character of the former. Though the temple was of paramount importance, it operated on a different plane from the city of Jerusalem, the land of Israel, and the people of Israel. Each of the latter maintained a stable identity and function through the varied and tumultuous epochs of Jewish history. This was never the case with the temple, which from its beginnings combined the holiness of a particular place with that of sacred furniture and architecture, resulting in a fragile and often disrupted structure. Moreover, the temple always functioned as a symbolic pointer to realities beyond itself in a way that distinguished it dramatically from city, land, and people. In those eras when the temple imperfectly incorporated its diverse components, or ceased its institutional operation entirely, the realities to which it pointed never lost their existence or their hold on the Jewish imagination.

Among its most important symbolic functions, the temple represented the presence of the God of Israel in the midst of the people and land of Israel. In this role the temple was closely identified with the city of Jerusalem in which it resided. When the city of Jerusalem was taken by the Romans in 70 CE, it was the destruction of the temple that caused the greatest grief, and that encapsulated in one fiery image the catastrophe of the entire war. Thus, in the New Testament and in Jewish tradition as a whole, the destruction of the city is represented by the destruction of the temple. In his death, Jesus participates in the suffering that Jerusalem will endure four decades later, and in so doing his body bears the blows that will fall on the temple that was her heart and soul. Nevertheless, the city, land, and the people remain in existence—wounded, but still breathing—even after the massive stones of the temple have been torn asunder. If the Babylonian destruction of the temple was any precedent, and the message of the prophet Ezekiel at that time is still to be believed, then the God of Israel continues to dwell among his people, and the city and land remain the proper objects of their hope.

The second negative conclusion concerns the New Testament focus on the heavenly temple, the human temple (i.e., temple-Christology and temple-ecclesiology), and the eschatological temple. We have shown that this orientation derives not from a critique of the Jerusalem institution but is inherent in the temple's essential symbolic role. The temple always served as a symbolic marker pointing to realities beyond itself, and the New Testament expressions of this symbolism do not differ in kind from those found in Hebrew scripture or Jewish tradition. In texts outside the New Testament such symbolism coheres with respect for the temple institution itself, and with reverence for the city, land, and people. There is no reason to assume without evidence that the New Testament is an exception to the rule.

My first positive conclusion concerns John's temple-Christology. I have argued that this distinctive Johannine approach to the temple builds upon the foundation of his Israel-Christology. Jesus sums up the people of Israel in his individual person, and the temple signifies God's dwelling in the midst of the people of Israel; therefore Jesus in his individual person is the ultimate temple. We may go further than this, and propose that Jesus likewise embodies in his person *the land* of Israel, which is connected indissolubly to the people of Israel, and which is the place where God promised to dwell.[129] If this truly expresses John's logic—if

129. "To say 'I am the true vine" ([John 15] v. 1) is to say "I am the true Israel" . . .

Israel-Christology in the broadest sense is the presupposition of his temple-Christology—then John's message confirms our earlier premise that the temple structure points to realities greater than itself, one of which is God's commitment to dwell in the midst of Israel.

The writings of Jewish theologian Michael Wyschogrod are relevant at this point. Wyschogrod draws insights from the New Testament and ecclesial tradition concerning incarnation, and employs those insights in his understanding of the Jewish people. As he states in an article entitled "Incarnation," the "indwelling of God in the people of Israel is the foundation of my theology."[130] He expresses the same point in his most extensive work of Jewish theology, *The Body of Faith*: "The existence of this people is the medium by means of which God enters the universe."[131] Wyschogrod also articulates the connection between this conviction and classical ecclesial (i.e., Johannine) Christology: "The church concentrates all this incarnation of the people of Israel, all of the incarnation of God into the people of Israel, in one Jew, Jesus of Nazareth."[132]

My proposal in the present volume is that the resurrected Jesus continues to identify with the Jewish people. If that is true, then his incarnation, death, and resurrection fulfill the gift of the divine presence among the Jewish people by intensifying the reality of that presence rather than removing it. This means that ecclesial theologians may embrace Wyschogrod's theology concerning the "indwelling of God in the people of Israel"—while also asserting a divine indwelling in the *ekklēsia* that confirms rather than negates its temple-partner.[133] In this way, Johannine temple-Christology supports and advances my central thesis.[134]

Christ recapitulates the living mystery of his people and their land. If the parable is read in this manner, Israel (people and land) is not left behind but is taken up into the mystery of Christ and glorified in him" (Vall, "Man is the Land," 153).

130. Wyschogrod, "Incarnation," 217.

131. Wyschogrod, *The Body of Faith*, 13.

132. Wyschogrod, "Incarnation," 215.

133. Robert W. Jenson is an example of a Christian theologian who has learned from Wyschogrod, and who makes a similar assertion in explicitly Christological terms: "Can there be a present body of the risen Jew, Jesus of Nazareth, in which the lineage of Abraham and Sarah so vanishes into a congregation of gentiles as it does in the church? . . . [T]he embodiment of the risen Christ is whole only in the form of the church *and* an identifiable community of Abraham and Sarah's descendants. The church and the synagogue are together and only together the present availability to the world of the risen Jesus Christ" (Jenson, "Toward a Christian Theology of Judaism," 13).

134. I am not arguing here that the human author or editor of the Fourth Gospel drew the implications from his Christology that I am drawing. I am only arguing that

My second positive conclusion concerns the temple-theology discerned in Luke and Acts. This temple-theology advances our discussion by highlighting the enduring significance of the Temple Mount (i.e., "the place") as a geographical site. Stephen's speech focuses on a sacred element of the temple that is distinct from the temple structure or its furniture—and that element endures as long as the earth endures. In this way, Acts 7 strengthens the case for the enduring significance of the city of Jerusalem in the very text that challenges misunderstandings of the temple and prophetically anticipates its destruction. Likewise, the Lukan *kavod*-Christology provides an eschatological complement to the Johannine temple-Christology by underlining an as-yet-unrealized dimension of the incarnation. In both John and Luke/Acts, Jesus embodies the divine presence; but in Luke/Acts the full reality of the temple is only realized when the people of Israel and the *ekklēsia* attain their fullness, as Jesus himself returns to the Temple Mount via the Mount of Olives. Thus, both the Jewish people and the *ekklēsia* of Jews and gentiles await the "return of the LORD to Zion."

Our study of the temple has only strengthened our thesis regarding the city of Jerusalem, the land of Israel, and the prophetic *euangelion*. But what about the Jewish people? How can we uphold its continuing covenantal identity and constructive mission in history in light of its communal failure to embrace its Messiah? In our next chapter we will examine Luke and Acts for clues to answer this difficult question.

---

such implications are reasonable when the text is read according to the theological method articulated in the Introduction of this book.

Chapter 3

The Resurrected Messiah and the Jewish People

According to Acts of the Apostles, thousands of Jews respond positively to the message concerning the resurrected Messiah (Acts 2:41; 5:14–16; 6:7; 9:31; 21:20). But Israel's leaders fail to follow suit, and the book ends with contention over that message. What is the perspective of Acts regarding those Jews outside the *ekklēsia*, and regarding the organized Jewish community as a whole? Does failure to believe in Jesus and join the community of his disciples result in the exclusion of Jews from the people of Israel?

The Gospel of Luke presents the death of Jesus as an anticipation of the judgment of Jerusalem in 70 CE, and hints that the suffering of the Messiah will render that judgment redemptive in its effects. Luke and Acts likewise imply that the resurrection of Jesus anticipates Jerusalem's future restoration. This suggests that genealogical-Israel retains its covenantal status and its constructive mission in the world, despite its corporate failure to embrace the resurrected Messiah.

Nevertheless, many commentators interpret Luke and Acts as teaching the contrary. For them, these books assert that Jews who fail to enter the *ekklēsia* forfeit their status as members of the covenant community. The arguments marshaled by these commentators draw upon two themes of Acts of the Apostles, one of which is knit into the basic fabric of the narrative, the other enunciated in two particular texts. The first theme concerns Jewish opposition to the apostolic message, which leads Paul to forsake the synagogue in various locations and "go to the gentiles." This narrative pattern reaches a climax in the final chapter of the book of Acts, in which Paul addresses the elders of the Roman Jewish community. For many commentators, this way of concluding the book suggests that the era in which Jews have a distinctive covenantal status outside the *ekklēsia* has come to a definitive end.

The second theme concerns Jesus' role as the prophet like Moses described in Deuteronomy 18:15–19. This text is cited in speeches by Peter (Acts 3:22–23) and Stephen (Acts 7:37). Peter's version of the text departs from both the Masoretic Hebrew and Septuagint Greek by including the statement, "everyone who does not listen to that prophet will be utterly rooted out of the people" (Acts 3:23). For many commentators, this verse provides the biblical and theological warrant for the exclusion from Israel of those Jews who fail to believe in and obey Jesus.

In this chapter I will examine the arguments offered by these interpreters of Luke and Acts, and attempt to show that both themes support rather than undermine the enduring covenantal status of the Jewish people. Before taking up these arguments, however, I will offer preliminary comments on the speeches of Acts and their differentiated character according to their Jewish and gentile settings. This will enable us better to appreciate the significance of Paul's consistent pattern of establishing—and then abandoning—the synagogue as his base of operations.

The Differentiated Missiology of the Book of Acts

Acts of the Apostles tells the story of the expansion of the *ekklēsia* in the power of the Spirit as the disciples of Jesus carry the *euangelion* to the far reaches of the Roman Empire. What is the content of that *euangelion*, and how does it relate to the various audiences to whom it is presented? To answer that question, one must pay careful attention to the speeches that play a prominent role in the book.

Differentiated Audience and Modes of Address

I have counted twenty-two speeches in the Acts of the Apostles.[1] Of these, sixteen are directed exclusively or primarily to Jewish audiences (eleven to Jews outside the *ekklēsia*, five to Jews within). Only five speeches are

1. This figure does not include Jesus' interaction with the eleven at the beginning of the book (Acts 1:6–8) or the words of the angels to the eleven after the ascension (Acts 1:11). It also does not include the prayer of the community in Acts 4:24–30.

directed to gentile audiences; one of those consists of an address to a group already loyal to the God of Israel (i.e., the household of Cornelius), and another is delivered before a Roman official responsible for the government of Judea (Acts 24:10–21). Of the three remaining speeches in a gentile setting, one is Paul's exhortation to his fellow shipmates summoning them to be courageous in the midst of danger (Acts 27:21–26).[2] Thus, only two of the twenty-two speeches of Acts qualify as proclamations of the *euangelion* to gentiles totally outside the Jewish sphere, aiming at their repentance and faith (Acts 14:15–17; 17:22–31). This figure is surprising, given the traditional assumption that Acts has as its main concern the *ekklēsia*'s transition from being a Jewish to a gentile entity with a mission to gentiles and not to Jews.

Even more surprising is the mode of address adopted by the leaders of the *ekklēsia* when speaking to Jewish audiences who have not yet accepted their message. The speakers generally refer to their hearers as *andres adelphoi*, "men, brothers" (Acts 2:29; 13:16, 26, 38; 23:1, 6; 28:17), or more simply as *adelphoi*, "brothers" (Acts 3:17; 23:5). On two occasions, both in Jerusalem, the speakers adopt an expanded and even more respectful phrase to characterize their diverse Jewish audience: *andres adelphoi kai pateres*, "men, brothers, and fathers" (Acts 7:2; 22:1). The term *adelphoi* and the phrase *andres adelphoi* are noteworthy in these contexts, for they recur in speeches which these leaders deliver *within the ekklēsia* (*adelphoi*: Acts 6:3; 21:20; *andres adelphoi*: Acts 1:16; 15:7, 13). There is nothing in these texts to indicate that the speakers considered their relationships within the *ekklēsia* to be different *in kind* from their relationships with fellow Jews who had not yet joined their circle, as though the former involved spiritual kinship whereas the latter consisted merely of a fleshly bond.

In contrast, the leaders of the *ekklēsia* never refer to members of a gentile audience as *adelphoi*—not even when the gentile in question is a pious God-fearer who loves the Jewish people, such as Cornelius. In Peter's opening words to Cornelius and his household, the apostle acknowledges that "God has shown me that I should not call anyone profane or unclean" (Acts 10:28). It is this conviction, provided by his vision in Joppa, that gives Peter the boldness to respond positively to Cornelius' invitation. Nevertheless, at this point in the narrative Peter cannot

2. This accounts for twenty-one of the twenty-two speeches. The Jewish and/or gentile composition of the audience for the remaining speech is uncertain, as the group gathered is a set of leaders from one of Paul's Diaspora congregations (Acts 20:18–35).

address Cornelius as "brother," for this gentile is not yet a member of the people of the covenant.

If that is the case with God-fearing gentiles, how much more so with idolaters. When Paul speaks to the gentiles of Lystra (Acts 14:15), or his gentile shipmates en route to Rome (Acts 27:21, 25), he merely calls them *andres*, "men." When he addresses the people of Athens, he employs the phrase *andres Athenaioi*, "men, Athenians" (Acts 17:22). This formal and impersonal terminology, expressing the absence of a relational bond, conveys the unambiguous distinction between the status of Jewish and gentile audiences in Acts of the Apostles.

The speeches also signal the honored spiritual status of their Jewish audiences in other ways. Employing multiple expressions, the speakers identify their hearers as heirs of the biblical tradition and sharers in a common covenant. Members of the audience are addressed as *andres Israelitai*, "men, Israelites" (Acts 2:22; 3:12; 13:16), as those who are part of "the whole house of Israel" (Acts 2:36) or "all the people of Israel" (Acts 4:10). They are "descendants of Abraham's family" (Acts 13:26), "descendants of the prophets and of the covenant that God gave to your ancestor" (Acts 3:25), and recipients of "the promise" (Acts 2:39). As members of the same covenant family, the Jewish leaders of the *ekklēsia* identify with their hearers and designate Abraham, Isaac, Jacob, and biblical Israel in general, as "*our* ancestors" (Acts 7:2, 11, 12, 15, 19, 39, 44; 13:17, 32–33; 26:6; 28:17). More significantly, they speak of the Holy One as "the God of *our* ancestors" (Acts 3:15; 5:30; 24:14) and "the God of this people Israel" (Acts 13:17).

As seen in our chapter on Jerusalem, failure to respond adequately to the proclamation of the *euangelion* exposes these Jewish audiences to divine judgment. However, there is no evidence in Acts of the Apostles that such judgment entails a change in covenantal status, such that disobedient Jews forfeit their identity as "Israelites," "descendants of Abraham's family," "descendants of the prophets and of the covenant," and recipients of "the promise." There is no evidence that Peter or Stephen or Paul withhold from their unfaithful kin the designation of "brothers," or are reluctant to include them when speaking of "the God of *our* ancestors."

In fact, the evidence suggests the opposite. According to Acts, the priestly council in Jerusalem, presided over by the high priest, consistently opposes the apostles and their message. The members of the council also bear primary responsibility for the crucifixion of Jesus. Nevertheless, the Holy One is also the God of *their* ancestors (Acts 5:30); they are addressed as "brothers and fathers" (Acts 7:2); and the high priest (despite his culpable conduct) is acknowledged as "a leader of your people" (Acts 23:5). In the disaster of 70 CE, the ruling council will be judged for its wrongdoing and the priestly caste will lose its governing privileges, but the priests who survive the debacle retain their priestly status, just as the people of Israel as a whole remain the people of Israel.

Differentiated Content and Goals

The Jewish setting of most of the substantive speeches of Acts, along with the terms of honor employed by the speakers to refer to their hearers, together suggest that the mission of the *ekklēsia* is uniquely oriented to the Jewish people. Acts tells the story of how this mission expands to include gentiles, but speeches to gentile audiences play a minor role in the book, and these audiences are never addressed with the terms of honor reserved for "the house of Israel." This missiological differentiation between Jews (as a communal reality) and gentiles (as aggregated individuals or families) is rooted in the content and goal of the *euangelion* that the leaders of the *ekklēsia* proclaim.

Our study of the significance of Jerusalem in Luke and Acts anticipated this observation concerning the speeches of Acts. There I examined the significance in Acts of Jesus' role as the heir of King David, whose name and destiny were inseparable from that of the city of Jerusalem. The speeches of Acts proclaim Jesus as the Davidic Messiah by virtue of his resurrection from the dead (e.g., Acts 2:24–36; 13:22–23, 32–37). They also imply that the resurrection of the Messiah ensures and will ultimately effect the resurrection of the entire Jewish people along with its capital city, a glorious corporate future that constitutes the "hope of Israel" and the core of the apostolic message (Acts 26:6–8, 23; 28:20). We concluded that this constellation of texts demonstrates that the question of the eleven in Acts 1:6 ("Lord, is this the time when you will restore the kingdom to Israel?") reflects an accurate grasp of the eschatological goal of the apostolic message. However, their question also demonstrated an ignorance of the "times" in which they were situated, a temporal sphere defined already by the words of Jesus in his eschatological discourse: "Jerusalem will be trampled on by the gentiles, until the *times* of the gentiles are fulfilled" (Luke 21:24). Thus, the "kingdom" which is the content of the apostolic message involves God's reign in Israel through the risen and glorified Son of David. While inaugurated in the midst of Israel's intensified exile (anticipated by the Messiah's suffering and death), the kingdom will be consummated in a restored Jerusalem, capital of a regathered and resurrected Israel.

Peter's speech in Acts 3 confirms this summary of the content of the *euangelion*, and also shows why the response of the Jewish audience to the message has unique significance. After recounting the death and resurrection of Jesus, Peter offers this appeal to his fellow Jews:

> 17 "And now, brethren [*adelphoi*], I know that you acted in ignorance, just as your rulers did also. 18 But the things which God announced beforehand by the mouth of all the prophets, that His Christ [i.e., God's Messiah] would suffer, He has thus fulfilled. 19 Therefore repent and return, so that your sins may be wiped away, in order that times [*kairoi*] of refreshing may come from the presence of the Lord; 20 and that He may send Jesus, the Christ [i.e., Messiah] appointed for you, 21 whom heaven must receive until [*achri*] the period [*chronoi*, lit. "times"] of restoration [*apokatastasis*] of all things about which God spoke by the mouth of His holy prophets from ancient time. (Acts 3:17–21; NASB)

Peter summons the people of Jerusalem to "repent and return"—that is, acknowledge the wrong done in putting Jesus to death, and embrace him as Israel's Messiah. Here the role of Jesus is explained in striking fashion: he is "the Messiah appointed for you." Acts of the Apostles shows that the redemptive work of Jesus brings blessing to all nations, but first and foremost he is and remains "the Messiah appointed *for you*." If the people of Jerusalem (and the entire nation whom they represent) respond properly to this appeal, a divine intervention of cosmic proportions will ensue: the Messiah they have embraced will usher in a new era described as "times of refreshing" (*kairoi anapsyxeōs*) and "times of restoration" (*chronoi apokatastaseōs*).

It is unclear whether these parallel expressions refer to a single period of time or to two distinct phases of a redemptive process. Nevertheless, it is perfectly clear that Israel's proper response will *culminate* in the sending of "Jesus, the Messiah" and his inauguration of "the period of restoration of all things about which God spoke by the mouth of His holy prophets" (v. 21). This translation is to be preferred to the NRSV's "the time of universal restoration that God announced long ago through his holy prophets."[3] The context concerns the fulfillment of "all" that God has promised Israel—that is, Israel's national restoration, with its implications for the world—rather than the restoration of the cosmos itself.

Acts 3:19–21 alludes to and interprets two crucial Lukan texts discussed previously: Luke 21:24 and Acts 1:6–7. The use of the words *kairoi* ("times") and *achri* ("until") in Acts 3:19–21 recalls Luke 21:24: "Jerusalem will be trampled on by the gentiles, *until* the *times* of the gentiles are fulfilled" (*achri hou plērōthōsin kairoi ethnōn*). This implies that the "times of refreshing" and "restoration" of Acts 3 concern the city of Jerusalem, and culminate in the decisive termination of the "times of the gentiles" (i.e., the era of Israel's exile and Jerusalem's subjection to foreign powers). Even more noteworthy is the connection between Acts 3:19–21 and 1:6–7: "So when they had come together, they asked him, 'Lord, is this the time [*chronos*] when you will restore [*apo-kathistaneis*] the kingdom to Israel?' He replied, 'It is not for you to know the times [*chronoi*] or periods [*kairoi*] that the Father has set by his own authority'" (Acts 1:6–7). As in Acts 3:19–21, the two roughly synonymous nouns, *chronoi* and *kairoi*, are paired. More significantly, Acts 1:6 employs the verb *apo-kathistemi* ("restore"), whose cognate nominal form *apo-katastasis* ("restoration") appears in Acts 3:21. This verb is a technical term that refers in other Jewish literature of the period to the restoration of Israel to its own land.[4] The contexts in Acts 1 and Acts 3 suggest that the author uses both

3. As the comparison of the NASB and the NRSV demonstrates, the phrase *apokatastaseōs pantōn* in Acts 3:21 ("restoration of all things") has been interpreted—and translated—in two significantly different ways. In the NASB (and also in the RSV), "all things" refers to the full range of promises contained in the prophetic writings of scripture. In this rendering, no comma separates the phrase "all things" from the phrase "about which God spoke." More often, however, the "restoration of all things" is taken as a self-contained phrase, meaning "universal restoration" (see NRSV, NIV, JB, KJV). In such translations a comma is often inserted: "the times of restitution of all things, which God hath spoken . . ." (KJV). The evident connection between this verse, Luke 21:24, and Acts 1:6–7, and the use of the Greek word *apokatastasis* as a technical term in Jewish writings describing the restoration of Israel, imply that the reference here is not to the cosmic scope of the restoration but instead to the comprehensive fulfillment of biblical prophecy concerning Israel. (See Bauckham, "The Restoration of Israel in Luke-Acts," 363.) This undermines Peter Walker's contention that Acts 3:21 intentionally emphasizes God's universal goal of restoration in order to challenge the disciples misplaced hope for a restored "kingdom of Israel" in Acts 1:6 (Walker, *Jesus and the Holy City*, 95–96). Walker assumes the second interpretation and translation of *apokatastaseōs pantōn*, rather than arguing for it.

4. Oepke, "Apokathistēmi," 388. See LXX Hos 11:11; Jer 16:15, 24:6; Josephus, *Antiquities* 11.2, 63.

the verbal and nominal forms with precisely that meaning. Thus, the second "sending" of the Messiah (Acts 3:20) will result in the restoration of the kingdom to Israel and the consequent end of Israel's exile.[5]

Peter's speech in Acts 3 conveys two important facts. First, the return of Jesus will initiate the end of Israel's exile and the restoration of Israel's kingdom—with "Israel" here, as always in Luke and Acts, referring preeminently to the Jewish people as a corporate and covenantal reality. Second, the return of Jesus will occur only after, and as a consequence of, the faithful response by his own flesh and blood to his words and person. Thus, the *euangelion* of the resurrected Messiah concerns the Jewish people in a unique fashion—they are an inextricable part of its essential content. Moreover, their corporate response to that message is required for its full cosmic substance to be realized.

These inferences from Acts 3:19–21 receive further support from the final words of Peter's speech. The NRSV translates Acts 3:26 in this way: "When God raised up [*anastēsas*] his servant, he sent him first to you, to bless you by turning each of you from your wicked ways." This translation implies a temporal progression—after raising Jesus from the dead, God sends him (through the apostolic testimony) *first* to the Jewish people.[6] While this translation is possible, the word order in the Greek text warrants another rendering which fits better with Peter's previous appeal: "It was for you in the first place that God raised up his servant and sent him to bless you" (New Jerusalem Bible).[7] This alternate translation implies a precedence not only in the temporal mission of Jesus, but also in the basic purpose of his resurrection. His resurrection is intended to bring the ultimate blessing of Jerusalem's and Israel's resurrection—a

5. "At Acts 1:6–11 the reader did not have enough information to determine the relationship between the kingdom and Jesus' return. Acts 3:12–26 provides the missing information. . . . Now, Peter speaks concerning the "time" of the restoration (*apokatastaseōs*) of all things (3:21), echoing the disciples' concerns from 1:6" (Salmeier, *Restoring the Kingdom*, 93–94).

6. The Greek word *anastēsas* (the aorist participle of the verb *anistēmi*) appears often in the Lukan writings in reference to the resurrection from the dead (Luke 16:31; 18:33; 24:7, 46; Acts 2:24, 30, 32; 13:32–34; 17:3, 31). Here it refers to the prophet like Moses whom God would "raise up for you" (Acts 3:22; Deut 18:15), and thus could have a more general meaning inclusive of Jesus' earthly life. However, since the author is interpreting Deuteronomy 18 with Jesus in mind, it is likely that the word highlights the resurrection.

7. See also the Jerusalem Bible, the New American Standard, and the New American Bible for similar readings.

blessing that individual Jews can attain and hasten by "turning," and being turned, "from your evil ways."[8]

Most readers of Acts assume that the *euangelion* is the same for Jewish and gentile audiences: individual Jews and gentiles are called to repent, believe in Jesus, be baptized, and enter the renewed Israel, which is the *ekklēsia*. When they respond properly, they receive forgiveness of sins, the gift of the Holy Spirit, and the assurance of eternal life. The message is the same, and the consequences of accepting or rejecting the message are the same. However, when we pay close attention to the composition of the audiences of the speeches recounted in Acts, to the way these audiences are addressed, and to the content of the words that are spoken, we reach a different conclusion. The *euangelion* is indeed for all—but its implications are different for Jewish and gentile audiences. Though often unobserved, this is a crucial point, and will provide us with the insight needed to deal with the challenges posed in the rest of this chapter.

With this perspective in view, let us examine the key texts summoned by exegetes who argue that Luke and Acts nullify Jewish covenantal identity for those Jews outside the *ekklēsia*.

Jewish Opposition and Paul's "Going to the Gentiles"

The Argument for Covenantal Exclusion

In Acts, the phrase *hoi Ioudaioi* ("the Jews/Judeans") is often employed to designate Jewish opponents of the apostolic message. Many see this as evidence that Luke views Jews outside the *ekklēsia* as having forfeited their status as members of the people of God.

The phrase *hoi Ioudaioi* does not appear in Acts before the account of Paul's encounter with the risen Jesus on the road to Damascus (Acts 9:1–19). After that event, the phrase is found often, especially in contexts where groups of Jews are opposing the work of Paul (Acts 9:23; 13:45, 50; 14:4; 17:5; 18:5–6, 12, 28; 20:3; 22:30; 23:12, 20; 24:9; 26:2; 28:19). The phrase thus arises with negative connotations almost exclusively in diaspora settings where Jews live as a minority community in the midst of gentiles.[9]

8. The Greek word translated here as "turning" could be either transitive (i.e., God acts through Jesus to turn one from evil) or intransitive (i.e., the individual himself or herself does the "turning").

9. The exception is in the account of the persecution of the *ekklēsia* under King

However we interpret the significance of this phrase in Acts, we must avoid the anachronistic presupposition that the author distinguishes the category "Jew" from that of "Christian" (i.e., disciple of Jesus). While Luke does speak of "*the* Jews" as a group hostile to the Jesus-movement, he also sees that movement as a *Jewish* reality, led by Jews and adhered to by many Jews. When Luke first introduces Aquila, he identifies him not as a Jesus-follower but as "a *Jew* named Aquila" (Acts 18:2). The narrator introduces Apollos in the same way (Acts 18:24). Paul identifies himself as "a *Jew*" (Acts 21:39; 22:3). Pagan critics of Paul and Silas in Philippi bring them before the Roman magistrates of the city, and accuse them of wrongdoing by stating, "These men are disturbing our city; *they are Jews* and are advocating [Jewish] customs that are not lawful for us as Romans to adopt or observe" (Acts 16:20–21). Speaking of the city of Jerusalem, James tells Paul, "You see, brother, how many thousands of believers there are *among the Jews*, and they are all zealous for the law" (Acts 21:20). When Jewish leaders attack Paul before the Roman authorities, they portray him as "an agitator *among all the Jews* throughout the world, and a ringleader of *the sect* of the Nazarenes" (Acts 24:5). They see Paul as a Jew who has a prominent position within a Jewish *sect* or party. Undoubtedly Luke recognizes the Jewish character of the Jesus-movement, and the Jewish identity of its leaders and its pioneering core membership.[10]

It is thus evident that the phrase *hoi Ioudaioi* in Acts does not encompass all Jews in a particular location, for the author knows and states that those whom *hoi Ioudaioi* are opposing are also *Ioudaioi*. Moreover, we are informed that in Corinth "the Jews" oppose and revile Paul (Acts 18:6) and make "a united attack" by bringing him before the proconsul Gallio (Acts 18:12); yet, the author also informs us that "Crispus, the official of the synagogue, became a believer in the Lord, together with all his household; and many of the Corinthians who heard Paul became believers and were baptized" (Acts 18:8). In order to make sense of these texts, we must interpret the phrase *hoi Ioudaioi* to mean the Jewish community in a particular diaspora location, acting—officially or unofficially—as a corporate entity.

Herod Agrippa (Acts 12:3, 11). This can be explained by the fact that Agrippa ruled over gentile as well as Jewish subjects and territories (as is clear from the story of his death in Acts 12:20–23).

10. This paragraph is drawn from my earlier work, *Postmissionary Messianic Judaism*, 116–17.

Three texts that mention the response to Paul's message given by this corporate entity deserve special attention. In his initial missionary journey, Paul delivers a lengthy speech in the synagogue of Antioch of Pisidia in Asia Minor (Acts 13:16–41). At first the Jewish audience welcomes Paul's message (Acts 13:42–43), but the following week they turn hostile:

> 45 [W]hen the Jews [*hoi Ioudaioi*] saw the crowds, they were filled with jealousy; and blaspheming, they contradicted what was spoken by Paul. 46 Then both Paul and Barnabas spoke out boldly, saying, "It was necessary that the word of God should be spoken first to you. Since you reject it and judge yourselves to be unworthy of eternal life, we are now turning to the gentiles. 47 For so the Lord has commanded us, saying, 'I have set you to be a light for the gentiles, so that you may bring salvation to the ends of the earth.'" (Acts 13:45–47)

In his second missionary journey, Paul receives a vision beckoning him to leave Asia Minor in order to begin a new work across the Aegean (Acts 16:9–10). Paul eventually makes his way to Corinth, a city situated on an isthmus and described by Strabo in 7 BCE as "master of two harbors, of which the one leads straight to Asia, and the other to Italy."[11] Corinth thus represents the progress of the Pauline mission to the continent of Europe. At this point, Luke describes briefly a scene that resembles what occurred earlier in Antioch of Pisidia (in the continent of Asia):

> 5 Paul was occupied with proclaiming the word, testifying to the Jews [*hoi Ioudaioi*] that the Messiah was Jesus. 6 When they opposed and reviled him, in protest he shook the dust from his clothes and said to them, "Your blood be on your own heads! I am innocent. From now on I will go to the gentiles." 7 Then he left the synagogue and went to the house of a man named Titius Justus, a worshipper of God; his house was next door to the synagogue. (Acts 18:5–7)

Then, in the final chapter of Acts, Paul reaches Rome, the heart of Europe and the Empire. There he meets with the local leaders of the Jewish community, and speaks to them about "the kingdom of God" and Jesus (Acts 28:23). Their attitude toward his message is more welcoming than that of the Jews of Pisidian Antioch or Corinth: "Some were convinced by

11. Cited by Hays, *First Corinthians*, 3.

what he had said, while others refused to believe. So they disagreed with each other" (Acts 28:24–25a). Nevertheless, Paul responds in a fashion similar to the previous two episodes: "Let it be known to you then that this salvation of God has been sent to the gentiles; they will listen" (Acts 28:28). Some ancient manuscripts recount what follows: "And when he had said these words, the Jews [*hoi Ioudaioi*] departed, arguing vigorously among themselves" (Acts 28:29).

Paul's declaration that he is "going to the gentiles" is recounted three times in three geographical settings, which represent the crucial stages of Paul's expanding apostolic sphere (Asia Minor, Greece, Rome). As with the three accounts of Paul's vision on the road to Damascus (Acts 9:1–19; 22:6–16; 26:12–18), and the three accounts of Peter's encounter with Cornelius (Acts 10:1–48; 11:4–16; 15:7–9), the literary technique of threefold repetition emphasizes the importance of these words of Paul in the eyes of the author. The fact that the book concludes with the third of these episodes further underlines the significance of the sequence.

What is that significance? Hans Conzelmann articulates the traditional exegetical consensus when he asserts, "Israel's turning away from salvation is final, as is clear in Paul's concluding statement in Acts 28:28."[12] While Joseph Tyson considers Luke's view of Judaism to be more complex, his assessment of Acts 28:28 echoes that of Conzelmann: "The text that exhibits such profound ambivalence in regard to Jews and Judaism [i.e., Luke/Acts as a whole] moves toward a resolution without ambivalence or ambiguity: an image of Jewish people as rejecting the gospel and thus as a people without hope."[13]

Hoi Ioudaioi and the Differentiated Missiology of Acts

The picture looks dramatically different if we view the threefold turning to the gentiles and the negative usage of *hoi Ioudaioi* against the background of the differentiated missiology of Acts presented above. When Peter or Paul address a Jewish audience, they are speaking to an organized community—their own community—that is the rightful recipient of the blessings brought by the Messiah. Jesus has been raised from the dead not just to "save" individual Jews, but to accomplish "the redemption of Jerusalem." On the other hand, when Peter addresses Cornelius and his

12. Cited in Tyson, *Luke, Judaism, and the Scholars*, 88.

13. Tyson, *Luke, Judaism, and the Scholars*, 144–45.

household, or when Paul speaks to gentiles in Lystra or Athens, they aim merely to win as many gentiles as possible to Jesus-faith. No "corporate" gentile response from each of the "nations" is sought or required.[14]

As we have seen, *hoi Ioudaioi* in Acts refers to the communal body of Jews ordered under its leaders and acting in an official or semi-official capacity. As noted at the beginning of this chapter, one of the central themes of Acts is that a large number of Jews respond with faith to the message of the resurrected Messiah. At the same time, the Jewish community as a whole, as embodied in its leadership and its official communal institutions, does not respond with faith, but instead seeks to thwart the efforts of the new movement. This communal failure to receive the national redemption offered in Messiah Jesus is also a central theme of Acts.

Robert Tannehill interprets the threefold turning to the gentiles in light of this communal dimension:

> Paul's announcement that he is going to the Gentiles indicates a shift from a synagogue-based mission, addressed to Jews and to those Gentiles attracted to Judaism, to a mission in the city at large, where the population is predominantly Gentile. . . . Paul . . . has fulfilled his obligation to speak God's word to God's people. They are now responsible for their own fate. The pattern of speaking first to Jews and only later turning to the Gentiles testifies to Paul's sense of prophetic obligation to his own people. He is released from this obligation only when he meets strong public resistance within the Jewish community. Then he can begin the second phase of his mission within a city, a phase in which the conversion of individual Jews is still possible, although Paul is no longer preaching in the synagogue nor addressing Jews as a community.[15]

Tannehill notes that the last of these three texts actually describes the Jewish leadership as divided in its response, with some accepting Paul's message and others rejecting it (Acts 28:24–25). Nevertheless, Paul understands this divided response as equivalent to communal rejection, since most of the leaders would need to respond favorably in order for his work to continue as a publicly sanctioned activity. "The presence

14. However, according to Acts, all those from the nations who respond to the message then become "a people for his name" (Acts 15:14)—a corporate reality bound to the people of Israel. (I thank Isaac Oliver for this observation.)

15. Tannehill, *The Narrative Unity of Luke-Acts*, 1:222–23.

of disagreement among the Jews is enough to show that Paul has not achieved what he sought. *He was seeking a communal decision, a recognition by the Jewish community as a whole that Jesus is the fulfillment of the Jewish hope.* The presence of significant opposition shows that this is not going to happen."[16] By ending his two volumes with this scene, Luke acknowledges that for the foreseeable future the Jewish community in its public settings would constitute an environment unconducive to the presentation of the apostolic message.[17] However, this does not imply a nullification of that community's covenantal status, nor a surrendering of hope for an eschatological reversal of that communal response.[18]

In fact, these texts point to the opposite conclusion. The threefold turning to the gentiles signifies a prophetic announcement of judgment that will be carried out beyond the narrative limits of Acts in the destruction of Jerusalem in 70 CE. The severity of that judgment derives less from the particular acts of wrongdoing committed by *hoi Ioudaioi*, considered in abstract and universal terms, and more from the heightened responsibility consonant with their distinguished covenantal status.[19] Israel's repentance and faith would have triggered the Messiah's return and the establishment of his royal reign in Jerusalem; its failure to offer such a corporate response results not only in the delay of the restored kingdom but in an intensification of the sufferings of exile. This means that *the*

16. Tannehill, *Narrative Unity*, 2:347. Emphasis added.

17. This is the practical reason for Paul's "going to the gentiles," as is evident from Acts 19:8–10: "He entered the synagogue [in Ephesus] and for three months spoke out boldly, and argued persuasively about the kingdom of God. When some stubbornly refused to believe and spoke evil of the Way before the congregation, he left them, taking the disciples with him, and argued daily in the lecture hall of Tyrannus. This continued for two years, so that all the residents of Asia, both Jews and Greeks, heard the word of the Lord." While only "some" —and not all or even most—"speak evil of the Way before the congregation," their actions render the environment as a whole inhospitable to Paul's message. As a result, Paul is no longer able to address "the Jews" as a community, yet he continues to bring his message to individual Jews (as well as gentiles).

18. This is the view of Tannehill. Joseph Tyson endorses Tannehill's insight into the communal dimension of Paul's efforts among the Jewish people, but he disagrees with Tannehill's suggestion that Israel's future is still open. Tyson thinks that Luke sees Israel as "a people without hope." See Tyson, "The Problem of Jewish Rejection in Acts," 126–27, and *Luke, Judaism, and the Scholars*, 142–45. Given the promises to Israel recorded in the infancy narrative, and Luke's confidence in the ultimate triumph of the divine plan/*boulē* (see chapter 5), Tyson's conclusion is without merit.

19. "From everyone to whom much is given, much will be required; and from the one to whom much has been entrusted, even more will be demanded" (Luke 12:48b).

coming judgment actually confirms rather than annuls the enduring covenantal bond between God and the Jewish people. Like the covenant curses of Leviticus and Deuteronomy, the fierce judgment of Jerusalem anticipated in Luke and Acts demonstrates in history the difficult demands imposed on Israel as God's covenant partner. If, as many exegetes claim, Jerusalem had been definitively divorced from her husband, she would become like any other city or nation, and the punishment designated for violation of the covenant would no longer be applicable.[20]

Acts reports that leaders and groups within local Jewish communities actively oppose the spread of the *euangelion*. Even when opposition was neither official nor an expression of the will of the majority, it was sufficient to make Jewish public settings inhospitable to the message and to indicate that the apostolic goal would not be realized. As Tannehill describes that goal, Paul (and the early *ekklēsia* as a whole) "was seeking a communal decision, a recognition by the Jewish community as a whole that Jesus is the fulfillment of the Jewish hope." While no such positive communal decision was forthcoming, Luke and Acts avoid portraying the Jewish community as uniformly hostile to the *euangelion*. The disciples of Jesus have friends and sympathizers in the wider Jewish world (e.g., the women who grieve for Jesus at his crucifixion, or the men who bury Stephen), and even among the Jewish leadership (e.g., Joseph of Arimathea, Gamaliel, the Pharisees of the Jerusalem Council to whom Paul appeals).[21] While the pre-70 narrative world of Acts gives nothing away about the future, the author and his readers both know that the chief villains of this drama (i.e., the high priest and his Sadducean colleagues) have lost their power, and the friendly elements among the pre-70 leader-

20. Like many other traditional Christian interpreters, Peter Walker assumes rather than demonstrates that the judgment on Jerusalem and Israel anticipated in Luke and Acts differs from previous biblical judgments of the same sort in its definitive and final nature: "Previous judgments upon the city had been severe but temporary; this one was final" (Walker, *Jesus and the Holy City*, 105).

21. As Robert Brawley puts it: "Luke does not simply set Christianity over against Judaism. Rather, he divides Israel into two camps—believers [in Jesus] and unbelievers. Then, he associates certain groups more closely with one or the other of the two camps. Luke differentiates Sadducees and the high priestly circle and connects them with recalcitrant Israel. On the other hand, he presents Pharisees as on the brink of Christianity. . . . Although the Pharisees can yet be distinguished as unbelievers [in Jesus], they are more closely related to [Jesus-]believing Israel than to recalcitrant Israel. . . . Luke does not merely usurp the prerogatives of Israel; he also *includes* a significant portion of Israel [in the *ekklēsia*] and has other reputable and influential Jews waiting in the wings" (Brawley, *Luke-Acts and the Jews*, 153).

ship (i.e., the Pharisees) are in the ascendancy. Judgment has come upon Jerusalem, but it has brought purification rather than eradication.

This suggests that the author/editor of Luke and Acts retains hope for Israel's future, and regards Israel's exilic present as enfolded within the covenantal purposes of God. The opposition to the *euangelion* of some within the Jewish community, and Paul's consequent threefold "going to the gentiles," pose no problem for this conclusion. Israel finds itself once again in exile, but once again also awaits its restoration.

The Intertextual Framework of Paul's Final Words

This picture draws further support from the intertextual echoes of Paul's final words in Acts, which represent the third instance of his "going to the gentiles." Paul's speech to the Jewish elders of Rome concludes as follows: "Let it be known to you then that this salvation of God [*to sōtērion tou Theou*] has been sent to the gentiles; they will listen" (Acts 28:28). The Greek word *sōtērion* is rare in the New Testament, appearing only five times.[22] Three of those occurrences are found in Luke and Acts. The most important of the three, which illuminates the others, is Luke 3:4–6. Here Luke parallels Mark and Matthew by characterizing the mission of John the Baptist in terms of Isaiah 40:3, but then goes beyond Mark and Matthew by citing Isaiah 40:4–5 as well:

> 4 as it is written in the book of the words of the prophet Isaiah,
> "The voice of one crying out in the wilderness:
> 'Prepare the way of the Lord,
> make his paths straight.
> [The citation of Isaiah 40 in Mark and Matthew ends here.]
> 5 Every valley shall be filled,
> and every mountain and hill shall be made low,
> and the crooked shall be made straight,
> and the rough ways made smooth;
> 6 and all flesh [*pasa sarx*] shall see the salvation of God [*to sōtērion tou Theou*]." (Luke 3:4–6)

In Acts 28:28, Paul states that "the salvation of God" [*to sōtērion tou Theou*], which Israel is now failing to receive, will be experienced by gentiles. Yet, citing Isaiah 40:5, Luke 3 tells us that this "salvation" will

22. The more common Greek word for salvation in the New Testament (appearing forty-five times) is *sōtēria*.

be seen (i.e., experienced) by "*all* flesh." It thus appears that Acts 28:28 witnesses to only a partial fulfillment of Isaiah 40:5.

How does Luke understand the phrase "all flesh" (*pasa sarx*) in Isaiah 40:5 (LXX)? Who are those who are destined to "see the salvation of God"? Luke's intention becomes clear in the Song of Simeon, the remaining text in which the word *sōtērion* is found.[23]

> 29 Master, now you are dismissing your servant in peace,
> according to your word;
> 30 for my eyes have seen your salvation [*sōtērion*],
> 31 which you have prepared
> in the presence of all peoples [*pantōn tōn laōn*],
> 32 a light for revelation to the gentiles
> and for glory to your people Israel. (Luke 2:29–32)

Simeon's "all peoples" (*pantōn tōn laōn*) is equivalent to Isaiah's "all flesh" (*pasa sarx*), and the meaning of "all peoples" is then explained in the line that follows: the phrase refers to Israel and the gentiles (i.e., the nations) together. Verse 32 alludes to Isaiah 49:5–6:

> 5 And now the LORD says,
> who formed me in the womb to be his servant,
> to bring Jacob back to him,
> and that Israel might be gathered to him,
> for I am honored in the sight of the LORD,
> and my God has become my strength—
> 6 he says, "It is too light a thing that you should be my servant
> to raise up the tribes of Jacob and to restore the survivors of Israel;
> I will give you as a light to the nations,
> that my salvation may reach to the end of the earth." (Isa 49:5–6)

God sends the servant to accomplish a dual mission: he is to be a "light to the nations" (i.e., gentiles), but also "to raise up the tribes of Jacob."

Luke treats these verses of Isaiah as fundamental to the divine purpose, and they shape his overall narrative. When Paul bears witness before King Agrippa, Isaiah 49:5–6 underlies his formulation of the mission of the risen Messiah conducted through the *ekklēsia*: "I stand here

23. The importance of Isaiah 40 as an intertextual reference in the Song of Simeon is highlighted by the way Luke introduces the figure of Simeon: "Now there was a man in Jerusalem whose name was Simeon; this man was righteous and devout, looking forward to the consolation [*paraklēsin*] of Israel" (Luke 2:25). The phrase "the consolation of Israel" alludes to the opening words of Isaiah 40: "Comfort, comfort [*parakleite, parakleite*] my people" (Isa 40:1 LXX).

. . . saying nothing but what the prophets and Moses said would take place: that the Messiah must suffer, and that, by being the first to rise from the dead, *he would proclaim light both to our people and to the gentiles*" (Acts 26:22–23, emphasis added). Even more telling is the explicit citation of Isaiah 49 in Paul's words to the Jewish community of Antioch in Pisidia, the first of his threefold "going to the gentiles": "It was necessary that the word of God should be spoken first to you. Since you reject it and judge yourselves to be unworthy of eternal life, we are now turning to the gentiles. For so the Lord has commanded us, saying, 'I have set you to be a light for the gentiles, so that you may bring salvation to the ends of the earth'" (Acts 13:46–47). While the Song of Simeon refers to both parts of the dual mission of the servant, and the reference to "all flesh" in Luke's citation of Isaiah 40:5 likewise asserts a comprehensive salvific purpose in the work of the Messiah (i.e., including both the gentiles and the "tribes of Jacob"), Paul in Acts 13 ignores Isaiah 49:5–6a (which speaks of Israel) and mentions only Isaiah 49:6b (which speaks of the gentiles). As we have seen, this anticipates the final scene of Acts 28 in which Paul rebukes the Jewish elders of Rome and announces for the third and last time his "going to the gentiles."[24]

Luke never tires of asserting that the prophetic words of scripture must be fulfilled, and Isaiah 40:5 ("*all flesh* will see the salvation of God")—understood in light of Isaiah 49:5–6 ("all flesh" = Israel + the nations)—is prominent among the prophetic words he cites. Because of Israel's corporate resistance to the *euangelion*, Jerusalem and the nation as a whole will be judged. While large numbers of individual Jews enter the *ekklēsia*, Israel *as a community* withholds its assent. Since Luke evidently interprets Isaiah 49 as referring to Israel's corporate redemption by the servant, it appears that only the gentile portion of Isaiah 49 will be realized in the immediate future. That is the significance of Paul's "going to the gentiles."

However, Jesus has come not only as "a light for revelation to the gentiles"; he is also destined to bring "glory to your people Israel" (Luke 2:32). Isaiah 49:5–6a will be accomplished, but only in a future beyond the events of 70 CE and Israel's second exile, when "the times of the

24. The subtle use of Isaiah 40 and 49 in Luke and Acts refutes the contention of some commentators that the author thinks that "Israel" has already been restored in the person of the "myriads" (Acts 21:20) of Jews who entered the *ekklēsia*. This is the view of Jervell, *Luke and the People of God*, 41–74.

gentiles are fulfilled" (Luke 21:24).[25] Just as in its original context Isaiah 6 pronounced a judgment of exile whose goal and result was to purify Israel and lead to its ultimate restoration, so Paul in Acts 28:26–27 cites these words of Isaiah with the same intent and meaning.[26]

Thus, the consistent opposition to the apostles by *hoi Ioudaioi*, Paul's threefold "going to the gentiles," and the climax of that threefold pattern in the final verses of Acts all fit well with the hopeful long-term perspective on the Jewish people that we have discerned in the two Lukan volumes.

Deuteronomy 18 and the Judgment of Unfaithful Israel

The Argument for Covenantal Exclusion

Many commentators find decisive refutation of this thesis in Peter's treatment of the prophet-like-Moses motif of Deuteronomy 18:15–19 (Acts 3:23) and Stephen's reference to the same text (Acts 7:37, 39). Peter cites Deuteronomy 18:19 in this form: "And it will be that everyone who does not listen to that prophet will be utterly rooted out of the people [*ex-olethreuthēsetai ek tou laou*]" (Acts 3:23). The phrase "will be utterly rooted out of the people" is found in neither the Masoretic text (which reads "I myself will require [a reckoning] from him") nor the Septuagint (which reads "I will execute judicial-punishment on him").[27] It appears that Luke has taken *ex-olethreuthēsetai ek tou laou* from the Septuagint

25. Charles B. Puskas skillfully identifies the intertextual network discussed here, and its relevance to the interpretation of Acts 28. Unfortunately, ignoring the evidence to the contrary, he thinks that Acts 28 indicates the fulfillment of the promises of Isaiah 40 for "all flesh," i.e., *both* gentiles and Jews: "Paul at Rome brings the universal significance of God's salvation in the person of Jesus, to its completion" (*The Conclusion of Luke-Acts*, 103). This reading of Acts 28 fails to attend to the *lack of completion* that Luke conveys by ending his narrative in Rome, with Israel about to fall under divine judgment.

26. Justin Taylor takes a similar approach to Paul's use of Isaiah 6 in Acts 28: "as in the original context in the Book of Isaiah, it is a call to conversion [i.e., repentance] rather than a declaration of rejection" ("Paul and the Jewish Leaders of Rome: Acts 28:17–31," 323). Moreover, Taylor argues that the Lukan Paul "who meets with representatives of the Jewish community in Rome in Acts 28 is in substantial agreement in his attitude to Israel with the Paul of Romans 9–11" (321).

27. The Masoretic Hebrew is *anochi edrosh mey'imo*; the Septuagint Greek is *egō ekdikēsō ex autou*. My English rendering of the Masoretic Hebrew is drawn from the translation of Everett Fox (*The Five Books of Moses*, 934).

version of another passage in the Torah, Leviticus 23:29: "For anyone who does not practice self-denial during that entire day [i.e., the Day of Atonement] shall be cut off from his people [*ex-olethreuthēsetai ek tou laou autēs*]."[28] The substitution of this phrase for the one in Deuteronomy 18:19 highlights the gravity of the commandment and the severity of divine punishment for its violation.

According to Jacob Jervell and those who follow his lead, the use of this phrase also implies that those who reject the *euangelion* are immediately excluded from the people of Israel: "The rejection of the missionary preaching . . . is to result in the purging of the unrepentant portion of the people from Israel[;] . . . a portion of Israel has forfeited its right to belong to the people of God."[29] To maintain their covenantal status, Jews must embrace Jesus as Israel's Messiah. Paul's "going to the gentiles" means that the Jews in those regions who have failed to do so have been stripped of their identity as "descendants of the prophets and of the covenant that God gave to your ancestors" (Acts 3:25). Furthermore, the threefold repetition of this "going to the gentiles," which culminates in Rome, means that the world-wide Jewish community outside the *ekklēsia* has now definitively lost its vocation as the people of Israel.

This is a bold conclusion to draw from one verse, especially given all the reasons presented above for holding a contrary thesis. However, Jervell is justified in highlighting the Lukan alteration of Deuteronomy 18:19, just as others before him were justified in emphasizing the threefold "going to the gentiles." I do not dispute the *importance* of this verse, but only its meaning.

Acts 3:23 and *Karet*

The Hebrew verb translated *ex-olethreuō* by the Septuagint in Leviticus 23:29 (and frequently elsewhere) is *karat*, "to cut off." The term appears often in the Torah as a severe penalty for offenses against God (such as the failure to fast on the Day of Atonement) that only indirectly affect other people. In rabbinic literature, the term appears in a nominal form,

28. See Tiede, *Prophecy and History in Luke-Acts*, 42, and Bock, *Acts*, 179.

29. Jervell, *Luke and the People of God*, 54. See also Juel, *Luke-Acts*, 110; Weatherly, *Jewish Responsibility for the Death of Jesus in Luke-Acts*, 165; Fitzmyer, *Luke the Theologian*, 191.

karet, in reference to this type of penalty. Jacob Milgrom summarizes the various opinions in rabbinic texts regarding the meaning of *karet*:

> (1) Childlessness and premature death (*Rashi* on *b. Shabb.* 25a);
>
> (2) Death before the age of sixty (*Mo'ed Qat.* 28a);
>
> (3) Death before the age of fifty-two (Rabad);
>
> (4) Being "cut off" through the extirpation of descendants (Ibn Ezra on Gen 17:14);
>
> (5) At death, the soul too shall die and will not enjoy the spiritual life of the hereafter (Maim., *Teshuva* 8.1; cf. *Sifre* Num 112; Ramban on Lev 20:2).[30]

Two features of all these interpretations of *karet* deserve attention here: first, the penalty is carried out directly by God rather than by a human authority; second, the penalty is not executed immediately but only (and sometimes remotely) after the fact. If the offender is youthful, the punishment may not take effect for decades.

Robert Tannehill notes the absence of any temporal markers in Acts 3:23 to indicate *when* those who reject the prophet-like-Moses are to be "destroyed from the people."[31] Tannehill does not have in mind a delayed judgment of the sort posited by rabbinic tradition, but instead seeks to define "rejection" as a firm disposition rather than a transitory reaction: "We remain within the parameters of Lukan thought if we say that it applies whenever the rejection of God's prophetic messenger becomes *definitive and irreversible*, a possibility that must be continually tested by calls to repentance."[32] Judgment is immediate rather than delayed, but the behavior that elicits the judgment must be sustained over an extended period of time to qualify as authentic "rejection." This clarification of the concept of "rejection" is helpful, but the rabbinic approach to the absence of temporal markers in regard to *karet* also deserves attention here.

Of the five rabbinic interpretations of *karet* listed by Milgrom, two are especially relevant for Acts of the Apostles: the fourth (extirpation of

30. Milgrom, *Leviticus 1–16*, 57.

31. Reflecting on the theological problem posed for the author of Luke-Acts by the notion of "two peoples of God" (i.e., the *ekklēsia* and the Jewish people), and the attempt of Jervell and others to solve this problem by recourse to Acts 3:23, Tannehill writes: "Some interpreters would see the threat of exclusion from God's people in 3:23 as an effort to solve this problem by eliminating Jews once and for all. *However, we are not told when that threat will take effect*" (*Narrative Unity*, 2:225).

32. Tannehill, *Narrative Unity*, 2:225. Emphasis added.

descendants) and the fifth (extirpation from the world to come).[33] The focus on *descendants* points to the long-term consequences of *karet* for one's impact on the life of the people of God in this world. The focus on *spiritual death* points to the long-term consequences of *karet* for one's individual future in the world to come.

Karet and Life in the World to Come

I propose that the Lukan writings adopt an approach to *karet* that resembles the rabbinic approach, and that these two long-term consequences of *karet*—posterity in this world and spiritual death in the next—enable us to unlock the significance of Acts 3:23. The latter consequence becomes visible when Paul makes his first transition from synagogue to general proclamation: "It was necessary that the word of God should be spoken first to you [as Jews]. Since you reject it and judge yourselves to be *unworthy of eternal life*, we are now turning to the gentiles" (Acts 13:46). Those whose unambiguous "rejection of God's prophetic messenger" has proven "definitive and irreversible" will be deemed "unworthy of eternal life," and as a result will forfeit their place among the people of Israel in the world to come. This sentence is severe indeed, but it neither negates nor qualifies the covenantal status of these Israelites *in this world*.[34]

This conclusion draws support from Stephen's citation of Deuteronomy 18 in Acts 7. Speaking of Moses' "wonders and signs in Egypt, at the Red Sea, and in the wilderness" (v. 36), and of his mediation of divine revelation at Sinai (v. 38), Stephen states: "This is the Moses who said to the Israelites, 'God will raise up a prophet for you from your own people as he raised me up'" (v. 37). Stephen then proceeds to castigate the wilderness generation for its rejection of Moses: "Our ancestors were unwilling to obey him" (v. 39). The point of Stephen's narration is transparent: he himself had been accused of speaking against Moses and the Torah (Acts 6:13–14), and he now refutes that charge by arguing that

33. There is also overlap between the first rabbinic interpretation of *karet* (i.e., its inclusion of childlessness) and the fourth which refers to extirpation of descendants.

34. The sad history of Christian distortions of the *euangelion*, combined with criminal acts against Jews perpetrated in the name of Jesus, have radically altered the context in which Jews of later generations have heard the message concerning Jesus. As a result, these texts from Luke and Acts are insufficient warrant for the claim that Jews today who remain skeptical of Jesus' messianic status have unambiguously "rejected the word of God."

the rejection of Jesus—the prophet spoken of in Deuteronomy 18—constitutes the real rejection of Moses and the Torah. Those who brought false charges against Jesus and now bring false charges against his servant show themselves to be as much like Israel's wilderness generation as Jesus is like Moses.

The relevance of this text to our understanding of the phrase "utterly rooted out of the people" in Acts 3:23 becomes evident once we recognize the way ancient Jewish exegesis commonly interpreted the promise of the land in eschatological terms. The Mishnah provides the following midrash on Isaiah 60:21: "All Israelites have a share in the world to come, for it is written, 'Thy people also shall all be righteous, they shall inherit the land for ever'" (*m. Sanhedrin* 10:1).[35] This rabbinic text then proceeds to identify those Israelites who forfeit their share in Israel's eternal inheritance. Notably, the list includes the wilderness generation: "The generation of the wilderness have no share in the world to come nor shall they stand in the judgment, for it is written, 'In this wilderness they shall be consumed and there they shall die'" (Num 14:35; *m. Sandhedrin* 10:3).[36] Just as they failed to enter the land of Israel under Joshua, so they shall fail to enter the eschatological inheritance of which that land was a foretaste.

The Jews of Jerusalem who hear Peter and Stephen are in danger of becoming like the wilderness generation who proved unworthy of Israel's inheritance. This threat contains fearsome long-term penalties, but it does not challenge the covenantal status of those Jews in the present age. This is evident from the parallel case of the wilderness generation. That generation did not die immediately after sentence was passed upon them, nor did they forfeit their covenantal status in this age. If their disobedience had disqualified them from legitimate Israelite identity, then they would have been barred from worship at the wilderness sanctuary, and their children would have been disqualified along with their parents as heirs of the promise. However, the Torah places no such restriction on their involvement with the sanctuary (e.g., Num 17:1–11), and the children of the wilderness generation are the ones who inherit the land in place of their parents.[37] The people of the wilderness generation remain

35. Danby, *The Mishnah*, 397.

36. Danby, *Mishnah*, 397–98.

37. Stephen says that "God turned away" from the wilderness generation, and "handed them over to worship the host of heaven" (Acts 7:42). This refers to the recurring idolatrous behavior of the wilderness generation, but it does not imply that they

Israelites, and the people of the generation of Peter and Stephen likewise remain Israelites. Their long-term future is in danger, but their present covenantal status remains intact.

Karet and Spiritual Posterity in This World

The other long-term consequence of *karet* relevant to Acts 3:23—the cutting-off of posterity in this world—sheds light on a crucial-but-neglected speech in Acts that appears midway between the speeches of Peter (in Acts 3) and Stephen (in Acts 7). I refer to the advice of Gamaliel, which he offers to his fellow members of the ruling council in Jerusalem (Acts 5:33–39). His colleagues are inclined to seek the execution of the apostles, but Gamaliel dissuades them from this course of action. After recounting the stories of two messianic pretenders whose movements came to naught, Gamaliel concludes: "So in the present case, I tell you, keep away from these men [i.e., the apostles] and let them alone; because if this plan or this undertaking is of human origin, it will fail; but if it is of God, you will not be able to overthrow them—in that case you may even be found fighting against God [*theo-machoi*]!" (Acts 5:38–39). Gamaliel argues that God's judgment on particular leaders, movements, and teachings among the people of the covenant will become evident in God's providential oversight of Israel's future history. In the long-term, the true prophets will have spiritual "posterity," whereas those who reject the true prophets will have no spiritual "posterity."

All commentators recognize the primary intent of these words of Gamaliel from the perspective of the author of Acts: as the author and his readers know, with more than a half-century distance between them and the Pharisaic sage, the Jesus-movement has not dissipated but instead has spread throughout the Empire and beyond. While this fact is insufficient to prove that the movement is divinely authorized, it is a necessary condition for reaching such a conclusion.

Beyond that primary positive implication, the author of Acts likely also intends a secondary negative inference from Gamaliel's advice, and that inference bears on the meaning of Acts 3:23. Gamaliel's main audience consists of the Sadducean priestly hierarchy that handed Jesus over to the Romans and has now arrested the apostles. With greater care than the other Gospels, Luke (and Acts) distinguish between the Sadducees

were excluded from participation in the legitimate worship of the desert sanctuary, a claim that would be in clear contradiction to the narrative of Numbers.

as adversaries of the Jesus-movement and the more ambivalent role of the Pharisaic party, whom Gamaliel represents.[38] While the Sadducean hierarchy accepts Gamaliel's recommendation in the current instance, their hostility to the apostolic community increases as the narrative unfolds, and eventually results in the execution of Stephen (Acts 6:12–7:1), the persecution of the Jerusalem *ekklēsia*, the heresy-hunting mission of Paul to Damascus (Acts 9:1–2), and finally the arrest and trial of Paul himself (Acts 23:1–9).[39] The Sadducean chief priests have thereby shown themselves to be *theo-machoi*—those "fighting against God" (Acts 5:39).

If the spiritual "posterity" of the apostolic community in the post 70 era demonstrates for the author/editor of Luke and Acts that its "plan" and "undertaking" are likely "of God," so the lack of spiritual "posterity" of the Sadducean priestly hierarchy in the same period demonstrates that it was "fighting against God." The destiny of the Sadducees will be the same as that of Theudas and Judas the Galilean: they will die, and "all who follow them" will be "dispersed" and will "disappear" (Acts 5:36–37). The Sadducees in fact deserve a worse fate than Theudas and Judas, for those two were only initiating divinely unauthorized movements, whereas the Sadducees are actively opposing a movement that has divine authorization. They definitively reject the prophet-like-Moses. Therefore, they will be "utterly rooted out of the people"—i.e., their spiritual posterity will vanish. They themselves do not forfeit the status of Israelites, or even the status of "*leaders* of Israel" (Acts 23:4–5), but their long-term prospects, in both this world and the next, are dim.[40]

To these two implications of Gamaliel's speech, I would add a third that has even more significance for the thesis of this chapter. Just as the post-70 Jewish readers of Acts know that the Jesus-movement has flourished and the Sadducean hierarchy has perished, they also may know that the *grandson of Gamaliel* (Gamaliel II) has assumed a position of leadership among the remnant of the Jewish people in the land of Israel. Gamaliel did not join the ranks of the Jesus-movement, but neither

38. See Brawley, *Luke-Acts and the Jews*, 85–132.

39. According to Acts, the Sadducean hierarchy initiates many of these actions in collaboration with Jews from the diaspora who reside in Jerusalem (Acts 6:9–12; 9:28–29; 21:27–29). While the Sadducees are not the only *theo-machoi* in the Lukan narrative, the Pharisees do not qualify as members of this genus. (I thank Isaac Oliver for this observation.)

40. A decisive judgment upon the Sadducees as a party is not equivalent to judgment on the priestly and levitical class as a whole. According to Luke and Acts, there remain many righteous priests (Luke 1:5–6; Acts 6:7) and Levites (Acts 4:36).

did he become one of its opponents—i.e., one of the *theo-machoi*. He counseled against persecuting the *ekklēsia*, and his party defended Paul against Paul's Sadducean accusers (Acts 23:9). In keeping with the theme of Gamaliel's own speech, we may say that his "plan" and the "undertaking" of his party—at least to some extent—are "of God." Unlike the Sadducean hierarchy, but like the disciples of Jesus, Gamaliel and the Pharisees enjoy an abundance of spiritual posterity. They are not among those who "definitively and irreversibly" reject the prophet-like-Moses, and they certainly are not among those who are "utterly rooted out of the people."

This implicitly favorable assessment of the Pharisees as future leaders of Israel fits with other Lukan texts that portray this party in a positive light. Pharisees warn Jesus, in response to Herod's attempt to arrest him (Luke 13:31); Pharisees seek to exonerate Paul, in response to the accusations against him leveled by the Sadducees (Acts 23:6–9); there are members of the *ekklēsia* in Jerusalem who continue to identify as Pharisees (Acts 15:5); and even Paul speaks of his Pharisaic loyalties in the present rather than the past tense (Acts 23:6). In Luke, the Pharisaic party bears no direct responsibility for Jesus' arrest and prosecution, and they are the Jewish party most sympathetic to the apostolic community. As Robert Brawley asserts, "In the two volumes, Luke presents the Pharisees as possessing serious character flaws, but nevertheless as respected and authoritative representatives of Judaism who can hover close to the edge of Christianity."[41]

Of special significance in this context is the Parable of the Two Sons (Luke 15:11–32).[42] Found only in Luke, the parable displays the author/editor's fundamental attitude toward the Pharisees in their post-70 role as emerging leaders of the Jewish community. The story focuses not on the returning younger son, who had abandoned his father and squandered his inheritance, but instead on the older son who had never left home. The opening verse of the chapter sets the parable in the context of criticisms of Jesus offered by Pharisees for his eating with "sinners." Thus, in Luke's narrative frame the older brother represents these Pharisaic critics. In this way, Luke shows his disappointment that many Pharisees fail to rejoice in the success that the Jesus-movement is having among less pious Jews—and, eventually, also among gentiles.

41. Brawley, *Luke-Acts and the Jews*, 84. Brawley's chapter on the Pharisees (84–106) is worthy of careful study.

42. See Kinzer, *Postmissionary Messianic Judaism*, 121–22.

Luke's evident dissatisfaction here with the Pharisaic response to Jesus and the *ekklēsia* can easily obscure what this parable actually shows of his attitude toward them. Three features of the parable are especially noteworthy in this regard. First, the father in the parable leaves the banquet hall and goes to the older son, who had sullenly refused to join the celebration. The father does not wait for the older son to come to him, but actively pursues his alienated child. Second, the father does not rebuke or threaten his son. Instead, he appeals to him and reassures him of his filial status: "Then the father said to him, 'Son, you are always with me, and all that is mine is yours. But we had to celebrate and rejoice, because this brother of yours was dead and has come to life; he was lost and has been found'" (Luke 15:31–32). Third, the parable *ends* with the father appealing to the older son. It does not tell us whether the son eventually accompanies his father into the banquet hall, or remains outside on his own. Like the book of Acts itself, the parable is unfinished. It will only be finished when the "older brother" hears the parable, realizes that it is addressed to him, and makes the appropriate response. In the meantime, the parable conveys the Lukan vision of how God relates to that group which became a leading force in Jewish affairs after the destruction of Jerusalem. They are "always with him," and "all that he has is theirs."[43]

Read in this light, Gamaliel's speech cautions us to be wary of interpreting Acts 3:23 as a universal disinheriting of individual Jews who do not accept Jesus as the Messiah, or of the organized Jewish community as a whole. In fact, that speech may imply the exact opposite conclusion—namely, that the Jewish community has been purified by the fire of 70 CE, and now remains with the Father.

In sum, the two explicit citations of Deuteronomy 18 in Acts (in the speeches of Peter and Stephen) cohere well with the rabbinic understanding of *karet* as a delayed rather than immediately-enforced penalty. Both speeches have in view the varied consequences of the destruction of Jerusalem forty years hence (i.e., exile from Israel's inheritance *in this world*) and the threat of divine punishment in a future life (i.e., exile from Israel's inheritance *in the world to come*). Gamaliel's speech midway

43. N. T. Wright applies the parable to the situation of Jews outside the *ekklēsia* (*Paul and the Faithfulness of God*, 1180–81, 1204), with an acknowledgement that it implies God's "continuing commitment" to those Jews (1180). However, he does not elaborate on the meaning or implications of this "continuing commitment," nor does he explore the various dimensions of the father's relationship to the older son discussed above.

between those of Peter and Stephen reinforces this interpretation of Deuteronomy 18:19/Leviticus 23:29, and provides a subtle legitimization of his grandson's future role of leadership in Israel at the time Acts was composed. While some Jews have been "utterly rooted out of the people," and all experience the impact of an intensified exile, the Jewish people as a whole retain their covenantal status even after the debacle of 70. Rather than undermining our core thesis regarding the standing of the Jewish people, the prophet-like-Moses theme of Acts confirms that thesis.

Acts 3, Lukan Eschatology, and the Enduring Covenantal Status of the Jewish People

Our discussion of the differentiated missiology of Acts highlighted the significance of Acts 3:19–21: "Therefore repent and return, so that your sins may be wiped away, in order that times [*kairoi*] of refreshing may come from the presence of the Lord; and that He may send Jesus, the Christ [i.e., Messiah] appointed for you, whom heaven must receive until [*achri*] the period [*chronoi*, lit. "times"] of restoration [*apokatastasis*] of all things about which God spoke by the mouth of His holy prophets from ancient time" (NASB). At this point in our study of Luke and Acts it will be helpful to pause and reflect on the impact of Acts 3:19–21 on our assessment of Lukan eschatology as a whole. Like the narrative of the ascension in Acts 1:9–11, Peter's conditional promise of the Messiah's return plays a pivotal role in a web of interlocking texts whose cumulative implications are rarely examined. As we will see, those implications include the enduring covenantal status of the Jewish people.

As noted above, Acts 3:19–21 shares vocabulary and theme with the dialogue of the resurrected Jesus and his disciples in Acts 1:6–8. The overlap signals to the reader that the disciples' question betrays no misunderstanding of Jesus' eschatological purpose. He *will* restore the kingdom to Israel, but only after Israel "repents" and "returns."

Read together with Acts 1:6–8, Peter's conditional promise of national restoration similarly sheds light on the prophecy of Jerusalem's "trampling by the nations" in Luke 21:24. As seen above, the three texts are interconnected and mutually interpretative. The Lukan passage informs the reader that the restoration of the kingdom to Israel will be preceded by Jerusalem's demise in the war of 70 CE. The two texts in Acts confirm the natural inference from Luke 21:24 that the "trampling" of

Jerusalem by the nations and the "times of the nations" will be followed by Jerusalem's repentance and restoration. It is the failure of many commentators to read Luke 21:24 in light of Acts 1:6–8 and 3:19–21 that leads them to treat Jesus' prophecy as vague and uncertain in its eschatological import for Israel.

Acts 3:19–21 sheds just as much light on Jesus' words in Luke 13:35: "You [Jerusalem] will not see me until the time comes when you say, 'Blessed is the one who comes in the name of the Lord.'" Both texts represent what Dale Allison calls "conditional prophecy": *if* Jerusalem welcomes Jesus, *then* God will bring her redemption. Acts 3 thus confirms Allison's exegesis of Luke 13. When Acts 3 is taken together with Acts 1:6–8 and Luke 21:24, however, it becomes clear that Israel's repentance is not merely a *sufficient* condition for the return of Jesus and the full restoration of the kingdom. If it were merely a *sufficient* condition, then Israel's resistance might never abate; Jesus would still return at his own chosen hour, and Israel would simply forfeit its kingdom blessings.[44] Acts 3:19–21 and Acts 1:6–8, taken together with Luke 21:24 (and the ascension narrative of Acts 1:9–11), demonstrate that Luke sees Israel's repentance as both a *sufficient* and a *necessary* condition for the Messiah's return: *if—and only if*—Jerusalem welcomes Jesus, will God restore "all things about which God spoke by the mouth of His holy prophets from ancient time" (Acts 3:21).

Thus, Luke 13:35 articulates a *sufficient* and *necessary* condition not only for Jerusalem's seeing God/Jesus but also for the *sending of the Messiah* (Acts 3:20). This insight enables us to form a proper judgment of Luke's purpose in his narrative of Jesus' "non-triumphal entry" to Jerusalem (Luke 19:28–40). Here Jesus' disciples offer the welcoming words of Psalm 118:26 (Luke 19:38), but the city remains silent. In light of Acts 3:19–21, the reader realizes that the conditional prophecy of Luke 13:35 remains in effect, and therefore views Jesus' descent from the Mount of Olives to the Temple Mount as a prophetic sign-act pointing to a future descent when Jerusalem will offer a more suitable welcome. This reading finds decisive confirmation in the narrative of Jesus' ascension in Acts 1:9–11, with its allusion to Zechariah 14 and Ezekiel 11 and 43.

44. Steve Smith accepts Allison's exegesis of Luke 13:35, but treats Jesus' "conditional prophecy" as depicting Jerusalem's repentance as a *sufficient* but not a *necessary* condition for the realization of God's redemptive purpose. In Luke 19, Jerusalem was given its chance to welcome Jesus, and it failed. For Smith, that is the end of the story for Jerusalem. See Steve Smith, *The Fate of the Jerusalem Temple in Luke-Acts*, 52–53.

Finally, the above network of texts shows that Luke expects his readers to take seriously the national hopes for redemption that pervade the Lukan infancy narrative (Luke 1–2). Like the mature John the Baptist himself, the characters of Luke 1–2 understand neither the *timing* nor the *means* by which the kingdom will be restored to Israel. The Messiah must first suffer, and so must Jerusalem. But in the end Jerusalem will be redeemed (Luke 2:38) and Israel will be consoled (Luke 2:25).

It only requires modest historical and theological reflection on this tight interlocking network of Lukan texts to expose the implausibility of the notion that Jews outside the *ekklēsia* forfeit their covenantal status as members of the people of Israel. Luke writes at least a generation after the death and resurrection of Jesus. He knows that Jerusalem and its temple are in ruins. He also knows that the vast majority of Jews throughout the world are ignorant of the salvation that Jesus promised. They have not believed in Jesus, received baptism, and entered the *ekklēsia.* As a result, have they all lost their right to be called *beney Yisrael*, members of the people of Israel? Are they no longer participants in the covenant? If that were the case, then all their children, grandchildren, great-grandchildren, etc., would be no more nor other than gentiles. But if that is true, who are the people whose repentance and returning fulfills the *necessary* and *sufficient* condition for the sending of the Messiah? And who are the people who will receive the kingdom that God will restore to Israel? If those who will ultimately fulfill the conditional prophecy of Luke 13 and Acts 3:19–21 are the descendants of untold generations of Jews who have not believed in Jesus, then those generations have successfully preserved and transmitted Israel's covenantal identity. After all, those who "repent" and "return" must themselves already *be* Israel in order for their repentance and returning to have eschatological significance.

This line of reasoning reinforces the exegetical arguments found earlier in the present chapter. For Luke the Jewish people remain Israel, despite their inadequate communal response to the prophetic *euangelion.*

Conclusion

Does the heavenly installation of Jesus as Messiah through resurrection entail the immediate exclusion from the covenant of those Jews who have not yet acknowledged him as their king?

Our earlier study of Jerusalem had suggested that such a conclusion was unlikely, and our examination of the speeches in Acts has confirmed that view. Furthermore, our study of the major arguments for this unlikely conclusion has revealed a serious misreading of Lukan missiology and historiography. The theme of communal Jewish opposition becomes prominent in Acts *because of Israel's enduring covenantal status, not as the basis for its nullification*. The Jewish people retain their unique position within the divine plan; the Messiah rises from the dead first for them, and his kingdom will have their beloved city as its capital. That kingdom will only come in its fullness when they are able to honor him as their appointed sovereign.

For the author/editor of Luke and Acts, God shapes the history of Israel according to God's own purposes and according to Israel's response to those purposes. Some fall (such as the Sadducean hierarchy), others rise (such as the heirs of both the apostles and Gamaliel), but Israel itself stands unbroken (Luke 2:34). While some deliver an unambiguous "no" to the *euangelion*, and others offer an unequivocal "yes," an ambivalent middle group remains. Luke and Acts hint at their significance, but those who share the theological and historiographical assumptions of the author will need to reflect further on this matter in the light of the two intervening millennia.

Before taking up this task, I will consider a topic that is as closely related to the identity of the Jewish people as the topic of the temple was to the significance of Jerusalem—namely, the Torah. Our study of the temple confirmed our conclusions regarding the city and the land. It is fitting to inquire whether the Lukan perspective on the Torah can do the same for the conclusions reached in the present chapter.

Chapter 4

The Jewish People and the Torah

Before the Jewish religious consensus was shattered in the modern era, the Torah (i.e., the Pentateuch) provided the Jewish people with its communal constitution and by-laws. Daily, weekly, and yearly patterns of life derived their structure from the Torah, and the boundaries that distinguished the Jewish community from those outside were defined by reference to its rules. Just as important, the narrative frame of the Torah shaped the Jewish worldview, tracing the ideal outlines of communal desire and hope.

I have argued in the previous chapters that the Gospel of Luke and Acts of the Apostles affirm the covenantal identity of the Jewish people and assert an eschatological hope that coheres with traditional Jewish expectation. If that is true, then these books should likewise affirm the Jewish way of life rooted in the Torah. In the present chapter, I will contend that a study of Luke and Acts reveals that such is indeed the case. As in our study of the temple, we will find that the Lukan perspective on the Torah is not a neutral factor but one that reinforces our central thesis.

That is not what the history of ecclesial exegesis of Luke and Acts would suggest. Two texts from Acts have determined the contours of that exegesis. The first text is Acts 10–11, which describes Peter's dream in which he is commanded to kill and eat non-kosher animals. This was universally interpreted as "an abrogation of ceremonial food laws and much else of the same character."[1] Peter's refusal to obey the command paints him as "vacillating," and illustrates the truth that "even the heroes

1. Bruce, *The Book of Acts*, 206.

of Acts are shown emphatically to have feet of clay."[2] If the dietary laws "which marked out the Jews from their pagan neighbors" were now "redundant," then God was "redefining Israel" and, in the process, showing that all of "the traditions which attempted to bolster Israel's national identity were out of date and out of line."[3] Peter's dream demonstrates that the Torah no longer serves as the constitution of the people of God, and the Jewish people no longer have the right to claim that national designation for themselves.

The second proof-text for the abolition of the Torah is Acts 15, a passage describing the Jerusalem Council. At this meeting the Jewish leaders of the *ekklēsia* decided that gentiles who embrace the *euangelion* of the resurrected Messiah needed neither to be circumcised nor to take on the distinctive Jewish national customs ordained in the Torah. The traditional interpretation of the official Council decree assumed as a given the demise of the Torah-observant "Jewish Church," and viewed Acts 15 as the definitive "report of how the Gentile Church is declared free from the Law."[4] In the absence of a "Jewish Church," freedom from the Torah also meant complete independence from the Jewish people—who were themselves now deemed to be separated from God and alienated from their covenantal status.

Before examining these two seminal texts, I will look at the overall message of Luke and Acts regarding the Torah. We do justice to Acts 10–11 and Acts 15 only when we read them in the broader narrative framework in which the passages are set. To discern that overall message regarding the Torah, I will focus attention on the infancy narrative of Luke, and argue that it is carefully composed to serve as an introduction to both the Gospel and Acts. The perspective of Luke and Acts on the Torah becomes clear when viewed through the lens of the infancy narrative. That perspective includes a strong affirmation of the Torah as the basis for the enduring national customs of the Jewish people, as well as the source of its eschatological hope for renewed life in the land of promise.[5]

2. Wright, *The New Testament and the People of God*, 452.

3. Wright, *Jesus and the Victory of God*, 398.

4. Conzelmann, *The Theology of St. Luke*, 212.

5. The first to challenge the existing consensus regarding Luke/Acts and the Torah was Jacob Jervell (see his *Luke and the People of God: A New Look at Luke-Acts* [1972] and *The Unknown Paul: Essays on Luke-Acts and Early Christian History* [1984]). Jervell was followed by David L. Tiede, *Prophecy and History in Luke-Acts* (1980) and *Luke* (1988); Donald Juel, *Luke-Acts: The Promise of History* (1983); Robert C.

The Infancy Narrative in Luke and Acts

One cannot read the first two chapters of Luke without noticing their emphasis on the city of Jerusalem, the temple, and the Jewish people. The main narrative occurs in or near *the city of Jerusalem*, and longing for the city's future "redemption" (2:38) animates the central characters. The story opens with a revelation to a priest in *the Jerusalem temple* (1:5–23), and returns to that holy place for prophetic announcements concerning the child-Messiah (2:22–38) and for a description of that child's coming of age (2:41–51). The salvation heralded by angelic messages and inspired songs concerns *"the people of Israel"* (1:16)—also referred to as "your people Israel" (2:32), "his servant Israel" (1:54), "the house of Jacob" (1:33), and the descendants of Abraham (1:55). The almighty sovereign who will accomplish this salvation is "the Lord God *of Israel*" (1:68).

Within such a context rich in traditional Jewish imagery, we are unsurprised to find repeated mention of obedience to *the Torah* and its commandments (1:7; 2:22–24; 2:27; 2:39). Because of that context, we are confident that these verses mentioning Torah-obedience are not incidental to the narrative but are deliberately included to enhance the Jewish texture of the chapters. Here the Torah functions as an essential mark of the Jewish people, ordering its life centered on the temple and shaping its hope toward a redeemed city and land.

What is the purpose of the traditional Jewish imagery of the Lukan infancy narrative? Is it merely a nostalgic attempt to establish continuity with the "Old Testament" and to buttress an ecclesial claim to the inheritance of Israel's promises, despite the obsolescence of city, land, people, and Torah? If that were the case, we would expect to find in the remainder of the Gospel and in the Acts of the Apostles a gradual or sudden distancing from these hallmarks of Jewish identity and hope. We have already

---

Tannehill, *The Narrative Unity of Luke-Acts: A Literary Interpretation; Volume One: The Gospel of Luke* (1986) and *Volume Two: The Acts of the Apostles* (1990); Robert L. Brawley, *Luke-Acts and the Jews* (1988); Joseph A. Fitzmyer, S.J., *Luke the Theologian: Aspects of His Teaching* (1989); Jon A. Weatherly, *Jewish Responsibility for the Death of Jesus in Luke-Acts* (1994); David Ravens, *Luke and the Restoration of Israel* (1995); William Loader, *Jesus' Attitude towards the Law: A Study of the Gospels* (1997); and Robert W. Wall, "The Acts of the Apostles," *The New Interpreters Bible, Volume X* (2002). A recent volume that continues this new tradition of Lukan scholarship is Isaac W. Oliver, *Torah Praxis After 70 CE: Reading Matthew and Luke-Acts as Jewish Texts* (2013). Oliver's work is the most thorough treatment of the topic of Torah praxis in the Lukan writings to date, and his arguments and conclusions are compelling. I will draw upon his volume extensively in the current chapter.

seen that this is not the case in regards to the city or the land, and we have argued the same concerning the Jewish people. What about the Torah?

In what follows, I will attempt to show that the presentation of the institutions and commandments of the Torah in the Lukan infancy narrative anticipate later words and events to be recounted in the Gospel and in Acts. Luke's opening chapters serve as a carefully crafted introduction to all that will follow. They are not a remote retrospective glance at the *ekklēsia*'s honored-yet-transcended Jewish origins, but instead a narrative paradigm expressing the enduring hopes and convictions of late first- or early second-century disciples of Jesus.[6]

In its Torah-perspective the infancy narrative serves as an especially effective introduction to the teaching and practice of the disciples of Jesus, particularly in Acts of the Apostles. I will demonstrate a close correlation between the language, images, and events of Luke 1–2 that deal with institutions and commandments of the Torah and their later parallels in the lives of Jesus' followers. Before doing so, however, I will examine the teaching and practice of Jesus himself in the Gospel of Luke, and show that it *coheres* with what is found in the infancy narrative. While I will only argue for *coherence* between Luke 1–2 and the teaching and practice of Jesus, I will propose a direct and intentional *correlation* between those two chapters and the teaching and practice of the disciples.

The Teaching and Practice of Jesus

The author of the Gospel of Luke acknowledges in his prologue that he relies on traditional sources for his account of the teaching and practice

6. In his chronicle and analysis of the history of critical Christian scholarship on the Lukan writings and Judaism (*Luke, Judaism, and the Scholars*), Joseph B. Tyson documents the various strategies scholars have employed to sever the tie between the Lukan infancy narrative (with its unqualified expression of Jewish particularism) and the remainder of the two volumes (with their alleged theme of Pauline universalism). Tyson's treatment of the work of Ferdinand Christian Baur (24–26) and Hans Conzelmann (83–85) is especially revealing on this point. Tyson also underlines the significance of an article by Paul S. Minear ("Luke's Use of the Birth Stories") in refuting the thesis of a radical disjunction between the infancy narratives and the Lukan writings as a whole. Minear argues in compelling fashion that interpreters must "recognize the degree to which the mood and motifs initiated in the prologue continue to characterize the later narratives. . . . [T]he first two chapters of the Gospel 'set the stage' for all subsequent speeches and actions" (129, 130). In the section that follows, I will support Minear's contention with reference to one aspect of the infancy narratives, namely, the role of the Torah.

of Jesus (Luke 1:1–4). That fact is confirmed by material that the book shares with Mark and Matthew. Since those traditional sources were widely known in the Jesus-movement, the author has less compositional discretion in his gospel than in Acts.

Nevertheless, the distinct viewpoint of the author becomes evident through material unique to his gospel, and through redactional details that distinguish his narrative from that of Mark or Matthew. In what follows, I will show that these features render his account of the Torah teaching and practice of Jesus fully coherent with the perspective of the Lukan infancy narrative.

Supplementing, not Cancelling, the Torah

While Jesus refers to the Torah on a number of occasions in Luke, he rarely makes general statements about the Torah itself. The primary exception to this rule is found in Luke 16:16–18:

> 16 The law and the prophets were in effect until John came; since then the good news of the kingdom of God is proclaimed, and everyone tries to enter it by force. 17 But it is easier for heaven and earth to pass away, than for one stroke of a letter in the law to be dropped. 18 Anyone who divorces his wife and marries another commits adultery, and whoever marries a woman divorced from her husband commits adultery.

Many scholars treat verse 16 as the key to Luke's overall scheme of history.[7] In line with the NRSV translation above, they interpret the verse as meaning that the Torah is no longer "in effect." Of course, verse 17 then becomes highly problematic. The extreme measures resorted to by some commentators to resolve this predicament are typified by the following interpretation given to verse 17 by G. B. Caird, the teacher of N. T. Wright:

> It is not so clear what Luke believed to be the meaning of the second saying. It has usually been taken to mean that, although Jesus made the Law obsolete as a religious system and abrogated many of its ritual commandments, its great moral principles remained unchanged. But it is doubtful whether this sense can

7. The most influential of these scholars has been Hans Conzelmann. In his words, "Luke xvi, 16 provides the key to the topography of redemptive history" (*Theology of St. Luke*, 23).

> be got from the text. The word translated "*dot*" [NRSV "stroke"] really means a serif or ornamental flourish added to a letter, and to say that not a serif of the Law can become void is to say that the whole Law, word for word and letter for letter, with all its minutiae and all its rabbinic embellishments, remains valid in perpetuity. Any rabbi might have said this, but we cannot imagine it on the lips of Jesus. . . . This being so, the simplest expedient is to regard the saying as an ironical attack on the pedantic conservatism of the scribes: it was easier for heaven and earth to pass away than for the scribes to surrender that scrupulosity which could not see the Law for the letters.[8]

Caird acknowledges that traditional attempts to understand verse 17 in terms of verse 16 (the latter being read as a statement of the Torah's obsolescence) are unconvincing. Verse 17 speaks with unmistakable clarity about the Torah as a seamless garment, authoritative in all its "minutiae" (though Caird's reference here to "rabbinic embellishments" is an anachronism). Unwilling to consider the possibility that verse 16 should instead be understood in terms of verse 17, Caird advances an interpretation of verse 17 in which Jesus ironically means the *exact opposite* of what he says. This may be the best that can be done by those who "cannot imagine" such a saying, taken in its straightforward sense, "on the lips of Jesus." But perhaps what is needed here is less exegetical ingenuity and a more expansive imagination.

If we expound verse 16 in light of verse 17 rather than the reverse, the exegetical results are more satisfying. We are aided here by the Greek text, which contains nothing to correspond to the NRSV's explanatory phrase "in effect." The Greek simply says "the law and the prophets were until John." For Luke, the work and teaching of Jesus inaugurates a new era in the life of the people of God, in which "the good news of the kingdom of God is proclaimed." The Lukan Jesus refers to the former era by the phrase "the law and the prophets." Elsewhere in Luke, we read that "the law of Moses and the prophets and the psalms" all point forward to the coming of Jesus the Messiah (e.g., Luke 24:27, 44–5). The distinction in eras thus relates especially to the prophetic dimension of scripture, as Matthew's version of Jesus' saying makes explicit: "For all the prophets and the law *prophesied* until John came" (Matt 11:13; emphasis added). However, as verse 17 indicates, the normative function of "the Law of Moses and the prophets" for Israel's way of life remains "in effect."

8. Caird, *The Gospel of St. Luke*, 191–92.

While the Torah loses none of its commanding force, the new era inaugurated by Jesus and embodied communally in his *ekklēsia* radicalizes and re-centers the Torah's demands. This accords with the interpretation of Joseph Fitzmyer: "[T]he sense of Luke 16:16b has to be that Jesus' kingdom-preaching is a *supplement* to the law and the prophets of the Period of Israel. Now in the Period of Jesus, when he appears in the Lucan Gospel as the kingdom-preacher par excellence, he views the law and the prophets as normative, and his preaching of the kingdom is *supplemental* to it."[9] The notion of "supplement" captures well Luke's intent. The work and teaching of Jesus *adds* something decisive to the Torah but does not *subtract* from it. This clarifies Luke's understanding of Jesus' prohibition of divorce, cited in the verse that follows (v. 18). Here Jesus *adds* to the Torah by intensifying its stringency.[10] What Jesus adds is not a *new law* but the gift of the Holy Spirit which will enable Israel to obey the true intent of the Torah given at Sinai in the way that Jesus himself does. From this perspective, Jesus is the supplement in his own person—and, accordingly, the re-centering of the Torah around him and his teaching does not merely lay an additional brick on an inert structure but re-orders the entire building. At the same time, the building itself and its constituent materials remain intact.

Torah, the Two Great Commandments, and Eternal Life

The normative function of the Torah features prominently in the Parable of the Rich Man and Lazarus, which Luke places next in his narrative (Luke 16:19–31). The rich man of the parable suffers torment in "Hades" as punishment for his indifference to the needy. He asks Abraham to send the poor man Lazarus—now exalted to Abraham's side—to warn his family of what awaits them if they imitate the conduct of their deceased relative. This sets the stage for the climactic interaction of the parable's

9. Fitzmyer, *Luke the Theologian*, 182 (emphasis added). Fitzmyer accepts Conzelmann's view that Luke divides history into three eras, that of Israel, Jesus, and the church, but he rejects Conzelman's assertion that the Torah is nullified in the era of the church: "the Mosaic Law continues for Luke to be a valid norm of human conduct in all three periods of salvation history and also as a means of identifying God's people" (176).

10. As William Loader states, "In the Lukan context the point is to say that, despite the new age of the kingdom, the Torah still applies and that this is evident in the instance of Jesus' exposition of marriage law which Jesus applies in the strictest possible terms." (Loader, *Jesus' Attitude towards the Law*, 337).

final verses: "Abraham replied, 'They have Moses and the prophets; they should listen to them.' He said, 'No, father Abraham; but if someone goes to them from the dead, they will repent.' He said to him, 'If they do not listen to Moses and the prophets, neither will they be convinced even if someone rises from the dead'" (Luke 16:29–31). Abraham indicates that Israel's scripture provides sufficient guidance to enable the rich man's family to avoid future punishment. The Torah requires generosity to the poor, and the rich man himself should have known what awaited him. Abraham then asserts that the appearance of a resurrected messenger will carry no weight for the family of the rich man if they are not already attentive to the commands and promises of the Torah and the prophets. As in Luke 16:16 and the conversation between Jesus and the disciples on the road to Emmaus (Luke 24:13–32), the Torah and the prophets here point to Jesus as the crucified and resurrected Messiah. More significant for the parable, however, and for our purposes in this chapter, Abraham's words echo the message of Luke 16:17: *the practical demands of the Torah remain foundational to Israel's way of life*. Far from negating or supplanting the Torah, the life to which the resurrected Jesus summons his disciples is only comprehensible in terms of that same Torah. If the family of the rich man desires eternal life, they need only follow what is written in the Torah.

Jesus enunciated this teaching earlier in Luke's Gospel when responding to the question of a lawyer (*nomikos*; i.e., an expert in the Torah).

> [25] Just then a lawyer stood up to test Jesus. "Teacher," he said, "what must I do to inherit eternal life?" [26] He said to him, "What is written in the law? What do you read there?" [27] He answered, "You shall love the Lord your God with all your heart, and with all your soul, and with all your strength, and with all your mind; and your neighbor as yourself." [28] And he said to him, "You have given the right answer; do this, and you will live." (Luke 10:25–28)

This passage in Luke resembles a story in Mark and Matthew that occurs in Jerusalem the week before Jesus' crucifixion. According to Mark and Matthew, the incident begins with a different question from a scribe (*grammateus*; Mark 12:28) or lawyer (*nomikos*; Matt 22:35): "Which commandment in the law is the greatest?" (Matt 22:36). In Mark and Matthew, the question is posed as an academic inquiry concerning the ranking of the *mitzvot*, and it is the inquirer who raises the topic of the Torah. In contrast, Luke's lawyer initiates the discussion with the existential question also posed by the rich ruler of Luke 18:18, and it is Jesus rather than the inquirer who brings up the topic of the Torah. In response to both the ruler and the lawyer, Jesus indicates that the way to enter the life of the coming age is to obey the commandments of the Torah (Luke 10:28b: "Do this, and you will live"). Thus, whereas Mark and Matthew include only one passage in which the existential issue of eternal life is addressed by reference to the commandments of the Torah (i.e., the story of the rich ruler), Luke has three: the story of the inquiring lawyer (Luke 10:25–28), the story of the rich ruler (Luke 18:18–39), and the Parable of the Rich Man and Lazarus (Luke 16:19–31).[11]

However, the lawyer of Luke 10:25–28 is not satisfied. He now shifts the discussion away from the existential sphere to the academic, asking, in regards to the second of the great commandments, "And who is my neighbor?" (Luke 10:29). This elicits from Jesus the Parable of the Good Samaritan, which offers no answer to the lawyer's academic question but instead returns the discussion to the existential level of his initial query. The parable mentions the familial-tribal status of the potential actors (priest, Levite, Samaritan) who must decide whether they will obey the commandment to love their neighbor, but leaves undisclosed the status of the recipient of their action (i.e., the wounded traveler). In a narrative twist typical of Jesus' parables, the man whose Israelites status is ambiguous by Jewish standards is the one who fulfills the commandment. "Go and do likewise" (Luke 10:37), says Jesus to the lawyer. In other words, the most basic question is who *you* are, not who *they* are. Concentrate first on *living as a neighbor* (i.e., as a true Israelite) to those around you rather than on analyzing their precise status. Then you will fulfill the commandment, and attain eternal life.

As noted above, Luke formulates his version of the story dealing with the two great commandments in a way that connects it to the story of the rich ruler. Both begin with a question concerning the path to eternal life. The first story provides the general answer: obey the Torah, as

11. See Loader, *Jesus' Attitude towards the Law*, 345: "In two accounts Luke's Jesus responds to the fundamental question: what must I do to inherit eternal life? On both occasions Jesus points to the Law. In 10:25–28 he points to the commandment to love God and one's neighbor and proceeds to expound the latter in the parable of the Good Samaritan. In 18:18–23 he points to the ethical commandments of the decalogue. Both passages make such adherence to Torah crucial. The same is assumed in the parable of Lazarus and the rich man (16:19–31 [esp. v. 31]). All three accounts imply a close connection between obeying the Law's demands and responding to the demands of Jesus."

summarized in the commandments to love God and neighbor. It then focuses on the latter of these commandments, which constitutes the practical obstacle in the way of the lawyer's attaining what he ostensibly desires. The second story offers the same general response: "You know the commandments" (Luke 18:20). Jesus then lists the imperatives of the second table of the Decalogue, which deal with human relationships. The ruler replies that he has observed all these since he was young (Luke 18:21). Jesus then issues the call to discipleship. "When Jesus heard this, he said to him, 'There is still one thing lacking. Sell all that you own and distribute the money to the poor, and you will have treasure in heaven; then come, follow me.' But when he heard this, he became sad; for he was very rich" (Luke 18:22–23). Jesus does not challenge the veracity of the ruler's claim to have obeyed the commandments of the "second table," but instead summons him now to obey also the commandments of the "first table," which deal with divine worship. As Jesus says elsewhere, "you cannot serve God and mammon" (Luke 16:13). Thus, this second story concerning qualifications for the life of the coming age focuses on the commandment to love God with all one's heart, soul, and strength, just as the first story focused on the commandment to love one's neighbor. Reinforcing this interpretation are the words of Jesus that introduce his call to discipleship: "There is still *one thing* lacking." This alludes to the words of the *Shema* (Deut 6:4) which are inseparable from the first commandment (Deut 6:5).

That Luke has the latter story of the rich ruler in mind as he tells of Jesus' conversation with the lawyer is confirmed by the verses that immediately follow the Parable of the Good Samaritan. There Luke recounts the visit of Jesus to the house of Martha and Mary (Luke 10:38–42). Martha's diligence in practical service manifests her obedience to the commandment of neighbor-love, which Jesus had emphasized in his instruction to the lawyer. Similarly, Mary's determination to remain in Jesus' presence and learn from his teaching manifests her love of God. When Jesus tells Martha that "there is need of only *one thing*," we have a preview of what Jesus will say to the rich ruler, and another allusion to the words of the *Shema*. To follow Jesus is to fulfill the commandment to love God with all one's heart, soul, and strength. Thus, the two stories of Luke 10:25–42 should be viewed as a unit that comments on the commandments of the Torah as the path that leads to eternal life.

Luke's special concern for the two great commandments appears again in the midst of his account of Jesus' rebuke of the Pharisees: "But woe to you, Pharisees! For you tithe mint and rue and herbs of all kinds, and neglect justice and the love of God; it is these you ought to have practiced, without neglecting the others" (Luke 11:42). Matthew's version of this saying has the Pharisees neglecting "justice and mercy and faith" (perhaps an allusion to Micah 6:8). Luke includes only two neglected duties, and the description of the second of them as "the love of God" suggests that the first (i.e., "justice") should be seen as equivalent to the love of neighbor. Like Matthew, Luke refuses to set these commandments in opposition to the ritual minutiae of the Torah; Jesus here urges obedience to *all* the commandments. He does, however, fault his Pharisaic critics for their inability to see the forest for the trees.

Repentance

Luke also shows his high regard for the Torah by portraying Jesus as a preacher of repentance. This theme plays a prominent role in Jewish thought, and always refers to an attitudinal *and* behavioral change defined in relation to the commandments of the Torah.

Therefore, when we discover in Luke not only an emphasis on the commandments as the path to life but also a preoccupation with the theme of repentance, we should view the latter as an expression of the former.

As E. P. Sanders has noted, "repentance has a prominence in Luke that it does not have in Matthew and Mark."[12] This distinction among the Gospels appears in striking fashion when Jesus, having been criticized by Pharisees for eating with sinners, describes the shape of his mission. According to Mark and Matthew, Jesus says "I have come to call not the righteous but sinners" (Mark 2:17; Matt 9:13). These words could be construed as meaning only that Jesus summons sinners to join his company. However, Luke's version of the saying includes an additional explanatory phrase: "I have come to call not the righteous but sinners *to repentance*" (5:32; emphasis added). Luke makes explicit what remains at best implicit in the other Gospels: to follow Jesus, sinners must repent and reorient their lives to the commandments of God.

Further emphasizing this point, Luke features an entire chapter devoted to the theme of repentance (Luke 15). The chapter begins with the same criticism of Jesus by the Pharisees as seen in Luke 5:30: "And

12. Sanders, *The Historical Figure of Jesus*, 231.

the Pharisees and the scribes were grumbling and saying, 'This fellow welcomes sinners and eats with them'" (15:2). Jesus proceeds to tell three parables. The first parable focuses on the activity of a shepherd searching for a lost sheep, and the second depicts a woman hunting for a lost coin. Neither parable speaks directly about repentance (i.e., an activity that, in the narrative world of these parables, would have been undertaken by the sheep and the coin). Yet, each parable concludes with a description of the heavenly celebration that greets the *repentance* of a sinner (vv. 7 and 10). Divine grace seizes the initiative, but apparently the lost sheep and coin must somehow let themselves be found. The final parable (i.e., that of the prodigal son and his older brother) deals more directly with the theme of repentance. As noted in our previous chapter, this parable also performs a crucial function in conveying the distinctive Lukan perspective on the Pharisees. Jesus calls *all* to repentance and the heavenly banquet— Pharisees (represented by the older brother) along with prodigals.

Luke's treatment of the complex rhythm of divine and human initiative inherent in the act of repentance also finds vivid expression in the story of Zacchaeus. This tax collector takes great pains to catch a glimpse of Jesus, and Jesus responds by choosing to stay at his house (Luke 19:1–6). At this point, the chorus of criticism reported in Luke 5:30 and 15:2 reappears: "All who saw it began to grumble and said, 'He has gone to be the guest of one who is a sinner'" (Luke 19:7). Zacchaeus welcomes Jesus with joy, and then acts in a manner that establishes him as a Lukan paradigm of repentance: "Zacchaeus stood there and said to the Lord, 'Look, half of my possessions, Lord, I will give to the poor; and if I have defrauded anyone of anything, I will pay back four times as much'" (Luke 19:8). As E. P. Sanders notes, Zacchaeus here fulfills the basic requirement of the Torah, but also goes beyond it: "Zacchaeus offered a lot more than the law requires, which is that a person who defrauds another should repay him, add 20 percent as a fine, and then sacrifice a ram as a guilt offering (Lev 6.1–7). A person who did this, and who did not return to his former life, was no longer wicked."[13] As in all forms of Judaism, Luke shows that repentance requires concrete action, and that such action must be shaped by the commandments of the Torah. While the Torah still provides the normative template for repentance, Luke assumes that a generous penitent will transcend the Torah's minimal demands.

13. Sanders, *Historical Figure of* Jesus, 230.

The connection between the Torah and repentance is likewise underlined in the Parable of the Rich Man and Lazarus discussed above. The rich man asks Abraham to send Lazarus to his family to persuade them to adopt a different way of life so they might escape the judgment that has befallen him. Abraham replies, "They have Moses and the prophets; they should listen to them" (Luke 16:29). Unsatisfied, the rich man argues that "if someone goes to them from the dead, they will repent" (Luke 16:30). He deems the Torah and the prophets insufficient to motivate or shape a repentant response. Abraham disagrees: "If they do not listen to Moses and the prophets, neither will they be convinced even if someone rises from the dead" (Luke 16:31). The way of repentance proclaimed by Jesus is not a substitute for the message of the Torah, but its fullest and most powerful embodiment. Those unaffected by the sovereign claims of the Torah will likewise ignore the words of the resurrected Messiah.

The Jewish "Customs" Given by the Torah

The commandments of the Torah that we have shown to be central to Jesus' teaching in Luke concern matters such as the prohibitions of idolatry (the rich ruler) and defrauding others of their goods (Zacchaeus), and the injunctions to help the poor (the rich man and Lazarus) and care for the afflicted (the good Samaritan). These are all practical expressions of the two commandments of love, which summarize the demands of the Torah as the path to life (the question of the lawyer). As for the "sinners" who flock to Jesus and who are despised by his pious critics, and who are represented in parable form by the prodigal son, we may assume that repentance includes turning from "dissolute living" (Luke 15:13; see 15:30) and obeying the Torah's commandments regarding marriage and sexual relations. For critics from the party of the Pharisees, on the other hand, who appear in the parable as the prodigal's elder brother, repentance will mean surrendering their judgmental attitude and learning to celebrate the return of many prodigals.

These concerns coincide with what we learn about Jesus in the other Gospels. For this Galilean prophet, "mercy" is more important than "sacrifice" (Matt 9:13; 12:7), "love" than "ritual." However, we have also encountered the following saying of Jesus: "But it is easier for heaven and earth to pass away, than for one stroke of a letter in the law to be dropped" (Luke 16:17). As G. B. Caird noted, these words resist an interpretation that divides the Torah into "moral" (i.e., permanently valid) and "ritual" (i.e., now obsolete) commandments. Likewise, we have examined Jesus' rebuke of Pharisaic Torah practice: "But woe to you, Pharisees! For you tithe mint and rue and herbs of all kinds, and neglect justice and the love of God; it is these you ought to have practiced, *without neglecting the others*" (Luke 11:42). Jesus here condemns the observance of ritual minutiae rooted in the Torah when such observance is severed from "justice" and "the love of God"—but he commends those ritual practices when they are part of an integral obedience to the Torah in its fullness.

How does Luke present the teaching and practice of Jesus in regard to those commandments of the Torah that are particular to Israel's vocation as a distinct people? To answer this question, we should begin with the Jewish institution that occupies a privileged position in the Torah and that all the Gospels recognize as a point of contention between Jesus and his critics, namely, the Sabbath. The Gospels provide a unified witness to Jesus' practice of healing on the Sabbath and to the controversy that this practice evoked. How does Luke present Jesus' understanding of the Sabbath? Does Jesus heal on the Sabbath in order to demonstrate his inauguration of a new era in which such "ritual" prescriptions have been transcended or relativized?

After Jesus has been baptized in the Jordan River by John, and has fasted for forty days in the wilderness of Judaea, he returns to Galilee to begin his public mission. All three of the Synoptic Gospels introduce this new phase of Jesus' life with a generalized description of his activity. Mark and Matthew focus on his "proclaiming" the kingdom of God.

> Now after John was arrested, Jesus came to Galilee, proclaiming the good news of God, and saying, "The time is fulfilled, and the kingdom of God has come near; repent, and believe in the good news." (Mark 1:14–15)

> Now when Jesus heard that John had been arrested, he withdrew to Galilee. He left Nazareth and made his home in Capernaum. . . . From that time Jesus began to proclaim, "Repent, for the kingdom of heaven has come near." (Matt 4:12, 13a, 17)

Luke's introductory description differs from that of Mark and Matthew, including elements that express his distinctive concerns: "Then Jesus, filled with the power of the Spirit, returned to Galilee, and a report about him spread through all the surrounding country. He began to teach in their synagogues and was praised by everyone" (Luke 4:14–15). Luke speaks of Jesus' "teaching" (an act associated with Torah) rather than "proclaiming," and the location of his pedagogical activity is the synagogue. Elsewhere in Luke, Jesus' "teaching in the synagogue" is explicitly identified as a Sabbath practice (Luke 4:31, 33; 6:6; 13:10), and we may assume that a Sabbath reference is implicit in Luke's introduction to Jesus' Galilean mission. Thus, alone among the Gospels, Luke begins by characterizing Jesus' central activity as *teaching*, identifying the characteristic location of that activity as the *synagogue*, and implicitly pointing to the *Sabbath* as the archetypical time in which that activity took place.[14]

The opening event in Galilee narrated by Mark and Matthew involves the calling of Jesus' first disciples. Luke diverges from that chronology, beginning instead with two events that both occur in a *synagogue* on a *Sabbath*. The first of these is of signal importance to Luke, as it conveys at the outset of Jesus' public mission his fundamental understanding of that mission. The unit begins as follows: "When he came to Nazareth, where he had been brought up, he went to the synagogue on the Sabbath day, as was his custom (*kata to eiōthos autō*)" (Luke 4:16). The phrase "as was his custom" is particularly noteworthy.[15] Luke stresses that Jesus made a habit of worshipping in the synagogue on the Sabbath. Since this habitual behavior is noted in reference to his conduct in "Nazareth, where he had been brought up," readers are to presume that such Sabbath observance characterized the entirety of Jesus' life, both before and after his baptism.

In describing Jesus' "custom" of Sabbath observance and synagogue attendance, Luke employs a Greek construction that appears often in his work to convey a particular message: "the preposition *kata* followed by a noun in the accusative frequently appears in Luke-Acts in contexts that . . . emphasize the fidelity of Jesus and his followers to Jewish custom."[16] In other words, Jesus' *personal* "custom" conformed to the *communal* "custom" of the Jewish people rooted in the Torah. Moreover, Luke often describes Torah practices intended specifically for the Jewish people with the plural nominal form (*ethē*, "customs") of the Greek verb translated

14. Chance, *Jerusalem, the Temple, and the New Age in Luke-Acts*, 59.

15. Luke uses the same phrase to characterize Paul's habitual synagogue attendance (Acts 17:1–2), presumably also on the Sabbath day (see Acts 13:14). See pp. 180–81 later in this chapter.

16. Oliver, *Torah Praxis after 70 CE*, 72. For Oliver's list of the texts in Luke-Acts that employ this construction with this purpose, see 72–73n86.

here as "his custom."[17] Luke does not use this term, as we moderns might employ its English equivalent, as a way of minimizing the normative authority behind such practices (i.e., merely *human* customs as opposed to *divinely* given patterns of life). Instead, he uses this term to distinguish commandments of the Torah applicable only to the Jewish people from those which are universally binding (i.e., applicable also to the gentiles). While directed only to Jews, the former are still divine *commandments*, as is seen in another *kata* phrase found near the end of the Gospel: "On the Sabbath they rested *according to the commandment* [*kata tēn entolēn*]" (Luke 23:56).[18]

Having established the typical character of the event, Luke now portrays Jesus as taking a central role in the worship of his home synagogue. "He stood up to read, and the scroll of the prophet Isaiah was given to him" (Luke 4:16b–17). We are not told whether Jesus selected this particular prophetic text, or if it had been determined in some fashion by his community. In either case, Jesus views the passage he will read (Isa 61:1–2a) as emblematic of the mission he now inaugurates:

> 18 'The Spirit of the Lord is upon me,
> because he has anointed me
> to bring good news to the poor.
> He has sent me to proclaim release [*aphesin*] to the captives
> and recovery of sight to the blind,
> to let the oppressed go free [*en aphesei*],
> 19 to proclaim the year of the Lord's favor.'

Isaiah here depicts the prophetic mission of the servant of the Lord by employing the imagery of the Jubilee year, in which slaves are freed, debts are remitted, and land is restored.[19] The Jubilee occurs every forty-nine years, and functions as a sabbatical year of sabbatical years. Thus, the principle taking effect in the Jubilee year is that of the Sabbath day, in which Jews remember their slavery in Egypt and display to their families,

17. Luke 1:9; 2:42; 6:14; 15:1; 21:21; 28:17.

18. "[T]he fact that the law is for the most part limited to Jews does not suggest that Luke believes it is not of divine origin . . . rather, the God of Israel had intended the law in its entirety to apply to Jews alone, with only specific laws applying to Gentiles. . . The circumscribed application of the law in no way entails its diminishment" (Thiessen, *Contesting Conversion*, 124).

19. The Greek word *aphesis*, found twice in the Isaiah verses cited by Luke, is the technical term in the Septuagint for the Jubilee year (LXX Lev 25:10–13, 28, 30–31, 33, 40–41, 50, 52, 54; 27:17–18, 21, 23–24; Num 36:4). It is also used to refer to the sabbatical year (LXX Exod 23:11; Deut 15:1–3, 9; 31:10).

servants, and domestic animals the same mercy God showed them when he released them from bondage (e.g., Deut 5:14–15). This is the liberating mercy that Jesus proclaims and manifests in his message of repentance and forgiveness (*aphesis*) and in his work of healing, which Luke sees primarily in terms of liberation from demonic forces.[20]

This constellation of texts and images illuminates the multiple levels of meaning in Jesus' comment on Isaiah 61: "Today this scripture has been fulfilled in your hearing" (Luke 4:21). The "Spirit of the Lord" came upon Jesus at his baptism (Luke 3:22), led him into the wilderness (Luke 4:1), and empowered him as he returned to Galilee (Luke 4:14). The purpose of this "anointing" with the Spirit was so that Jesus might accomplish the task enunciated in Isaiah 61. The task is only just beginning, but the "anointing" has already taken place; the one feature of the prophetic mission detailed in Isaiah 61 that is described in the past tense has now been "fulfilled" in Jesus. The time has come for him to "fulfill" the task itself, and that task entails "fulfilling" the meaning of the Jubilee year, which is also the meaning of the Sabbath day: to set free the captives and bring them into their inheritance of rest. Thus, what better way to inaugurate the fulfillment of that task than to read Isaiah 61 in the synagogue on the Sabbath?

As noted above, Luke has departed from the Markan chronology by inserting this Sabbath episode before the calling of the first disciples. He further departs from that chronology in the unit that follows by proceeding directly to Jesus' teaching and healing in the Capernaum synagogue on another Sabbath (Luke 4:31–37). In the Gospel of Mark, Jesus begins his Galilean mission by calling disciples, and then afterwards teaches and heals in the synagogue. In the Gospel of Luke, the calling of the first disciples is delayed until after these two Sabbath synagogue scenes, in which Jesus first announces what he has come to do (i.e., bring a sabbatical release to the captives), and then begins doing it (i.e., freeing a man from the oppressive power of an unclean demon). In this way, Luke further highlights the significance of the Sabbath and the traditional Jewish mode of honoring the day by gathering together for the reading of

20. "Luke seems to think that diseases generally originate from demonic sources. . . . [R]eference to demonic origins, which are responsible for human suffering, plays an integral role in Luke's attempt to justify Jesus' need to intervene on the Sabbath on behalf of the oppressed children of Israel. Demonic cruelty demands immediate divine intervention, making it lawful for Jesus to do good and save life on the Sabbath (Luke 6:9)" (Oliver, *Torah Praxis after 70 CE*, 60, 64).

Scripture. In his teaching and healing on the Sabbath, Jesus fulfills both the words of Scripture and the sabbatical institutions founded by those words.

Controversy over Jesus' approach to the Sabbath only emerges later in the narrative. Luke's perception of this controversy becomes clear in an episode found only in his Gospel.

> [10] Now he was teaching in one of the synagogues on the sabbath. [11] And just then there appeared a woman with a spirit that had crippled her for eighteen years. She was bent over and was quite unable to stand up straight. [12] When Jesus saw her, he called her over and said, "Woman, you are set free [*apo-lelusai*] from your ailment." [13] When he laid his hands on her, immediately she stood up straight and began praising God. [14] But the leader of the synagogue, indignant because Jesus had cured on the sabbath, kept saying to the crowd, "There are six days on which work ought to be done; come on those days and be cured, and not on the sabbath day." [15] But the Lord answered him and said, "You hypocrites! Does not each of you on the sabbath untie [*luei*] his ox or his donkey from the manger, and lead it away to give it water? [16] And ought not this woman, a daughter of Abraham whom Satan bound for eighteen long years, be set free [*lythēnai*] from this bondage on the sabbath day?' [17] When he said this, all his opponents were put to shame; and the entire crowd was rejoicing at all the wonderful things that he was doing. (Luke 13:10–17)

Jesus does not defend his action by nullifying the laws of the Sabbath but by alluding to the Torah's injunctions to free "your ox or your donkey" from burdens on the Sabbath (Deut 5:14) and to "remember that you were a slave in the land of Egypt, and the LORD your God brought you out from there" (Deut 5:15). Jesus tells this "daughter of Abraham," who had been "bound" by Satan, that she has now been "set free." Luke here portrays Jesus as bringing a messianic liberation that completes the redemptive purpose of the exodus, thereby also fulfilling the intent of the Sabbath. Far from relativizing the Sabbath, Luke actually underlines its messianic significance as a fundamental institution of Jewish life.

The Sabbath was the most important of Israel's "customs" commanded in the Torah. Of similar weight, and linked in various ways to the Sabbath, were the laws associated with the Jerusalem temple. As we will see later in this chapter, Luke shows intense concern for these laws in his infancy narrative (Luke 1–2) and in Acts of the Apostles. But how does he portray Jesus' own approach to the temple and its "customs"?

Following the pattern of Mark and Matthew, and in contrast to John, Luke tells his readers nothing of Jesus' adult experience in Jerusalem before his arrival in the capital a week before his death. Luke does, however, narrate a revealing incident that occurs on Jesus' journey to Jerusalem. Entering a village near Samaria, Jesus encounters ten lepers who seek his help (Luke 17:11–13). He responds by commanding them to show themselves to the priests (Luke 17:14a). According to the laws of the Torah, a leper would only do this *after* being healed (Lev 14:1–32). In the earlier story of the healing of a leper (Luke 5:12–16), which is also found in Mark and Matthew, Jesus commands the man to go to a priest subsequent to his healing. In this later story, unique to Luke, Jesus demands more from his petitioners: they are to put faith in his word, and to set out on their journey to the priest with the confidence that they will be healed en route. It is their obedience to Jesus' command that leads to their healing, but the story *presumes* that the action the lepers are commanded to undertake is one that would be obligatory for a person healed of this disease. The point of the story is the obedience of faith shown by the ten lepers, and (even more) the gratitude shown by the Samaritan who returned to Jesus after the healing "to give praise to God" (Luke 17:15–19). But the drama of the narrative depends upon an assumption shared by its author, readers, and characters that the priestly customs ordained by the Torah are sacred duties for all the children of Abraham (Jews and Samaritans alike).

Assuming that Luke is familiar with the Gospel of Mark, and utilizes that volume in order to structure his own narrative, it is also instructive to attend to incidents or narrative details that are present in Mark and *absent* in Luke. Apart from the laws of the Sabbath and the temple, no distinctive "customs" were more essential to Jewish life than the dietary laws. The Gospel of Mark describes a controversy between Jesus and the Pharisees over the ritual washing of hands and "the tradition of the elders' (Mark 7:1–23). In responding to the criticism of the Pharisees (v. 5), Jesus finds fault with the way these critics use their tradition to evade the commandments of the Torah (vv. 6–13). Mark then provides an editorial aside which has been taken by past commentators to entail an abolition of the Torah's dietary laws (v. 19b). Matthew follows Mark in his telling of this story, but he deletes the Markan aside; this fits with Matthew's polemical treatment of the Pharisees, and his unswerving devotion to the Torah. Luke, on the other hand, deletes the entire episode from his narrative. Like Matthew, he wants to avoid the slightest implication that Jesus undermined the Jewish way of life given in the Torah. Adopting a more irenic posture toward the Pharisees and their tradition than does Matthew, Luke also wants to avoid the implication that Jesus attacked even the Jewish "customs" that were rooted in the Torah but not explicitly taught there.[21]

In conclusion, we have seen that the Gospel of Luke presents Jesus as a Torah-faithful Jew in both his teaching and his practice. The Lukan Jesus considers adherence to the commandments to be the way to eternal life, and summons all who hear him to repentance in response to the Torah. While focusing upon the two great commandments of loving God and neighbor, and supplementing the Torah by demanding an even more radical conformity to its inner intent, the Lukan Jesus also honors the distinctive Jewish institutions of the Sabbath and the temple, and shows no discomfort with basic Jewish customs rooted in the Torah such as the dietary laws. Thus, there is nothing in Luke's portrayal of the Torah teaching and practice of Jesus that conflicts with the picture painted in the infancy narrative. Their coherence is evident.

As regards the Torah teaching and practice of Jesus' disciples and its relationship to the infancy narrative, *coherence* is too weak a term. Here we will insist on *intentional correlation.*

The Teaching and Practice of Jesus' Disciples

Kata ton Nomon

Before considering how the *content* of Luke's infancy narrative anticipates the Torah teaching and practice of Jesus' disciples, I will examine a stylistic idiom related to Torah-observance that is central to the infancy narrative. This idiom is repeated later in Luke and Acts in describing the Torah-observance of both Jesus and his disciples, and serves as a stylistic clue to the function of the infancy narrative in relation to the rest of Luke and Acts.

21. "The important section in Mark 7:1–23, dealing with ritual cleanliness, is missing in Luke. . . . Luke does not offer any criticism concerning the rejection of God's commandments 'in order to maintain the tradition of men' (Mark 7:8; Matt. 15:3ff.). Luke, on the contrary, asserts that the 'customs from the fathers' are in harmony with the law (Acts 6:14; 21:21; 28:17, cf. 10:14ff.; 11:3, 8)" (Jervell, *Luke and the People of God*, 139–40).

In my earlier discussion of Jesus' "custom" of observing the Sabbath by worshipping with his community in the synagogue, I cited the comment of Isaac Oliver that "the preposition *kata* ['according to'] followed by a noun in the accusative frequently appears in Luke-Acts in contexts that . . . emphasize the fidelity of Jesus and his followers to Jewish custom." This usage is most pronounced in the infancy narrative:

> . . . he [Zechariah] was chosen by lot, according to the custom of the priesthood [*kata to ethos tēs hierateias*], to enter the sanctuary of the Lord and offer incense. (1:9)
>
> When the time came for their purification according to the law of Moses [*kata ton nomon Mōuseōs*], they brought him up to Jerusalem to present him to the Lord (as it is written in the law of the Lord [*kathōs gegraptai en nomō kuriou*], "Every firstborn male shall be designated as holy to the Lord"), and they offered a sacrifice according to what is stated in the law of the Lord [*kata to eirēmenon en tō nomō kuriou*], "a pair of turtledoves or two young pigeons." (2:22–24)
>
> Guided by the Spirit, Simeon came into the temple; and when the parents brought in the child Jesus, to do for him what was customary under the law [*kata to eithismenon tou nomou*] . . . (2:27)
>
> When they had finished everything required by the law of the Lord [*panta ta kata ton nomon kuriou*], they returned to Galilee . . . (2:39)
>
> And when he was twelve years old, they went up as usual [*kata to ethos*] for the festival. (2:42)

All of these texts speak of what have traditionally been called "ritual" elements of the Torah. Sometimes Luke refers to them as "customs" (*ethos/ethē*), sometimes simply as "the law," and sometimes he combines the two terms (as in 2:27). As noted above, Luke does not employ the word "custom" to minimize the normative character of the practices in question but to identify them as distinctive covenantal rites required only of Jews.

As we have seen, Luke uses this Greek construction when describing Jesus' Sabbath appearance in the synagogue at Nazareth: "When he came to Nazareth, where he had been brought up, he went to the synagogue on the Sabbath day, as was his custom (*kata to eiothos auto*)" (Luke 4:16). The identical phrase recurs in Luke's description of Paul's conduct in Thessalonica, "where there was a synagogue of the Jews. And Paul went in, as was his custom (*kata to eiōthos*), and on three Sabbath days argued with them from the scriptures" (Acts 17:1b–2). The personal "custom" of both Jesus and Paul conforms to the corporate "custom" of the Jewish people, who gather together in their local synagogues on the Sabbath, just as the personal custom of Mary and Joseph (when they made pilgrimage to Jerusalem for Passover) conformed to the corporate custom of the Jewish people as shaped by the Torah (Luke 2:42). Moreover, the customary activity displayed by Jesus and Paul in these narratives conforms to that of other Jews—they read from and interpret "the scriptures." This network of terms and concepts establishes a solid link between the *kata* phrases of the infancy narrative (which emphasize the commandments of the Torah and Jewish corporate custom) and these two later *kata to eiothos* verses (which emphasize the personal custom of Jesus and of Paul).

Elsewhere in Luke and Acts we find this *kata* construction employed in a way that is unambiguously parallel to what is seen in the infancy narrative. The clearest example in the Gospel appears in the description of the actions of the women in Jesus' company who follow Joseph of Arimathea as he lays Jesus' body in the tomb: "Then they returned, and prepared spices and ointments. On the Sabbath they rested according to the commandment (*kata tēn entolēn*)" (23:56). *Kata* here takes as its object a "commandment" of the Torah. While it is the Sabbath rest of these women that is explicitly in view, their commitment to bury Jesus in an appropriate manner likewise demonstrates their fidelity to the Torah, just as the same commitment confirms the characterization of Joseph of Arimathea as "a good and righteous man" (Luke 23:50). In this way, the women who accompanied Jesus from Galilee to Jerusalem at the end of his earthly life (Luke 23:55) become partners with Mary and Joseph who brought him from Galilee to Jerusalem at the beginning of that life. They are united in their love for Jesus and in the way that love takes shape according to the commandments of the Torah.

The clearest example of this *kata* construction from Acts of the Apostles derives from Paul's speech to the crowd in the temple after his arrest. He describes his blinding encounter with the risen Jesus on the road to Damascus, and then tells of the disciple whom God sent to baptize him and restore his sight: "A certain Ananias, who was a devout man according to the law (*kata ton nomon*) and well spoken of by all the Jews living there, came to me . . ." (Acts 22:12–13a). Ananias here fulfills a role for Paul analogous to that which the parents of Jesus undertook in circumcising (Luke 2:21) and redeeming (Luke 2:22–23) their son. In each case the primary figure finds himself in a condition in which others must do for him what he cannot do for himself. Implicitly in view is more than particular acts, but the entire process of rearing a child or initiating a neophyte. To be qualified for such a role in the life of the Messiah or the emissary to the nations, those called to the task must be "devout . . . according to the Torah."

These texts provide the necessary background for another striking *kata* phrase in the book of Acts. This occurs in Paul's speech before King Agrippa:

> [4] "The Jews all know the way I have lived ever since I was a child, from the beginning of my life in my own country, and also in Jerusalem. [5] They have known me for a long time and can testify, if they are willing, that according to the strictest sect of our religion, I lived as a Pharisee (*kata tēn akribestatēn hairesin tēs hēmeteras thrēskeias ezēsa pharisaios*). [6] And now it is because of my hope in what God has promised our fathers that I am on trial today. [7] This is the promise our twelve tribes are hoping to see fulfilled as they earnestly serve God day and night. O king, it is because of this hope that the Jews are accusing me. [8] Why should any of you consider it incredible that God raises the dead? (Acts 26:4–8; NIV)

Paul speaks here of his upbringing and his early education, testifying that he was raised to live "according to [*kata*] the strictest sect of our religion . . . as a Pharisee." The Greek adjective translated here as "strictest" appears only here in the New Testament, but its cognate adverb is used by Luke elsewhere to refer to his own "careful" investigation of the life of Jesus and to the "accurate" teaching of Apollos concerning the same matter. Thus, the word has positive ("careful") rather than negative ("overly-scrupulous") connotations for Luke. This is also clear from the context, in which Paul frames his own message concerning resurrection in reference to the Pharisaic teaching in which he was reared. Setting this text beside the other *kata* passages already examined, we see Paul's Torah-faithful Pharisaic upbringing as anticipating his instruction in the apostolic message by the Torah-faithful Ananias, and as echoing the more humble yet still Torah-faithful family environment of Jesus. In all these cases, the *kata* construction refers to the authoritative character of the Jewish way of life.

Thus, the use of *kata* phrases in the infancy narrative in reference to the Torah prepares readers for similar constructions later in Luke and

Acts. This characteristic of Luke's literary style is the first piece of evidence suggesting a deliberate correlation between the Torah's role in the infancy narrative and in the two volumes which follow. Now let us shift our focus from style to content, and look at the way the people, events, and themes of the infancy narrative point forward to later material in the Gospel and Acts related to the Torah-fidelity of faithful Israel.

Righteousness, Devotion, and the Torah

Luke's infancy narrative is populated by a rich cast of "righteous" Jews. We have already seen how Luke depicts the Torah-fidelity of Joseph and Mary. Before this Galilean couple appear on the scene, however, the reader encounters two Judeans, Zechariah and Elizabeth: "Both of them were righteous [*dikaioi*] before God" (Luke 1:6a). This statement occurs as the main predication of the first two verses of the book following the introductory dedication to Theophilus, and as such deserves special attention. The statement informs us that the Jewish world of the time included people who were truly "righteous," and offers a traditional Jewish definition of what such "righteousness" entailed: "living blamelessly according to all the commandments and regulations of the Lord" (Luke 1:6b). For the Lukan infancy narrative, "righteousness" and the Torah are inseparable.

Another such character appears on the scene when Joseph and Mary bring the child Jesus to the temple. Simeon displays his prophetic gift in his recognition of the child as the Messiah (Luke 2:26–27), and in his words concerning the messianic mission that the child-become-adult would undertake (Luke 2:29–35). Simeon is introduced in this way: "Now there was a man in Jerusalem whose name was Simeon; this man was righteous [*dikiaios*] and devout [*eulabēs*], looking forward to the consolation of Israel, and the Holy Spirit rested on him" (Luke 2:25). Simeon is not only "righteous," he is also "devout" (*eulabēs*). The latter term "is expressive of reverence and awe in God's presence."[22] Like the word "fear" when used in Jewish texts to speak of a proper orientation toward God, the term also implies the careful fulfillment of religious duties.[23] Thus, while *eulabēs* describes an all-encompassing posture in relation to God,

22. Fitzmyer, *The Gospel According to Luke I–IX*, 426.

23. Marshall, *The Gospel of Luke*, 118.

it also suggests a way of life that conforms to the standards of the Torah (see Acts 22:12).

The "righteous" and "devout" Jews of the infancy narrative combine in their persons careful attention to Torah-observance with expectant hope in the promises to Israel contained in the Torah and the Prophets. Here we see model Jews who "look forward to [*prosdechomenos*] the consolation of Israel" (Luke 2:25) (or, as Luke 2:38 will put it, "who were looking for [*prosdechomenois*] the redemption of Jerusalem"), and whose piety is expressed in Torah-fidelity. These "righteous" and "devout" people anticipate other figures who will appear later in the Gospel and Acts. Fitting this pattern is Joseph of Arimathea, who is described by Luke as a "righteous man" (Luke 23:50).[24] His righteousness is manifested by his unwillingness to consent to the sentence against Jesus issued by the Council (Luke 23:51), his concern to provide Jesus with a proper burial (Luke 23:52–53), and his "waiting [*prosedecheto*] for the kingdom of God" (Luke 23:51). Joseph's "waiting" for the kingdom recalls Simeon's and Anna's "looking for" and "looking forward to" consolation and redemption (the Greek verb in all these texts is *prosdechomai*). His righteous conduct in fidelity to the Torah likewise reminds readers of the godly Jews of the infancy narrative. They had performed appropriate deeds of kindness at the beginning of Jesus' earthly life; Joseph performs an appropriate deed of kindness at its end.

Paralleling the burial of Jesus in the Gospel of Luke is the burial of Stephen in Acts. After Stephen is stoned to death, Luke tells us that "devout [*eulabeis*] men buried Stephen and made loud lamentation over him" (Acts 8:2). Nothing in the text suggests that these men are already disciples of Jesus. Like the disciples, however, they are pious Jews, and as such they recognize, as did Joseph of Arimathea, that a grave miscarriage of justice has occurred. Following the pattern established by Joseph, they express their grief and indignation by burying the victim and weeping at his tomb. Joseph is described as "righteous," and these men as "devout"—a fact that confirms the way Luke links the two terms outside the infancy narrative just as he does within it. In the case of both burials, the act fulfills a cardinal imperative of the Torah.

24. While Matthew refers to Joseph of Arimathea as a disciple of Jesus (Matt 27:57), Mark and Luke make no mention of this fact. If one were only reading Mark or Luke, one would presume that Joseph was a righteous Jewish leader who recognized that an injustice had occurred, and sought some way to express his dissent from the rest of the Council. See Oliver, *Torah Praxis After 70 CE*, 148–49n2.

The infancy narrative portrayed Joseph and Mary as making pilgrimage to Jerusalem "every year" to celebrate the Passover holiday (Luke 2:41). In Acts we read of "devout [*eulabeis*] Jews from every nation under heaven living in Jerusalem" during the feast of Pentecost (Acts 2:5). Most likely, we are to think of these Jews as having made their long journey to Jerusalem for Passover and remaining in the city for the seven weeks that ended with the second pilgrimage feast. Their "devout" character is reflected in their commitment to fulfill the commandment of the Torah enjoining such a journey at the time of the holidays. They are the natural audience for Peter's Pentecost sermon, and from their number arises the post-Pentecostal *ekklēsia*.

All of the "righteous" and "devout" figures considered to this point either precede the mission of Jesus (Joseph, Mary, Zechariah, Elizabeth, Simeon, Anna) or are outside the Jesus-community (Joseph of Arimathea, Stephen's mourners). Does Luke view their Torah-faithful righteousness and devotion as practice that is transcended by the life of discipleship? Here the example of Ananias proves decisive. Paul describes this disciple of Jesus who was sent to baptize, heal, and commission him as "a devout [*eulabēs*] man according to the law and well spoken of by all the Jews living there" (Acts 22:12). As the "devout" Simeon held the baby Jesus in his arms and spoke to the child's parents of his future mission, so the "devout" Ananias lays his hands on Saul (Acts 9:17) and tells of the task that the man from Tarsus must perform (Acts 22:14–15). This verse also makes explicit what was only implicit in the other texts that mention "devotion": to be "devout" (*eulabēs*) is to live according to the Torah.

Only one gentile is described as "righteous" in Luke or Acts: the centurion Cornelius (Acts 10:22). While he is a non-Jew and a Roman soldier, Cornelius adheres as fully as his circumstances allow to the teaching of the Torah: "he gave alms generously to the people [i.e., to the needy among the Jewish people] and prayed constantly to God" (Acts 10:2). The Greek phrase translated here as "constantly" (*dia pantos*) is used by the Septuagint to render the Hebrew word *tamid* (e.g., LXX Lev 24:2, 8), especially when the latter term refers to the burnt-offering presented twice-daily as the fulfillment of Israel's corporate worship according to the Torah (e.g., LXX Num 28:10, 15, 23, 24, etc.). It thus refers not to the prayerful orientation to life that Cornelius demonstrated every moment of every day, but to his adoption of the specific Jewish custom of praying twice daily at the time when the burnt-offering was presented by the priests at the temple in Jerusalem.[25] It is while adhering to this custom that the angel visits Cornelius and tells him to send for Peter (Acts 10:3–4; 30–31).

Like Ananias, Cornelius is a man "well spoken of by the whole Jewish nation" (Acts 10:22; see 22:12). His love for the people of Israel and the God of Israel is a publicly acknowledged fact. As a righteous gentile who lives according the provisions of the Torah that fit his status and circumstances, he becomes the perfect representative and first-fruit of those from the nations who are to be sanctified and joined to the people of God. His story will be recounted by Peter at the Jerusalem Council (Acts 15:7–9), and, as we will discuss below, the decree issued by that Council summons baptized gentiles to conform to those commandments of the Torah which apply to those from the nations who dwell "in the midst" of Israel.

The cast of "righteous" and "devout" characters depicted in the infancy narrative anticipates a similar cast that will appear in the chapters of Luke and Acts that follow. The ranks of Torah-faithful Israelites (and gentile lovers of Israel) who await the coming kingdom is not limited to the infancy narrative, but colors the entire canvas of the two volumes.

Prayer, the Daily Offerings, and the Gift of the Spirit

From the opening verses of Luke, this Torah-fidelity finds expression in a pattern of daily prayer that is closely linked both to the priestly institutions of the Jerusalem temple and to reception of the gift of the Holy Spirit.

As seen above, the first verse following the book's prefatory dedication introduces Zechariah and Elizabeth as "righteous before God, living blamelessly according to all the commandments and regulations of the Lord" (Luke 1:6). The book's initial scene then unfolds in the Jerusalem temple, where the priest Zechariah is chosen by lot to enter the holy place and present Israel's offering of incense on the golden altar (Luke 1:8–9). The burning of incense on that altar occurred twice daily as part of the *tamid* ("constant") sacrifice which fulfilled Israel's corporate duty of worship as ordained in the Torah (Exod 29:38–42; Num 28:1–8). As already noted, a custom had developed among "devout" Jews of praying at the

25. See our earlier discussion on pp. 111–12 of chapter 2. See also Hamm, "The Tamid Service in Luke-Acts," 219n11; 222.

time when the *tamid* was offered in the temple. Luke informs us that this custom took its paradigmatic form at the temple itself: "Now at the time of the incense-offering, the whole assembly of the people was praying outside" (Luke 1:10).

Luke also implies that Zechariah himself mingled prayer with the incense he burned, for, when Gabriel appears to him on the right side of the altar (Luke 1:11), the angel begins his revelatory announcement by saying, "Do not be afraid, Zechariah, for your prayer has been heard" (Luke 1:13). What is the content and object of Zechariah's prayer? Perhaps he prays for a son, since he and his wife are childless and of advanced age (Luke 1:7). However, if that were the content and object of Zechariah's prayer, it seems strange that he would doubt an angelic communication foretelling the conception and birth of a son. While the gift of a child to aged parents would be a wondrous sign, Zechariah would not pray for it if he did not think it possible, and such a sign would not exceed in wonder the appearance of an angel. More likely, Luke suggests that Zechariah's prayer in the temple has the same content as the prayer of those Jews in the outer court, and as the prayer of those Jews, proselytes, and righteous gentiles (like Cornelius) who turn toward Jerusalem and call upon the God of Israel at the time of the twice daily offering: they all pray for the "redemption of Jerusalem" and the "consolation of Israel." That is the prayer that God is answering with the conception and birth of this child, and even more with the conception and birth of another child whose way he will prepare (Luke 1:17).

The son to be born to Zechariah and Elizabeth will be distinguished by a special divine gift: "he will be great in the sight of the Lord . . . even before his birth he will be filled with the Holy Spirit" (Luke 1:15). Mention here of the Holy Spirit may seem like an incidental detail, but what follows in Luke and Acts should make us think otherwise. As an unborn child, John is moved by the Spirit when his mother is visited by the mother of the unborn child whose way he is destined to prepare (Luke 1:41, 44). Luke tells us that at that moment Elizabeth was "filled with the Holy Spirit" (Luke 1:41), for her womb contains one who is already "filled with the Holy Spirit" (Luke 1:15). When, as an adult, John describes the mission of the one whose way he prepares, he says that the coming one "will baptize you with the Holy Spirit and fire" (Luke 3:16). Thus, the incense offering of Zechariah and his prayer, along with the prayers of devout Jews in Jerusalem and around the world, receive a divine response in the birth of a child filled with the Holy Spirit, and in the birth of another child who will become the agent who bestows the Holy Spirit on faithful Israel.

In summary, the opening scene of Luke combines imagery associated with the temple, the Torah, and faithful Israel. It also relates the daily temple service, ordained by the Torah, to the daily practice of prayer undertaken by "devout" Jews, proselytes, and righteous gentiles, and sees both as ordered toward the "redemption of Jerusalem." Finally, the opening scene of Luke hints that the long-awaited redemption begins with the impartation of the Holy Spirit.

Before leaving this scene, let us consider a question that will have significance for our interpretation of later scenes in Acts. Does Zechariah offer incense as part of the morning or afternoon *tamid*?[26] Joseph Fitzmyer and I. Howard Marshall argue that Luke 1 refers to the afternoon/evening *tamid*.[27] Their conclusion rests on parallels between Luke 1:8ff and the angelic revelation of Daniel 9, which takes place at the time of the *afternoon/evening* sacrifice. The parallels are indeed noteworthy. Like Zechariah, Daniel prays for the redemption of Jerusalem at the time of the *tamid* sacrifice (Dan 9:17–20); like Zechariah, Daniel's prayer is followed by a visitation from the angel Gabriel (Dan 9:12); like Zechariah, Daniel receives from Gabriel a promise of Jerusalem's ultimate restoration (Dan 9:24). The post-70 reader of Luke also perceives another parallel that Zechariah could not have discerned: in both Daniel 9 and Luke 1, the promise of Jerusalem's redemption will be realized only after the city endures another tragic destruction (Dan 9:26).

These substantive parallels support the contention of Fitzmyer and Marshall that Luke draws upon Daniel 9 in his crafting of the opening scene in his Gospel. However, differences between the two narratives should also be noted. Unlike Zechariah, Daniel has no priestly pedigree or role (Dan 1:6). Unlike Zechariah, Daniel prays from a distant land rather than in the holy city, and, even if Daniel had been in Jerusalem rather than in eastern exile, he would have been unable to pray in the temple, for that structure was in ruins. Thus, while Daniel can pray at *the*

26. The Torah states that the second *tamid* offering of the day should be presented "between the evenings" (*beyn ha'arbaim*; Exod 29:39; Num 28:4, 8). Modern translators usually render this phrase as "at twilight." However, in the late Second Temple period the sacrifice was presented in the late afternoon, at the ninth hour (i.e., around 3:00 pm). The Passover sacrifice was also to be slaughtered *beyn ha'arbaim* (Exod 12:6), and Josephus (*Jewish War*, 6.9.3) informs us that this occurred from the ninth to the eleventh hours (i.e., from around 3:00 to 5:00 p.m.).

27. Fitzmyer, *Luke I–IX*, 324; Marshall, *Luke*, 54.

time of the afternoon/evening sacrifice (Dan 9:21), no such sacrifice was actually offered at that time; he prays at the time when the sacrifice *would have been offered*, if the temple had not been destroyed. These significant differences challenge the claim that without further evidence we may import a detail from the Daniel 9 narrative (i.e., its evening setting) into a Lukan narrative that makes no mention of it.

Dennis Hamm agrees with the conclusion of Fitzmyer and Marshall, but on different grounds. Luke 1 implies that the incense offering of Zechariah should be followed immediately by the priests' blessing of the people (vv. 21–22). Hamm asserts that this sequence is unique to the afternoon *tamid*.[28] However, that is not the case. Hamm bases his assertion on the Mishnah, but the relevant tractate states that the priestly blessing follows the incense offering also in the morning *tamid* (*m. Tamid* 6:3; 7:1–2).

Unlike Fitzmyer, Marshall, and Hamm, I would argue that Luke expects his readers to assume a *morning* setting for Luke 1:8–22. There are three reasons for holding such a proposition. First, the morning *tamid* enjoyed greater prominence than the afternoon/evening service. Illustrating this fact, the Mishnah devotes an entire tractate to the order of service for the *tamid* offering, but that tractate focuses exclusively on the morning *tamid*. If no explicit time designation is provided in a narrative that refers to the *tamid*, we are therefore justified in assuming a morning setting.[29] Second, this assumption is confirmed by the other Lukan texts that refer or allude to the *tamid*, for, as we will see, they all deal with the afternoon/evening sacrifice, and they are explicit in their temporal designation (Acts 3:1; 10:2–4; 10:30). If Luke 1:8–22 also has an afternoon/evening setting, we would expect Luke similarly to mention the fact. In light of the special prominence of the morning *tamid*, the absence of a contrary mention suggests that Luke assumes a morning setting. Third, a morning setting for this story fits its position at the beginning of Luke's narrative, and also fits the final words of the Song of Zechariah: "the dawn from on high will break upon us, to give light to those who sit in darkness and in the shadow of death, to guide our feet into the way of peace" (Luke 1:28b–29). While Zechariah speaks these words nine months later, at the circumcision of his son, he had been unable to speak since his encounter

28. Hamm, "The Tamid Service," 221.

29. Alfred Edersheim reaches this conclusion with the same reasoning: "We presume, that the ministration of Zecharias (St. Luke 1.9) took place in the morning, as the principal service" (Edersheim, *The Life and Times of Jesus the Messiah*, 1:133n1).

with the angel, and the blessing that breaks his silence represents the response he should have given immediately to the angelic promise (Luke 1:68). The morning *tamid* began with the break of dawn (*m. Tamid* 3:2), and it thus provides the appropriate setting for an introduction to Luke and Acts and for the announcement of the "light" that will shine in the midst of the darkness.

We are now ready to examine Acts to see if the prayer/sacrifice/Spirit constellation of Luke 1:8–22 recurs there. The first text to consider is Acts 2. The only element of the tripartite constellation that receives emphasis in the narrative is the bestowal of the Holy Spirit (Acts 2:4, 17–18, 33, 38). The other two elements (prayer and the *tamid* sacrifice) are at best implicit—but the hints of their presence should be noted. After the ascension of Jesus on the Mount of Olives, the eleven apostles returned to the city and "went to the room upstairs where they were staying" (Acts 1:13). The main activity in which they were there engaged was prayer: "All these were constantly devoting themselves to prayer" (*proskarterountes homothymadon tē proseuchē*, Acts 1:14). Acts 2 then begins in this way: "When the day of Pentecost had come, they were all together in one place. And suddenly from heaven there came a sound like the rush of a violent wind, and it filled the entire house where they were sitting" (Acts 2:1–2). The "one place" of Acts 2:1 and the "house" of Acts 2:2 are equivalent to the "room upstairs" of Acts 1:13, and the author likely expects his readers to envision the apostolic community as engaged in the same activity in that place that had been mentioned previously (Acts 1:13), namely, the activity of prayer.

Luke makes no mention of the *tamid* in Acts 2, but he does indicate the time at which the Spirit was given: it was the third hour, or approximately 9:00 am (Acts 2:15). According to rabbinic texts, the morning *tamid* commenced at daybreak with the slaughtering of the burnt-offering, but the sacrificial rites would take hours to complete. The service would normally conclude no later than the fourth hour (i.e., 10:00 or 11:00 am; *m. Eduyot* 6:1; *b. Berachot* 26b–27a). Since the morning incense-offering was presented before both the priestly benediction and the placement of the burnt-offering on the altar of sacrifice, it would take place approximately at the third hour (i.e., 9:00 am).[30] This means that the apostolic community received the Holy Spirit at approximately the same time as the priests offered incense in the temple, and thus also at the same time

30. Edersheim, *The Temple*, 107–8.

of day as Zechariah had entered the holy place and received the promise of redemption from the angel Gabriel.

If Acts 2 has the prayer/sacrifice/Spirit constellation in view, then it likely also has in view the biblical texts that speak of the dedication of the tabernacle in the wilderness and the temple in Jerusalem. Both of these rites reach their climax when fire falls from heaven and consumes the sacrifice on the altar (Lev 9:24; 2 Chr 7:1). On Pentecost "divided tongues, as of fire" appeared among the apostolic community, and "a tongue rested on each of them. All of them were filled with the Holy Spirit and began to speak in other languages [i.e. tongues], as the Spirit gave them the ability" (Acts 2:3–4). The "tongues of fire" represent the Spirit who fills them. The praying community has now become the sacrifice, yet they are not consumed by the fire from heaven but instead transformed and empowered by it. Filled with the Spirit before birth at the inauguration of the era of redemption, John the Baptist had foretold that his successor would "baptize with the Spirit and with fire" (Luke 3:16). While the fire of which he spoke refers primarily to the eschatological purification and judgment (Luke 3:17), Luke may also understand it to be an image characterizing the transformative power of the Spirit.

If the prayer/sacrifice/Spirit constellation of Luke 1 is at best below the surface in Acts 2, it rises to incontestable visibility in Acts 10–11. The author introduces Cornelius as a man who "prayed constantly " [*dia pantos*] to God" (Acts 10:2). As noted above, the Greek phrase *dia pantos* is employed by the Septuagint to translate the Hebrew word *tamid*; Cornelius is thus portrayed from the outset of the narrative as a person who habitually prays to the God of Israel at the time of the *tamid* offering. The author then describes a particular scene in which Cornelius is engaged in that activity. The centurion is praying at the hour of the afternoon *tamid* when an angel appears to him, as also happened to Zechariah (Acts 10:1–3) and Daniel. The angel tells him that his prayers and alms "have ascended as a memorial before God" (Acts 10:4). The terminology employed by the angel ("ascended," "memorial") derives from the sacrificial system, and suggests that the prayer of Cornelius (like that of Zechariah) has been mingled with the incense of the Jerusalem temple and received with favor. For Zechariah (in Luke 1) and for the apostolic community (in Acts 2), the acceptance of prayer and sacrifice results in a direct intervention of God by the Spirit. The case of Cornelius requires a different kind of intervention, since he is not part of the people of Israel. The angel therefore commands him to send for Peter, who will be the human agent (representing the people of Israel) through whom the saving message will be proclaimed and the Spirit bestowed. While the gift of the Spirit in this case is humanly mediated (albeit without the laying on of hands seen in Acts 8:14–17 and 19:1–6), and thus a temporal hiatus divides the prayer/sacrifice from the giving of the Spirit, the final result is the same as in Luke 1 and Acts 2: the prayer of a righteous person, accompanying Israel's sacrifice ordained by the Torah, leads to the bestowal of the Holy Spirit.

The unmistakable reappearance of the prayer/sacrifice/Spirit constellation in Acts 10 also has implications for our understanding of Acts 2. When Peter enters the home of Cornelius and proclaims to his household the message of Jesus, "the Holy Spirit fell upon all who heard the word" (Acts 10:44), and the presence of the Spirit was manifested among them through their speaking in tongues (Acts 10:46). This astounds the Jewish disciples of Jesus who had accompanied Peter, who evidently thought that the Spirit could only be poured out on Jews (Acts 10:45). Peter's response is telling: "Can anyone withhold the water for baptizing these people who have received the Holy Spirit *just as we have*?" (Acts 10:47; emphasis added). In other words, Peter compares the experience of Cornelius and his household to the experience of the apostolic community on the day of Pentecost. This comparison is reiterated in even more explicit form when Peter in Jerusalem defends his visit to Cornelius and his baptizing of the centurion's gentile household:

> [15] And as I began to speak, the Holy Spirit fell upon them just as it had upon us at the beginning. [16] And I remembered the word of the Lord, how he had said, "John baptized with water, but you will be baptized with the Holy Spirit." [17] If then God gave them the same gift that he gave us when we believed in the Lord Jesus Christ, who was I that I could hinder God?' (Acts 11:15–17)

Here Peter refers back to the day of Pentecost, but also to the words of John the Baptist. In this way a linkage is established in the text between the Cornelius episode, the reception of the Spirit at Pentecost, and the figure of John the Baptist (and thus also to the angelic announcement of John's conception and birth in Luke 1). Given this linkage, we are justified in seeing the prayer/sacrifice/Spirit constellation as a paradigm anticipated in the Lukan infancy narrative and played out in the community history of the disciples of Jesus.

At this point we can appreciate the significance of establishing the timing of the *tamid* in Luke 1. If Luke presents Zechariah's incense-offering as an element of the morning *tamid*, then this episode directly foreshadows the narrative of Pentecost, which also occurs at the time of the morning *tamid*. On the other hand, a contrast is drawn between these two events and the Cornelius incident, which occurs during the afternoon *tamid*. This pattern reflects a feature of the narratives that we have already commented upon: the divine action following the prayer/sacrifice is direct and temporally immediate in the cases of Zechariah and the apostolic community, whereas it is indirect (i.e., humanly mediated) and temporally delayed in the case of Cornelius. This likely expresses Luke's view of the Jew-gentile distinction, which shapes the contours of "salvation history." God works first and in a direct way with faithful Israel, and then works through these Jews to bring "light" to the gentiles. For the author of the infancy narrative and Acts, the two daily *tamid* offerings correspond to the renewal of Israel accomplished at Pentecost (i.e., at the dawn of the messianic age) and to the calling of the gentiles through renewed Israel (i.e., in the afternoon of the messianic age).

At the same time, the author does not so spiritualize the meaning of these Jewish customs ordained by the Torah as to rob them of their enduring institutional value. After receiving the Spirit on Pentecost, the apostolic community cultivated a pattern of daily life in which "they spent much time together in the temple" (*proskarterountes homothymadon en tō hierō*, Acts 2:46), echoing the description of their life of prayer in the upper room before Pentecost (*proskarterountes homothymadon tē proseuchē*, Acts 1:14). They gather for prayer in the temple, and they do so not only as a matter of practical convenience (i.e., because the temple was the only site that could accommodate such a large group), but as a matter of religious devotion. Furthermore, they do not pray only on their own, but also as part of the wider people of Israel. All this becomes evident in the next incident that Luke recounts: "One day Peter and John were going up to the temple at the hour of prayer, at three o'clock in the afternoon" (Acts 3:1). Peter and John ascend the Temple Mount at the time of the afternoon *tamid*, in order to join their prayer to the offerings and prayers of all Israel. This suggests that it was not only the temple site but also its pattern of worship (shaped by the Torah) that attracted the apostolic community and ordered its way of life. The traditional customs of Jewish worship are now filled with new power and "supplemented" in their significance, but they are neither nullified nor sublated (i.e., fulfilled in meaning yet discarded as concrete practice).

We find another likely allusion to the custom of praying twice daily at the time of the *tamid* in a phrase found in the infancy narrative and Acts. The Gospel introduces the eighty-four-year-old prophet Anna by describing her as one who "never left the temple but worshiped there with fasting and prayer night and day [*latreuousa nykta kai hēmeran*]" (Luke 2:37). Almost the identical language is found in Paul's defense before King Agrippa: "And now I stand here on trial on account of my hope in the promise made to our ancestors, a promise that our twelve tribes hope to attain, as they earnestly worship day and night [*nykta kai hēmeran latreuon*]" (Acts 26:6–7). Paul here characterizes the righteous and devout men and women of Israel throughout the world as adhering to the same custom exemplified by Anna—prayer twice daily at the time of the *tamid* offering. Moreover, he indicates that the content and object of this prayer is the same as that found in the prayers of Daniel, Zechariah, and Anna: they pray for the fulfillment of the "promise made to our ancestors," i.e., "the redemption of Jerusalem" (Luke 2:38).

In this context, it is noteworthy that post-70 rabbinic Judaism decided that the practice of offering a set petitionary prayer (i.e., the Eighteen Blessings, or *Shemoneh Esreh*) twice daily—at the time of the morning and afternoon/evening *tamid*—should be treated as a commandment rather than a commendable custom.[31] As transmitted by Jewish tradition, that prayer focuses on "the redemption of Jerusalem." In this way, the Jewish people fulfill as best they can in the present era the commandments of the Torah that prescribe Israel's daily worship duties (Exod 29:38–42; Num 28:1–8). Writing in the period when the rabbinic movement (under the leadership of the Gamaliel dynasty) was making such decisions, the author of the infancy narrative and Acts lays out a theological foundation for a similar Torah-practice among the disciples of Jesus.

Once again, we find the Torah-related features of Luke 1–2 re-cast and re-played in later chapters of the Lukan narrative. It is difficult to deny that we find here intentionally correlated texts.[32]

31. See Kinzer, *Searching Her Own Mystery*, 128–37.

32. For further discussion of the *tamid* in Luke, Acts, and Second Temple Jewish literature, see Kinzer, "Sacrifice, Prayer, and the Holy Spirit: The Daily Tamid Offering in Luke-Acts.

The Family of Jesus and the Jerusalem *Ekklēsia*

Of the six major characters who surround the young Jesus in Luke's infancy narrative, four of them are members of his family. Elizabeth, wife of Zechariah and mother of John the Baptist, is a "relative" (*syngenis*) of Mary (Luke 1:36), and Mary resides with her Judean kin for the last three months of Elizabeth's pregnancy (Luke 1:56; see 1:36). Luke alone informs us that John the Baptist himself is part of Jesus' extended family, and we only learn that through the infancy narrative.

As we have seen, Luke portrays Zechariah, Elizabeth, Joseph, and Mary (along with Simeon and Anna) as "righteous and devout according to the Torah." In particular, the author presents Joseph and Mary as obeying specific Torah commandments related to ritual purity, circumcision, and the redemption of a first-born son (Luke 2:21–24). Of the two, Mary takes center stage as the model of Torah obedience because of her faithful response to the message of the angel Gabriel. After being told that she would be the mother of the Messiah, Mary answered, "Here am I, the servant [*doulē*] of the Lord; let it be with me according to your word [*genoito moi kata to rēma sou*]" (Luke 1:38). Unlike Zechariah, who, though "righteous before God" (Luke 1:6), doubted Gabriel's message, Mary takes the posture of a "servant" and places herself humbly at God's disposal. In this way, she demonstrates the kind of "devotion" (*eulabēs*) to God that underlies whole-hearted Torah-faithfulness.

As the infancy narrative unfolds, Luke again calls attention to Mary's response to the divine word spoken to her through Gabriel. When Mary visits her Judean kinswoman, Elizabeth proclaims, "And blessed [*makaria*] is she who believed [*pisteusasa*] that there would be a fulfillment of what was spoken to her by the Lord" (Luke 1:45). Mary is pronounced "blessed" (i.e., divinely favored and happy) because she responded to God's word as God's faithful servant, that is, with trusting fidelity (*pistis*). Mary then offers praise to God, "for he has looked with favor on the lowliness of his servant [*doulē*]. Surely, from now on all generations will call me blessed [*makariousin*]" (Luke 1:48). These words allude both to the angelic visitation [i.e., Mary as *doulē*] and to the inspired blessing pronounced by Elizabeth [*makariousin*] in its aftermath. Later in the narrative, angels appear to shepherds outside Bethlehem, who then find Mary, Joseph, and the newborn Jesus, and recount what they had heard from the heavenly messengers concerning the child. Luke tells us that "Mary treasured [*synetērei*] all these words [*ta rēmata*] and pondered them in her heart" (Luke 2:19). Just as Mary took seriously the word (*to rēma*) of Gabriel (Luke 1:38) and offered herself as a servant in its realization, so she received and "guarded" (*syn-tēreo*) in her heart the "words" (*ta rēmata*) concerning another angelic appearance as a confirmation of what she had heard originally.[33] In this way, Mary demonstrates the orientation to God's word that marks Torah-faithful Israel.

So much for the infancy narrative and its depiction of the family of Jesus. To see how this theme is echoed later in Luke and Acts, let us begin with a short dialogue between Jesus and a woman that is found only in Luke: "While he was saying this, a woman in the crowd raised her voice and said to him, 'Blessed [*makaria*] is the womb that bore you and the breasts that nursed you!' But he said, 'Blessed [*makarioi*] rather are those who hear the word of God and obey it! [*hoi akouontes ton logon tou Theou kai phylassontes*]'" (Luke 11:27–28). This female bystander praises the teacher and wonder-worker from Nazareth by acknowledging the divine favor shown to the woman who bore and raised him. At first glance, it seems that Jesus corrects her by honoring obedient response to the divine word *rather than* physical transmission of life ("womb," "breasts")—in effect, saying "Do not honor my mother, but instead honor those who obey God's law." However, the "correction" turns out to be only a shifting of the basis for honoring Mary, for verse 28 alludes back to the infancy narrative and the "blessedness" of the servant-girl who received the divine word with humility and faith and thereby proved herself worthy to be the mother of the Messiah.[34] In other words, Jesus agrees with "the woman in the crowd" that his mother should be seen and honored as "blessed," but wishes to focus less on the bodily life he derived from her and more on her faithful hearing of the divine word that made her worthy to bestow that life. Here Mary becomes the paradigmatic disciple, hearing and performing the living word of the Torah.

33. In Luke 2:51, Mary takes the same approach to the words of her twelve year old son: "His mother treasured [*di-ēterei*] all these things [*ta rēmata*; lit., "words"] in her heart."

34. The Greek word translated here by the NRSV as "obey," *phylasso*, appears often in the LXX of Proverbs (see Prov 2:11; 13:3; 16:17; 19:16) in synonymous parallelism with the word *tēreo* ("guard"), which Luke 2:19 employs in compound form (*syn-tēreo*) to speak of Mary's "treasuring" the words she had heard from the shepherds. The compound Greek word itself appears in Sirach 4:20 as a synonym of *phylasso*. Elsewhere in LXX Sirach, *syn-tēreo* appears frequently with reference to obedience to the commandments or teaching of God (see Sirach 15:5; 35:1; 37:12; 44:20).

Luke's concern to portray Mary as a paradigmatic disciple becomes evident in another story, which appears also in Mark, and in which Luke's distinctive perspective is manifested when the two versions of the story are compared. Following an account of Jesus' selection of the twelve (Mark 3:13–19a), and preceding a conflict between Jesus and certain scribes in which they accuse him of acting with demonic power (Mark 3:22–30), Mark notes briefly the fears of Jesus' family: "Then he went home; and the crowd came together again, so that they could not even eat. When his family heard it, they went out to restrain him, for people were saying, 'He has gone out of his mind'" (Mark 3:19b–21). In Mark's narrative, the family of Jesus has little comprehension of what he is doing. They may not agree with what the people are saying, but they want him to give the crowds less fodder for gossip. After recounting the conflict with the scribes, Mark returns to the topic of Jesus' family.

> [31] Then his mother and his brothers came; and standing outside, they sent to him and called him. [32] A crowd was sitting around him; and they said to him, "Your mother and your brothers and sisters are outside, asking for you." [33]And he replied, "Who are my mother and my brothers?" [34] And looking at those who sat around him, he said, "Here are my mother and my brothers! [35] Whoever does the will of God is my brother and sister and mother." (Mark 3:31–35)

Mark has already informed his readers of the worries of Jesus' family, and so when we learn that they are standing outside and looking to speak with him, we assume that their purpose is "to restrain him" (Mark 3:21). Jesus responds by pointing to his disciples ("those who sat around him") and declaring that they are his true family, for they are doing "the will of God" (apparently in contrast to his flesh-and-blood kin).

Luke's version of the story (Luke 8:19–21) differs from that of Mark in five significant ways. First, Luke deletes the introductory verses, which depict the fears of Jesus' family and their desire to "restrain him." Thus, when we learn from Luke that Jesus' mother and brothers are seeking him, we have no reason to suspect their motives. Second, here Jesus does not ask the question. "Who are my mother and my brothers?" The question itself implies a challenge to the claim of his "mother and brothers" to be his true relatives, and Luke regards such a challenge as misguided. Third, Luke does not introduce Jesus' proclamation concerning his true family by indicating that he said it only in reference to "those who sat around him" (Mark 3:34). Luke's intention is to *include* rather than *exclude* the relatives who stand outside the building. Fourth, whereas Mark describes the true family of Jesus as "Whoever does the will of God" (Mark 3:35), Luke characterizes them as "those who hear the word of God and do it (*hoi ton logon tou Theou akouontes kai poiountes*)" (Luke 8:21). This phrase is nearly identical to the one that appears in Jesus' response to the woman who calls his mother "blessed" (Luke 11:28: "those who hear the word of God and obey it! [*hoi akouontes ton logon tou Theou kai phylassontes*]"). The purpose of the phrase here is also nearly identical to its purpose in the later text. Fifth and finally, Luke's readers encounter this description of the true family of Jesus in a literary context established by the Lukan infancy narrative, in which all the flesh-and-blood kin of Jesus are "righteous and devout," and in which Mary in particular is the exemplar par excellence of responding to the divine word as a humble and faithful servant (Luke 1:38). The result of Luke's redaction of this story is to *expand* the meaning of Jesus' family to *include* his disciples (rather than to *exclude* his flesh-and-blood), and also to implicitly single out his mother as a model for all of his disciples to follow.[35]

Luke's high regard for the mother (and brothers) of Jesus also surfaces in his version of the failure of Jesus' home village to receive his message. In Mark Jesus' neighbors show their contempt for him by saying, "Is not this the carpenter, the son of Mary and brother of James and Joses and Judas and Simon, and are not his sisters here with us?" (Mark 6:3). Even though these are the words of characters who lack credibility, Luke prefers to avoid the slightest intimation that Jesus' connection to his flesh-and-blood relatives might undermine his messianic credentials. Thus, in Luke's version of the story, the people of Nazareth say, "Is not this Joseph's son?" (Luke 4:22). As the readers of the infancy narrative know (see also Luke 3:23), Jesus is not in fact the son of Joseph. So, the only family connection these neighbors mention is one which Luke's readers know to be limited in extent. They are wrong in their assumption that Jesus is Joseph's flesh-and-blood offspring, and they are just as wrong in their assessment of Jesus' place in the divine plan.

Given Luke's treatment of Jesus' family in the infancy narrative and in the Gospel as a whole, readers are not surprised when they learn in Acts about the composition of the apostolic community in Jerusalem after the ascension of Jesus but before Pentecost: "All these [i.e., the eleven

35. Joseph Fitzmyer draws the same conclusions from these texts: "Luke has eliminated all criticism of Jesus' family and casts Mary, his mother, as the ideal hearer of the Word of God" (*Luke the Theologian*, 76).

apostles] were constantly devoting themselves to prayer, together with certain women, including *Mary the mother of Jesus, as well as his brothers*" (Acts 1:14). If Mark had written a history of the early Jesus-community in which this statement had appeared, readers would be puzzled at the absence of an account of how "the mother of Jesus" and "his brothers" had reversed course and come to believe in him. Readers of Luke, however, sense no such lacuna, for the family of Jesus have been treated with honor throughout the narrative. Their presence with the apostles in the upper room seems as appropriate as the association of Mary and Joseph with the shepherds of Bethlehem and the prophets of the temple.[36]

Most importantly, the Lukan infancy narrative and the later Gospel incidents that refer to Jesus' family members anticipate the appearance of a crucial figure in Acts of the Apostles whose role would otherwise be inexplicable—namely, James, the brother of the Lord. When Peter is forced to flee from Jerusalem, he treats James as the leader of the community (Acts 12:17). When the Jerusalem Council meets to determine which commandments of the Torah will be required of the gentiles who have come to believe in Jesus, James delivers the final word (Acts 15:13–21). When Paul arrives in Jerusalem amidst rumors that he is undermining Torah-fidelity among diaspora Jews, James directs him to participate in a public act of Torah-piety as proof that the rumors are false (Acts 21:18–25).[37] In explaining to Paul the need for this action, James describes the members of the Jerusalem *ekklēsia* as "all zealous for the law," i.e., the Torah (Acts 21:20b). Those most zealous for Torah-fidelity could honor James as their leader because he himself was widely regarded as a preeminent model of such zeal.[38] In this regard, James is continuing the family tradition that Luke portrays so vividly in his infancy narrative.

36. Another figure whom Luke's first readers may have recognized as a family member of Jesus appears in Luke's account of the resurrection. Cleopas is one of the two disciples who encounter Jesus on the road to Emmaus (Luke 24:18). Richard Bauckham suggests that this is the man referred to as "Clopas" in John 19:25. Regarding this man, Bauckham writes, "There is . . . little room for doubt that he is the Clopas to whom Hegesippus refers, as the brother of Joseph and therefore uncle of Jesus, and the father of Symeon or Simon who succeeded James the Lord's brother in the leadership of the Jerusalem church (Hegesippus, *ap.* Eusebius, *HE* 3:11; 3:32:6; 4:22L:4)" (Bauckham, *Jude and the Relatives of Jesus in the Early Church*, 16). Thus, this apparently inconsequential detail in the Lukan story of the Emmaus Christophany may connect Jesus' family to the appearances of the resurrected Lord.

37. We should not miss the authoritative tone of the "advice" that James gives to Paul: "So do what we tell you" (Acts 21:23a).

38. For the description of James in Hegesippus, see chapter 1, pp. 23–24.

The description of the Jerusalem *ekklēsia* that James offers—"they are all zealous for the Torah" (Acts 21:20b)—contains no note of criticism. Earlier in the narrative Luke had recounted the controversy that resulted when "some [Jesus-]believers who belonged to the sect of the Pharisees" in Jerusalem had argued, in regard to gentile believers in Jesus, that "It is necessary for them to be circumcised and ordered to keep the law of Moses" (Acts 15:5). While James rules against their opinion, he bases his judgment on the Torah itself (see below), and there is no evidence in the remainder of Acts suggesting that these Pharisaic disciples of Jesus rejected his authoritative decree. Thus, in Acts 21, James does not fault members of his community whose "zeal" he considers excessive. Rather than aiming to correct their view of the Torah, James instead attempts to disprove a rumor circulating among them about Paul's approach to Torah-fidelity for *Jewish* disciples of Jesus. The action that James asks Paul to undertake has the purpose of showing that Paul himself "guards [*phylassōn*] the Torah" (Acts 21:24b). James assumes that Paul is also "zealous for the Torah" in his own way of life, and that the rumors to the contrary are false.

In fact, the statement "they are all zealous for the Torah" captures well the Lukan portrait of the family of Jesus—and the Torah-faithful Jerusalemites who surround them—in both the infancy narrative and the two volumes which that narrative introduces. Just as Mary, Joseph, Zechariah, Elizabeth, Simeon, and Anna are all "righteous" and "devout" according to the Torah, so are also the twelve, Mary and James, and the entire Jerusalem *ekklēsia*. As these six pious Jews (and the adolescent Jesus) show special reverence for the temple and for the Torah-mandated rites performed in its midst, so also the Jerusalem *ekklēsia* in Acts does the same both under the leadership of the twelve (Acts 2:46; 3:1; 5:12; 5:19–21; 5:42; 6:7) and under James (21:23–24, 26). As goes the infancy narrative, so goes the rest of the two volumes. The imagery of Torah and Torah-faithful Israel, so prominent in the infancy narrative, remains central throughout the story that Luke tells.

The Infancy Narrative and the Lukan Paul

James and the Jerusalem *ekklēsia* function in the Lukan account of the early Jesus-community as natural heirs of the Torah-piety first described in the infancy narrative. James is a member of the family that occupied center-stage in the opening chapters of Luke, and the holy city provides the geographical setting for both the initial paradigm and its later ecclesial expression. While the figure of James and the city of Jerusalem anchor Luke's ecclesial narrative, the story's featured protagonist is not James, leader of a community of Jewish disciples of Jesus, but Paul, light to the nations. Therefore, it is significant that Luke's portrait of Paul adheres to the pattern established in the infancy narrative as closely as does his portrait of James.

Three particular practices that enrich the Torah-observant texture of the infancy narrative recur in Luke's telling of Paul's story. Notably, each plays a more significant role in the latter than in the former. In the infancy narrative, these practices merely add to the already-overflowing Torah imagery; in the story of Paul, however, each is pivotal to the plot, and all three coalesce at one of its climactic moments. This suggests that Luke has composed the infancy narrative in such a way that it sheds as much light on the Pauline mission as on that of James; it may even suggest that Luke paints his portrait of James in order to clarify the aims of Paul.

The first Torah practice to receive mention in both narrative contexts is that of the journey to Jerusalem for one of the three pilgrim feasts. The opening chapters of Luke tell of Joseph and Mary's custom of traveling each year to Jerusalem for the holiday of Passover (Luke 2:41), and then recount an incident that occurred on one of those occasions (Luke 2:42–51). As the Gospel of Luke unfolds, Jesus' journey to Jerusalem with his disciples to celebrate Passover becomes the scaffolding around which Luke arranges his main narrative (see Luke 9:51). Just as Luke places at the beginning of his Gospel an incident dealing with the family of Jesus and the Passover pilgrimage, so he places at the beginning of his ecclesial history a foundational event occurring during the pilgrim-feast of Pentecost (Acts 2:1–5) in which the family of Jesus is also present (Acts 1:14). And just as Jesus' journey to Jerusalem for Passover establishes the narrative tension that will reach its climax in his arrest, trial, and execution, so Paul's journey to Jerusalem for Pentecost functions in a similar way in Acts (Acts 20:3–6, 13–16, 25, 36–38; 21:4, 10–15). Immediately upon arriving in Jerusalem for the holiday, Paul meets with James (one of "the brothers of Jesus" of Acts 1:14), and this meeting raises the issue that will dominate the final eight chapters of the book—namely, the issue of Paul's approach to Judaism and the Jewish people. Thus, the pilgrim feast of Luke 2 becomes the model on which the following three stories are patterned, and the final story in the sequence introduces the drama to which the entire book has been leading.[39]

The second Torah practice that receives mention in the infancy narrative and recurs in more momentous form in the story of Paul is the custom of the Nazirite vow. When the angel Gabriel appears to Zechariah in the temple, he bears a promise and two commands: Zechariah's wife will bear a son (Luke 1:13a; the promise), and Zechariah must name him John (Luke 1:13b; the first command); this son will be "great in the sight of the Lord" and will be filled with the Holy Spirit from the womb (Luke 1:15a and 15c; the promise continued), and "he must never drink wine or strong drink" (Luke 1:15b; the second command). The prohibition of "wine and strong drink" was a central component of the Nazirite vow (Num 6:3). Such vows were normally temporary in duration, but in unusual circumstances individuals became lifelong Nazirites (Judg 13:3–7; see also Jer 35:1–10).[40] The Nazirite vow imposed obligations upon an individual similar to those that bound the high priest, and imparted to the person a status of sanctity that was appropriate to John as one filled with the Holy Spirit from before birth.

John's lifelong status as a Nazirite prepares the reader for a temporary Nazirite vow which Paul undertakes just before traveling to Jerusalem at the end of his second missionary journey (Acts 18:18–23).[41] As in the infancy narrative, Luke does not use the term "Nazirite," but the informed reader understands from the details of the text that this Torah practice is in view. In Luke 1, the relevant fact is the prohibition of wine and strong drink; in Acts 18, the key details are the "vow" and the cutting of Paul's hair (v. 18; see Num 6:1, 5, 18). Luke's reference here to Paul's

39. N. T. Wright minimizes the significance of Paul's approach to the Sabbath and Jewish holidays according to Acts, and thinks that the reference to Pentecost may have more to do with weather and travel conditions than with Paul's Torah piety: "Acts indicates that Paul himself was aware of the Jewish festivals, including the regular sabbaths, but whether these have simply become markers within the year and its changing seasons is not clear. Paul may perhaps simply have wanted to get to Jerusalem before Pentecost because he wanted a quick turnaround to get off to Rome while the Mediterranean was still safe for sailing; in which case he was disappointed" (N. T. Wright, *Paul and the Faithfulness of God*, 364). Had Wright considered these references in the wider literary context of Luke-Acts rather than as isolated incidents in the life of Paul, he would have recognized that it is indeed quite "clear" that the Sabbath and the holidays in this narrative function as basic Torah practices and not merely as "markers within the year and its changing seasons."

40. On John as a lifelong Nazirite, see Fitzmyer, *Luke I–IX*, 318–19, 325–26.

41. See Fitzmyer, *The Acts of the Apostles*, 633–34.

Nazirite vow appears at first sight to be incidental to the narrative and of no great consequence. It portrays Paul as a devout Jew who chooses to express his faith in forms drawn from the Torah, but seems to play no other role in the narrative.

This initial impression is undermined once Paul reaches Jerusalem for Pentecost after his third missionary journey, and meets with James and the Jerusalem elders. At that point James explains the problem that must be addressed: rumors are circulating within the Jerusalem *ekklēsia* that Paul has been teaching "all the Jews living among the gentiles to forsake Moses" (Acts 21:21). James knows this to be false, as does the knowledgeable reader, who has just read about Paul's Nazirite vow and his exertions to reach Jerusalem for Pentecost.[42] But how can Paul prove this fact to the members of the Jerusalem *ekklēsia*, who are "all zealous for the Torah"? James has the solution: "So do what we tell you. We have four men who are under a vow. Join these men, go through the rite of purification with them, and pay for the shaving of their heads. Thus all will know that there is nothing in what they have been told about you, but that you yourself observe and guard the law" (Acts 21:23–24). The solution is for Paul to participate in the concluding ceremonies for four members of the Jerusalem *ekklēsia* who are completing their own Nazirite vows. Now we see the importance of Luke's earlier mention of Paul's vow. A reader who has heard the same rumors about Paul which circulated at that time in Jerusalem (i.e., virtually *everyone* who has ever read Acts of the Apostles) might think that Paul could comply with James' direction only by rejecting its stated purpose of showing that he is a Torah-observant Jew. (In other words, Paul might act in accordance with the direction of James, but for reasons of expediency rather than principle.) However, having read that Paul had earlier taken upon himself a Nazirite vow, in a context that implied no motive other than devotion to God, we are prepared to believe that he would sincerely participate in the vows of these four fellow Jewish disciples of Jesus in order to make known to others what was the simple truth—namely, that he also was a Jew "zealous for the Torah."[43]

42. "Since Paul arrives in Jerusalem as a pilgrim to celebrate Pentecost (see 20:16), his easy accommodation of a purification ritual is not due to church politics but to its agreement with his religious practices as a devout Jew" (Wall, *Acts of the Apostles*, 291).

43. N. T. Wright portrays the choice set before Paul by James as a no-win situation, in which Paul was forced to select the least worst option: "'Do this and we will know you are loyal to Torah; don't do it and everyone will believe you have torn up the scriptures!' Faced with that loaded and dangerous alternative, Paul would unhesitatingly choose the former, since everything he believed was predicated on the assumption

These first two Torah practices—the pilgrimage feast and the Nazirite vow—converge when Paul reaches Jerusalem at Pentecost after his third missionary expedition. As we shall see, the third practice becomes significant on the same occasion. The Torah practice in question is circumcision. The first chapter of Luke's infancy narrative reaches its climax at the circumcision of John (Luke 1:59–79). The second chapter of the infancy narrative focuses on events that take place in Bethlehem immediately after the birth of Jesus (Luke 2:1–20) and in Jerusalem several weeks later when the family fulfills its Torah obligations in the temple (Luke 2:22–39). After the revelation given to the shepherds near Bethlehem and before the prophetic pronouncements of Simeon and Anna in the temple, at the center of the chapter's story of the infant Jesus, Luke recounts briefly the circumcision of the Messiah: "After eight days had passed, it was time to circumcise the child; and he was called Jesus, the name given by the angel before he was conceived in the womb" (Luke 2:22). No heavenly visions, no ecstatic songs of praise, no ominous prophecies, no mention even of those who attend the joyful event—the boy is circumcised (as the Torah required) and named (as the angel commanded), and that is enough.

Circumcision receives attention once again in Acts, but now it is more than background to great events that are external to the rite itself. Here the matter of circumcision becomes a major point of contention, representing metonymically the entire framework of Jewish Torah-observance, and shaping the drama surrounding the figure of Paul. Following the first missionary journey of Paul and Barnabas, who had been commissioned for this work by the *ekklēsia* at Antioch (Acts 13:1–3), the author sets the stage for the Jerusalem Council as follows:

> [1] Then certain individuals came down from Judea [to Antioch] and were teaching the [gentile] brothers, "*Unless you are circumcised according to the custom of Moses, you cannot be saved.*" [2] And after Paul and Barnabas had no small dissension and debate with them, Paul and Barnabas and some of the others were

that the law and the prophets were fulfilled in the Messiah" (*Paul and the Faithfulness of God*, 1441n113). This makes sense if one interprets the Pauline letters as Wright does, and then read Acts 21 in light of that interpretation rather than in light of the wider narrative of Luke and Acts. If instead we begin with Luke and Acts and attempt to understand Acts 21 in *that* context, it is nearly impossible to uphold such a reading. As Robert Wall notes, "From Acts 16:3 [i.e., the circumcision of Timothy] forward, the reader of Acts knows full well that these unfavorable reports are a canard, . . . Paul is an exemplary Jew . . . careful to safeguard a Jewish *ethos*" (*Acts of the Apostles*, 293).

> appointed to go up to Jerusalem to discuss this question with the apostles and the elders. . . . [4] When they came to Jerusalem, they were welcomed by the church and the apostles and the elders, and they reported all that God had done with them. [5] But some believers who belonged to the sect of the Pharisees stood up and said, *"It is necessary for them to be circumcised and ordered to keep the law of Moses."* (Acts 15:1–2, 4–5; emphasis added)

The issue at hand concerns the Torah as a whole and its application to gentiles who become disciples of Jesus. The particular commandment of circumcision symbolizes and sums up the general issue, for these Pharisaic members of the *ekklēsia* regard circumcision as the doorway for gentiles to join the Jewish people. In this way these proselytes would also become subject to the Torah as a whole. After the question has been debated by the apostles and elders, Peter recounts his experience with Cornelius (Acts 15:6–11), and James issues his decree that implicitly rejects the argument proposed by the Pharisaic disciples of Jesus regarding circumcision. He does so by indicating the limited set of commandments of the Torah which are incumbent upon gentile members of the *ekklēsia* (Acts 15:13–21). As far as Acts of the Apostles is concerned, the issue has been resolved once and for all.

But another question arises for both the first readers of Acts and for those of subsequent generations: what about the *Jewish* disciples of Jesus? Are they still obliged to circumcise their sons, and to keep the Torah? As Michael Wyschogrod has pointed out, the narrative of Acts 15 implies that this is not a question that the "apostles and elders" would have deemed worthy of consideration. *Of course* Jewish disciples of Jesus must circumcise their sons! If that were not a solemn duty for all Jews, what is the point of arguing about whether it is also a duty for gentiles?[44] This must be the opinion of Peter and James as depicted in Acts 15—but what about Paul? The readers of Acts have heard of Paul, and may even have read his letters. They may reasonably wonder whether Paul quietly disagreed with Peter and James on this matter. It is thus of enormous significance that the next chapter of Acts begins with Paul's circumcision of Timothy, son of a Jewish woman and a gentile man (Acts 16:1–3), and with Paul and Timothy's joint transmission of the rulings issued by the Jerusalem Council (Acts 16:4).

Why does Paul circumcise Timothy? The author tells us that it was "because of the Jews who were in those places, for they all knew

44. Wyschogrod, *Abraham's Promise*, 209.

that his father was a Greek" (Acts 16:3). If Paul assumes the principle of matrilineal descent and views Timothy as unambiguously Jewish, and if he believes that all Jews should be circumcised, why does the narrator even mention the practical problems in Paul's relations with the Jewish community posed by his traveling with an uncircumcised Jew?[45] Shaye Cohen argues that the matrilineal principle was not yet commonly accepted among first-century Jews, and thus the author considers Timothy a gentile.[46] But then Paul's circumcision of Timothy causes problems for the integrity of the narrative, since the authoritative decisions from the "apostles and elders" that Paul and Timothy are transmitting include the ruling that gentiles should not (or, at least, need not) be circumcised. Isaac Oliver has articulated a third position in response to this question, and his reading of Acts 16:1–4 has much to commend it. According to Oliver, as the child of a mixed marriage Timothy's status was ambiguous—he was neither clearly Jewish (for the matrilineal principle was not yet the consensus position of the entire Jewish world), nor clearly gentile (for at least some Jews likely held matrilineal descent sufficient to establish Jewish status). This ambiguity caused problems for Paul as he enlisted Timothy as his travel companion and partner in conveying the Apostolic Decree.

> The major decision that had been reached in Jerusalem, according to Luke, was that Gentiles did not need to be circumcised but only observe the commandments of the Apostolic Decree. Of course, in Luke's eyes, this decision presupposes that Jewish followers of Jesus continue to observe the Torah *in toto*, including circumcision. An uncircumcised follower of Jesus, whose mother was Jewish and father Greek, might not have proved the most adequate candidate for proclaiming the Apostolic Decree. On the contrary, Timothy's ambiguous background could raise further halakic questions and headaches: As an uncircumcised

45. Accepting these premises, David Rudolph offers a creative answer to this question: "The literary context suggests that Luke's explanatory statement ("because of the Jews who were in those places") does not mean that the *act of circumcision* was an expedient, but that the *timing of the circumcision* was an expedient. . . . Paul thought that the optimum time for Timothy to be circumcised (in order to confirm his covenant identity as a Jew) was prior to visiting his home region" (Rudolph, *A Jew to the Jews*, 27). But if Paul considered Timothy Jewish, and if he held that all Jews needed to be circumcised, why does the issue of timing arise in the first place? Timothy should be circumcised immediately to fulfill the commandment, and no further reason need be given.

46. Cohen, *The Beginnings of Jewishness*, 363–77.

> Jew (to those who would have considered him as such), did he necessitate circumcision or not? Could his non-circumcised status imply that Jewish followers of Jesus need not circumcise their children, precisely the rumor spreading around in Luke's day about Paul's teachings (Acts 21:21)? The circumcision of Timothy resolves this ambiguity and allows Luke at the same time to refute the allegations directed against Paul concerning his alleged abrogation of Torah observance for Jews. If Luke's Paul is even willing to circumcise a "semi-Gentile," how much more would he affirm the circumcision of Jews. Timothy's circumcision provides a buffer protecting Paul against accusations stating to the contrary that he opposed Jews who upheld the Torah.[47]

Oliver thus contends that the author includes this incident of Timothy's circumcision to prepare the reader for Paul's meeting with James and the Jerusalem elders. In that meeting James informs Paul of the rumors that are circulating about him within the Jerusalem *ekklēsia*: "They have been told about you that you teach all the Jews living among the gentiles to forsake Moses, and that *you tell them not to circumcise their children* or observe the customs" (Acts 21:21; emphasis added). To prove this rumor false, Paul submits to James' direction to participate publicly in temple rites celebrating the completion of the temporary vow of several Nazirites from the Jerusalem *ekklēsia*. Just as Paul's own Nazirite vow earlier in the narrative demonstrates that his compliance with the plan of James reflects rather than obscures his actual approach to Torah-praxis, so Paul's circumcision of Timothy shows that the rumors about him are false. Moreover, the fact that both of these Torah practices (the Nazirite vow, circumcision) are anticipated in the infancy narrative suggests that the issues that surface in Acts 21 are central rather than peripheral to the author's concerns in the composition of the infancy narrative and Acts of the Apostles.[48]

47. Oliver, *Torah Praxis After 70 CE*, 433. Oliver here draws upon the work of Matthew Thiessen, who likewise sees the Jewish status of Timothy as ambiguous. Thiessen further proposes that the author of Acts rejects the validity of all circumcision conducted beyond the eighth day from birth, and so sees the circumcision of Timothy as problematic even if his status as a Jew is accepted on genealogical grounds. Thiessen contends that this lies behind the narrator's apparent ambivalence in recounting the event. See Thiessen, *Contesting Conversion*, 120–22.

48. In an important 1973 article entitled "The Circumcised Messiah," Jacob Jervell argued persuasively for the importance of the topic of circumcision in the infancy narrative, and its literary function of preparing for Paul's circumcision of Timothy in

Further support for this view of Luke's purpose derives from Paul's speeches in the remaining chapters of Acts. Defending himself against the charges that have been brought against him by the priestly leaders of Jerusalem—charges that in effect reiterate the rumors recounted by James—Paul repeatedly asserts his fidelity to the Torah and to the Jewish people.

> Paul said in his defence, "I have in no way committed an offence against the law [i.e., the Torah] of the Jews, or against the temple, or against the emperor." (Acts 25:8)

> [4] All the Jews know my way of life from my youth, a life spent from the beginning among my own people and in Jerusalem. [5] They have known for a long time, if they are willing to testify, that I have belonged to the strictest sect of our religion and lived as a Pharisee. (Acts 26:4–5) (see Acts 23:6: "Brothers, I am a Pharisee, a son of Pharisees.")

> Brothers, though I had done nothing against our people or the customs of our ancestors, yet I was arrested in Jerusalem and handed over to the Romans. (Acts 28:17)

Robert Tannehill stresses the connection between the rumors cited by James in Acts 21:21 and the charges Paul faces in subsequent chapters of Acts, and the way Paul's defense against these charges highlights the Lukan treatment of "the problem of Judaism":

> The importance of the charge against Paul [in Acts 21:21] is also underlined when we look forward in the narrative. To be sure, the Jerusalem church will drop out of the narrative after this scene, and the charge in 21:21 may seem to disappear with it. In reality, the charge is absorbed into a larger accusation of continuing importance throughout the rest of Acts. This accusation comes from Jews and claims that Paul teaches "against the people and the law and this place (the temple)" (21:28), that is, that Paul and his mission are anti-Jewish. The reference to the temple reflects the temple setting of the scene. *The references to the people and the law parallel the charge in 21:21, for circumcision is the distinctive mark of the Jews as God's special people. Abandoning it and the Mosaic customs means the dissolution of the Jews as a separate and unique people.* The charge that Paul

---

the Book of Acts and for Paul's sincere efforts to refute the false allegations mentioned by James in Acts 21:21. The article was later included in Jervell's collection of essays, *The Unknown Paul*, 138–45.

> leads Jewish Christians to abandon their Jewish way of life can disappear because it is one aspect of a larger issue: Paul's attitude toward Judaism in general. This larger issue does not disappear. Again and again in the following chapters Paul will seek to convince his hearers that he is a loyal Jew and that his mission is not an anti-Jewish movement. He will still be arguing his case in 28:17–20, after he arrives in Rome. The importance of this issue in Acts 21–28 is one major indication of the importance throughout Luke-Acts of the problem of Judaism . . . .[49]

As the most prominent theme in the final eight chapters of Acts, the question of Paul's attitude toward Judaism obviously concerns the author. The rumors that James cites and that later surface in new form in the mouths of Paul's priestly antagonists likely also circulated among the book's potential readers. The aim of defending Paul against these charges gives shape to the narrative in significant ways.

The three key Torah practices of Paul—his journey to Jerusalem for the feast of Pentecost, his Nazirite vow, and his circumcision of Timothy—all point us to the temple act that Paul undertakes in accordance with the guidance of James, and that ultimately leads to his arrest. Moreover, Paul's purpose in undertaking that temple act then defines the terms in which he defends himself against his detractors: he has always been and now remains a faithful Jew, observing the Torah and living in loyalty to his people. These three Torah practices repeat in emphatic fashion elements from Luke's infancy narrative that in their earlier location appeared incidental to the major events being described. The annual pilgrimage to Jerusalem of Jesus' family, the Nazirite status of John the Baptist, and the circumcisions of John and Jesus all increase the symbolic weight of a text already laden with traditional Jewish motifs, but they do not immediately strike the reader as intrinsically important. However, in light of the Pauline narrative that concludes Luke's two volumes, readers are able to realize for the first time the significance of these three particular practices as mentioned in the infancy narrative, and similarly to recognize how the rich Torah imagery of Luke's first two chapters applies to the messianic era inaugurated by Jesus.

In conclusion, we have seen that the emphasis on Torah-observance in the Lukan infancy narrative is not a nostalgic evocation of Israel's honored-yet-transcended past, but instead establishes a paradigm for the

49. Tannehill, *The Narrative Unity of Luke-Acts*, 2:269–70 (emphasis added). See also Weatherly, *Jewish Responsibility for the Death of Jesus*, 156–57.

teaching and practice of Jesus and his disciples in the imminent future. Moreover, this material is not marginal to the author's concerns, but plays a prominent role in the unfolding narrative. The author's appreciation for the distinctive character of the Jewish way of life attests to the enduring centrality of the Jewish people in the Lukan theological vision.

Texts Allegedly Undermining Torah

Implicit Critique?

As noted at the beginning of this chapter, commentators have traditionally assumed that Luke and Acts view the Torah as inapplicable in the new era inaugurated by Jesus. The key texts summoned to confirm this assumption have been Acts 10 (Peter's dream) and Acts 15 (the decree of the Jerusalem Council). I will examine these two narratives in the following pages, but first let us look at units that are commonly interpreted as "implicit critiques" of the Torah.

Illustrative of such passages are those Lukan texts discussed above in which Jesus *supplements* the Torah by his call to discipleship or by his intensifying of the Torah's demands (e.g., in regards to divorce). In his short book dealing with Luke and the Torah, S. G. Wilson looks at the story of the rich young ruler (Luke 18:18–23) and claims that "An ambivalent attitude towards the law is expressed in this incident."[50] What is the ambivalence that Wilson discovers? "On the one hand the law's commands are quoted approvingly as a guide for those who wish to inherit eternal life; yet on the other hand it is clearly implied that the law has been supplemented by the teaching of Jesus."[51] But should this really be described as *ambivalence*? As we have seen, Fitzmyer takes full account of this supplementation, yet finds it entirely compatible with a wholehearted affirmation of the Torah: "[Jesus in Luke] views the law and the prophets as normative, and his preaching of the kingdom is *supplemental* to it."[52] Isaac Oliver adopts the same perspective: "What Israel needs, in Luke's eyes, is a *supplement* (not a supplanter!) to the Torah to assist in fulfilling its vocation and destiny."[53]

50. Wilson, *Luke and the Law*, 28.

51. Wilson, *Luke and the Law*, 28.

52. Fitzmyer, *Luke the Theologian*, 182.

53. Oliver, *Torah Praxis*, 447.

Wilson also argues that the Lukan Jesus offers an "implicit critique of the Sabbath" by condoning the plucking of grain on the holy day and asserting that "The Son of Man is lord of the Sabbath" (Luke 6:1–5).[54] "As lord of the Sabbath he stands above the law and implicitly claims the right to define it."[55] Jesus does indeed claim such a right, but his authority in relation to the Torah need entail no "implicit critique" of its normative character or enduring value. This fact is demonstrated by an element of the narrative that Wilson notes but misinterprets:

> In this connection it is important to observe that the charge of illegality in 6:2—"Why do they do that which is unlawful [*ouk exestin*] to do on the Sabbath"—is not denied or disputed. Indeed, the example of David confirms it by echoing the charge, since he eats "that which it is not lawful [*ouk exestin*] except for the priests alone to eat." The repetition of *ouk exestin* and the fact that it is precisely the element of illegality which binds the two incidents together, confirm that evasion of the charge of illegality is not intended, at least in the terms in which Jesus' opponents pose it. Whatever other ramifications there may be in the assertion that Jesus is lord of the Sabbath, one remains clear: it can be used to justify a rejection of current Sabbath practice.[56]

Wilson rightly stresses the significance of the repetition of *ouk exestin* and the parallel drawn between the example of David and the actions of his disciples. However, Wilson's conclusion is unwarranted by his premises. As those premises indicate, Jesus acknowledges that it is generally inappropriate to pluck grain on the Sabbath. Far from constituting "a rejection of current Sabbath practice," such an acknowledgment *affirms* that practice as normative. Jesus asserts his christological authority to make exceptions to normative practice, just as David did in the incident Jesus cites as an analogy supporting his authority (as the promised Son of David). But here the exception truly proves the rule—for Jesus explicitly treats his own act and that of David as exceptions rather than new norms. The plucking of grain by Jesus' disciples did not involve a "rejection of current Sabbath practice" any more than David's eating of the bread of the presence entailed a "rejection" of current *temple* practice.[57]

54. Wilson, *Luke and the Law*, 34.

55. Wilson. *Luke and the Law*, 33.

56. Wilson, *Luke and the Law*, 33–34.

57. It should also be noted that the incident recounted in Luke 6:1–5 is attested in Mark and Matthew, and thus does not reflect a distinctively Lukan perspective. In

While not explicitly undermining any of the commandments, two passages from Acts have often been treated by scholars as expressing a dismissive attitude toward the Torah. The first derives from Paul's synagogue sermon in Acts 13: "Let it be known to you therefore, my brothers, that through this man forgiveness of sins is proclaimed to you; by this Jesus everyone who believes is set free [*dikaioutai*; 'justified'] from all those sins from which you could not be freed [*dikaiōthēnai*; 'justified'] by the law of Moses" (Acts 13:38–39). This has often been taken to mean that "the law of Moses" provided *no* forgiveness or justification (two concepts that are here equated), and thus that the coming of Jesus defines an era of grace in which the Torah no longer shapes Israel's daily life. However, the words themselves do not say this, and the Lukan vision discerned elsewhere points to a more subtle reading. William Loader rightly rejects such a strict polarity: "It does not say that prior to the gospel there was no forgiveness, as popular Christianity has taught. Rather it speaks of *more* forgiveness than was possible before."[58] Joseph Fitzmyer recognizes here another instance of Luke's theme of messianic supplementation: "the gospel that Paul is preaching is understood once again as a *supplement* to the law. . . . It does not follow that the law has been done away with or that it no longer has a role to play in Jewish or Jewish-Christian piety."[59]

The second passage that has often been treated as dismissive of the Torah derives from Peter's speech to the Jerusalem Council in which he

---

the current chapter, I have focused on material that is unique to Luke or distinctive Lukan redaction of shared material. In the case of Luke 6:1–5, the Lukan version (like that of Matthew) deletes the Markan statement of Jesus, "the Sabbath was made for humankind, and not humankind for the Sabbath" (Mark 2:27). It is likely that Luke (along with Matthew) deletes this saying because he thinks it could be misconstrued as providing grounds for disregarding customary Sabbath norms. It is typical that Wilson rejects this explanation of the deletion because, as he understands Luke, it "scarcely concurs with the radical implications of the Lucan narrative as it stands" (Wilson, *Luke and the* Law, 34). However, Wilson has failed to demonstrate that such "radical implications" exist.

58. Loader, *Jesus' Attitude towards the Law*, 371–72. Emphasis added.

59. Fitzmyer, *Luke the Theologian*, 187. We should also allow for the possibility that "forgiveness of sins" and "justification" in this text have a corporate and prophetic meaning, and—in line with N. T. Wright's treatment of the theme—speak primarily of Israel's national restoration rather than the salvation of individuals. Since Paul is addressing a synagogue audience of his fellow Jews, and since Peter's sermons to Jewish audiences in Jerusalem have such a corporate and prophetic thrust (e.g., Acts 3:19–21), this reading of Acts 13:38–39 should be taken seriously. See Wright, *Jesus and the Victory of God*, 268–74.

argues against requiring circumcision and full Torah-observance from the gentile believers in Jesus:

> [8] God, who knows the heart, showed that he accepted them [i.e., Cornelius and his household, all gentiles] by giving the Holy Spirit to them, just as he did to us [i.e., Jews who received the Spirit on Pentecost]. [9] He did not discriminate between us and them, for he purified their hearts by faith. [10] Now then, why do you try to test God by putting on the necks of gentiles a yoke that neither we nor our ancestors have been able to bear? [11] No! We believe it is through the grace of our Lord Jesus that we are saved, just as they are." (Acts 15:8–11 NIV)

The heart-purification that these gentiles received when God gave them the Holy Spirit is the same as that received by the Jewish disciples of Jesus at Pentecost, and is also identical to that which Ezekiel prophesied as essential to Israel's national restoration (Ezek 36:25–27). The allusion here to Ezekiel is significant, as it provides a clue for interpreting the meaning of "the yoke that neither we nor our ancestors have been able to bear" (v. 10b). This is not an attack on the burdensome character of the Torah, nor is it an assertion that every individual Jew has failed to keep its commandments in an adequate way. Luke himself contradicts this latter claim in his infancy narrative when he describes Zechariah and Elizabeth as "righteous before God, walking in all the commandments and ordinances of the Lord blameless" (Luke 1:6). The former claim likewise seems incompatible with the attitude of those "thousands" of Jerusalem disciples of Jesus who were "zealous for the Torah" (Acts 21:20). They appear to have embraced this supposedly "unbearable burden" with enthusiasm.

The allusion to Ezekiel 36 suggests that Peter refers here to Israel's *corporate* failure in the past (i.e., the generations of "our ancestors") and the present ("nor we," i.e., the Jewish people of our own generation) to keep the Torah adequately, *a corporate failure that led to the exile spoken of by the prophet*. To address that situation, God has acted through the Messiah to pour out the Holy Spirit—not to free the sons and daughters of Israel from the burden of the Torah, but to empower them to "follow my statutes and be careful to observe my ordinances" (Ezek 36:27). By giving the same Spirit to the gentile believers in Jesus, God has shown that there is a place for them within an expanded Israel *as gentiles* who keep those "statutes" and "ordinances" of the Torah appropriate to them. Thus, Peter's words are not a critique of the Torah but instead a critique of

Israel, past and present, in its corporate response to the Torah. As Loader states, "It is doubtful that Luke understands 'hard to bear' negatively, i.e., as 'burdensome.' The Law's demands are to be borne; Luke has Peter acknowledge of the Jews: we have not kept them well."[60]

After denying that gentile believers in Jesus should be required to be circumcised (i.e., to become Jews) and to keep all the provisions of the Torah incumbent upon Jews, Peter offers an affirmation that provides the basis for this denial: "No! We believe it is through the grace of our Lord Jesus that we are saved, just as they are" (Acts 15:11).What does the author mean when he speaks of "being saved"? In the Lukan writings "salvation" (*sōtēria*) and its related verb (*sōzō*) refer to the proleptic experience now, in this world, of the deliverance, healing, restoration, and renewal that constitute Israel's eschatological blessing.[61] The "yoke" that Israel failed to bear was the corporate responsibility of fulfilling the Torah *as a condition for* receiving that blessing. This is the "yoke" that the Torah-zealous Jewish disciples of Jesus are seeking to impose on the new gentile disciples when they insist that "Unless you are circumcised according to the custom of Moses, *you cannot be saved*" (Acts 15:1). Thus, to "be saved" here does not refer to a special juridical status that entitles particular individuals to go to heaven after they die; instead, it means sharing *now* in the eschatological life of the people of Israel as it receives the foretaste of its promised inheritance. Peter rejects the demands of these contending leaders because he sees a different logic at work in his experience with Cornelius (Acts 10) and in the prophetic text (Ezek 36) by means of which he interprets that event. The gift of the Spirit bestows the saving power of God. That saving power opens access to the eschatological blessing promised to Israel by purifying the heart and inspiring obedience to the commandments —for *both* Jews and gentiles (though

60. Loader, *Jesus' Attitude towards the Law*, 373. Isaac Oliver shares this perspective on Acts 15:10, and compares the verse with other Jewish texts that were written in the same era. "Luke's Peter's reference to the Law as a yoke is not negative. He blames *Israel* for failing to fulfill the Law, not the supposedly overwhelming stipulations contained in the Mosaic Torah. . . . Luke joins the authors of 2 *Baruch* and 4 *Ezra* and other Jewish thinkers of his time in recognizing that history confirms Israel's collective failure to follow God's Law" (Oliver, *Torah Praxis After 70 CE*, 446–47).

61. For Luke, the word "salvation" refers not to a future life in "heaven" for individual disembodied souls but instead to the full-orbed restoration of Israel and the world envisioned by Ezekiel, Isaiah, Jeremiah, and Jewish scripture as a whole. Luke usually employs the term in the past or present tense rather than the future, for he believes that Israel's eschatological blessing is already available in seed form in the *ekklēsia* by the gift of the Spirit. See Fitzmyer, *Luke I–IX*, 222–23.

in a differentiated manner). This grace of salvation is manifested in the gift of the Holy Spirit as a result of the work of Jesus and the response to him of faith.[62]

Therefore, Acts 15:10–11 should be read in the context in which it appears. It is not a critique of the Torah, but of Israel's obedience to it; it is also a critique of those Jews who fail to perceive Israel's corporate condition of spiritual need, and consequently misunderstand the relationship between the Torah and the divine gift of eschatological blessing. In accordance with Ezekiel 36, Luke sees Israel's corporate life of full-orbed Torah-obedience as a component and consequence of that blessing, rather than as a condition for its realization.[63] He also envisions Torah-obedience as differentiated in its expression for Jews and gentiles (who remain gentiles while being attached to Israel).

These two passages from Acts of the Apostles, in which Paul and Peter acknowledge the limits of the Torah, pose no challenge to the thesis

62. It could be asked whether this teaching from Acts about Torah-obedience as a condition for salvation conflicts with the emphasis in the Gospel of Luke on keeping the commandments as the path to "life." While a certain tension exists between these two perspectives, they are not incompatible once the concepts involved are clarified. First, the term "life" in the Gospel of Luke refers to the reward bestowed upon the righteous in the world to come, and in context the question always concerns the ultimate destiny of particular individuals. In contrast, the term "salvation" in both Lukan volumes refers to a restored wholeness that is experienced primarily (or at least initially) in the present world, and this wholeness includes incorporation into a community in which God's saving power now resides. Second, when the question is "what must I do to inherit eternal life?" (Luke 10:25; 18:18), Jesus' response points the questioner to the most essential elements of the Torah (i.e., love of God; love of neighbor; the Ten Commandments) which apply equally to Jews and gentiles. When the question concerns "salvation," as in Acts 15, emphasis falls on the direct response that those in view are giving to the person and work of Jesus, and on the insufficiency of Israel's integral Torah-obedience (encompassing the entire spectrum of moral and ritual commandments) apart from such a response to the Messiah.

63. As was indicated in the previous footnote and in the previous chapter, the author envisions Israel's "salvation" as contingent upon its corporate response to the person and work of Jesus. Since Jesus is portrayed in Acts as the prophet like Moses (Deut 18:15–19) to whom the Torah itself commands obedience (Acts 3:22–23; 7:37), we should be careful not to overstate the contrast in these volumes between Torah-obedience and faith in Jesus. In a certain sense, then, the author does see Torah-obedience (i.e., faith in Jesus) as a condition for receiving "salvation." He singles out this one element of Torah-obedience as fundamental to Israel's capacity to faithfully fulfill all the rest. However, *that one element is common to the Torah-obedience demanded of both Jews and gentiles.* Having fulfilled this commandment of the Torah that applies to them both, Jews and gentiles are then called to and equipped for a differentiated life of Torah-observance.

proposed in this chapter. In these texts the author presents the Torah as subordinate to Jesus and his saving work—but he still upholds the authority of the Torah and its role as a pillar of Israel's national life.

Peter's Dream

Having demonstrated the emphatically positive approach to the Torah displayed by the overall narrative of Luke and Acts, and having dismissed assertions of its "implicit critique," we are now ready to take up the two texts whose critique of the Torah is allegedly explicit.

The first of these concerns Peter's vision in Acts 10:9–16 and its aftermath at the home of Cornelius (Acts 10:17–48). In his vision Peter beholds a host of animals, clean and unclean according to the Torah, and is told "Get up, Peter; kill and eat" (v. 13). F. F. Bruce represents the older commentary tradition when he suggests that this vision may have reminded Peter of Jesus' words concerning unclean food (Mark 7:14–19a): "This [i.e., the teaching of Jesus recorded in Mark 7] was in effect an abrogation of ceremonial food laws and much else of the same character, but it was not until much later, as a result of his experience on the roof at Joppa, that Peter appreciated this."[64]

Since F. F. Bruce wrote these words the interpretive consensus that he expressed has dissolved. While no new consensus has yet replaced it, the trajectory of Lukan scholarship appears to be in the direction of a Torah-positive reading of Acts 10. Isaac Oliver represents that trajectory in its most recent and potent form. In his 2013 volume, he devotes an entire chapter to the Cornelius incident, and offers a compelling argument against the view that Acts 10 implies the abrogation of the dietary laws of the Torah.[65] I will summarize Oliver's case in eight points.[66]

64. Bruce, *The Book of Acts*, 206. In passing, it is noteworthy that the old consensus of New Testament scholars concerning Mark 7 itself and that chapter's "abrogation of ceremonial food laws" no longer holds. Many twenty-first-century studies argue persuasively that the scope of Jesus' critique in that chapter is far more limited, and the position advanced far less radical. For examples of such recent research, see Kister, "Law, Morality and Rhetoric in Some Sayings of Jesus"; Rudolph, "Jesus and the Food Laws"; Crossley, *The Date of Mark's Gospel*, 183–205; Kinzer, *Postmissionary Messianic Judaism*, 52–58; Furstenberg, "Defilement Penetrating the Body"; and Boyarin, *The Jewish Gospels*, 102–28.

65. Oliver, *Torah Praxis After 70 CE*, 320–64.

66. This list of eight points is my attempt to cull key elements from Oliver's argument, which is not ordered in this manner. His treatment of Acts 10 is rich in its

(1) The narrative emphasizes Peter's refusal to obey the heavenly directive, "Get up, Peter, kill and eat," which is addressed to him three times. Despite his hunger (v. 10), on each occasion Peter boldly replies, "By no means, Lord; for I have never eaten anything that is profane [*koinon*] or unclean [*akatharton*]" (v. 14). Peter's response contrasts with Cornelius' immediate compliance with the command he had received in a vision (vv. 1–8). The two narratives are otherwise symmetrical, and so the difference in the responses of Cornelius and Peter stands out.[67]

(2) Following the threefold vision, command, and refusal, Luke tells us that "Peter was greatly puzzled about what to make of the vision that he had seen" (v. 17). Peter's perplexity suggests that he assumes that the vision has symbolic import. It could not mean literally "eat unclean food," for the Torah forbids Jews to act in that way. So the heavenly command, and its explanation in verse 15 ("What God has made clean [*ekatharisen*], you must not call profane [*koinou*]"), must have symbolic meaning. This fits well the with the prophetic and apocalyptic genre, in which visions (often involving animals) convey their message in vivid images that evoke from the seer initial bewilderment and that require inspired interpretation.[68]

(3) As Peter puzzles over the vision, the messengers sent by Cornelius arrive at the place he is staying (v. 17). The Spirit then speaks to Peter and tells him to "go with them without hesitation" (v. 20). Whereas Peter had earlier refused to comply with the command given in the vision, he now obeys the voice of the Spirit without complaint. Peter's response to the Spirit's guidance now completes the symmetry of the two visions, in which both men receive practical direction and both men act as directed. The relation between the command in Peter's vision ("Get up, Peter, kill and eat") and the Spirit's command to go to the home of a gentile is then expressed explicitly in Peter's opening words to those gathered with Cornelius: "You yourselves know that it is unlawful [*athemiton*] for a Jew to associate with [*kollasthai*] or to visit a gentile; but God has shown me that I should not call anyone profane [*koinon*] or unclean [*akatharton*]. So when I was sent for, I came without objection" (vv. 28–29). Peter here interprets the animals of his vision as symbolizing various groups of

analytical framework, exegetical detail, use of Second Temple literature, and engagement with secondary sources, and the summary provided here fails to do justice to its persuasive power.

67. Oliver, *Torah Praxis After 70 CE*, 323–24; 340–41.

68. Oliver, *Torah Praxis After 70 CE*, 324; 341–44.

human beings—the clean animals representing Jews, the unclean animals gentiles. The command to "eat" referred to the type of social interaction exemplified by "eating *with*."[69]

(4) Oliver notes that the verb in verse 28 translated as "associate with" (*kollasthai*) refers to "extended, intimate association and interaction" rather than "superficial, formal contact."[70] The issue is not whether Peter may sit at table with Cornelius on one isolated occasion, but whether he may enter into a relationship in which table-fellowship becomes a normal feature of life. Once again, we see that the controversy has nothing to do with kosher and non-kosher food, but instead concerns communal relationships.

(5) When Peter returns to Jerusalem, he receives criticism for his actions in Caesarea. His critics ask, "Why did you go to uncircumcised men and eat with them?" (Acts 11:3). They do not charge him with violating the dietary laws of the Torah, which would be a far more serious accusation. They focus not on *what* Peter ate, but on *those with whom* he ate.[71]

(6) Luke recounts the Peter-Cornelius incident three times (Acts 10:9–48; 11:4–17; 15:7–9). This parallels the three reports given of Paul's vision on the Damascus road (Acts 9; 22:6–21; 26:9–20), and highlights the significance of the event. In none of these accounts is there the slightest indication that the food laws of the Torah have been abolished or modified.[72]

(7) Luke stresses that Cornelius was a righteous gentile who loved the Jewish people and had adopted various Jewish practices. The knowledgeable reader would assume Cornelius's familiarity with the dietary laws of the Torah and appreciation for the significance of a Jew entering his home. In accordance with elementary principles of hospitality, Cornelius would never serve Peter food items that would require his transgression of the Torah commandments.[73]

(8) The heavenly voice that responds to Peter's refusal to eat (Acts 10:15), and the interpretation of the vision that Peter later provides (Acts 10:28; 11:12; 15:8–9), challenge the way Peter's community has been "making a distinction" (*diakrinō*) between people who are "clean" and

69. Oliver, *Torah Praxis After 70 CE*, 344–45.

70. Oliver, *Torah Praxis After 70 CE*, 358.

71. Oliver, *Torah Praxis After 70 CE*, 362

72. Oliver, *Torah Praxis After 70 CE*, 325.

73. Oliver, *Torah Praxis After 70 CE*, 337–40, 357, 362.

"holy" (i.e., Jews) and those who are "unclean" and "profane" (i.e., gentiles). While commentators often treat the two negative adjectives as synonyms, Oliver argues that *akathartos* ("unclean") and *koinos* ("profane") should be understood as translations of the Hebrew words *tamē* and *chol*. The former (*akathartos/tamē*) refers to the moral (and not ritual) impurity that derives from idolatry, sexual immorality, and murder. Cornelius and other gentiles who enter the *ekklēsia* have repented of these gentile practices, and thus should no longer be viewed by Jews as unclean. The latter term (*koinos/chol*) refers to that which has not been sanctified or set apart for God. Israel is holy (*kadosh*), and the nations are *chol* (common). However, the reception of the Holy Spirit by Cornelius and his household demonstrates that these gentiles have now also been sanctified and rendered part of the holy people. Thus, Jews in the *ekklēsia* may no longer "distinguish" (*diakrinō*) themselves from all gentiles according to these categories. At the same time, Oliver emphasizes that the categories themselves remain in effect, and that it is not *all gentiles* but only gentiles who enter the *ekklēsia* whose status is altered from "impure" to "pure" and from "profane" to "holy."[74] Moreover, while this change in gentile status within the *ekklēsia* was symbolized in Peter's vision by the purification of formerly unclean animals, there is no evidence in the narrative that this symbolic change in animal status implied an abolition of the dietary laws of the Torah.[75]

These eight points provide a compelling refutation of the claim that Peter's vision in Acts 10 entails the abolition of the dietary laws of the

74. Oliver, *Torah Praxis*, 345–57; 360–62. Oliver also stresses that Peter only agrees to stay at the home of Cornelius *after* these gentiles have received the gift of the Holy Spirit, and have thus manifestly been set apart as holy (361–62).

75. Traditional commentators have often asserted that the symbol and its referent in Peter's vision are so intertwined that they cannot be separated as Oliver has done. "Within the framework of the vision it is food that God has cleansed by dominical pronouncement, but in the wider narrative it is men and women, even Gentiles, whose hearts he has cleansed by faith (cf. 15:9). Yet the cleansing of food is not wholly parabolic: there is a connection between the abrogation of the levitical food restrictions and the removal of the barrier between believing Jews and Gentiles, for it was in large measure the Gentiles' eating of food which was 'unclean' (not *kosher*) by Jewish law that made association with them a source of 'defilement' for Jews" (Bruce, *Book of the* Acts, 206). Oliver demonstrates in compelling fashion the falsity of this claim. The "uncleanness" of gentiles was not ritual in character, but moral; it derived not from the food they ate or the substances they touched, but from the idolatrous practices in which they engaged. Richard Bauckham approaches this text, and its categories of "unclean"/"profane," in much the same way as Oliver. See his article, "James, Peter, and the Gentiles."

Torah. When viewed in the wider context of Luke and Acts—in which the Torah plays such a prominent role and the distinctive customs (*ethē*) of the Jewish people ordained by the Torah are repeatedly affirmed—this staple of traditional exegesis loses the slightest trace of plausibility.

The Jerusalem Decree

The last passage to be examined is especially significant, since it was traditionally viewed as the definitive "report of how the Gentile Church is declared free from the Law"[76] but is considered by many recent interpreters to imply the exact opposite. I refer to the report in Acts of the Jerusalem Council (Acts 15:1–29), and especially of its official decree (Acts 15:19–21; 23–29). In response to the demand of some Jewish disciples of Jesus that all gentiles who received the apostolic message must be circumcised and instructed to keep all the provisions of the Torah, the Council ruled that these gentiles need only adhere to four particular practices: abstention from "what has been sacrificed to idols and from blood and from what is strangled and from fornication" (v. 29; see also v. 20). In keeping with the words of Conzelman cited above, traditional commentators treated the decision of the Council as a declaration of independence from the Torah for the (gentile) *ekklēsia*. The call to avoid the four behaviors listed by the Council was treated as a pastoral "recommendation" aimed at facilitating "harmony between Jews and Gentiles."[77] In other words, these practices were handed on because Jewish members of the *ekklēsia*, by force of upbringing and environment, found the excluded behaviors to be "repulsive."[78] Thus, gentile believers in Jesus were being asked to bear in love with some of the excessive scruples of their Jewish brothers and sisters.

As in so many other matters, it was Jacob Jervell who championed a dissenting vision of Acts 15, a vision that has gathered substantial momentum among exegetes since the publication of his seminal volume on Luke in 1972. Examining the four practices enjoined by the Apostolic Decree, Jervell asserted that they derive from commandments found in Leviticus 17–18 that apply to "'strangers' that sojourn among Israelites."[79] When

76. Conzelman, *Theology of St. Luke*, 212.

77. Marshall, *Acts*, 253, 255.

78. Marshall, *Acts*, 253.

79. Jervell, *Luke and the People of God*, 143–44.

James concludes his ruling by stating, "For in every city, for generations past, Moses has had those who proclaim him, for he has been read aloud every Sabbath in the synagogues" (Acts 15:21), the leader of the Jerusalem *ekklēsia* means that "Everyone who truly hears Moses knows that the decree expresses what Moses demands from Gentiles in order that they may live among Israelites."[80] Jervell infers from this that the significance of the Jerusalem Council in relation to the Torah is the exact opposite of what has usually been thought: "The apostolic decree enjoins Gentiles to keep the law. . . . It is false to speak of the Gentiles as free from the law. The church, on the contrary, delivers the law to the Gentiles as Gentiles. Thus Luke succeeds in showing complete adherence to the law as well as the salvation of Gentiles as Gentiles."[81]

In a series of probing exegetical articles, Richard Bauckham has studied the provisions of the Apostolic Decree in minute detail.[82] His careful analysis supports Jervell's thesis that the Apostolic Decree derives from Leviticus 17–18. Building upon the seminal research of Jonathan Klawans on the laws of purity, Bauckham identifies these particular four practices as "the offenses that are . . . most often regarded as constituting the moral impurity of the Gentiles."[83]

Thus, the decree is not a pastoral directive delivered for the purpose of enabling gentiles to live in community with overly scrupulous Jews, but instead a statement regarding the authoritative teaching of the Torah as it applies to these gentiles: "Nor is the enabling of table fellowship between Jews and Gentiles its [the apostolic decree] primary purpose. . . . But the decision taken addressed in principle the issue of Gentile Christians' obligation to the Law of Moses. The four prohibitions would have been regarded as in principle binding on Gentile Christians quite irrespective of whether they had any contact with Jewish Christians."[84] This conclusion has been confirmed by many exegetes.[85] Far from constituting

80. Jervell, *Luke and the People of God*, 144.

81. Jervell, *Luke and the People of God*, 144.

82. See Bauckham, "James and the Jerusalem Church"; "James and the Gentiles (Acts 15.13–21)"; "James, Peter, and the Gentiles"; "James and the Jerusalem Council Decision."

83. Bauckham, "James and the Jerusalem Council Decision," 183. See Klawans, *Impurity and Sin in Ancient Judaism*.

84. Bauckham, "James and the Jerusalem Church," 464.

85. See, for example, Juel, *Luke*-Acts, 90, 106–7, and Loader, *Jesus' Attitude towards the* Law, 374–75, 378. Isaac Oliver's chapter on the Apostolic Decree (*Torah Praxis*

a declaration of independence from the Torah, the Apostolic Decree actually constitutes a decisive demonstration of the Torah's enduring power in the age of the Messiah.

If the Jerusalem Council affirms the authority of the Torah for the lives of *gentile* disciples of Jesus, how much more so does it do so for the lives of *Jewish* members of the *ekklēsia*. As noted above, this exegetical conclusion was reached by Orthodox Jewish theologian Michael Wyschogrod, even apart from consideration of the meaning of the decree for gentiles. Wyschogrod bases his judgment on the nature of the controversy that sparked the convening of the Jerusalem Council: "But it is clear that both parties [of the dispute] agreed that circumcision and Torah obedience remained obligatory for Jewish Jesus believers since, if this were not the case, one could hardly debate whether circumcision and Torah obedience was obligatory for gentiles."[86] Once it is recognized that the Jerusalem decree imposes a form of Torah obedience also on gentile members of the *ekklēsia*, Wyschogrod's conclusion becomes even more compelling. Thus, when Paul arrives in Jerusalem, and is instructed by James to show publicly once and for all that "you yourself observe and guard the Torah" (Acts 21:24), readers of Acts behold a scene that should hold no surprises for them. Acts 21 merely makes explicit what was already implicit in Acts 15.

I have argued that Luke interprets the death of Jesus as a bearing of Israel's judgment and a proleptic participation in the suffering that Jerusalem would endure at the hands of the Romans in 70 CE. When that event occurred, the Torah-observant Jewish disciples of Jesus lost their center, and their position in the now gentile-dominated *ekklēsia* became tenuous. The author/editor of Luke and Acts writes in that period, and one of his purposes may be to encourage these Jewish disciples of Jesus to persevere in hope. They are privileged now to share in the atoning suffering of their Lord, who took upon himself Israel's sin and its judgment. But these two books also hint that the resurrection of Jesus serves as a promise and pledge of Jerusalem's ultimate redemption. In the same way, the Torah-observant Jewish disciples of Jesus—now in exile—may look with hope to a future day when they will share the glory of their Messiah in a renewed Jerusalem. In that day, they will also see the *ekklēsia* renewed along with Jerusalem, as a community of Jews and gentiles in

---

After 70 CE, 365–98) deserves special attention.

86. Wyschogrod, *Abraham's Promise*, 209.

which the Torah is honored and observed in a differentiated manner appropriate to each group.

In conclusion, we find no texts in Luke or Acts that undermine the thesis of this chapter: according to Luke, the Torah remains in effect in the messianic age inaugurated by the death and resurrection of Jesus, and retains its significance as a fundamental sign of Israel's election and vocation.

Conclusion

We have taken up the issue of the Torah as a way of continuing our discussion of the Jewish people, just as our treatment of the temple was a continuation of our discussion of the city and the land. Our conclusion here is much the same as it was in chapter 2: the Lukan approach to the Torah confirms and strengthens our thesis regarding the Lukan approach to the Jewish people. Luke and Acts affirm the enduring applicability of the Torah, and they do so in a way that underlines the connection between the Torah and Jewish national life. As Jacob Jervell writes, "Luke is concerned about the law *because it is Israel's law*. . . . It is significant that Luke is most concerned about the ritual and ceremonial aspects of the law. *The law is to him not essentially the moral law, but the mark of distinction between Jews and non-Jews. The law is the sign of Israel as the people of God* . . . ."[87]

Luke and Acts focus their attention upon the faithful Torah practice of Jesus and his disciples. At the same time, the fact that Jesus and his disciples treat the Torah as authoritative implies that the Torah retains its role as the constitution of the Jewish people as a whole. If the death and resurrection of Jesus and the gift of the Spirit have not ushered the *ekklēsia* into a Torah-free eschatological zone, then the same is true for all Jews. Moreover, Acts of the Apostles portrays the Pharisees in a positive light, and hints that they will replace the priestly Sadducean party as the guiding force in the post-70 Jewish world. But the authority of the Pharisees is based on their strict adherence to "our ancestral law" (see Acts 22:3; 26:5). The future role of the Pharisees and its connection to Torah point to the enduring covenantal status of the Jewish people as a whole.

The results of this examination of the Torah in Luke and Acts also fit perfectly with the results of chapter 1 regarding the city and the land.

87. Jervell, *Luke and the People of God*, 137. Emphasis added.

There we saw that the universal *eschatological* vision of Luke and Acts remains rooted in Israel's particular national hopes expressed in the Torah and amplified in the prophets. The particular is not drowned in the ocean of the universal, but is lifted up and sustained as its orienting center. Here we have seen that the universal *ecclesial* vision of Luke and Acts remains rooted in Israel's particular identity as defined by the Torah as its national constitution and way of life. The particularity of the Jewish people is never lost even within the ever expanding horizon of the universal *ekklēsia.*

Furthermore, the relationship between this chapter and our chapter on the temple goes beyond the functional parallel between Torah and temple in the structure of our argument. The Torah and the temple are themselves intrinsically connected. A large proportion of the commandments contained in the Torah deal with temple rites, and the destruction of the temple renders them inoperable in their straightforward sense. However, just as the Temple Mount remains a holy place when the temple building has disappeared, so also the distinctive Jewish national customs (*ethē*) of the Torah emphasized in Luke and Acts—circumcision, Sabbath, holidays, and dietary laws—continue to define the identity of the Jewish people even when the sacrificial service is defunct. This relationship between the Torah and the temple is also reflected in the way the Pharisaic family of Gamaliel remains in authority among the Jewish people after his Sadducean colleagues on the council have disappeared along with the temple building which gave them priestly legitimacy.

Thus, this chapter on the Torah ties together the three previous chapters and provides them with a suitable exegetical conclusion. We have now finished our compositional analysis of Luke and Acts. It has revealed much about the prophetic *euangelion* and its message concerning the resurrected Messiah and his relationship to the Jewish people and the land of promise. But it also raises a host of new questions. How should the perspective of Luke and Acts affect our reading of the Pauline writings? What do we make of an ecclesial tradition that failed to absorb the message of Luke and Acts regarding the Jewish people and the land? What do we make of the long history of the Jewish people and its tradition? In particular, what do we make of the momentous events of Jewish history in the twentieth century? These are the questions that will occupy us in our final chapters.

Chapter 5

The Divine *Boulē* and the Fractured *Euangelion*

The thesis I have articulated and tested over the past four chapters concerns the content of the *euangelion* as a message dealing with the crucified and resurrected Jesus and his enduring relationship with both the Jewish people and the land promised to its ancestors. Jesus the king of Israel represents and embodies the people of Israel and the land of Israel, and realizes in his person the incarnational presence of God to which the Jerusalem temple pointed. In his suffering and death he bore Israel's suffering, past, present, and future, but with special reference to the judgment that the Jewish people would endure forty years later at the hands of the Romans. In doing so he transformed the character of that suffering, granting it a redemptive power that it would not have possessed apart from his atoning work. As a result, the Jewish people are ontologically (though not yet epistemologically) knit to Jesus through their experience of exile, and his renewing power is manifested in the post-70 flourishing of Jewish life. Moreover, the resurrected Messiah—representing and embodying the land as well as the people—serves as the pledge and power of Israel's ultimate eschatological restoration. That restoration will constitute the definitive end of exile, establishing a renewed Jerusalem as the jewel at the heart of a renewed cosmos. In this way, the Jewish people—and the *ekklēsia* joined to it ontologically—are redeemed not only *from* exile but also *through* exile.

This means that the *euangelion* of the resurrected Messiah is in important respects *a prophetic message about the future of the Jewish people*. Moreover, the future implied by that message includes not only the ultimate eschatological restoration of the Jewish people but also that people's exilic journey, which culminates in restoration. If this is correct, then interpreters of the *euangelion* are compelled to reflect theologically on the history of the Jewish people.

How should a disciple of Jesus assess the history of the Jewish people and its tradition, which developed in apparent opposition to the messianic claims of Jesus? And what are we to make of the history of the *ekklēsia* and its tradition, which developed in apparent opposition to Jewish claims concerning the covenant, the land, and the messianic hope? Those questions will direct our reflections in the present chapter. In the chapter that follows we will take up questions that relate to the momentous events of modern Jewish history.

Luke and Acts themselves offer wise counsel concerning the presuppositions that should guide such theological reflection on history. In light of that fact, I will begin by discussing the perspective of Luke and Acts regarding divine action in history. I will then take up issues related to the compositional context and aims of Luke and Acts. These matters may at first appear tangential to our purposes, but are in fact essential to obtaining a canonical vision of the patterns in Jewish and ecclesial history that begin to take shape in the second century. I will give special attention to the author's concerns regarding Paul's early anti-Jewish interpreters and the ecclesial response to the emergence of Pharisaic-influenced Judaism. Finally, I will look briefly at the way the *ekklēsia* and the Jewish tradition developed historically in relationship to one another, and in relation to the Lukan *euangelioin* of the crucified and resurrected Messiah.

Luke, Acts, and the Divine *Boulē*

The author/editor of Luke and Acts is a historian and a theologian, but he pursues his historical and theological objectives in an integrated fashion. He does his history as a theologian and his theology as a historian. His fusion of theology and history expresses his convictions regarding God's action in the midst of human affairs.

The most explicit articulation of these convictions within the narrative comes from Gamaliel, the leader of the Pharisees. As seen in chapter 3, Gamaliel's speech to his fellow members of the Jewish council plays an important role in Acts. The Pharisaic leader warns the Sadducean party against suppressing the apostles, and bases his warning on a theological conviction: "if this plan (*boulē*) or this undertaking is of human origin, it will fail; but if it is of God, you will not be able to overthrow them" (Acts 5:38–39). As already noted, in the author's post-70 context this statement vindicates the apostles *and* the Pharisees, and condemns the Sadducees, for the former now flourish while the latter have faded away. But this statement also enunciates a theological conviction shared by the apostles and the Pharisees, and denied by the Sadducees, namely, that God is intimately involved in the affairs of human history.[1] As the apostles and Gamaliel both affirm, the God of Israel has a "plan" (*boulē*) or intention for human history, and that plan will be achieved despite all human efforts to oppose it.[2]

According to Acts, the revealed content of the divine *boulē* constitutes the substance of Paul's proclamation. In the Lukan account of Paul's farewell address to the Ephesian elders at Miletus (Acts 20:18–35), Paul solemnly asserts, "I did not shrink from declaring to you the whole purpose [*pasan tēn boulēn*] of God" (Acts 20:27). Echoing the argument of Heinz Schürmann, Brevard Childs views this speech as a "summary of Luke's purpose in writing Acts."[3] The speech fulfills this function by describing Paul's proclamation of "the whole purpose of God," and presenting this proclamation as determining the parameters for all future ecclesial preaching and teaching. Childs and Schürmann interpret the phrase *pasan tēn boulēn* to mean "the sacred tradition (*paradosis*) he [Paul] had received," i.e., the interpreted *euangelion*. This reading is sustainable only if one understands "the sacred tradition" as a revelation of the divine *plan* for the *history* of Israel and the world, a prophetic plan that has been inaugurated decisively but not yet fully realized. The divine *boulē* centers on the death, resurrection, ascension, and return of the Messiah, but it also concerns the mission in history of the Jewish people and the *ekklēsia* as intertwined communities related to that Messiah.

In Acts of the Apostles, human attempts to thwart the divine *boulē* often become the means by which it is realized. The speeches of Acts emphasize that the decisive event of this plan takes effect through the evil action of the Jewish council in its handing over of Jesus to the Roman authorities (Acts 2:23–24; 4:27–28). That pattern becomes the paradigm for the advance of the apostolic community and message in Acts. The

1. For more on this point, see Brawley, *Luke-Acts and the Jews*, 116–17.

2. The Greek word *boulē* appears twelve times in the New Testament, and nine of those twelve verses are found in Luke and Acts.

3. Childs, *The Church's Guide for Reading Paul*, 228. See Schürmann, "Das Testament des Paulus für die Kirche."

persecution that follows Stephen's death scatters the disciples from Jerusalem and enables the *ekklēsia* to expand its mission and horizon (Acts 11:19–21). Saul's violent opposition to the new movement only makes him a more effective herald of the Messiah he formerly persecuted (Acts 22:3–11; 26:4–11). The failure of the diaspora synagogues to embrace the message of Paul leads to his fruitful work among gentiles (Acts 13:45–49; 18:5–11; 28:23–31). Paul's arrest enables him to proclaim his message to a large audience in the temple (Acts 21:37–22:21), to the ruling Jewish council (22:30–23:9), to King Agrippa (25:23–26:32), and to the leadership of the Roman Jewish community (28:17–28).

Within the Torah, the story of Joseph best exemplifies this pattern of divine action, in which God works redemptively *despite* and even *through* the evil deeds of human beings. It is therefore fitting that the story of Joseph occupies a prominent place in Stephen's speech before the Jewish council (Acts 7:9–16). Like Moses, Joseph suffers opposition from his brothers, only to be raised up as their leader and deliverer. Stephen narrates Joseph's story in language that echoes similar stories in Acts. Just as Joseph's brothers were "jealous" (*zēlōsantes*) of their sibling (Acts 7:9), so Jewish communal leaders react with jealousy to the apostles (Acts 5:17) and to Paul (Acts 13:44–45). And just as God "rescued (*exeilato*)" Joseph from his afflictions (Acts 7:10), so God rescued Peter (Acts 12:11) and Paul (Acts 23:27; 26:16–17). Significantly, Stephen's account of the Joseph story, like the Genesis narrative that it summarizes, features a happy ending for Joseph's brothers: "On the second visit Joseph made himself known to his brothers. . . . Then Joseph sent and invited his father Jacob and all his relatives to come to him" (Acts 7:14). The author of Acts likely expects his readers to recall the words of Joseph in this scene from Genesis: "I am your brother, Joseph, whom you sold into Egypt. And now do not be distressed, or angry with yourselves, because you sold me here; for God sent me here before you to preserve life. . . . So it was not you who sent me here, but God . . ." (Gen 45:4–5, 8). Joseph's brothers sought to do evil, but the overruling *boulē* of God accomplished good despite their malicious intent (Gen 50:20). In the same way, God will work redemptively through the evil actions of the leaders of the Jewish people, in order to bring blessing not only to the nations but also to the Jewish people. While Acts cannot recount that happy ending as an accomplished event, the narrative points beyond itself to a coming day when Joseph and his brothers will be reconciled.

Luke and Acts do not present a mechanical predestinarian vision of God's action in human history. The author/editor assumes that human beings make their own decisions, and are held accountable for those decisions (e.g., Acts 24:25). Even when God brings good out of evil, as with the crucifixion of Jesus, the martyrdom of Stephen, and the destruction of the temple, Luke and Acts acknowledge the tragic character of those events by depicting the intense human grief the events rightly evoke (Luke 23:27; Acts 8:2; Luke 13:34; 19:41–44). Human beings are not marionettes, and history is not a puppet show in which a manipulative divinity hovers intrusively above the stage. Human beings act freely, and often badly. Luke and Acts accept this fact, but also affirm God's power to bring good out of evil, and to effect a benevolent purpose despite—and even through—the tragic twists and turns of history.

If indeed the God of Israel is the Lord of history, it is necessary to inquire about "the whole purpose/plan of God" as manifest in Luke and Acts, and regarding the shape of its outworking in the later history of the *ekklēsia* and the Jewish people. How does the paradigmatic story of Jesus of Nazareth and his early disciples shed light on the subsequent story of those related to him by flesh and/or by Spirit? Before asking that question, however, let us inquire about an intermediate and mediating history: what do we know of the setting from which the Gospel of Luke and Acts of the Apostles emerged as canonical texts?

The Context and Aims of Luke and Acts

It may seem strange to raise this question only after several chapters of intensive exegesis of these volumes. Why not address the matter at the outset? The answer lies with my canonical presuppositions. I read Luke and Acts as a theologian seeking divine wisdom from authoritative sources rather than as an antiquarian probing ancient artifacts. To that end, it was sufficient to know that these two texts were closely related to one another, that they were each composed within a hundred years of the death and resurrection of Jesus, and that they have been treated as canonical by all the disciples of Jesus for more than eighteen centuries.

I raise the question of date and authorship at this point because I am now discussing the perspective of these books on the divine plan enacted *in history*, and the implications of that perspective for our theological understanding of the centuries that follow their composition. The final author/editor of these volumes faced a particular historical situation, and looked to past events in the life of Jesus and the *ekklēsia* for wisdom in responding to his circumstances. We cannot know for certain what those circumstances were, and so all proposals are hypothetical. (That is another reason why I have waited till now to explore the question.) Nevertheless, the hints provided by the texts themselves and our knowledge of the period enable us to narrow the range of plausible options. As we consider the author/editor's response to his own historical situation, we may gain theological insight into the historical developments that later ensued.

Most New Testament scholars of the late twentieth century agreed that Luke and Acts were written by the same author between 80 and 90 CE. Luke's use of the Gospel of Mark, his preoccupation with the destruction of Jerusalem in 70 CE, and the nature of his redaction of Mark 13:14ff (see Luke 21:14ff) make an earlier date for his gospel unlikely.[4] A revisionary hypothesis has gained currency in the twenty-first century, according to which a first edition of the Gospel of Luke was produced between 80 and 90, but Acts of the Apostles was not composed until 110–120 CE.[5] The author of Acts may or may not have written the early edition of Luke, but was certainly responsible for a new edition that made the Gospel an even more suitable companion volume to Acts. This redactional activity included the addition of the infancy narrative (Luke 1–2) and supplementary material related to the resurrection (some of Luke 24).[6] One leading representative of the revisionary school argues that the Marcionite controversy had already erupted in the second decade of the second century, and that Acts and canonical Luke (as he calls the final form of that gospel) were a response to that ultra-Pauline movement.[7]

Scholarly debate over the dating of Acts is unresolved, and the argument advanced in the preceding chapters is unaffected by its ultimate result. However, the revisionary hypothesis underlines a dominant concern driving canonical Luke and Acts regardless of their chronological origins: these volumes aim to defend the authentically Jewish character of Paul's life and teaching, and to assert the commonality of his vision with that

4. On Luke 21:14ff as a post-70 redaction of Mark 13:14ff, see chapter 1, pp. 34–37.

5. See Pervo, *Dating Acts*; Tyson, *Marcion and Luke-Acts*; and Smith and Tyson, eds., *Acts and Christian Beginnings*.

6. See Tyson, *Marcion and Luke-Acts*, 79–120.

7. See Tyson, *Marcion and Luke-Acts*, 24–49.

of the twelve (led by Peter) and the family of Jesus (led by James). This explains the apologetic character of Paul's speeches in the final chapters of Acts, which uphold the Pauline legacy while combating its antinomian and anti-Jewish interpreters. The Paul of Acts displays no disagreement with James or Peter regarding the responsibility of Jews to observe the Torah and teach their children to do likewise. Paul himself observes the Torah, honors the holy city of Jerusalem, worships in its temple, and does all of this as a matter of conscience rather than expedience. Despite these characteristics of the Lukan Paul, his successful efforts in the diaspora among gentiles lead many Jews in the narrative to believe that he is an apostate who no longer acknowledges the authority of Jewish institutions. While the focus of Acts falls on the misunderstandings of Paul that exist among Jews *outside* of the *ekklēsia*, the author also hints at the proliferation of such misunderstandings *within* the *ekklēsia* (Acts 21:21). In fact, an antinomian and anti-Jewish reading of Paul among those claiming to be heirs of the apostle at the end of the first and the beginning of the second centuries may have intensified the Jewish community's hostile reaction to the Jesus-movement. The Book of Acts is written, in part, to correct such a misconstrual of the Pauline legacy.

Furthermore, the Lukan Paul's version of the *euangelion*, like his teaching regarding the Torah, replicates that of Peter and James. This prophetic message concerns the ultimate restoration of Israel through its crucified and risen Messiah, and the renewal of the world that will accompany Israel's restoration. The process by which this restoration and renewal will take place involves, on the one hand, a purifying judgment of Jerusalem (the "cross" that precedes the "resurrection"), and, on the other hand, the expansion of Israel through the adoption from among the gentiles of "a people for his name" (Acts 15:14). Those adopted from the gentiles adhere to the people of Israel, but are exempt from observing the full scope of Israel's national "customs" (*ethē*). The result is a twofold community with a bilateral constitution. Through the gift of the Holy Spirit the bilateral *ekklēsia* experiences proleptically the first-fruits of Israel's eschatological inheritance, and summons the entire community of Israel and individual gentiles to repentance and faith in the Messiah. Like the prophetic *euangelion* announced by Peter and James, Paul's proclamation concerns "hope in the promise made by God to our ancestors, a promise our twelve tribes hope to attain, as they earnestly worship day and night" (Acts 26:6–7).

For my purposes it makes no difference whether the author of canonical Luke and Acts is prescient about a future ultra-Pauline distortion of the apostolic message and way of life, or responds to such a phenomenon that has already emerged. In either case, a primary aim in his writing remains the same—namely, to preserve the prophetic Jewish character of both the *ekklēsia* and the *euangelion* of the resurrected Messiah that has brought her into being.

Most scholars of Luke and Acts continue to assert or assume that the author is a gentile, that he addresses a gentile audience, and that the *ekklēsia* he knows is overwhelmingly gentile in composition and way of life. According to that view, the author/editor seeks to preserve continuity with the Jewish heritage of the *ekklēsia* by honoring the Jewish Bible and presenting the *euangelion* as the fulfillment of biblical prophecy, but he has no interest in fostering communities or collections of Jewish disciples of Jesus who live according to Jewish national customs and share Jewish national hopes. While most of these scholars dismiss the traditional ascription of these books to the gentile physician who accompanied Paul (Phlm 24; Col 4:11, 14; 2 Tim 4:11), they still accept the tradition of gentile authorship.[8] Given what we have seen in the previous chapters, is this majority position warranted by the evidence?

I think not. More compelling is Jacob Jervell's assessment offered in 1980: "It is not decisive whether Luke himself was by birth a Jew or Gentile. What is important is that he thinks as a Christian Jew and that he is using the categories typical of Jewish Christianity. And so we have the main point: Luke conceives of the Jewish Christian element in the church as the center and kernel of the church."[9] The Lukan emphasis on the eschatological destiny of Jerusalem and the Jewish people—and on the strict Torah obedience of the story's Jewish heroes—appear to be rhetorical overkill if the only aim is to stress the value of the Jewish past without regard for the Jewish present and future. As Robert Wall observes, "Luke's interest in protecting the Jewish heritage of Christian faith is not wholly expected and must be viewed as somewhat radical given the evidence."[10]

8. Irenaeus is the first to associate these books with Luke. He writes at the end of the second century, and does not cite earlier ecclesial authorities as the historical basis for his claim.

9. Jervell, *The Unknown Paul*, 40, 42–43. The title of the chapter (originally published in 1980 as an independent essay) is "The Mighty Minority," a phrase he uses to describe the Jewish disciples of Jesus in the *ekklēsia* of Luke's experience.

10. Wall, "The Acts of the Apostles," 214.

Moreover, whether few or many, Jewish disciples of Jesus existed in the early second century. For them, Luke and Acts would support the imperative of maintaining a distinctive Jewish hope and way of life. Given what we know from second-century authors such as Ignatius, Barnabas, and Justin Martyr, that would have been a hotly contested proposition.

So far, we have considered matters related to the internal Jewish life of the *ekklēsia* which appear to have animated the composition/redaction of Luke and Acts. But the author/editor also responds to an external Jewish reality—namely, a post-70 Jewish movement influenced by the remnants of the Pharisees. This external factor is closely related to the internal ecclesial dynamics that drive the Lukan narrative. While the Pharisees of Luke and Acts represent devout Jews *outside* the *ekklēsia* who fail to grasp the significance of Jesus' outreach to those "children of Abraham" (Luke 13:16; 19:9) located on the margins of Jewish religious life (e.g., the three parables of Luke 15), they also represent devout Jews *within* the *ekklēsia* who fail to grasp the significance of the apostolic outreach to gentiles residing beyond those margins (e.g., Acts 15:5). The presence of Pharisees both *outside* and *within* the *ekklēsia* shows that they occupy a special place in the Lukan social landscape. They stand near and on both sides of the indistinct boundary distinguishing the *ekklēsia* from the wider Jewish world of which she was part. Within the *ekklēsia*, Pharisees are those faithful Jews scrupulously concerned for Israel's tradition and reluctant to accommodate surprising new developments initiated by the Holy Spirit. But outside the *ekklēsia*, Pharisees are those Jews most open to Jesus and the apostles, sharing with them a belief in the resurrection of the dead (Acts 23:6–10), the mediation of angels (Acts 23:9), and the providential action of God in human history (Acts 5:33–39). Gamaliel and company continue to stand outside the banquet hall, but hope remains that they will yet enter and join the celebration (Luke 15:25–32).

Like Josephus, who in his histories also assigns a prominent place to the Pharisees, the author/editor of Luke and Acts shapes his narrative in light of the growing influence of the Pharisaic legacy in the Jewish world after the destruction of the temple. According to Jewish tradition, the successor to Yochanan ben Zakkai as the head of the early rabbinic movement in the post-70 period was another Gamaliel, grandson of the figure treated by the author of Acts with such respect (Acts 5:33–39). From that point on the leader or "patriarch" (*nasi*) of the rabbinic movement in the land of Israel would be chosen from among the descendants of Gamaliel. Among those descendants was Judah the Patriarch (Yehudah Hanasi), author of the Mishnah at the end of the second century. While the early rabbinic movement arose as a coalition, with the Pharisaic stream constituting only one of its parties, Pharisaic tradition certainly played a significant role in the formation of rabbinic Judaism.[11]

The author/editor of Luke and Acts thus implicitly acknowledges two powerful religious currents at work at the time he composes his volumes: the Pauline tradition, which was becoming ascendant in the Jesus-movement, and the Pharisaic tradition, which was growing in strength in the wider Jewish world. Moreover, *he relates one to the other* by portraying Paul as a proud disciple of Gamaliel (Acts 22:3) who continues to identify as a Pharisee (Acts 23:6; 26:5). We have already seen how the author of Acts presents Paul's mission and teaching as in harmony with the mission and teaching of both Peter and James. We now see that he likewise presents Paul as sharing much in common with a rising extra-ecclesial Jewish movement of his own day—particularly on matters related to the Jewish eschatological hope. The tragedy of 70 CE has intensified Israel's exile, but the redemptive power of the crucified and risen Messiah is visible not only in the *ekklēsia* but also in the midst of Israel's re-organized exilic life.

What is going on here? I would suggest that the author/editor of Luke and Acts assesses the Jewish and ecclesial circumstances of his own day with prophetic clarity. He sees the dangers posed by an anti-Jewish reading of Paul, and seeks to counter those threats. He also sees the opportunities opened by the emerging rabbinic movement, and seeks to encourage the *ekklēsia* to adopt the same attitude toward them as is shown by the father in the parable of the two sons. Moreover, the author/editor of Luke and Acts recognizes that the aspects of the *euangelion* threatened by the anti-Jewish Paulinists are the very convictions that the Lukan Paul shares with his fellow Pharisees. To get their proper bearings in proclaiming the *euangelion*, the disciples of Jesus may eventually need to look outside the boundaries of their ecclesial environment.

11. Jacob Neusner's articulation of the historical roots of the rabbinic movement reflects the current scholarly consensus: "Rabbinic Judaism . . . did not begin in 70. It drew in part upon teachings and traditions of the Pharisees, who had formed a sect within the larger Judaic world of the land of Israel. *After 70, the Pharisees formed the single most influential group*. . . . But the rabbinic Judaism that was aborning took within itself a second group, the heirs and continuators of the scribes from the period before 70. . . . The sect of the Pharisees and the profession of the scribes—together with the surviving priests who joined them—framed a Judaism to take the place of the Judaism of temple and cult" (Neusner, *A Short History of Judaism*, 51–52. Emphasis added).

In conclusion, we may say with confidence that canonical Luke and the Book of Acts were composed no later than the second decade of the second century, and that a primary aim of these books was to preserve the Jewish character of the *euangelion* in the face of an anti-Jewish reading of the Pauline letters. The author's strategy for countering this real or potential movement involved a reframing of Paul rather than a dismissal of the Pauline legacy. That reframing positioned Paul as a Torah-observant *Pharisaic* Jew, conducting a mission distinct from that of the twelve and the family of Jesus but in unity with them on all matters of fundamental importance. Furthermore, that reframing underlined the unique position of the Pharisees as the external Jewish party closest to the *ekklēsia*, and pointed to a post-70 future when the divine *boulē* would unfold within the Jewish world in surprising ways.

Post-Lukan History in Lukan Perspective: Fractured Community, Fractured *Euangelion*

While the Gospel of Luke and Acts of the Apostles attained canonical status in the *ekklēsia*, the Lukan interpretation of the Pauline legacy was received only in part. With the help of Luke and Acts, the *ekklēsia* resisted the extreme anti-Jewish Paulinism of Marcion and his followers, and preserved Jewish scripture as an essential component of her biblical canon. But the prophetic *euangelion* of the resurrected Messiah was not preserved in its seamless integrity.

In addition to Jewish scripture, the *ekklēsia* received and transmitted the teaching and the story of the crucified and risen Messiah, Jesus of Nazareth; the call he extended to gentiles through his apostles to repent, believe in his name, be baptized, and receive the Holy Spirit; a way of life founded on the apostolic teaching, communal sharing and relationship, the Lord's Supper, and prayer (Acts 2:42); and the hope that Jesus would return to establish the fullness of his reign. The *ekklēsia* guarded this rich treasure and kept it safe for generations through fierce storms, and we should be grateful for her faithful stewardship.

But the *ekklēsia* also lost sight of other crucial elements of the prophetic *euangelion*. As described in chapter 1, she soon dismissed the significance of the earthly Jerusalem and the land of Israel as sacred Jewish sites with universal implications. She similarly denied or downplayed the enduring covenantal status of the Jewish people and its priestly vocation, nullifying the Torah as Israel's defining national constitution. In keeping with this hostility to Jews and Judaism beyond her walls, the *ekklēsia* also actively suppressed distinctive Jewish expression within her own life, rejecting her original bilateral character as a communion of Jews and gentiles.[12] The eschatological vision of the *ekklēsia* became so spiritualized and individualized that the New Testament hope for a transformed earth peopled by resurrected nations seemed alien and threatening.[13]

As recounted by the Gospel of Luke and Acts of the Apostles, the Jewish people had corporately refused or ignored the heart of the *euangelion*, namely, the message concerning the crucified and risen Messiah. As a result, the eschaton was delayed, and Israel's exile intensified. However, as the dust settled following the failure of the second Jewish revolt against Rome (135 CE), and the Gamaliel-dynasty of the Galilean patriarchate grew in power and influence, a strange phenomenon gradually became visible. The very elements of the prophetic *euangelion* that the *ekklēsia* had abandoned were preserved as central components of the Jewish worldview. Guided in part by the Pharisaic component of its heritage, the rabbinic movement preserved the Torah as Israel's national constitution and the narrative guide to Israel's eschatological hope; the earth as the necessary locus of redemption; the geographical centrality and messianic significance of the land of Israel, Jerusalem, and the Temple Mount; and the irrevocable bond between the God of Israel, the Messiah of Israel, and the genealogical descendants of Abraham, Isaac, and Jacob.

There is nothing novel in the assertion that the people of God were fractured when the *ekklēsia* and the Jewish people became estranged. However, it was traditionally thought that this fracture occurred because of the Jewish rejection of the *euangelion*. In light of the previous chapters, that assumption no longer seems viable. In reality, each side rejected that part of the prophetic *euangelion* that the other side preserved. In its fullness and integrity, the message of the crucified and resurrected Messiah of Israel is transmitted and received only through both communities and both traditions.

Viewed from the perspective of the prophetic *euangelion*, the history of post-70 Judaism displays vivid signs of providential oversight. The rabbinic movement traced its own inner tensions to pre-70 debates between the school of Hillel and the school of Shammai. Apparently the

12. On the early history of these developments, see Kinzer, *Postmissionary Messianic Judaism*, 181–212.

13. See Wright, *Surprised By Hope*; Farrow, *Ascension Theology*.

Shammaites rather than the Hillelites predominated in the decades before the destruction of the temple.[14] That is significant, since the teaching of Jesus and the apostle Paul have more in common with the perspective of the Hillelites.[15] In the post-70 era, the Hillelites became ascendant, and so the rabbinic movement took shape under the inspiration of teaching that was closer to the Jesus' movement than would otherwise have been the case. Just as the Pharisees rose after the destruction of the temple while the Sadducees fell, so the Hillelites gained at the expense of the Shammaites. In both cases, Gamaliel's judgment concerning divine providence was vindicated.

In reaction to the two disastrous revolts against Rome, the second-century rabbinic movement rejected apocalyptic enthusiasm and focused instead on the cultivation of a sanctified communal life.[16] That was a wise and necessary response, and effectively countered futile efforts at political revolt on the one hand, and gnostic denials of the goodness of creation on the other.[17] At the same time, the focus on sanctification resulted in an attenuated concern for the messianic outworking of the divine purpose in Israel's history. The retreat from history and eschatology threatened to rob the Jewish people of the prophetic treasure deposited in its midst, a treasure that it carried not only for its own sake but also for the sake of the *ekklēsia* and the world. Paradoxically, it was the political triumph of the *ekklēsia* in the fourth century that provoked the rabbinic movement to rediscover the prophetic inheritance it had hitherto neglected. That, at least, was the conclusion reached by Jacob Neusner in comparing the earlier Mishnaic emphasis on *sanctification* with the later Talmudic stress

14. Neusner, *From Politics to Piety*, 36–37. See Wright, *The New Testament and the People of God*, 194, and *Jesus and the Victory of God*, 378–79. Wright interprets the controversy between these two schools as primarily political in nature, with the Shammaites favoring confrontation with Rome and the Hillelites opting for accommodation. While it is plausible to posit such a disagreement as existing, the evidence does not warrant the conclusion that political issues were at the heart of their multiple disputes.

15. See Weinfeld, "Hillel and the Misunderstanding of Judaism in Modern Scholarship," 56–70, and Tomson, *Paul and the Jewish Law*, 245–54.

16. "The genius of the Judaic system of sanctification that took shape after 70 and reached its full expression in the Mishnah was to recognize that the holy people might reconstitute the Temple in the sanctity of its own community life. Therefore the people had to be made holy, as the Temple had been holy" (Neusner, *An Introduction to Judaism*, 162).

17. On Mishnaic Judaism as a response to Gnosticism, see Neusner, *Introduction to Judaism*, 172–74.

on national and historical *salvation*: "In the Yerushalmi [i.e., the Jerusalem Talmud] we witness, among the Mishnah's heirs, a striking reversion to biblical convictions about the centrality of history in the definition of Israel's reality. The heavy weight of prophecy, apocalyptic, and biblical historiography, with their emphasis upon salvation and on history as the indicator of Israel's salvation, stood against the Mishnah's quite separate thesis of what truly mattered."[18] While the rise of Constantine was by no means an unmitigated blessing for the Jewish people, it did contribute to the consolidation of the rabbinic tradition in a form that would endure through the centuries and ultimately enrich its ecclesial antagonist.[19]

I could continue with further reflection on the providential course of Jewish history, but what has been said is sufficient to make my point. Once one construes the prophetic *euangelion* as a proclamation about Jesus *and* about the Jewish people, the marks of the divine *boulē* in that history are readily discerned. In his resurrection as the first-fruits of Israel's eschatological rebirth, Jesus the Messiah establishes an unbreakable bond with the Jewish people as a whole. Those Jews who fail to acknowledge his sovereignty are not thereby released from his hold. In his death on the cross, Jesus anticipates and bears in himself the punishment that will fall on Jerusalem forty years later. In this way, he transforms that event, rendering it not only a punishment for the rebellion of past generations but also a purifying fire capable of producing spiritual renewal. Accordingly, the destruction of Jerusalem in 70 CE ends the reign of the priestly aristocrats whom Luke and Acts portray as responsible for the execution of Jesus and the persecution of his early disciples, and prepares the way for the dominance of the Pharisees under the overall leadership of Gamaliel's descendants. The Jewish tradition develops providentially under the unrecognized authority of the risen Messiah, who, like Joseph the son of Jacob, acts for the welfare of his family while keeping his true identity hidden. In its mature talmudic form, that tradition derives its power from the hope of a messianic future—a hope that is animated and sustained by the veiled Messiah whose resurrection provides the irrevocable pledge that he will one day "restore the kingdom to Israel" (Acts 1:6).

According to this reading of Luke and Acts, and our theological interpretation of the subsequent events of Jewish and ecclesial history, we

18. Neusner, *Introduction to Judaism*, 221–22.

19. According to Seth Schwartz, the rise of Constantine produced a wide range of unintended positive effects in the life of the Jewish people. See *Imperialism and Jewish Society 200 B.C.E. to 640 C.E.*

know the crucified and risen Messiah of Israel in his undivided fullness only when we recognize his presence in *both* the *ekklēsia and* the Jewish people. Likewise, we receive the prophetic *euangelion* in its undivided fullness only when we see its truth transmitted through *both* ecclesial and Jewish traditions. The bad news is that the *euangelion*, like the people of God itself, suffered fracture. The good news is that the *euangelion* is still accessible in its fullness and integrity—but only through a restored partnership between the two fragments of that fractured community.

As in the paradigmatic story of Joseph recounted by Stephen at his trial, and as in many incidents in the narrative of Luke and Acts, God works with the flawed material presented to him by human error, failing, and sin, in order to bring good out of evil. The people and its message are in fragments, but those fragments have endured, and the pieces can still be reassembled. It is now our task to repair the garment that was torn asunder, and, as imitators of God, to show that we too can convert the consequences of what was evil into the ingredients for something that is good.

Conclusion

Surprisingly, the Jewish religious tradition is essential not only to sustain the identity of the Jewish people but also to complete the *euangelion* of Jesus the Messiah. The preservation of the Jewish people and the Jewish tradition are thus a gift of divine providence for the *ekklēsia* and the entire world.

But this discussion of the work of divine providence in preserving the prophetic *euangelion* deals only with ancient history, and with rival communities of biblical faith driven by rival claims to that biblical inheritance. What, if anything, do we make of the extraordinary developments in modern Jewish history, enacted not on the plane of religious debate, but on the political, diplomatic, and military stage of the secular world? The answer to that question will occupy our next chapter.

Chapter 6

The Divine *Boulē* and Modern Jewish History

If the God of Israel is the Lord of history, one cannot be faithful to the covenant while neglecting the challenge of seeking some meaning in that history. That was the conviction of the author/editor of Luke and Acts, and I am proposing that it should be ours as well. While interpretation of God's historical action in the post-biblical period will always be tentative and open to debate, we are on safer ground when assessing events remote in time, such as those discussed in the previous chapter. At least their long-term consequences are now visible. It is more difficult to judge the meaning of events that are still fresh in historical memory. Nevertheless, those events are the ones that summon our most urgent response, and so we must do our best to respond to the challenge they present.

In this chapter I will offer an assessment of two modern historical developments that each claim to reverse or qualify the exilic status of the Jewish people and the *ekklēsia*. Each is associated with features of the prophetic *euangelion* discerned from our study of Luke and Acts, and each correlates in surprising ways with the other. My main topic will be Zionism, and that will occupy most of this chapter. I will conclude by commenting briefly on a second historical development of no less controversial nature, namely, Messianic Judaism.

A Theological Appraisal of Zionism

Employed here, the term "Zionism" refers to an ideology and a movement that asserted the practical priority of establishing a "national home for the Jewish people" in the land promised to the biblical patriarchs and matriarchs.[1] With the establishment of the Jewish State in 1948, the term refers to an ideology and movement that views the reality of this "national home" as an essential component of Jewish identity and destiny, and which aims to support and strengthen Jewish life in the land.[2]

I will first explore the relationship between Zionism and the Jewish tradition. I will then offer a general theological assessment of Zionism, and conclude by addressing several specific theological questions related to the status of the Jewish State and its policies.

Zionism and the Jewish Tradition

In the previous chapter I proposed a general theological assessment of the Jewish religious tradition from the perspective of Luke and Acts. I now seek to discover the extent to which Zionism shows signs of continuity with that tradition. Was the modern movement to establish a culturally vibrant autonomous Jewish community in the land of Israel a radical tear in the seams of Jewish history, or is the movement's novelty explicable only in terms of that same history?

If one listens exclusively to the voices of its early secularist advocates and religious critics, one might conclude that Zionism breaks decisively with the Jewish way of life forged in exile and oriented to a transcendent horizon. If one listens exclusively to students of modern political history, one might conclude that Zionism is merely a Jewish expression of a nineteenth-century European political phenomenon, i.e., nationalism. All of these voices deserve our attention, for they reveal important aspects of the Zionist reality. But they only tell part of the story.

Emanuele Ottolenghi captures well the paradox inherent in Jewish diaspora existence before the rise of Zionism:

1. This language is drawn from the Balfour Declaration adopted by the British government in 1917. In this text, addressed by the British Foreign Secretary, Arthur James Balfour, to Lord Rothschild, the following is conveyed: "I have much pleasure in conveying to you, on behalf of His Majesty's Government, the following declaration of sympathy with Jewish Zionist aspirations. . . . His Majesty's Government view with favor the establishment in Palestine of a national home for the Jewish people . . . ." The vagueness of the phrase "national home" was one of its advantages in 1917—it could refer to a state, but it could also refer to another form of national existence.

2. "To be a Zionist is to be personally committed or loyal to the existence of the State of Israel as a Jewish polity" (Novak, *Zionism and Judaism*, 1).

> For centuries, the idea of return to the Land of Israel in Jewish tradition coexisted with a passive acceptance of exile. Longing for Zion was central to Judaism, yet no collective action was undertaken to actively pursue it. A Jewish community—albeit small—had always existed in the Holy Land. Individual Jews moved there. And the bond with the land remained paramount in Jewish self-image. Jews understood themselves not only as a minority, but as a minority in exile. Their intimate bond with the land, rather than merely distinct beliefs and practices, prevented their shift to being simply a religious community. Yet, despite the longing for Zion and the sense of estrangement from host countries . . . few moved to Zion.[3]

Ottolenghi then considers how this paradox took a new form with the rise of Zionism: "Tradition loosened its grip on Jewish identity. But Zionism, though openly revolting against tradition, made return [to the Land of Israel] central to the idea of Jewish continuity."[4] The eschatological tension that previously existed between present life in exile and future life in Zion now morphs into a tension between present life in Zion and a past life which longed for Zion yet remained distant from it.

"Longing for Zion was central to Judaism." Anyone familiar with Jewish liturgy knows this to be a fact. Prayer for Israel's return to the land of its ancestors occupies a central position in the *Amidah* (recited three times daily); the *Birkat Hamazon* (recited after every meal); the mystical prayer (known as "*Lecha Dodi*") which welcomes the Sabbath each Friday evening; the blessings after the weekly reading from the Prophets; and the Jewish wedding service. The saddest day in the Jewish liturgical year is the Ninth of Av, in which Jews remember the destruction of Jerusalem by the Babylonians (in 586 BCE) and the Romans (in 70 CE). The Passover Seder and the Day of Atonement each conclude with the same ecstatic words of hope: "Next year in Jerusalem!"

"A Jewish community—albeit small—had always existed in the Holy Land." The early rabbinic movement was centered in the Judean town of Yavneh after the destruction of Jerusalem in 70 CE . Following the Roman suppression of the Bar Kokhba revolt, the rabbinic leadership relocated to Galilee. There Judah the Prince edited the Mishnah (circa 200 CE), the foundational document of rabbinic Judaism. From the sixth to the tenth centuries a group of Jewish scholars (the Masoretes) labored

3. Ottolenghi, "A National Home," 56.

4. Ottolenghi, "A National Home," 56.

in Tiberias to standardize, vocalize, and punctuate the biblical text. Thus, even after the two wars with Rome, the "small" Jewish community in "the Holy Land" continued to exercise significant influence on the Jewish people worldwide.

"Individual Jews moved there. And the bond with the land remained paramount in Jewish self-image." The "individual Jews" who contemplated or made the move were often the giants of their generation. Judah Halevi (1075–1141) wrote exquisite poems of longing for Zion, and realized his desire by traveling and dying there.[5] Maimonides (1135–1204) passed away in Egypt, but asked that his remains be taken to the land and buried in Tiberias. Judah Halevi and Maimonides represented the Jewish ideal, which could envision no ultimate future for the Jewish people apart from the land.

"Longing for Zion was central to Judaism, *yet no collective action was undertaken to actively pursue it*" (emphasis added). Ottolenghi here identifies the paradox at the heart of the Jewish tradition's view of Jerusalem and the land of Israel. Individual Jews expressed their devotion to God by "going up" to the land, but the community as a whole took no "collective action" to make its ultimate future a present reality. To explain this phenomenon, one must consider traditional Jewish eschatological expectations. As Israel Yuval states, "according to the traditional view, the Messiah will ingather the dispersed of Israel wherever they are in Exile and return them to Zion, just as he delivered Israel from Egypt while they were still dwelling in an alien land. The Exodus from Egypt thus serves as a typological model for the future Redemption, from which it follows that the redemption will precede the return to Zion."[6] This view found its classical formulation in the writings of Maimonides: "After his [i.e., the Messiah's] manifestation in Palestine, Israel will be gathered in Jerusalem."[7] The obligation to wait for the divine initiative fits the penitential orientation to exile common within the tradition. As Ottolenghi notes, "Jewish tradition always had a passive attitude to exile: it was accepted as punishment for Jewish misdeeds, which divine intervention alone could reverse."[8]

5. For more on Judah Halevi, see Halkin, *Yehudah Halevi*.

6. Yuval, *Two Nations in Your Womb*, 268.

7. *Epistle to Yemen*. Cited by Yuval, *Two Nations in Your Womb*, 269.

8. Ottolenghi, "A National Home," 59.

Did this attitude remain stable among religious Jews before the modern era, to be rejected first by secularist Zionism at the end of the nineteenth century? Although satisfying in its simplicity, such a neat scheme based on the modern conflict between religious and secular Jews fails to account for the full range of facts. Already in the thirteenth century a new eschatological perspective emerges among French Jews. It finds initial literary expression in a text entitled "Homilies of King Messiah and Gog and Magog," composed by an anonymous student of the renowned French scholar Rabbi Yitzhak ben Abraham (Ritzbah).[9] According to this text, the Messiah will only appear *after* the community of pious students of the Torah has grown large in the land of Israel. At that point the Messiah will reveal himself among them and gather the Jewish exiles who remain dispersed. Thus, Jews should not wait for the Messiah to come before "going up" to the land, for his manifestation depends on the "collective action" of their return to their ancestral home. This message did not fall on deaf ears. As Yuval notes, "This call to prepare for the coming of the Messiah by immigrating to the Land of Israel . . . coincides with reports of the immigration of elitist groups of Talmudic scholars from France, which took place beginning from 1211, known in the sources as the immigration 'of the Three Hundred Rabbis.'"[10]

This new eschatological perspective arises in the context of messianic expectation concerning the year 1240. After the Messiah failed to appear, the ferment of anticipation and eschatological immigration diminished. Yet something new had been planted in the Jewish imagination. We see it in the great commentator and mystic, Nahmanides (1194–1270), who moved to the land of Israel in 1267 and died there three years later. Nahmanides restored the Jewish communal presence in Jerusalem, a presence that had been decimated by the Crusaders.[11] In his writings he displays the new orientation to Jewish life in the land by taking issue with Maimonides' numbering of the 613 commandments of the Torah. Nahmanides believed that living in the land of Israel comprised one of the 613 commandments, whereas Maimonides failed to list this duty as a distinct commandment. While Nahmanides does not make this Jewish

9. For discussion of this text, see Yuval, *Two Nations in Your Womb*, 267–73.

10. Yuval, *Two Nations in Your Womb*, 270.

11. Nachmanidies is known by his acronym Ramban. The Ramban synagogue in the old city of Jerusalem takes its name from him. The community he re-established remained in continuous existence until the 1948 Arab-Israeli War.

"collective action" a precondition for the coming of the Messiah, he does establish it as a duty which each Jew must reckon with.[12]

The role of individual and collective action in facilitating the arrival of the messianic era takes on new significance after the expulsion of the Jews from Spain at the end of the fifteenth century. Some of those expelled made their way to the land of Israel and settled in the Galilean town of Tzefat (Safed). Among them was Isaac Luria (1534–72), a mystic who taught that the redemption of the divine and created order depends upon Jews undertaking the fulfillment of the commandments with proper intentionality. According to Luria, this eschatological goal belongs at the center of Jewish life.[13] Lurianic mysticism gained a wide following, and inspired the eschatological zeal of the Italian Rabbi Moshe Chaim Luzatto (1707–47)—poet, dramatist, theologian, and mystic—who, like Nahmanides, immigrated to the land of Israel with his family and died there. Lurianic mysticism did not focus specifically on the commandment to live in the land of Israel, but the new mystical movement originated there, and it created a conceptual framework which brought the active eschatological program of "The Homilies of King Messiah and God and Magog" into coherence with the Jewish theological tradition.

The eighteenth century also witnessed the birth of the Hasidic movement, which, like Luzatto, derived inspiration from the teaching of Isaac Luria. According to Martin Buber, this movement was oriented to "the land" from its inception.[14] One of its most important early leaders, Rabbi Menahem Mendel of Vitebsk (1730–88), immigrated to Palestine in 1777 with three hundred of his disciples. He settled first in Tzefat, the city of Isaac Luria, and later moved to Tiberias.[15] This communal act of "going up" to the land replicates the move of the three hundred rabbis of the early thirteenth century, and implies a similar eschatological intention.[16]

12. On Nachmanidies' critique of Maimonides concerning the commandment to settle the land, see Novak, *Zionism*, 179–83.

13. As Gershom Scholem writes, "The distinguishing feature of Lurianic Kabbalism was the important part played by the Messianic element." The Lurianic school "placed this concept [of redemption] with all it implies in the center of religious life and thought" (Scholem, *Major Trends in Jewish Mysticism*, 327, 330).

14. Buber, *Tales of the Hasidim*, 23.

15. Buber, *Tales of the Hasidim*, 24.

16. Scholem argues that Hasidism as a whole de-emphasized the eschatological character of Lurianic kabbalah. However, he adds a qualifying note: "although some groups and two or three of their leaders transplanted themselves to Palestine in 1777"

The immigration of Menahem Mendel and his disciples anticipates a more ambitious and consequential project initiated some three decades later by the great adversary of Hasidism, the Vilna Gaon (Rabbi Elijah ben Solomon Zalman, 1720–97). While the Gaon opposed the Hasidic movement, he shared with its adherents a devotion to the teaching of Isaac Luria, especially as transmitted by Luzatto. As Yehudah Mirsky notes, the Gaon "saw in Luria's and Luzzatto's teachings the idea that redemption could be hastened by earthly means."[17] Like Luria and Luzzato, the Gaon himself set off for the land of Israel, but was unable to get beyond Germany.[18] However, more than five hundred of his disciples succeeded in making the voyage, and they became the guiding force in the Jewish community of the land (the "Old Yishuv"). Mirsky recognizes their importance:

> Modern settlement of the Land of Israel, and religious involvement with that enterprise, predated Theodor Herzl and the Zionist movement by decades. In a departure from traditional immigration for the purpose of dying in the land's physically desiccated but spiritually fragrant shade, religious Jews began arriving in the early 1800s *for the express purpose of building institutions*. A number of them were disciples of the Gaon. . . . The Old Yishuv took its modern shape in the early decades of the nineteenth century with the immigration of latter-day disciples of the Gaon of Vilna.[19]

The contrast between "traditional immigration" and the new type of immigration undertaken by the disciples of the Gaon concerns their respective purposes: the latter "went up" to the land "for the express purpose of building institutions." In other words, they were engaged in "collective action," as befitted the activist eschatological theology they received from Isaac Luria and Moshe Chaim Luzatto through their teacher, the Vilna Gaon.

The implicit vision of the disciples of the Gaon assumed a more programmatic character in the writings and practical efforts of Rabbi Yehudah Alkalai (1798–1878) and Rabbi Zvi Hirsch Kalisher (1795–1874).

(*Major Trends*, 330).

17. Mirsky, *Rav Kook: Mystic in a Time of Revolution*, 32.

18. According to legend, the Baal Shem Tov had the same experience (Buber, *Tales of the Hasidim*, 23).

19. Mirsky, *Rav Kook*, 32, 45. Emphasis added.

Ottolenghi recognizes their foundational role in laying the groundwork for the mature Zionism of the latter nineteenth century:

> Both . . . called on the Jewish people to initiate redemption by returning to their ancestral land. Neither saw any contradiction between messianic expectations and active human endeavors. Both believed redemption would be achieved gradually through a process of collective return and revival of Jewish observance which would prepare the ground . . . .
>
> Both thinkers still thought in traditional, redemptive and messianic terms. But their authoritative work, which inspired the first efforts of Jewish settlement in the Land of Israel by the Hibbat Zion movement in the latter half of the nineteenth century, was instrumental in bridging the gap between tradition and secular Zionism.[20]

While Alkalai and Kalisher provided this "bridge," they were themselves but the culmination of a current of religious thought that had its roots as far back as the thirteenth century.

The "cultural Zionism" of Ahad Ha'am (1856—1927) builds upon this foundation. While he discarded the theistic premises of his religious predecessors, Ahad Ha'am argued that vibrant Jewish life in the modern world—and in a future Jewish "national home"—demanded respectful engagement with the Jewish religious culture of the past. Because of this complex response to Jewish tradition, Arthur Hertzberg referred to him as "the Agnostic Rabbi" of Zionism.[21] Chaim Weizmann, the first President of the State of Israel, was one of the disciples of this "Agnostic Rabbi." Ahad Ha'am also exercised a powerful influence over intellectuals of the Zionist movement, many of whom (such as Martin Buber and Gershom Scholem) reincorporated the theistic component in their cultural Zionist

20. Ottolenghi, "A National Home," 59–60. See also Johnson, *A History of the Jews*, 374–75. David Novak views Kalisher and Alkalai through the lens of messianic forms of religious Zionism manifested after the establishment of the State of Israel, and thus criticizes their vision of redemption as "a slow incremental process rather than a sudden apocalyptic event" (*Zionism*, 234–35). I share Novak's reservations about messianic forms of religious Zionism which diminish the eschatological distance between the present age and the age of the Messiah. Nevertheless, I find his attack on all notions of a "redemptive process" to be excessive (see 238–40). One may expect the final act of redemption to be "a sudden apocalyptic event" initiated by God and not by human beings—an event discontinuous with the natural course of events in this age—and still believe that human beings participate in preparing for its advent.

21. Cited by Levenson, *An Introduction to Modern Jewish Thinkers*, 118.

vision, albeit in non-halakhic form.[22] Even Rabbi Abraham Isaac Kook (1865–1935), the most seminal thinker in the formation of religious Zionism, draws from this cultural Zionist stream. As Yehudah Mirsky notes, "He [Rav Kook] explores Zionism solely for its cultural possibilities, which are in turn inextricably tied to morality and spirituality. His interlocutors here are the cultural Zionists of Ahad Ha-Am, for whom national spirit, understood as ethical consciousness, was the defining feature of Jewish identity throughout history."[23]

While considerable tension existed between the cultural Zionists and the political Zionists (such as Theodor Herzl and David Ben Gurion), the two currents were bound together as integral components of the Zionist movement.[24] Unlike cultural and religious Zionism, which were deeply rooted in traditional Jewish life, political Zionism emerged largely as a pragmatic modern response to the crisis of Jewish survival in the midst of an increasingly anti-Semitic environment. The eventual establishment and flourishing of the Jewish State is inconceivable apart from the efforts of the political Zionists, but it owes a similar debt to the cultural Zionists—even though they often functioned in the political sphere as loyal opposition. Thus, it was fitting that the first Prime Minister of Israel, David Ben Gurion, should serve alongside its first President, Chaim Weizmann.

Given this history, it is unsurprising that traditional Jewish religious practice and the study of traditional Jewish religious texts have thrived in contemporary Israel. While most of the founders were "secular Jews,"

22. On Scholem's personal views on these matters (which are less accessible from his writings than those of Buber), see Scholem, *On Jews and Judaism in Crisis*, 34–36, 46–48. David Novak offers a critical philosophical assessment of cultural Zionism based on Ahad Ha'am's secularism (*Zionism*, 66–83). Novak's analysis of Ahad Ha'am is astute, but a comprehensive evaluation of cultural Zionism requires assessment also of its theistic stream represented by figures such as Buber and Scholem.

23. Mirsky, *Rav Kook*, 37. See also 189 for discussion of Kook's personal contact with Gershom Scholem and Samuel Hugo Bergmann. Kook was a friend of novelist and Nobel Laureate S.Y. Agnon, who was part of the cultural Zionist circle.

24. This tension is amply explored in Hazony, *The Jewish State*. However, Hazony is a partisan of the political Zionist camp, and his assessments of the cultural Zionists are often unfair. In contrast, David Novak is more critical of the political Zionists than of the cultural Zionists (*Zionism*, 50–66). In his view, the latter at least had "positive purposes" that inspired their "action," whereas the former had only "negative purposes" that motivated their "reaction" (50). At the same time, Novak sees the State of Israel that emerged from their efforts as a tremendous political achievement.

today a majority of Israeli Jews no longer identify with that label.[25] Israeli Jews speak and write the language of the Jewish literary classics, order their public and private lives according to the rhythm of the Jewish religious holidays, and live in cities with streets named after Rashi, Maimonides, and Judah Halevi. Even those who identify as "secular" often take an interest in Talmud, Midrash, Kabbalah, or Hasidism. Israel is unquestionably modern, but its ties to traditional Jewish life are manifold.

In light of all this, I concur with the conclusion reached by Ottolenghi: "Jews eventually embraced Zionism because it reflected elements of identity pre-dating the reformulation of Jewishness in modern nationalist terms."[26] The paradox of passivity at the heart of the traditional Jewish religious approach to the land was gradually resolved in many quarters in favor of collective action, just as the paradox of radical rupture at the heart of early secular Zionism has gradually been resolved in twenty-first-century Israel in favor of identification with the Jewish past. Zionism is indeed a distinctively modern movement, but it is also an expression of values, longings, and utopian dreams cherished by Jews for millennia.

General Theological Assessment

What is the theological significance of Zionism in light of the prophetic *euangelion* described in the previous chapters?[27] That *euangelion* envisions the eschatological restoration of Jewish life in the land of Israel as an essential fruit of the resurrection of Israel's messianic king, who embodies his people in his person. Once such an interpretation of the *euangelion* is given credence, the historical re-establishment of Jewish national life in the land, with Jerusalem as its capital, raises theological

25. See Pew Research Center, March 8, 2016, "Israel's Religiously Divided Society," 7.

26. Ottolenghi, "A National Home," 55–56.

27. In *Zionism and Judaism*, David Novak analyzes Zionist thinking from a philosophical perspective, and offers his own "new theory" of Zionism that is theistic, halakhic, democratic, and non-messianic (i.e., independent of any claim that the State of Israel is the "beginning of the redemption"). I am in sympathy with his project and with many of his conclusions. My purpose here, however, is quite different. I am reflecting on the historical events that preceded and followed the establishment of the State of Israel, and attempting to discern their theological significance in the light of the New Testament texts studied in previous chapters. My focus here is not Zionism as a set of ideas, but Zionism as a concrete historical phenomenon.

questions of great moment. Could this be a decisive outworking of the divine *boulē* in history, just as fundamental to the purposes of God as the flourishing of Jewish life under the heirs of Gamaliel and the irrepressible spread of the *euangelion* itself?

While the reading of Luke and Acts offered in the previous chapters points to the eschatological restoration of Jewish life in the land, it does not strictly require that a preliminary restoration occur in advance of the Messiah's final appearance. One could affirm what I have proposed and understand it in a manner similar to what was common to the Jewish tradition before the modern era: only *after* the Messiah comes will Israel return to the land and renew there its national life. However, now that Jewish national life in the land has revived *before* the Messiah's coming, one must inquire whether such a historical development fits the prophetic *euangelion* even if that message does not strictly demand it.

Some of the texts from Luke and Acts that we have considered seem to presume a form of Jewish national life in the land antecedent to Jesus' return. That is especially the case with regard to those crucial texts that anticipate (Luke 13:35), describe (Luke 19:28–46), or allude retrospectively (Acts 1:6–12) to Jesus' triumphal entry on Palm Sunday. In the first of these texts, Jesus grieves over Jerusalem, concluding his lament with words drawn from Psalm 118: "you will not see me until the time comes when you say, 'Blessed is the one who comes in the name of the Lord.'" As noted earlier, this points to the triumphal entry itself (Luke 19:28–46) as a prophetic typological sign, in which the enthusiastic acclamation of Jesus by his own disciples represents the welcome that the entire Jewish population of the holy city—including its leaders—will offer when the resurrected and returning Messiah comes to redeem his people. In light of Acts 3:19–21, which makes Jerusalem's repentance a condition for the messianic restoration, we should see the city's readiness to offer such a welcome as a catalyst and not merely a consequence of the Messiah's appearance. The prophetic character of Palm Sunday receives further confirmation from the ascension narrative of Acts 1:6–12, in which we learn that Jesus "will come in the same way as you saw him go into heaven" (v. 12). As previously noted, this implies that Jesus will first *descend* to the mount of Olives (i.e., to the place from which he earlier *ascended*), in order to enact in fullness what the prophetic sign of Palm Sunday signified. The typological triumphal entry began on the Mount of Olives (Luke 19:29), as an indication that the eschatological triumphal entry would commence from the same location (in accordance with Zechariah

14:4–5). If we interpret this Lukan prophecy in a straightforward manner, it suggests that Jerusalem will be in some sense a Jewish city *before* Jesus returns to it.

For disciples of Jesus who live after the establishment of a Jewish State in 1948, the question we are considering here is unavoidable. We face a political fact that cries out for theological interpretation. However, it is striking that this question first became a matter of lively ecclesial discussion centuries before Zionism emerged as an explicit program among Jews. Gerald McDermott recounts how the Anglo-American Protestant theological tradition of the seventeenth century first began to articulate an eschatological expectation of Jewish return to the land.[28] Commenting on Increase Mather's *The Mystery of Israel's Salvation* (1669), McDermott states that "[o]ne of Mather's innovations was to charge that the Jews would regain their ancient land *before* they would convert. It would be only 'after the Israelites shall be returned to their own Land again' that the Holy Spirit would be poured out on them."[29] This view eventually became widespread in Anglo-American Protestant circles, and rendered that theological setting especially favorable to the Zionist project once it was launched in the nineteenth century. Was this new theological proposition an aberration, or was it a prescient response to the illuminating work of the Holy Spirit? In light of our reading of Luke and Acts and early ecclesial and Jewish history, the latter alternative seems far more likely.

We have now noted four weighty pieces of evidence relevant to the theological assessment of Zionism and the Jewish State: (1) the restoration of Jewish life in the land of Israel is a fundamental component of the prophetic *euangelion*; (2) an expectation that this restoration would occur before the return of Jesus coheres well with the way this theme is treated in key texts of the New Testament; (3) some Christians began to understand the New Testament as teaching such a Jewish national restoration centuries before the emergence of the Zionist movement; and (4) the Zionist movement originates in part as a continuation of a trajectory intrinsic to a Jewish religious tradition which itself was providentially ordained by the divine *boulē*. From these four pieces of evidence, I conclude that the establishment of a Jewish national home in the land of Israel (i.e., the success of the Zionist enterprise) was itself providentially ordained by

28. McDermott, "A History of Christian Zionism," 59–61. See also Goldman, *God's Country*, 13–16, 28–42.

29. McDermott, "A History of Christian Zionism," 61.

the divine *boulē*, and constitutes a historical fact of enormous theological significance.

A grim fifth factor confirms this assessment. The establishment of the Jewish State occured three years after the conclusion of World War II. In the twelve years of Nazi rule the Jewish people suffered the most devastating catastrophe in their long history of persecution and martyrdom. One out of every three Jews in the world was murdered. As a result of this modern horror, many Christians began to revise their views of the theological significance of the Jewish people. Discarding the notion that Jewish suffering could be attributed solely to Jewish sin, they proposed that the Shoah—and the centuries of persecution that made it possible—revealed the unbreakable connection between the Jewish people and Jesus the Messiah. In a mysterious fashion, the Jewish people were participants in the suffering of Jesus.[30]

I have already argued that this perspective on the suffering and death of Jesus has a firm basis in the New Testament itself. The cross of Jesus involves his proleptic participation in the Jewish torments of 70 CE, so that Jewish faithfulness unto death in coming centuries might participate retroactively in his martyrdom. However, I have also argued that this dynamic correspondence between Jesus and the Jewish people likewise requires a connection between the resurrection of Jesus and the national redemption of Israel. If the Shoah reveals the bond between the Jewish people and the death of Jesus, then the establishment of the Jewish State three years later likewise reveals the bond between Jewish national life and the resurrection of Israel's Messiah on the third day.

Just as "modern antisemitism was the catalyst for the rise of Jewish nationalism rather than its cause," so the Shoah was the catalyst for the establishment of the Jewish State rather than its cause.[31] But effective catalyst it was, and there is more than an accidental historical connection between the Shoah and the birth of the State of Israel in 1948. Thus, we are not considering two events linked only by an immediate temporal succession, but a partial communal death that helped prepare for a par-

30. For examples of such theological perspectives, see Kinzer, *Postmissionary Messianic Judaism*, 226–30. I there refer to the comments of Edith Stein, Pope John XXIII, Clemens Thoma, Thomas Torrance, and Joel Marcus.

31. Ottolenghi, "A National Home," 59. See also the words of Martin Buber in 1946: "Modern political Zionism . . . was only prompted and intensified, but not caused by modern anti-Semitism" (Buber, *A Land of Two Peoples*, 181). On the theological relationship between the Shoah and the establishment of the State of Israel, see Novak, *Zionism*, 225–49.

tial communal rebirth. Together, these two events made the 1900s "the most dramatic century in the dramatic history of the Jewish people."[32] If we understand the Jewish people as the continued object of divine election, then the two-act drama of that century cannot be theologically insignificant.

My focus to this point has been on New Testament texts that have a prophetic character, and on the bearing they have on our view of Zionism and the Jewish State. Of course, these New Testament texts are rooted in *Tanakh* (i.e., the "Old Testament"). Christian Zionists usually base their arguments on prophecies from *Tanakh*, and their opponents raise an objection that deserves comment. As Gary Burge puts it, "these [Zionist] Christians fail to point out the indisputable biblical motif that [the] land promise is strictly tied to covenant fidelity."[33] Israel has "right" to the land only so long as it remains faithful to its God. Moreover, once expelled from the land for infidelity, Israel's return is promised only on condition of its repentance (Deut 4:26–31; 30:1–5). Did the Zionist movement arise as an expression of such renewed covenant fidelity? Was this movement not dominated by secular Jews who rejected the authority of the Torah and who often lacked even minimal faith in God?

Such critics of Christian Zionism have a point. The Deuteronomic tradition does make covenant fidelity a condition for Israel's national restoration. While it is a mistake to view Zionism as a strictly secular movement and the State of Israel as a strictly secular state, neither can be seen as primarily religious in nature. Furthermore, like all political movements and states, this movement and this state may reasonably be charged with acts of injustice that violate the ethical demands of the covenant.[34] Do these two facts undermine the claim that the Zionist movement and the Jewish State manifest historically the divine *boulē* and correlate in some manner with the words of Israel's prophets?

In order to answer that question, it is crucial to distinguish two strands of prophetic teaching about Israel's return from exile. As noted, the Deuteronomic strand requires Israel's repentance as a condition for its national restoration.[35] However, other strands of prophetic teaching

32. Shavit, *My Promised Land*, 412.

33. Burge, *Jesus and the Land*, 123.

34. "Christian Zionists who champion the prophetic fulfillments of modern Israel must likewise be ready to apply the prophetic ethical demands of these same writers" (Burge, *Jesus and the Land*, 124).

35. This Deuteronomic tradition is also found in prophetic texts such as Jeremiah 31:18–20.

approach the topic quite differently. For example, in Ezekiel 36 God restores Israel "for the sake of my holy name," and "not for your sake, O house of Israel" (vv. 21–23; 32). God acts not because Israel has fulfilled a covenantal condition, but because God's name is irrevocably tied to Israel, and because Israel's desolate state brings dishonor to God's name. This act of divine restoration involves *first* a return to the land (v. 24), and *then* an internal transformation that enables Israel to obey God's statutes and ordinances (vv. 25–27) and to abide in a renewed covenant relationship (v. 28). Here Israel's repentance (v. 31) is a *result* of God's restorative work rather than its *condition*. Moreover, Israel's repentance *follows* rather than precedes its return to the land. A similar eschatological scenario appears in Isaiah 40–66.[36]

If we read Luke and Acts as anticipating a return of Israel to its land before it welcomes Jesus with the words of Psalm 118:25–26, then Luke and Acts may combine these two strands of the prophetic tradition. First, God acts (in accordance with the teaching of Ezekiel and Isaiah) to partially restore Israel to its own land. Only afterward does God give Israel a new heart, so that the people are able to receive Jesus as the prophet like Moses (Acts 3:22). This second redemptive act then opens the way for the full restoration of Israel, and of all creation with it (Acts 3:19–21).

From this perspective, nothing prevents us from seeing Zionism as an integral yet imperfect expression of the divine *boulē* at work in human history.

Specific Theological Questions

I have deliberately formulated this conclusion in general terms. *Something* is happening in the Zionist movement of tremendous positive theological import. That *something* corresponds *in some way* with the prophetic *euangelion*. But what does this mean for the specific questions that disciples of Jesus must address as they reflect theologically on critical events taking place in the Middle East?

How disciples of Jesus answer these questions has a profound impact on how they respond to those events. Most of the direct participants

36. In these chapters of Isaiah, Israel in exile is described as a "worm" (41:14) and as "blind" (42:16). As Isaiah 44:22 states, "I have swept away your transgressions like a cloud, and your sins like mist; return to me, for I have redeemed you." Here the demonstration of divine forgiveness and redemption serves as the motive for Israel's repentance, rather than its result.

in the Middle East are not intentional disciples of Jesus, and we cannot expect the *euangelion* to shape their thinking and action. But disciples of Jesus around the world play a prominent role in supporting or opposing various courses of action adopted by those participants. Thus, we need to know what the prophetic *euangelion* requires or permits concerning these actions.

In what follows I am not advocating any particular political program or policy. My aim is to clarify the practical twenty-first-century imperatives of the New Testament teaching identified in the previous chapters. I seek only to define what that message requires concerning the Jewish people and the land of Israel, and where there is scope for prudential decisions based on the ethical teaching that is also central to the *euangelion*.

I will now address five specific questions.

Question #1: Does a positive theological assessment of Zionism in light of the prophetic euangelion mean that the Jewish State as currently constituted is the beginning of the redeemed order of the world?

Our theological reflection on these historical events suggests that *the rebirth of Jewish national life in the land of Israel is a divine work with profound eschatological implications.* This conclusion should be evident from the extraordinary form this history took and by its relationship to the Lukan *euangelion*. However, this does not mean that *the state* should be regarded in exactly the same way. Considered as a particular political arrangement for the ordering of Jewish national life, the state serves the nation but is not identical to it. It is an instrument, not an end in itself, and could take a variety of forms and still fulfill its purpose.

In 1948, the two chief rabbis of the new State of Israel composed a prayer for the state that is still used by many Jewish communities today. That prayer refers to the state as *reshit tzemichat ge'ulateynu*—literally translated, "the first-fruit of the sprouting of our redemption." The Hebrew word translated here as "sprouting" alludes to biblical and liturgical texts that speak of the eschatological reign of the Messiah.[37] There are ways of interpreting this phrase that would be compatible with the prophetic *euangelion*. The term "state" (*medinah*) may be understood as

37. See, for example, the fifteenth blessing of the daily *Amidah* prayer: "May the offshoot [*tzemach*] of Your servant David soon flower [*tatzmiach*], and may his pride be raised high by Your salvation, for we wait for Your salvation all day. Blessed are You, LORD, who makes the glory of salvation flourish [*matzmiach*]" (Sacks (ed.), *The Koren Siddur: Nusach Ashkenaz*, 124–25).

referring not primarily to a governmental structure but instead to the people served by that structure, and also to the entire historical sequence of events whereby they were regathered to the land as a self-governing community. These events may reasonably be viewed together as an eschatological sign manifesting God's faithfulness to the covenant promises, and pointing beyond themselves to a future messianic expression of that faithfulness beyond all imagining.

However, the phrase employed in the prayer for the State of Israel may also be interpreted in ways that are incompatible with the *euangelion*. This occurs whenever the State of Israel as a particular political order comes to be viewed as the first stage of the messianic redemption, with the ultimate reign of the Messiah merely adding the capstone to a nearly completed structure. Such an orientation to the Jewish State exaggerates the continuity between this broken world and the redeemed world, between Israel-now and Israel-then. The coming of the Messiah will heal the *nations* (Rev 21:24, 26; 22:2), but will end *states* as we now know them by establishing a *kingdom* in Israel (Acts 1:6).[38]

In this context, the approach taken to the reality of the Jewish State by Martin Buber has much to commend it. Before 1948, Buber had been aligned with those who had argued for a bi-national state in which the Jewish people would find a national home as an autonomous partner in a twofold Jewish-Arab political order. Displeased with the actual shape taken by the State of Israel in 1948, he nonetheless accepted it as his own. "I have accepted as mine the State of Israel, the form of the new Jewish community that has arisen from the war. I have nothing in common with those Jews who imagine that they may contest the factual shape which Jewish independence has taken. The command to serve the spirit is to be fulfilled by us in this state, starting from it."[39] While embracing the Jewish State, Buber still argued vigorously against an idolatry of that state. For him, the Zionist vision was fundamentally a moral and spiritual task given by God to the Jewish people, and the establishment of the state offered

38. According to David Novak, the notion of the state as the first stage of the messianic redemption is also problematic from a traditional Jewish theological perspective. See *Zionism*, 233–40. Novak argues that "the land of Israel exists for the sake of the people Israel; the people Israel do not exist for the sake of the land of Israel. . . . In the same way, the State of Israel is for the sake of the people Israel in the land of Israel; the people Israel in the land of Israel is not for the sake of the State of Israel. And, most importantly, the people, then the land, then the state all exist for the sake of God" (150, 151). I agree completely with Novak's formulation.

39. Buber, *Land of Two Peoples*, 292–93.

a decisive new opportunity to accomplish that task. Buber's biographer summarizes his view of the State of Israel in this way:

> "Every attempt to replace the living idea of 'Zion' through the establishment of a state must end in failure," wrote Buber [in 1959]. "The state is not, as Hegel thought, the 'self-determination' of the spirit in which alone man can have a rational existence. It is at best a supporting structure that the spirit employs in its work; but can also be a hindrance." Zion can grow out of a state that is faithful to the spirit but not out of one that forgets it unless it recollects itself and "turns." The people need the land and freedom to organize their own life in order to realize the goal of community, Buber wrote in *Israel and Palestine*. But the state as such is at best only a *means* to the goal of Zion, and it may even be an obstacle to it if the true nature of Zion as commission and task is not held uppermost. "Zion means a destiny of mutual perfecting. It is not a calculation but a command; not an idea but a hidden figure waiting to be revealed. Israel would lose its own self if it replaced [the land of] Palestine by another land and it would lose its own self if it replaced Zion by [the land of] Palestine."[40]

Buber was the prophetic conscience of the Zionist movement. His attitude to the State of Israel produced by that movement has as much prophetic power today as it did a half-century ago.

Question #2: Does a positive theological assessment of Zionism in light of the prophetic euangelion mean that the State of Israel must retain sovereignty over all the land it now controls?

If the State of Israel were the first stage of the eschatological redemption, destined to change gradually into the messianic kingdom, then one might justly argue against any territorial concessions on the part of the Jewish State. In that case, to yield land could mean delaying the day of final redemption. However, I have already denied such a status to the Jewish state. The State of Israel is at best a preliminary sign of the messianic kingdom, whose ultimate coming will rupture the order of this world as we know it.

In effect, I would argue that the Zionist ethos of collective action must be complemented and tempered by the traditional Jewish ethos of trusting expectation. Inspired collective action has providentially yielded

40. Friedman, *Martin Buber's Life and Work*, 351.

a Jewish national home in the land of promise. But collective action alone cannot initiate the messianic age. In light of the *euangelion* of Jesus' death and resurrection, one must hold that the existential condition of exile continues so long as sin and death dominate the created order. The corporate life of the Jewish people in the land of Israel constitutes a sign pointing beyond the exile to a world governed by the resurrected and glorified Messiah of Israel—yet the exile continues, even for Jews in the land. We will only see the true end of exile when God intervenes in an extraordinary and unilateral fashion to rend the heavens and transfigure the form of this world.

That is the eschatological perspective of the prophetic *euangelion*.[41] Viewed from this angle, the State of Israel is free to make territorial concessions if it determines that such decisions would advance the welfare of its people and promote the good of its region. Prudential judgments concerning security and other matters may make such concessions unwise in certain circumstances, but one should not confuse prudential judgments with theological imperatives.

Question #3: Does a positive theological assessment of Zionism in light of the prophetic euangelion mean that the State of Israel must retain total sovereignty over a politically united city of Jerusalem?

As seen in chapter 1, the *euangelion* acknowledges the unique bond joining the Jewish people to the holy city, and anticipates an eschatological day of redemption when that bond will be consummated. This means that disciples of Jesus must resist all attempts to equate theologically the Jewish relationship to the city with the religious attachment to the place held by Christians (i.e., gentile disciples of Jesus) and Muslims. Christians are joined to the city through their relationship with Jesus, the Messiah, who suffered, died, and rose from the dead there, and to whom the city ultimately belongs. However, the titulus under which he died identified him as "the king of the Jews," and the city belongs to him because he fulfills that role as the risen Son of David. Consequently, gentile disciples of Jesus are linked to the city through the Jewish people of which Jesus is the sovereign. Muslims, on the other hand, derive their devotion to Jerusalem from a tradition that Mohammed ascended to heaven on the Temple Mount in order to receive divine revelation. This tradition won a

41. This is also the eschatological perspective advocated by Jewish theologian David Novak, a perspective that he terms "transcendent messianism" (*Zionism*, 245).

special place in Islamic piety through the houses of worship constructed there to honor the event. Of course, disciples of Jesus will be disposed to view this story as legendary, but they cannot deny the attachment that has arisen as its result. What is crucial for our purposes is to note that, in historical perspective, the story likely arose because the early Islamic tradition acknowledged the site as the place of the Jerusalem temple, and thus treated it as suitable for such an ascent.[42] Thus, Muslim as well as Christian devotion to Jerusalem derive ultimately from the more basic Jewish connection to the site.

However, our answers to questions #1 and #2 underline the preliminary and provisional character of the Jewish state in relation to the messianic kingdom that is still to come. What is true of Jewish state sovereignty over the land as a whole applies also to Jewish state sovereignty over the holy city that is its heart. Of course, any political arrangement concerning Jerusalem must account for the city's unique role as the center not only of the Jewish state but also of the Jewish people throughout the world. Administration of the city must always be such as to enable Jewish life to thrive there, and to assure freedom of access to Jewish holy sites. Having met those essential conditions, the Jewish state could negotiate any number of possible political arrangements that would be compatible with the message of the resurrected Messiah. Disciples of Jesus should not impose theological constraints on the state's right and duty to develop creative solutions to complex political and diplomatic problems. The prophetic *euangelion* and the Zionist ideal (especially in the cultural Zionist tradition) share in common the imperative of joining ethical concerns, such as the priority of justice and peace, to national and religious concerns. As Buber argued, the "Zion" that animated the Zionist hope was not merely a place but also an ethical task, and the Jewish people should not be compelled to give up that task in the name of a particular expression of "state sovereignty."

At this point in history it is unlikely that the State of Israel would agree to any political arrangement that compromises its sovereignty in respect to Jerusalem. I am not arguing against that position, nor proposing any particular alternative. I merely seek to define the boundaries of

42. That does not mean that Muslims today generally recognize the site as the ancient home of a Jewish temple. Thus, Palestinian President Mahmoud Abbas has frequently stated that "there never was a Temple on the Temple Mount" (Yossi Alpher, "The Issues the Peace Process Should Avoid," *The Forward*, July 29, 2013).

permissible political options for those committed to the *euangelion* of the crucified and resurrected Messiah.

Question #4: Does a positive theological assessment of Zionism in light of the prophetic euangelion mean that the State of Israel should claim ownership of the Temple Mount and seek to rebuild the temple?

All Jews treat the Temple Mount as the holiest place on earth. For most of the past nineteen centuries Jews have been unable to worship on the mount itself, and have expressed their devotion to the place by praying at the Western Wall of the mount's supporting structure. Even after the Jewish State took control of the Old City of Jerusalem in 1967, rabbinic rulings prohibited Jews from visiting the Temple Mount in order to prevent the inadvertent profaning of the holy place.

According to our study of the temple in chapter 2, the Lukan writings continue to show reverence for the Temple Mount. Regardless of whether a Jewish temple adorns the site, the place itself retains its unique character as a central component in the Lukan vision of the cosmos. Just as Jerusalem remains the holy city, so the Temple Mount remains the holiest of the holy.

Therefore, disciples of Jesus should affirm the enduring connection between the Jewish people and the Temple Mount, and defend Jewish rights to worship freely at the Western Wall.[43] While Christians of the Roman and Byzantine eras may have treated the Mount with contempt, seeing it as a symbol of a people forsaken by God, disciples of Jesus today should show reverence for the site as a sacred symbol of a people chosen and beloved by God, whose identity and destiny are part and parcel of the *euangelion*.

Jews have traditionally believed that the temple would be rebuilt by the Messiah, and therefore Jewish longing for the temple was enfolded in a greater longing for the messianic era. Religious Zionists believed in collective action in order to return to the land and refashion Jewish national life, but they still assumed that the temple would be rebuilt only by the

43. This may appear to be a non-controversial statement. That this is not the case is demonstrated by an April 15, 2016 UNESCO resolution which spoke of the "Al-Haram Al Sharif" (the "noble sanctuary") solely as a "Muslim holy site of worship," and which referred to the Western Wall as "Al-Buraq Plaza" (with "Western Wall" mentioned parenthetically, in quotation marks). The resolution ignored the biblical connection between the Jewish people and the Temple Mount. See http://www.haaretz.com/israel-news/.premium-1.715442.

Messiah. So, when it came to the hope for a new temple, one could only pray and wait.

This approach coheres well with the New Testament orientation to the temple and the messianic era. Like many Jews of the first century, the early disciples of Jesus looked for a future temple "not made with hands," which would descend from heaven. For many of them, that temple was equivalent to the entire creation transformed and filled with the divine glory. Some of them may have hoped for a particular edifice in a renewed Jerusalem—but even they knew that it would not be constructed out of earthly stones by ordinary Jewish hands.

In the Six Day War of 1967 Israel took control of the Old City of Jerusalem for the first time in nearly nineteen centuries. After that dramatic event, a few Israelis began to think that the temple should be rebuilt *now*, before the coming of the Messiah.[44] The same type of collective action that resulted in the establishment of the Jewish state and the unification of the city of Jerusalem could now result in the renewal of Jewish temple worship. Such a program has gained momentum in recent years, and, while still marginal, has a growing number of Israeli adherents.[45]

Of course, this program also would likely entail destroying some or all of the Muslim religious sites that currently reside on the Temple Mount. That act would dishonor structures held sacred by a billion Muslims around the world, isolate the Jewish state even from its allies, and ignite a violent conflict with the Palestinians and other Muslim neighbors. Given the fact that building the temple before the coming of the Messiah is required by neither Jewish tradition nor the prophetic *euangelion*, and given the catastrophic geo-political consequences it would produce, this is not a course of action that disciples of Jesus need support or applaud.

I am not here suggesting that temple worship itself is incompatible with New Testament teaching. As we saw in our examination of the book of Hebrews in chapter 2, temple sacrifice is permissible in the current aeon. The early Jewish disciples of Jesus participated in temple worship before the destruction of Jerusalem in 70 CE, and there are no compelling theological reasons that would prevent Jewish disciples of Jesus from doing the same if the Jerusalem temple existed in our day. Thus, I am not here arguing against the *permissibility* of temple worship but instead

44. See Shavit, *Promised Land*, 215–17.

45. See Miller, "Temple Mount Revival Movement Revels in Crowd-Funded Passover Sacrifice—But at What Cost?" *The Forward*, May 2, 2016.

against the *necessity* or *wisdom* of advocating its restoration before the return of the Messiah.

Some may argue that disciples of Jesus must advocate the rebuilding of the temple because the New Testament expects the temple to be in existence in the period immediately preceding the return of the Messiah. As seen in chapter 2, Paul (or one of his literary disciples) evidently held such an expectation (see 2 Thess 2:1–4).[46] However, Paul apparently also believed that Jesus' return was imminent, and he does not seem to know what the author/editor of Luke/Acts knew—that the temple would be destroyed, and the history of Israel and the nations would continue in its absence. Since prophets do not always know how their words will be fulfilled, it is possible that Paul's reference to the temple in 2 Thessalonians should be taken in a figurative sense. The text may point only to the authority that "the lawless one" claims over the people of God, and the worship he demands from them. On the other hand, perhaps this text will indeed have a literal fulfillment, and the temple will be reconstructed at some point. Even if that is the case, it does not follow that such reconstruction is intrinsically a good and desirable act. There are many events that scripture anticipates at the end of this age that may be inevitable, but that in themselves are not good, and that should be resisted by the faithful rather than promoted. The initial triumph of "the lawless one" is itself the most extreme instance of just such an event, and (depending upon the circumstances) the reconstruction of the temple could be another.

While the prophetic *euangelion* does not require disciples of Jesus to advocate the reconstruction of the temple, it also does not require that they oppose such action. As noted above, circumstances in 2018 (as I finish this book) make the reconstruction of the temple a perilous and potentially disastrous venture that would dishonor a major world religion and violate the rights of its adherents. While it is difficult to envision a future scenario in which that is not the case, history takes many strange twists and turns that defy all attempts at prognostication. Should circumstances change in a way that makes the reconstruction of the temple a morally and prudentially acceptable action, disciples of Jesus would be free to support it. As I have already stated, there is nothing about temple worship that is incompatible with New Testament teaching.

46. See my discussion of this text in chapter 2, p. 82.

Nevertheless, our hope rests not on any such human project, but on the temple built without the help of human hands, whose holy of holies will be the New Jerusalem, and whose glory will fill the entire cosmos.

Question #5: Does a positive theological assessment of Zionism in light of the prophetic euangelion *mean that disciples of Jesus should always support the policies and actions of the government of the State of Israel?*

In contrast to the previous four questions, the answer to this one should be obvious: if disciples of Jesus need not approve of every policy and action undertaken by the governing authorities of their own ecclesial communities—which even Catholics are not obliged to do—of course they need not do so in regards to the Jewish state. Once again, if traditional Jews who consider themselves Zionists do not adopt such a posture—and none to my knowledge do—then why should Jewish or gentile disciples of Jesus be required to do so?

The reason for even asking this question is not in order to receive the expected negative response, but instead to clarify the attitude that disciples of Jesus should take in their moral evaluation of Israeli policy and action. Fundamentally, that attitude should be one of solidarity with the people who have elected the particular government in power and whose continued assent provides it with legitimacy. A disciple of the Jewish Messiah cannot adopt a neutral posture in thinking about Middle-East politics, standing at an equal distance from all parties and giving the benefit of the doubt to none.

At this final stage of our argument, the bases for such solidarity should be evident. First, all disciples of Jesus—gentile as well as Jewish—are bound inextricably to the Jewish people as brothers and sisters. As a consequence, one is considering the conduct of family members, not strangers. Second, disciples of Jesus should view the overall Zionist enterprise as a miracle of the Holy Spirit in history, tied intimately to the *euangelion* and reflecting the divine *boulē*. Just as we cannot consider the ovens of Auschwitz apart from the cross of the Messiah, so we cannot consider the life of this nation apart from his resurrection. Third, disciples of Jesus should be vividly aware that the diabolical forces whose machinations culminated in the Shoah have not been banished by its manifest horrors. The spirit of anti-Semitism is identical to the spirit of anti-Christ, and it is alive and well today in both guises. Not all anti-Zionism serves as a socially acceptable cloak for anti-Semitism, but some of it does. This fact makes us all the more eager to speak constructively, if not always positively, about the inevitably ambiguous fruit of Israeli politics.

We should begin from a place of faith in the work of God in history. Like every government enmeshed in a tangled web of inter-national, inter-cultural, inter-ethnic, and inter-religious hostility and violence, the government of Israel has committed, is committing, and will continue to commit misdeeds of varying degrees of gravity. But does this not echo the biblical narrative itself, in which God weaves his own redemptive tapestry out of our frayed and tangled cords? We can acknowledge the misdeeds of the Jewish state and pray and labor for their correction, while also acknowledging our limited capacity to discern the precise outlines of God's providential design in its historical outworking. At the same time, we are called to place our hope in the divine *boulē* that turned the sin of Joseph's brothers into salvation for both Jacob's family and the nations of the world.

Conclusion

Within the broad framework of this ecclesial Zionism, there is ample room for vigorous debate and disagreement concerning the practical details of the Israeli-Palestinian conflict. I am attempting to provide a set of theological parameters within which advocates of the right, left, and center can all take their stand. In other words, the approach presented here does not dictate a particular political stance in dealing with the issues at hand. In fact, the purpose is to limit the impact of theology to those essentials that draw the outer boundaries of discourse. I seek to free those in the debate from the heavy burden of theological imperatives in order to focus on the prudential and ethical considerations whose content should be decisive in shaping the argument. The theological framework is indispensable, but every attempt to draw detailed practical conclusions from this framework imprisons us in a dogmatic box from whose unyielding judgments we cannot escape, regardless of urgent ethical and prudential considerations.

We are now ready to take up our final topic as we reflect on historical events which are intimately connected to the prophetic *euangelion*.

A Theological Appraisal of Messianic Judaism

Just as our discussion of Jerusalem and the land in chapter 1 made the contemporary issue of Zionism unavoidable, so our treatment of the Torah in chapter 4 leads inevitably to a consideration of contemporary Messianic Judaism. The reading of the New Testament offered in the preceding pages implies that these two modern historical phenomena are of equal relevance to the *euangelion*. While this is itself a somewhat audacious conclusion, I intend here to propose an even more provocative thesis—namely, that *Zionism and Messianic Judaism are linked within God's providential design.* In support of that thesis, I will narrate briefly the history of Messianic Judaism in relation to the history of Zionism.

Jerusalem in Luke and Acts is the city of God and the Messiah, with the Temple Mount at its heart. It is the holiest point in the land of promise, the most precious part that represents the whole. But Jerusalem in Luke and Acts is also the city of Torah-faithful Jews who are devoted to both Jesus the Messiah and the people of Israel. Simeon, Anna, Joseph of Arimathea, James the brother of Jesus, the "thousands . . . among the Jews" who were "all zealous for the Torah" (Acts 21:20)—these are the citizens of Jerusalem whose lives represent for Luke the city's prophetic destiny. In his narrative they virtually reside in the temple, and the role they play in the worldwide *ekklēsia* makes them nearly equivalent to the place they inhabit.

The Jewish wars with Rome at the end of the first and beginning of the second centuries determined the contours of Israel's national existence in exile for almost two millennia. Communities of Jews continued to live in the land of promise, but for centuries Jerusalem was off-limits. These same wars also played a decisive role in weakening and eventually destroying the community of Jewish disciples of Jesus—the *ekklēsia ex circumcisione* ("the *ekklēsia* from the circumcision"), in the terminology of the patristic period. As it turned out, the "times of the gentiles" (Luke 21:24) would involve the elimination of a visible Jewish communal presence not only in Jerusalem but also in the *ekklēsia*. Sadly, most believers in Jesus of the second century and beyond celebrated the destruction of both the holy city and the *ekklēsia ex circumcisione*. They failed to recognize the beginning of their own ecclesial exile. The Jewish people had been expelled from a Jerusalem conquered by external enemies, but these Christians had fanned the flames that destroyed their own holy city and marched willingly into exile as if homeward bound.

The sufferings of exile were most cruel for the Jewish disciples of Jesus. Like the rest of the Jewish people, they had lost their beloved city and temple, and had endured national humiliation. But it soon became evident that they had also forfeited their place in both the Jewish community and the *ekklēsia*. To maintain their Jewish identity they were required to renounce their faith in Jesus. To maintain their faith in Jesus they were compelled to surrender their Jewish identity and be absorbed into the *ekklēsia ex gentibus* (i.e., the *ekklēsia* from the nations). The decision of that *ekklēsia* for a Jerusalem-less existence meant that Jewish disciples of Jesus, who would not renounce their faith in him, must suppress their intrinsic connection to the holy city and, as a consequence, be exiled from themselves.

Having lost Jerusalem and their national home in the land of Israel, the Jewish people never relinquished hope for a future restoration. When the Messiah would come, he would lead his people back to their promised inheritance. In the meantime, Jews could only pray and wait.

Correspondingly, the *ekklēsia ex gentibus* retained its own glimmer of hope for the Jewish people—a hope at the outer margins rather than the center of ecclesial existence, but noteworthy nonetheless. At the end of the age the Jews would be "converted to Christ," and then Jesus would return. This meant that the *ekklēsia* never utterly lost its consciousness of Israel's unique covenantal status among the nations of the earth. Of course, that status could only have positive significance when Jews believed in Jesus (and, paradoxically, gave up their Judaism). Still, this meant that the Jewish people were an essential part of the divine plan, for the final redemption of the world and the resurrection of the dead could not be realized in their absence. In the meantime, Jews lived under a curse, and the most that Christians could do was pray for them and wait.

Already in the seventeenth and eighteenth centuries some Christians began to envision a collective return of Jews to their ancestral land *before* the return of the Messiah.[47] These Christians were a century or two ahead of their time. Similarly, in the early eighteenth century some German pietist Christians began to envision the establishment of communities of Jewish disciples of Jesus who would adopt the essential components of a traditional Jewish way of life.[48] These Christians saw the Jerusalem

47. As noted above, some Jews had entertained the same notion in the medieval period, but this view lived on at best as a subterranean belief in Jewish circles until the nineteenth century.

48. Rudolph, "Messianic Judaism in Antiquity and in the Modern Era," 25–26.

community of Acts of the Apostles as a model worthy of emulation by latter-day Jewish disciples of Jesus.[49] They also were ahead of their time, as this vision would not gain traction among Jewish disciples of Jesus until the late nineteenth century.

The Jewish attitude toward exile took a decisive turn only at the beginning of the nineteenth century when disciples of the Vilna Gaon emigrated to Palestine "for the express purpose of building institutions."[50] In the same period, Jewish believers in Jesus in England took a step without precedent in the post-Constantinian era. Affirming publicly the enduring character of their Jewish identity and its spiritual significance, they began to form bonds with one another and institutions that could strengthen those bonds. In 1813, forty-one Jewish disciples of Jesus established a London association called *Beney Abraham* (the Children of Abraham). In 1866, the Hebrew Christian Alliance was born, again in England.[51] The participants in these organizations were loyal members of various churches, and were not attempting to construct a distinct Jewish ecclesial community. Nevertheless, they had broken with a centuries-long practice of total Jewish assimilation within the gentile *ekklēsia*.

Zionism as a movement assumed its mature form in the 1880s and 1890s. In 1881 Czar Alexander II of Russia was assassinated, and many blamed the Jews for his death. Pogroms and anti-Jewish legislation followed, as did massive emigration. This period is traditionally known as "the First Aliyah," when some 25,000 Jews made their way from Eastern Europe to Palestine. In January of 1882, a central committee was established in Romania to coordinate the transport of groups of Jews to the land, and to facilitate their inclusion in Jewish agricultural settlements in their new habitation. The first such settlement, Rishon Lezion, was founded in the same year. In 1895 Theodor Herzl wrote *The Jewish State* (published in 1896), and in 1897 he led the First Zionist Congress in Basel, Switzerland. In these decades Zionism emerged as a defined movement oriented to the founding of a distinct Jewish polity in the land of Israel.

49. Rudolph, "Messianic Judaism in Antiquity and in the Modern Era," 25–26n18.

50. Mirsky, *Rav Kook*, 32.

51. This organization continues to exist, now under the name "The Messianic Jewish Alliance." There are autonomous national branches of the Alliance (like the British Alliance, described above), as well as an international branch, which was founded in 1925.

One of those Eastern European Jews caught up in the Zionist discussions of the 1880s was Joseph Rabinowitz (1837–99). In 1882 he traveled to Palestine to investigate whether collective immigration to the land might be a solution to the ills plaguing the Jewish people. While gazing on the holy city from the Mount of Olives (where Jesus had been welcomed by his disciples on Palm Sunday), Rabinowitz was suddenly convinced that "*Yeshua Achinu*" (Jesus our Brother) was the Messiah, and that he alone could save Israel.[52] He returned to Kishinev in Bessarabia, and sought to gather a group of Jewish disciples of Jesus whom he called "Israelites of the New Covenant" (*Beney Israel, Beney Brit Chadashah*). This body would follow the biblically ordained practices of the Torah, such as circumcision, the Sabbath, and the Jewish holidays, and—while seeking cooperative relationships with the Christian churches—would guard their autonomy as a *Jewish* community. Unable to win governmental authorization to baptize individuals and to establish a congregation, Rabinowitz's group in Kishinev failed to survive his death in 1899. Nevertheless, this "Israelite of the New Covenant" enjoyed extraordinary success in gaining an international hearing for his program.[53] Following in his footsteps were other like-minded Jewish disciples of Jesus such as Isaac Lichtenstein in Hungary, Theodore Lucky in Galicia, Mark John Levy in the United States, Paul Levertoff in Britain, and Moshe Immanuel Ben-Meir in Israel. Kai Kjaer-Hansen calls Rabinowitz "the Herzl of Jewish Christianity," and the moniker is apt. As a result of his efforts, the vision of a distinct Jewish polity within the one *ekklēsia*, formerly inconceivable, had now become a matter of active debate among Jewish disciples of Jesus, and also among gentile disciples of Jesus who labored in Christian missions to the Jews.

As the ideas of Rabinowitz spread among sympathetic Jewish disciples of Jesus, who now employed the term "Messianic Jew" to describe themselves, the longstanding members of the Hebrew Christian alliance

52. Kjaer-Hansen, *Joseph Rabinowitz and the Messianic Movement*, 11–22.

53. Rabinowitz traveled to Germany, Hungary, England, Scotland, and the United States, attracting attention wherever he went (Kjaer-Hansen, *Joseph Rabinowitz,* 75–90, 171–78). He even became the subject of an essay by the great Russian philosopher, Vladimir Solovyov, who wrote about Rabinowitz in 1885. Urging the Russian government to grant legal status to the nascent congregation of Kishinev, Solovyov wrote: "[O]n what grounds and interest does our government remove independence from the Jewish commune which attained Christ by its own lawful path, receiving its Messiah on its and His own personal native soil, the soil of a historical, three-thousand-year-long tradition?" (Solovyov, *The Burning Bush*, 343).

reacted fiercely. In 1917 they officially denounced Messianic Judaism as a heresy.[54] This draconian measure succeeded in delaying the growth of Messianic Judaism for five decades, but it could not destroy the idea which Rabinowitz and others had championed.

The seismic events of the 1940s united the Jewish world in support of the nascent Jewish polity fighting for its life in a hostile Middle-East. The Hebrew Christian world experienced a similar shaking two decades later in the wake of the Six-Day War. That conflict had begun amidst the realistic fear of Israel's annihilation, and had concluded with Jews returning to pray at the Western Wall. In those days, Jewish disciples of Jesus shared the sense of wonder that prevailed within the Jewish world as a whole, and many now began to reconsider the Messianic Jewish "heresy" suppressed a half-century earlier. Perhaps the Jewish disciples of Jesus needed their own ecclesial polity to ensure their survival and flourishing, in solidarity with all Jews and especially with those in the restored Jewish commonwealth of Israel. After almost two millennia of exile, Jerusalem was once again the capital of the Jewish people. Was it not an appropriate time for the *ekklēsia* to renounce her self-imposed exile and recover her own communal embodiment of the holy city?

In this way the Messianic Jewish movement of the 1970s was born. As its fruit, congregations and groups of Jewish disciples of Jesus now exist who identify as Jews rather than as Christians, and who seek to live according to the Torah.[55] Some of them even embrace rabbinic tradition as an indispensable—or at least valuable—aid in shaping that life.[56] Since the heady days in which it first took root, the Messianic Jewish movement has developed diverse expressions—some of impressive theological and spiritual depth, others embarrassingly shallow. In producing mixed fruit Messianic Judaism once again resembles Zionism. But mistakes and failures do not preclude miracles of divine providence in history. Indeed, as Luke and Acts teach and illustrate, human frailty provides the normal material upon which providence works its redemptive craftsmanship.

54. On this conflict, see Rudolph, "Messianic Judaism," 26–29.

55. Messianic Jews refuse to identify as "Christians" because that term invariably connotes a form of religious life distinct from and incompatible with Judaism. They do not treat the term with contempt, but see it as an honorable designation appropriate for members of the *ecclesia ex gentibus*.

56. See, for example, the Messianic Jewish Rabbinical Council, of which I am a member: http://ourrabbis.org/main/.

Neither Zionism nor Messianic Judaism signify the decisive end of exile for the Jewish people or the *ekklesia*. While the crucified Jerusalem has not yet risen, intimations of her eschatological glory are now present among us. If we attend to those hints, the twenty-first century may yet witness the recovery of an integrated *euangelion*, which was fractured soon after its initial proclamation.

Conclusion

The flourishing of the Jewish people and tradition after the destruction of Jerusalem was a powerful sign of the divine *boulē* at work in human history. While the historical developments considered in the present chapter are still fresh in our memory and vision, and their long-term effects are uncertain, they reflect the outworking of the same divine counsel. For adherents of the prophetic *euangelion* whose eyes behold (however dimly) "the whole purpose of God," these historical realities point to the unquenchable love that the resurrected Messiah of Israel has for his people, and his determination to make his glory known through them. He dwells in his *ekklēsia*, but he also abides in hidden form among his own flesh and blood. Only together do these two communities bear witness to the saving purpose of God for the world.

Chapter 7

The Integrative Power of the Prophetic *Euangelion*

I have attempted in this volume to understand the *euangelion* of the resurrected Messiah as good news for the Jewish people and the land of promise. In the process I have explored dimensions of the *euangelion* than have traditionally been overlooked. So conceived, the message of the resurrected Messiah makes possible a coherent ecclesial vision of genealogical-Israel that is faithful to the apostolic witness and sensitive to the workings of divine providence in history. At the same time, this volume raises new questions in other theological spheres that require intensive exploration. In addressing those questions, the integrative potential of the prophetic *euangelion* will be revealed.

In this final chapter I will first underline the integrative force of this perspective on the *euangelion* in relation to ecclesial teaching on the Jewish people and the land. I will then describe four of the remaining theological challenges that this perspective brings into focus, and suggest directions that show promise of bearing fruit in the future. If my thesis is sound, it should bring greater coherence not only to ecclesial teaching directly related to the Jewish people and the land, but to the full scope of ecclesial theological reflection.

An Integrated Jesus-Centered Vision of Israel

In the previous chapters I have proposed a Jesus-centered vision of Israel that affirms the irrevocable election of the Jewish people; its priestly vocation throughout history; its unbreakable connection to the land of promise; and its rich eschatological destiny. Each of these elements is integrated with the others, and all find their center in the prophetic *euangelion* of the crucified and resurrected Messiah.

We have seen how early ecclesial views of the land developed, with the millenarian eschatology of Justin and Irenaeus provoking the spiritualized Platonist reaction of Origen, culminating in a sacramental Byzantine synthesis after the discovery of the tomb of Jesus. The holiness of the land was now treated as a given, but that holiness had nothing to do with either the Jewish people or the world's eschatological hope. It had everything to do with the death and resurrection of Jesus as accomplished facts that were unrelated to the Jewish people. Thus, the land was seen as intimately tied to the *euangelion* proclaimed by the *ekklēsia*, but that gospel was a message of an already-realized rather than a future redemption.

In the seventeenth century some Protestants rediscovered the eschatological connection between the land and the Jewish people. In the following centuries this modest theological current became a raging torrent, attaining classic formulation in nineteenth-century dispensationalism. At the same time, this tradition lost sight of the land's sacramental relationship to the Messiah, and failed to perceive Jesus' resurrection as the source of Israel's future national resurrection. Moreover, while this Protestant stream recovered the eschatological vocation of the Jewish people, it retained the standard ecclesial neglect or denial of genealogical-Israel's priestly vocation in the present age.

The growth of Pentecostalism in the last century has produced new theological grounds for Christian Zionism, with stress shifting from eschatological prophecy to earthly blessing in this life. In this ecclesial stream, focus is now placed on the land promise to Abraham, and on the divine assurance of Genesis 12:3 that "I will bless those who bless you, and the one who curses you I will curse."[1] Without losing the eschatological dimension, the Pentecostal perspective recovers appreciation for the Jewish vocation in this age—though this appreciation has little substantive theological content. Furthermore, the connection between the Jewish people, the land, and the *euangelion* remains obscure. Attention has shifted from eschatological prophecy to Abrahamic promise, but neither prophecy nor promise are conceived in a way that is centered in the death and resurrection of Israel's Messiah.

1. See Hummel, "The New Christian Zionism."

In the aftermath of the Shoah many segments of the *ekklēsia* have reassessed their traditional teaching of contempt for the Jewish people. The Catholic Church took the lead, declaring in *Nostra Aetate* (1965) that "the Jews remain very dear to God, for the sake of the patriarchs, since God does not take back the gifts he bestowed or the choice he made" (Rom 11:28–29).[2] Making clear the implication of this statement, the Catholic Catechism (1992) asserted that "Israel is the priestly people of God"—and the context leaves no doubt that "Israel" here means "the Jewish people" (*CCC* 63).[3] To the chagrin of its mainstream Jewish dialogue partners, Catholic teaching has nevertheless retained its eschatological conviction that the Jewish people will ultimately acknowledge Jesus as its Messiah, and that this acknowledgement is an essential condition of his return: "The glorious Messiah's coming is suspended at every moment of history until his recognition by 'all Israel'" (*CCC* 674).[4] Nevertheless, the Catholics have not yet affirmed the inseparable bond tying the Jewish people to the land, nor have they seen this bond as itself a proleptic eschatological "mystery." They have also been reticent in working out a Christologically-based theology of Israel, though their official documents provide rich resources for such a perspective.

In the preceding chapters I have attempted to weave all of these separate strands into an integrated Jesus-centered vision of Israel. Here the death and resurrection of the Messiah undergirds the present holiness of the land and the Jewish people, while also pointing forward to the eschatological fulfillment of both land and people in the holiness of the age to come. Here the modern historical surprises of Zionism and Messianic Judaism serve as interconnected witnesses to the divine purpose for Israel. Here the gentile *ekklēsia* loses nothing of its dignity, but instead gains a clearer sense of its own status as a messianic extension of Israel and an essential participant in Israel's mission among the nations.

Just as Israel provides the perspective needed for interpreting the death and resurrection of the Messiah, so Jesus himself provides the perspective needed for interpreting the identity of the Jewish people and its heritage of the land.

2. Flannery (ed.), *Documents of Vatican II*, 741.

3. *Catechism of the Catholic Church*, 26. On the context and the textual allusions, see Kinzer, *Searching Her Own Mystery*, 49.

4. *Catechism of the Catholic Church*, 193.

Canonical Coherence

Will the prophetic *euangelion* articulated in the previous chapters demonstrate the same integrating force in relation to other spheres of ecclesial theological reflection? Will it bring greater coherence to ecclesial teaching as a whole, or sow general theological confusion? To address these questions, I will consider four areas of theological reflection, and ponder the potential impact of my thesis in each context. Obviously, these four topics do not exhaust the issues that require attention, but merely illustrate what is demanded across the entire field of ecclesial teaching.

I will begin with ecclesial theology's biblical framework. My argument in the previous chapters rests on a reading of Acts of the Apostles and the Gospel of Luke. Concentrating upon these two related New Testament books fits the compositional orientation of my theological approach to the biblical text, for it enables me to take adequate account of the subtle literary cues employed by the author/editor to convey his message. This is especially important for Acts and Luke, which in the past have been overshadowed theologically by their imposing canonical neighbors.

Nevertheless, the compositional orientation is only the first of four aspects of a theological mode of reading described in the introduction to this volume. It must be followed and complemented by canonical reflection on the text. This involves the study of related biblical books in light of Acts and Luke, to see if those books can be interpreted in a manner that coheres with what we have proposed from the Lukan corpus. As the compositional principle implies, *coherence* does not mean *equivalence*. We do not expect diverse biblical authors, writing in different times to different audiences for different purposes, to say exactly the same thing in exactly the same way. But the theological mode of reading that I advocate and practice presumes that the varied books of the biblical canon are (at minimum) compatible, and (at best) shed clarifying light on one other.

In the case at hand, the crucial test of our thesis will come from study of the Pauline letters. Acts of the Apostles presents itself in part as a biographical introduction and defense of Paul. If it can be shown that the Pauline letters—studied with attention to their own compositional integrity—offer a view of the *euangelion*, the Jewish people, the Torah, and the land of Israel that contradicts my reading of Acts, then my thesis has failed the test. If, on the other hand, a reasonable case can be made for reading the Pauline letters in a way that coheres with what has been presented in the previous chapters, my thesis stands.

This testing process is easier said than done. From Marcion to Augustine to Aquinas to Luther to Barth, interpreters of Paul have wrestled with his writings and with the writings of one another. Over many centuries and among diverse readers certain constants have remained largely intact: the Torah has been abolished, the Jewish people are under divine wrath, the eschatological inheritance consists of heaven or a glorified universe (with no eschatological significance attached to the land of Israel), and the *euangelion* concerns the eternal destiny of individuals (or the *ekklēsia*) and has nothing to do with the national identity of the Jewish people. Given such a formidable cultural tradition, it is difficult for any reader even to consider an alternative model.

It is therefore noteworthy that such consideration is currently taking place in the scholarly world.[5] Given the importance of the covenantal/communal principle in my theological mode of reading scripture, and my conviction that the people in covenant with God includes both the Jewish people and the *ekklēsia*, it is even more noteworthy that Jewish scholars feature prominently in this re-reading of Paul.[6] These Jewish biblical scholars, along with their gentile colleagues, adhere to a historical rather than a theological mode of interpretation. Thus, their critique of the traditional ecclesial understanding of Paul derives from the letters themselves read in their historical context (including their *Jewish* context). These scholars do not begin with a theological commitment to read the Pauline letters in light of the Lukan text that precedes them in the established canon. This gives more weight to their findings from the perspective of the compositional principle of theological interpretation.

Unlike these historians of ancient literature, I do begin with a theological commitment to the biblical canon. As stated in the introduction of this volume, the canon speaks to us not only through its contents but also through its structure. That structure likely took shape in response to the Marcionite canon, which included a shorter de-Judaized version

5. To get acquainted with these provocative new interpretations of Paul, see two recent collections: Boccaccini and Segovia (eds.), *Paul the Jew: Rereading the Apostle as a Figure of Second Temple Judaism* and Nanos and Zetterholm (eds.), *Paul within Judaism: Restoring the First-Century Context to the Apostle.*

6. Especially noteworthy are the writings of Mark D. Nanos (e.g., *The Mystery of Romans* and *The Irony of Galatians*), Pamela Eisenbaum (*Paul Was Not a Christian*), and Paula Fredriksen (*Paul: The Pagan's Apostle*).

of the Gospel of Luke and ten letters of Paul, beginning with Galatians.[7] In response, the *ekklēsia* developed a canon that began with the Gospel of Matthew (and its Jewish genealogy), and that placed Acts before the Pauline letters (with Romans rather than Galatians at the head). This canonical arrangement conveyed a message: rather than reading the letters of Paul as anti-Jewish, the apostle to the gentiles should be interpreted in a way that coheres with the perspective of Peter, the twelve, and James the Just.

I propose that ecclesial readers should adopt a hermeneutic of suspicion toward a traditional reading of Paul, which retained certain Marcionite prejudices and which took inadequate account of the Lukan theological framework inscribed in the canon. One must still make the case that the Pauline letters can be read in a way that coheres with the thesis of the preceding chapters. The recent "Paul within Judaism" school of biblical scholarship suggests that such a case can indeed be made, and points the way forward in the sphere of biblical theology for those testing the adequacy of my interpretation of the prophetic *euangelion*.

Soteriological Coherence

The preceding chapters have unfolded a prophetic *euangelion* that links the death and resurrection of Jesus to the redemptive exile and eschatological restoration of the Jewish people. As noted in the introduction, I have not attempted a comprehensive study of the *euangelion* and its varied implications. If, however, my proposal is to be fully convincing, it must be shown to fit well within a wider vision of the saving work of Jesus the Messiah.

While I cannot provide such treatment here, I will offer a few suggestions as to how it might proceed. I will first consider the life of Jesus, and then his atoning death. I will conclude by reflecting on his resurrection in relation not only to soteriology but also incarnation and eschatology.

The Life of Jesus

Paul's capsule summary of the *euangelion* states that "Messiah died for our sins in accordance with the scriptures" (1 Cor 15:3). What is there about the Messiah's death that gives it atoning power? Elsewhere, Paul

7. See Miller, *How the Bible Came to Be*, 60–83.

connects the death of Jesus to his obedience, and views that obedience or "righteousness" as enabling others to become "righteous": "Therefore just as one man's trespass led to condemnation for all, so one man's act of righteousness leads to justification and life for all. For just as by the one man's disobedience the many were made sinners, so by the one man's obedience the many will be made righteous" (Rom 5:18–19). Stepping back a distance and taking a broader view of the Messiah's redemptive work, the apostle sets this messianic obedience "to the point of death" in the context of his entire life, and even of his pre-incarnate existence "in the form of God":

> [T]hough he was in the form of God,
> [he] did not regard equality with God
> as something to be exploited,
> but emptied himself, taking the form of a slave,
> being born in human likeness.
> And being found in human form,
> he humbled himself
> and became obedient to the point of death—
> even death on a cross. (Phil 2:6–8)

It was because of the Messiah's self-emptying humility and obedience that God "highly exalted him" by raising him from the dead (Phil 2:9).

Thus, the atoning death of Jesus cannot be separated from his obedient life. This calls to mind the rich theological concept of "recapitulation" (*anakephalaiōsis*) developed in the second century by Irenaeus. David Bentley Hart works out his own understanding of soteriology on the basis of this concept:

> Irenaeus describes with extraordinary felicity the necessary logic of all Christian soteriology. It is because Christ's life effects a narrative reversal, which unwinds the story of sin and death and reinaugurates the story that God tells from before the foundation of the world—the story of the creation he wills, freely, in his eternal counsels—that Christ's life effects an ontological restoration of creation's goodness[:] . . . he who is from the beginning the head of all things recapitulates the human entirely, in the shape and substance of a whole life lived for the Father . . . .[8]

8. Hart, *The Beauty of the Infinite*, 324. Hart summarizes his view of soteriology in this way: "Salvation occurs by way of recapitulation, the restoration of the human image in Christ, the eternal image of the Father after whom humanity was created in the beginning . . ." (318).

Irenaeus and Hart present Jesus' "whole life lived for the Father" as a recapitulation of the human story. Jesus is the new Adam who restores the divine image to humanity by living the way human beings were supposed to live. His obedience "to the point of death" opens the way so that "the many will be made righteous."

But the one who does this is "the Messiah," that is, the king of Israel. In accordance with that title, the Gospels focus on Jesus less as the "new Adam" and more as the true Israel. The salvific work of Jesus consists primarily in his recapitulation of Israel in the form of a life of true righteousness, that is, covenant faithfulness. When Jesus suffers and dies on the cross, bearing in advance the wrath of Rome that his people would face a generation later, entering into the depths of Israel's exile, his action is not an isolated event but the culmination of an entire life. The narrative of his life receives its shape and meaning by the way it ends, but that ending can only be understood in relation to the decisions he had already made, the actions he had already taken, the words he had already spoken.

As seen most vividly in the account of his temptation in the wilderness, this meant obeying God in the way Israel was always intended to do (Matt 4:1–11). Jesus responds to Satan with words drawn from Deuteronomy, a book that exhorts Israel at the end of its wilderness wandering to be faithful to the covenant and obedient to the Torah so that it might prosper in the land promised to the patriarchs and matriarchs. These temptations offer interpretive commentary on the shape of his life that will follow. Similarly, Jesus' prayer in Gethsemane offers commentary on the meaning of his coming death. When Jesus says "not my will but your will be done," he reiterates the message conveyed by Israel at Sinai—"All that the LORD has spoken we will do, and we will be obedient" (Exod 24:7). In contrast to Israel in the wilderness, he lives out this pledge blamelessly.

While Jesus' role as the one who recapitulates Israel deserves stress, it should not come at the expense of his universal human recapitulation. Irenaeus and Hart are right to underline the way Jesus recapitulates the human story as a whole. The Gospels also tell this universal story, but they do so at one step removed. *Jesus recapitulates the story of Israel, and only thereby recapitulates the human story—since the vocation of Israel was itself that of universal recapitulation.* As N. T. Wright contends, Jesus is Adam restored *by virtue of* being Israel restored.[9] If that is true, then the

9. Wright sees this as true not only for the Gospels, but also for the apostle Paul. See, for example, "Adam, Israel and the Messiah" in *The Climax of the Covenant*, 18–40.

emphasis in the preceding chapters on Israel-Christology coheres well with the soteriological message of the *euangelion* regarding the Messiah's life of obedience which extended "to the point of death."

The Death of Jesus

The *euangelion* also speaks of the Messiah's death as a distinct atoning act. The preceding chapters have focused on Jesus' suffering and death as redemptive participation in the future exile of the Jewish people. How does this aspect of Jesus' death cohere with the universal message of the *euangelion* that addresses Jews *and* gentiles throughout history?

The key connection between the Israel-Christology of the preceding chapters and a more universal vision of atonement may be found in Jewish martyr theology.[10] That is the path taken by N. T. Wright in his reading of Isaiah 52–53 and the use made of this text in Daniel, Maccabees, and the New Testament. Wright portrays the martyrdom of Jesus as the Messiah's voluntary acceptance of his people's ultimate plight—*exile*—in order to enact their final *restoration*.[11] Jesus recapitulates Israel's deepest suffering in order to effect Israel's final redemption. In doing so, Jesus fulfills Israel's universal salvific mission by opening the door for gentiles to become part of the restored people of God. By dying for the sins of Israel, the Messiah (as one-man Israel) has also died for the sins of the nations—since Israel represents the nations as a priestly people. Wright summarizes the logic of Paul's atonement theology in this way:

> (a) the saving plan for the world which the prophets had seen as Israel's vocation would always involve Israel (or righteous martyrs within Israel) becoming a kind of sacrifice through which not only Israel itself but also the whole world would be rescued from its sinful, rebellious state; (b) this was the sacrifice offered by Jesus, precisely in his capacity as Israel's representative Messiah.[12]

I have modified Wright's thesis by emphasizing the forward-looking dimension of Jesus' martyrdom for Israel rather than its retrospective

10. For further discussion of this topic, see Williams, *Maccabean Martyr Theology in Paul's Theology of Atonement.*

11. Wright, *The New Testament and the People of God*, 211, 276, 331–32; *Jesus and the Victory of God*, 582–92, 608–9; *Paul and the Faithfulness of God*, 845–46.

12. Wright, *Paul and the Faithfulness of God*, 845–46.

character, and qualifying his claim that the *euangelion* announces Israel's restoration as an accomplished fact. But the fundamental logic of his atonement theology remains intact.

Does the category of martyrdom compromise the unique character of Jesus' suffering and death by subsuming it within a broader genus to which others also belong? If Jesus is but the greatest of the martyrs, the difference between him and his fellow-sufferers is one of degree rather than kind. Such a Christology would unravel the fabric of ecclesial teaching on God's saving work in Jesus. While the New Testament does not present Jesus as the greatest of the martyrs, it does show him to be the quintessential martyr in whom and through whom all other martyrs offer their witness to God. He is not a preeminent example of a genus, but the paradigm and source of that genus, who sums up all its other members in himself. That is the import of Hebrews 11–12, which lists the heroes of faith who lived before Jesus (including the suffering prophets and the Maccabean martyrs [Heb 11:35–38]), and concludes the list by speaking of Jesus as the "pioneer (*archēgos*) and perfecter (*teleiōtēs*) of our faith" (Heb 12:2). He is the beginning and the end of that vast company, which now also includes those who have come after him (Heb 11:40); he is the origin (*archē*) of the path in which they all walk and the one who brings them to its destination (*telos*). The difference between Jesus and the "cloud of witnesses (*martyrōn*)" (Heb 12:1) is thus one of kind rather than degree. It resembles the difference between a Platonic archetype and its concrete expressions, except that *this* archetype is as concrete and particular as the instances that conform to its pattern. Or, to employ a different metaphor, Jesus is the musical theme and the cloud of witnesses are its innumerable variations. The uniqueness of Jesus is thus preserved—but so is the bond that connects him to his fellow witnesses.

If the saving work of Jesus involves his recapitulation (*anakephalaiōsis*) of Israel, then it necessarily entails his living as one Israelite among many, as one member of a particular "category" of human beings. If he is to serve as Israel's "head" (*kephalē*), then his life must manifest the fullness of what Israel was called to be. That call consists in a life of worship and obedience that bears witness to the identity of the God who made a covenant with Abraham. In a world of idolatry and hostility to that God, such witness involves suffering—or, rather, such witness *takes the form of suffering*. This is a vicarious suffering that possesses the power to bear the judgment deserved by others, even by those who inflicted it, thereby conquering idolatry and befriending those who were formerly God's enemies. As 2 Maccabees and Hebrews 11 demonstrate, many in Israel had already embraced that call. According to Hebrews 12, the life of Jesus, culminating in his suffering and death, sums up Israel's witness and renders it effective. It also empowers his disciples to walk the same path that he walked, sharing in his witness of righteous suffering.

In biblical tradition, martyrdom as a soteriological concept was associated with the tribulation that Israel was expected to suffer immediately before "the return of the LORD to Zion." This is evident in Daniel 12:1–3:

> There shall be a time of anguish, such as has never occurred since nations first came into existence. But at that time your people shall be delivered, everyone who is found written in the book. Many of those who sleep in the dust of the earth shall awake, some to everlasting life, and some to shame and everlasting contempt. Those who are wise shall shine like the brightness of the sky, and those who lead many to righteousness, like the stars forever and ever.

N. T. Wright shows how Daniel 12 draws upon the language and substance of Isaiah 52–53.[13] He also interprets the Isaiah text in the same manner: "The Servant, acting out the tribulation and future restoration of Zion . . . dies and rises again as a sin-offering."[14] In light of this biblical tradition, Wright confirms Albert Schweitzer's insight into Jesus' death as an atoning martyrdom in which the Messiah bears in his own body the eschatological suffering of Israel: "Schweitzer saw the second-Temple expectation of the 'messianic woes' as the vital clue to Jesus' understanding, both of the moment in history at which he was living, and of his own vocation in relation to that moment. . . . Schweitzer was right: Jesus believed that the messianic woes were about to burst upon Israel, and that he had to take them upon himself, solo."[15]

This martyrdom-tribulation nexus casts new light on the death of Jesus as proleptic participation in the destruction of Jerusalem of 70 CE and the Jewish exile that follows. One of the most noteworthy features of the eschatological discourse of Jesus in Mark 13 and Matthew 24 is the way the texts conflate reference to the events of 70 with prophecies of

13. Wright, *The Resurrection of the Son of God*, 115–16.

14. Wright, *New Testament and the People of God*, 276.

15. Wright, *Jesus and the Victory of God*, 578, 609. See also Pitre, *Jesus, the Tribulation, and the End of the Exile.*

the final tribulation. (Luke 21 distinguishes the two, but still juxtaposes one with the other.) This suggests that the events of 70 typologically anticipate the suffering that precedes "the return of the LORD to Zion." I would propose that such typology represents not only a foreshadowing but a relationship of "real presence" in which the eschatological reality of the archetype inheres proleptically in the type. In a certain sense, Israel experienced the final tribulation in 70 CE, and in a similar sense Jesus experienced the final tribulation by participating proleptically in the events of 70 through his suffering and death.

This is significant for the thesis of *Jerusalem Crucified* because Israel's suffering at the end is not primarily viewed in the biblical tradition as judgment for its sins. In Zechariah 12–14 the tribulation purifies Israel, but greater emphasis is given to the wickedness of the nations who attack Jerusalem. In Daniel 7 there is no mention of Israel's sins, but only of the evil beast who "made war with the holy ones" (v. 21). These images recur in the Revelation of John, where the suffering of the people of God derives not from its sins but from the fury of the dragon and the beast (Rev 12–13). As seen in the previous chapters of this volume, the suffering of Jerusalem in 70 is unquestionably portrayed in the New Testament as divine judgment. But the typological connection to the "messianic woes"—along with its role as link between the martyrdom of Jesus and those woes—reinforces the additional redemptive function of the Jewish exile proposed in the previous chapters.

I am not here proposing that the category of martyrdom exhausts the meaning of Jesus' "dying for our sins." I am only pointing to this category as a fruitful instrument in establishing the theological coherence between the thesis of *Jerusalem Crucified* and the wider field of soteriology.

The Resurrection of Jesus

"Messiah . . . was raised on the third day in accordance with the scriptures" (1 Cor 15:4). The preceding chapters have presented this assertion as a prophetic announcement confirming Israel's national and territorial hope and revealing how that hope would be realized. This fits well with the "scriptures" (such as Ezekiel 36 and Hosea 6) that depict Israel's national restoration in terms of resurrection. Moreover, this also fits well with an interpretation of the Messiah's death as atoning martyrdom, since, as N. T. Wright puts it, "Resurrection is the divine reward for martyrs; it is what will happen after the great tribulation."[16] "[T]he martyrs would be raised, and Israel as a whole would be vindicated."[17]

But even if this prophetic reading of 1 Corinthians 15:4 is warranted, surely these words of the *euangelion* refer to more than Israel's national restoration. How does this "more" cohere with the national hope articulated in *Jerusalem Crucified*?

Here is where our chapter on the temple becomes significant. That chapter showed how the biblical teaching regarding the temple supports rather than undermines our conclusions concerning Jerusalem, the land, and the Jewish people. The temple always pointed to heavenly, cosmic, and eschatological realities beyond itself, but did so in a way that bound those realities tightly to the earthly and embodied identity of the people of Israel. The temple represented Israel's role as the particular geographical location in which its God resided in the midst of the world. As such, Israel linked earth to heaven, served as a microcosm of the universe, and anticipated an eschatological future in which the entire creation would become God's temple, with Jerusalem as its holy of holies.

As seen in our examination of the Gospel of John, Jesus assumes the role of the temple by assuming the role of Israel. Israel-Christology provides the logic of temple-Christology. What John portrays as the truth of the incarnation and the life of Jesus is pictured elsewhere in the New Testament mainly in relation to Jesus' resurrection and return. Because Jesus has been raised from the dead, his *ekklēsia*—a community of Jews and gentiles anticipating the expanded Israel of the age to come—now serves as an intensified expression of the divine presence in the midst of Israel and the world. Because Jesus has been raised from the dead and ascended to heaven from the Mount of Olives, we may be confident that he will return in the same way and establish Jerusalem as "the joy of all the earth" (Ps 48:2). Because Jesus has been raised from the dead, we

16. Wright, *New Testament and the People of God*, 331.

17. Wright, *Resurrection of the Son of God*, 205. The wider context of this citation is worth quoting: "But it remains the case that resurrection, in the world of second-Temple Judaism, was about *the restoration of Israel* on the one hand and *the newly embodied life of all YHWH's people* on the other, with close connections between the two; and that it was thought of as the great event that YHWH would accomplish at the very end of 'the present age', the event which would constitute the 'age to come', *ha'olam haba*. All of this was concentrated, for many Jews, in the stories of the righteous martyrs, those who had suffered and died for YHWH and Torah. Because YHWH was the creator, and because he was the god of justice, the martyrs would be raised, and Israel as a whole would be vindicated" (emphasis original).

hope for the day when the glory of the LORD will fill the earth (Ps 72:19) and God will be all in all (1 Cor 15:28).

In this way, the prophetic Israel-Christology of the preceding chapters provides a framework in which the divinity of Jesus, the experience of ecclesial life and worship, and a cosmic eschatological vision cohere with the enduring covenantal identity of the Jewish people and its hope of national resurrection. Moreover, this understanding of the *euangelion* also sheds light on the traditional soteriological concept of *theōsis*. Creation attains consummation only when it becomes a temple for the God of Israel, and it only does so through the incarnation and resurrection of Israel's Messiah. Individual human beings also attain their full stature only when they are joined to that Messiah by his Spirit and are "filled with all the fullness of God" (Eph 3:19).

This is but a modest introduction to the long-term project of thinking through the soteriology of the prophetic *euangelion* in a way that ties Israel's national restoration to the wider scope of the Messiah's saving action. While much challenging work remains to be done, the task is doable, and worthy of the doing.

Ethical and Theo-political Coherence

In the preceding chapters, I have argued for an understanding of the *euangelion* that renders the message inseparable from the hope of Jewish national restoration. Furthermore, I have given reasons for concluding that the Zionist project emerged under a divine impulse, and deserves ecclesial support. At the same time, I have distinguished between Zionism (as a national, moral, and spiritual program) and the State of Israel (as an inevitably flawed political instrument of that program). Moreover, I have also insisted on the necessary distinction between the current reality of Jewish national life in the land and the eschatological restoration of Israel to which it gestures.

Such an interpretation of the *euangelion* and its relation to modern Jewish history raises important questions regarding the ethical and theo-political message of the *ekklēsia*. Does this view cohere with the kingdom teaching of Jesus and the universal scope of the love-commandment? What does this view imply about the theological significance and role of nations, nation-states, land, and territorial governance? On a more concrete level, what ethical standards should disciples of Jesus employ in assessing actions of the Israeli government and people? These are only a few of the questions that require attention.

Some of the spade work has already been done by Nicholas Brown in his recent volume, *For the Nation.*[18] Brown brings together the two topics at issue here—the *euangelion* as a message of Jewish national restoration, and the ethical implications of such a message. He first argues that historians, exegetes, and theologians have missed the territorial dimension of Jesus' message and mission. He then examines the landscape of ethical and theo-political teaching, and concludes that this teaching suffers loss when the territorial dimension of the *euangelion* is neglected. Expanding his conclusion to the entire sphere of ecclesial theology, Brown asserts that a territorially-rooted *euangelion* is not only coherent with the core ecclesial theological tradition but essential to it: "[T]he Christian theological imagination is not only hospitable to but indeed predicated upon the landedness of our existence."[19] Ultimately, this is because of the goodness of the material creation and the human body, and the role played by both in God's covenant with Israel: "[A] landless interpretation of Jesus' kingdom proclamation is no more theo-logically tenable than a docetic Christology for precisely the same reason the latter has been rejected as heterodox. That is because the insuperable materiality of YHWH's covenant with Israel presupposes and demands that the full corporeality of both be maintained."[20]

While embodiment is important for all spheres of theological concern, Brown contends that it is especially important in the ethical sphere. Here he emphasizes the role played by character formation. Brown summarizes recent studies stressing how moral agency "depends on our physically embodying certain moral virtues" and on doing so "in relation to embodied others."[21] He then extends this insight to the territorial realm. "[I]f one grants the premise that Christian morality is always and necessarily embodied, and deduces from this claim that embodiment is itself a Christian ethical modality, then one must extrapolate and apply this same logic to the reality of territoriality as well and admit that it

18. Brown, *For the Nation.*

19. Brown, *For the Nation*, 120.

20. Brown, *For the Nation*, 93. In the original the divine name is spelled out fully. In accordance with Jewish convention, I have included only the transliterated consonants.

21. Brown, *For the Nation*, 116.

too is a Christian ethical modality insofar as both Christians and their embodied moral practices are always territorially placed."[22]

By linking territoriality to Jesus' kingdom teaching and its ethical content, Brown seeks to critique both anti-Zionists and maximalist Zionists. Brown agrees with John Howard Yoder in seeing Jesus and his kingdom message "as the norm for Christian ethics." However, Brown thinks that Yoder's emphasis on diaspora and exile "detaches the kingdom from Israel's land." Brown then levels a parallel charge against maximalist Zionists: "[W]hat makes Christian Zionist arguments problematic is not that they take Israel's connection to the land seriously, but rather that they tend to detach that connection from Jesus' proclamation of the kingdom."[23] In contrast to both, Brown argues for an *euangelion* that binds Jesus' kingdom message to the people of Israel, the land of Israel, and the ethical demands of the good news.

As noted in chapter 6, the Zionist philosophy of Martin Buber illustrates this marriage between Jewish national and territorial renewal, on the one hand, and the ethical demands of the kingdom of God, on the other. Buber viewed the State of Israel as essential to the renewal of Jewish national life, but only as a subordinate instrument in the service of that higher aim. In similar fashion, ecclesial Zionism cannot focus exclusively on land, state, security, and sovereignty. It must also reflect the ethical and spiritual priorities embodied in the person, teaching, and work of the crucified and resurrected Messiah.

The volume of Nicholas Brown is itself only a preliminary engagement with this topic. Brown has succeeded, however, in fulfilling his objective of providing "a substantive basis from which it is possible to, if not develop a fully formulated set of normative practices, than at least distill the contours of a normative framework from which such practices should derive."[24] Brown's work suggests that the prophetic *euangelion* presented in the preceding chapters has the potential to bear much fruit in the sphere of ecclesial ethical reflection.

22. Brown, *For the Nation*, 117.

23. Brown, *For the Nation*, 192.

24. Brown, *For the Nation*, 191.

Missiological Coherence

The preceding chapters bring an equal measure of support and challenge to both sides of the longstanding debate concerning ecclesial mission to the Jewish people. Should disciples of Jesus seek to "evangelize" their Jewish neighbors? Should they support "Christian missionary efforts" aimed at "converting" Jews to "Christianity"?

On the one hand, *Jerusalem Crucified* shows that the identity and destiny of the Jewish people are bound up with the identity and destiny of Jesus as the Jewish Messiah. The calling of genealogical-Israel will be realized through the prophetic *euangelion* concerning Jesus' death and resurrection, and the return of Jesus to the Mount of Olives is contingent upon an official communal welcome of that messianic arrival by the Jews of Jerusalem. On that day, Jesus' triumphal entry to Jerusalem on Palm Sunday as a symbolic prophetic act will find its eschatological fulfillment. Furthermore, the present volume provides exegetical evidence for the theological significance of Jewish communal life within Messiah's *ekklēsia*, and suggests that the renewal of such life in the modern era should be treated as a sign of God's providential ordering of history. The *ekklēsia* is by definition a communion of Jews and gentiles, and ecclesial Jews have an essential role to play *as Jews.*[25]

On the other hand, *Jerusalem Crucified* demonstrates that the Jewish tradition has preserved essential elements of the *euangelion* that the *ekklēsia* abandoned early in its existence. That fracturing of the *euangelion* meant that through much of the past two thousand years it has been impossible for Jews to respond to the entire prophetic message of the resurrected Messiah by entering the *ekklēsia*. It also meant that it was possible to respond to essential elements of the *euangelion* by remaining part of a Jewish community that ostensibly rejected Jesus. Moreover, *Jerusalem Crucified* also proposes that the flourishing of that Jewish community under the inspiration of rabbinic Judaism should be attributed to divine providence, and that the Zionist project displays similar marks of providential design. Furthermore, in my discussion of the Jewish response to

25. The recent (2015) Vatican document entitled *The Gifts and Calling of God Are Irrevocable* provides a succinct formulation of this point: "It is and remains a qualitative definition of the Church of the New Covenant that it consists of Jews and Gentiles, even if the quantitative proportions of Jewish and Gentile Christians may initially give a different impression" (paragraph 43). For the text of the entire document, see http://www.vatican.va/roman_curia/pontifical_councils/chrstuni/relations-jews-docs/rc_pc_chrstuni_doc_20151210_ebraismo-nostra-aetate_en.html.

Jesus in Acts, I emphasized its communal dimension. The eschatological significance of the Jewish communal response to Jesus, combined with the historical fracturing of the prophetic *euangelion*, suggests that the consequences of Jewish acceptance of Jesus as the Messiah may now have more to do with the fulfillment of Israel's eschatological destiny than with individual recompense in the afterlife. In fact, one could reasonably infer that believers in Jesus who have rejected the irrevocable election and priestly vocation of genealogical Israel will be as accountable as Jews who have refused to acknowledge Jesus as Israel's Messiah. In either case, it is the *euangelion* itself which has been partially denied (and partially affirmed).

What does this mean for ecclesial mission in relation to the Jewish people? Just as Nicholas Brown points the way forward in the sphere of ethics, so Stuart Dauermann charts a missiological path that fits the prophetic *euangelion* presented in *Jerusalem Crucified*. In his recent volume entitled *Converging Destinies*, Dauermann formulates a missiological model that presumes two ecclesiological propositions: (1) the covenant people of God consists of "the church from among the nations and Israel . . . seen as one great people currently living in a state of schism destined to be healed";[26] (2) the *ekklēsia* is properly bilateral in composition and character, a united community with a twofold corporate expression—one Jewish, the other multi-national.[27] The missiological paradigm that Dauermann advocates possesses two key features, which correspond to these two ecclesiological presuppositions. (1) The "mission of God" (*missio Dei*) takes corporate form in the world through both Israel (i.e., the Jewish people) and the Christian church (i.e., the "church from among the nations"). Each community participates in the divine work in the world in its own distinct way. Moreover, each community has a mission in relation to the other.[28] Thus, the *ekklēsia* does have a mission in relation to the Jewish people, and that mission includes bearing witness to Jesus as the Messiah. But the Jewish people also has a mission in relation to the *ekklēsia*—a mission that includes bearing witness to the significance of the Jewish identity of the Lord confessed by the *ekklēsia*. (2) The mission of the *ekklēsia* in relation to the Jewish people has a twofold character that corresponds to its own bilateral constitution.

26. Dauermann, *Converging Destinies*, 145.

27. Dauermann, *Converging Destinies*, 188–90.

28. Dauermann, *Converging Destinies*, 85.

On this last point, Dauermann provides little in the way of substantive description concerning the mission of the "church of the nations" in relation to Israel. He devotes most of his attention to what he calls "the Messianic Jewish remnant," and its mission to the wider Jewish community—a mission that he calls "inreach" rather than "outreach," since "the Messianic Jewish remnant" is part of Israel rather than a branch of the "church of the nations." To make sense of what Dauermann has to say about Messianic Jewish *inreach*, we will first have to explain his understanding of the *euangelion*—the good news that is the basic message embodied and proclaimed by the twofold *ekklēsia.*

Dauermann views the national intent of the *euangelion* much as I have presented it in the previous chapters. It is a prophetic message concerning Israel's eschatological destiny that presumes Israel's continuing covenantal status as God's beloved. Unlike the present volume, Dauermann makes no attempt to show how this prophetic message is rooted in the proclamation of the death and resurrection of Jesus.[29] Instead, he attends to certain key texts from the Hebrew prophets. In particular, he highlights Ezekiel 37:21–28 (which he calls "the Ezekiel Agenda") as a summary of the eschatological destiny of Israel that the *euangelion* envisions:

> Ezekiel lists the facets of the good news in this order:
> - The ingathering of the Jewish [people] to our homeland, Israel (thus, Aliyah)
> - The restoration of the unity of the people of Israel
> - Repentance-renewal for the people as a whole
> - Messiah reigning in the center of this gathered people
> - Torah living as the communal life of this people
> - National experience of the divine presence
> - And because of the foregoing, and in the sight of the nations, the vindication of the Jewish people as the people of God, and the God of Israel as faithful to his promises[30]

29. A limitation inherent in Dauermann's way of treating the *euangelion* is that the restoration of the Jewish people might be taken to be merely a *consequence* of the message that is relevant only to Jews, rather than an intrinsic *element* of the message that is of universal relevance. This is a limitation that I seek to overcome in the previous chapters by viewing the resurrection of the Messiah and the restoration of Israel as two inseparable acts.

30. Dauermann, *Converging Destinies*, 164.

While noting that "Ezekiel places Messiah in the center of these items," Dauermann nevertheless emphasizes that the "gospel" as a message for the Jewish people includes all seven of these aspects of Israel's hope. "Anything less and anything other is at best someone else's truncated gospel."[31]

Dauermann draws the following practical conclusions concerning Messianic Jewish "inreach" from this exposition of Israel's "gospel": (1) Messianic Jews are to be a prophetic sign, demonstration, and catalyst of this eschatological vision in their corporate life.[32] This means living in unity with the Jewish people as a whole, observing the Torah in accordance with Jewish tradition, experiencing and expressing the presence of God's Spirit, supporting Jewish life in the land of Israel, and, at the center of all, following and proclaiming Jesus as Israel's Messiah. (2) Messianic Jews (and presumably gentile Christians as well) should speak boldly about Jesus, but in a way that honors the Jewish past and the Jewish present, and focuses on his role as the agent of Israel's corporate redemption rather than the savior who delivers individuals from hell.[33] (3) Messianic Jews should support and honor all efforts to advance any of the seven aspects of Ezekiel 37:21–28, even if they are pursued apart from faith in Jesus as the Messiah.[34] Thus, the "mission" involves promoting not only "Jesus," but the entire "Ezekiel Agenda" in which Jesus is the heart but not the whole.

As Dauermann shows, missiology takes shape in relation to ecclesiology and the content of the *euangelion.* He has succeeded in tracing the preliminary outlines of a missiology that coheres with the ecclesiology proposed in my previous writings and the prophetic *euangelion* explored in the present volume.[35] His efforts demonstrate the creative practical potential of these new theological paradigms.

31. Dauermann, *Converging Destinies*, 164.

32. Dauermann, *Converging Destinies*, 233–39.

33. Dauermann, *Converging Destinies*, 153–59, 169–70, 181–84, 202–4.

34. Dauermann, *Converging Destinies*, 185, 238, 242.

35. See especially Kinzer, *Postmissionary Messianic Judaism and Searching Her Own Mystery.*

Conclusion

Jerusalem Crucified is a book about the *euangelion*. It deals most directly with the meaning of God's saving action in the life, death, and resurrection of Jesus the Messiah. However, the interpretation here given to that saving action points to its proleptic and prophetic character. Therefore, *Jerusalem Crucified* is also a book about eschatology. Moreover, the prophetic and eschatological features of the *euangelion* uncovered in these chapters center on the Jewish people and their relationship to the city of Jerusalem and the land of Israel. Accordingly, *Jerusalem Crucified* is a book whose import is inescapably *ecclesiological*. If the saving *euangelion* is as I have portrayed it, and if we behold clues of its prophetic intent encoded providentially in the strange twists and turns of the last two millennia, then the twofold *ekklēsia*—that community called into being in order to embody and proclaim the *euangelion*—can rediscover in this "good news" for Israel her own identity as Israel's extension and partner.

In doing so, the *ekklēsia* also learns a harsh lesson about her fractured character and history. The wound is deeper than first imagined. It makes the divisions between Catholic and Protestant, East and West, look superficial and merely symptomatic of the more radical underlying condition.

But this harsh lesson also holds out hope for recovery. Renewed appreciation for the rich and multifaceted message that brought her into being can bring with it a renewal of her own identity and mission. She is the body of Jesus, the Messiah of Israel, and as such she lives and serves her Lord faithfully only as she is properly related to the Israel for whom, first, he died, and for whom, first, he was raised from death.

Hope also springs from a geographical place, a site that is indissolubly bound up with Jesus the Messiah and the Israel for whom, first, he died and now lives. The Jewish people have endured as one people through centuries of exile by never losing sight of that "place that the LORD your God will choose out of all your tribes" (Deut 12:5). Before 70 CE the holy city represented also for the disciples of Jesus, Jew and gentile alike, an institutional center and object of messianic hope. After 70 CE the gentile disciples of Jesus looked to other cities for identity and orientation—Rome, Alexandria, Constantinople, Moscow, Canterbury—but never again recovered a single site that could unite them all in love and eschatological longing. In the Byzantine era it appeared that Jerusalem might again claim the hearts of all disciples of Jesus as the unique geographical sacrament of his life, death, and resurrection, but this was a city detached from the Jewish people and from the coming kingdom concerning which the eleven had inquired of the risen Lord. The wars and conquests that began in the seventh century limited the city's institutional influence within the *ekklēsia*, but she never lost her hold on the imagination of many of the disciples of Jesus.

In the present volume, the earthly city of Jerusalem appears as a proleptic eschatological reality inseparable from both the Jewish people and the *euangelion* of the resurrected Messiah. In this concluding chapter, we have seen how the good news of Jerusalem, crucified and risen with her king, has the potential to integrate the various perspectives of ecclesial theological vision—canonical, soteriological, eschatological, ethical, and missiological. As the hope of both the Jewish people and the *ekklēsia*, she is also an *ecclesiological* reality that has the potential to unify the whole people of God—Jew and gentile, Protestant and Catholic, Eastern and Western. Her holy mountain is destined to be a "house of prayer for all peoples" (Isa 56:7; Mark 11:17), with all nations streaming to it (Isa 2:2). Just as Jews find their spiritual home in Jerusalem, so also shall those whose descent from Abraham and Sarah is only by faith and not by genealogy: "Among those who know me I mention Rahab and Babylon, Philistia too, and Tyre, with Ethiopia—'This one was born there,' they say. And of Zion it shall be said: 'This one and that one were born in it'" (Ps 87:4–5).

When the *ekklēsia* of the nations rediscovers this truth she will join with the Jewish people in taking the words of the Psalmist as her own sacred promise: "If I forget you, O Jerusalem, let my right hand wither! Let my tongue cling to the roof of my mouth, if I do not remember you, if I do not set Jerusalem above my highest joy" (Ps 137:5–6).

Bibliography

Allison, Dale C. Jr. "Matt. 23:39 = Luke 13:35b as a Conditional Prophecy." *Journal for the Study of the New Testament* 18 (1983) 75–84.

Alpher, Yossi. "The Issues the Peace Process Should Avoid." *The Forward*, July 29, 2013. https://forward.com/opinion/181261/the-issues-the-peace-process-should-avoid/.

Anderson, Charles P. "Who Are the Heirs of the New Age in the Epistle to the Hebrews?" In *Apocalyptic and the New Testament: Essays in Honor of J. Louis Martyn*, edited by J. Marcus and M. L. Soards, 255–77. Sheffield, UK: JSOT Press, 1989.

Armstrong, Karen. *Jerusalem: One City, Three Faiths*. New York: Ballantine, 1996.

Aviam, Mordechai. "Reverence for Jerusalem and the Temple in Galilean Society." In *Jesus and Temple: Textual and Archaeological Explorations*, edited by James H. Charlesworth, 123–44. Minneapolis: Fortress, 2014.

Baltzer, Klaus. "The Meaning of the Temple in the Lukan Writings." *Harvard Theological Review* 58.3 (1965) 263–77.

Barrett, C. K. *The Gospel according to St. John*. Philadelphia: Westminster, 1978.

Barth, Karl. *Church Dogmatics IV.4: The Doctrine of Reconciliation*. Translated by G. W. Bromiley. Reprint. London: T. & T. Clark, 2010.

Bauckham, Richard. "James and the Gentiles (Acts 15.13–21)." In *History, Literature, and Society in the Book of Acts*, edited by Ben Witherington III, 154–84. Cambridge: Cambridge University Press, 1996.

———. "James and the Jerusalem Church." In *The Book of Acts in its First Century Setting, edited by* Richard Bauckham, 415–80. Grand Rapids: Eerdmans, 1995.

———. "James and the Jerusalem Community." In *Jewish Believers in Jesus*, edited by Oskar Skarsaune and Reidar Hvalvik, 55–95. Peabody, MA: Hendrickson, 2007.

———. "James and the Jerusalem Council Decision." In *Introduction to Messianic Judaism: Its Ecclesial Context and Biblical Foundations*, edited by David Rudolph and Joel Willitts, 178–86. Grand Rapids: Zondervan, 2013.

———. "James, Peter, and the Gentiles." In *The Missions of James, Peter, and Paul: Tensions in Early Christianity*, edited by Bruce Chilton and Craig Evans, 91–142. Leiden, Netherlands: Brill, 2004.

———. *Jesus and the God of Israel*. Milton Keynes, UK: Paternoster, 2008.

———. *The Jewish World around the New Testament*. Grand Rapids: Baker Academic, 2010.

———. *Jude and the Relatives of Jesus in the Early Church*. Edinburgh: T. & T. Clark, 1990.

———. *The Testimony of the Beloved Disciple: Narrative, History, and Theology in the Gospel of John.* Grand Rapids: Baker, 2007.

———. *The Theology of the Book of Revelation.* Cambridge: Cambridge University Press, 1993.

Beasley-Murray, G. R. *Baptism in the New Testament.* Grand Rapids: Eerdmans, 1973.

Boccaccini, Gabriele. *Beyond the Essene Hypothesis: The Parting of the Ways between Qumran and Enochic Judaism.* Grand Rapids: Eerdmans, 1998.

———. *Middle Judaism: Jewish Thought 300 B.C.E. to 200 C.E.* Minneapolis: Fortress, 1991.

Boccaccini, Gabriele, and Carlos A. Segovia, eds. *Paul the Jew: Rereading the Apostle as a Figure of Second Temple Judaism.* Minneapolis: Fortress, 2016.

Bock, Darrell L. *Acts.* Grand Rapids: Baker Academic, 2007.

Borgen, Peder. "God's Agent in the Fourth Gospel." In *The Interpretation of John*, edited by John Ashton, 67–78. Philadelphia: Fortress, 1986.

Boyarin, Daniel. *The Jewish Gospels: The Story of the Jewish Christ.* New York: New Press, 2012.

Brawley, Robert L. *Luke-Acts and the Jews: Conflict, Apology, and Conciliation.* Atlanta: Scholars, 1987.

Brown, Nicholas R. *For the Nation: Jesus, the Restoration of Israel, and Articulating a Christian Ethic of Territorial Governance.* Eugene, OR: Pickwick, 2016.

Brown, Raymond E. *The Gospel according to John I–XII.* New York: Doubleday, 1966.

———. *The Gospel according to John XIII–XXI.* New York: Doubleday, 1970.

Bruce, F. F. *The Book of Acts.* Grand Rapids: Eerdmans, 1988.

Buber, Martin. *A Land of Two Peoples.* Edited by Paul Mendes-Flohr. Chicago: University of Chicago Press, 2005.

———. *Tales of the Hasidim.* New York: Schocken, 1991.

Burge, Gary M. *Jesus and the Land: The New Testament Challenge to "Holy Land" Theology.* Grand Rapids: Baker, 2010.

Cadbury, Henry J. *The Making of Luke-Acts.* 1927. Reprint. Grand Rapids: Baker Academic, 1999.

Caird, G. B. *Saint Luke.* Baltimore, MD: Penguin, 1963.

Catechism of the Catholic Church. New York: Doubleday, 1995.

Chance, J. Bradley. *Jerusalem, the Temple, and the New Age in Luke-Acts.* Macon, GA: Mercer University Press, 1988.

Charlesworth, James H. "The Temple and Jesus' Followers." In *Jesus and Temple: Textual and Archaeological Explorations*, edited by James H. Charlesworth, 183–212. Minneapolis: Fortress, 2014.

Childs, Brevard S. *The Church's Guide for Reading Paul: The Canonical Shaping of the Pauline Corpus.* Grand Rapids: Eerdmans, 2008.

———. *The New Testament as Canon: An Introduction.* Valley Forge, PA: Trinity, 1994.

Chilton, Bruce, and Jacob Neusner. *Judaism in the New Testament: Practice and Beliefs.* New York: Routledge, 1995.

Cohen, Shaye J. *The Beginnings of Jewishness: Boundaries, Varieties, Uncertainties.* Berkeley: University of California Press, 1999.

Conzelmann, Hans. *The Theology of St. Luke.* Translated by Geoffrey Buswell. Philadelphia: Fortress, 1982.

Crossley, James G. *The Date of Mark's Gospel: Insight from the Law in Earliest Christianity.* JSNTSup 266. London: T. & T. Clark, 2004.

Danby, Herbert. *The Mishnah*. Oxford: Oxford University Press, 1933.
Dauermann, Stuart. *Converging Destinies: Jews, Christians, and the Mission of God*. Eugene, OR: Cascade, 2017.
Dunn, James D. G. *The Partings of the Ways: Between Christianity and Judaism and Their Significance for the Character of Christianity*. Philadelphia: Trinity, 1991.
Edersheim, Alfred. *The Life and Times of Jesus the Messiah, Vol I*. 1883. Reprint. Grand Rapids: Eerdmans, 1971.
———. *The Temple: Its Ministry and Services*. 1874. Reprint. Peabody, MA: Hendrickson, 1994.
Eisenbaum, Pamela. *Paul was not a Christian: The Original Message of a Misunderstood Apostle*. New York: HarperCollins, 2009.
Elior, Rachel. *The Three Temples: On the Emergence of Jewish Mysticism*. Translated by David Louvish. Oxford: Littman Library of Jewish Civilization, 2004.
Esposito, Thomas. *Jesus' Meals with Pharisees and their Liturgical Roots*. Rome: Gregorian Biblical Press, 2015.
Evans, Craig A. "Jesus & the Continuing Exile of Israel." In *Jesus & the Restoration of Israel: A Critical Assessment of N. T. Wright's* Jesus and the Victory of God, edited by Carey C. Newman, 77–100. Downers Grove, IL: IVP, 1999.
Farrow, Douglas. *Ascension Theology*. London: T. & T. Clark, 2011.
Fiorenza, Elisabeth Schüssler. *The Book of Revelation: Justice and Judgment*. Philadelphia: Fortress, 1985.
Fitzmyer, Joseph A. *The Acts of the Apostles*. New York: Doubleday, 1998.
———. *The Gospel according to Luke I–IX*. Garden City, NY: Doubleday, 1981.
———. *Luke the Theologian: Aspects of His Teaching*. Mahwah, NJ: Paulist, 1989.
Flannery, Austin P., ed. *Documents of Vatican II*. Grand Rapids: Eerdmans, 1975.
Fox, Everett. *The Five Books of Moses*. New York: Schocken, 1995.
Fredriksen, Paula. "Judaizing the Nations: The Ritual Demands of Paul's Gospel." In *Paul's Jewish Matrix*, edited by Thomas G. Casey and Justin Taylor, 327–54. Mahwah, NJ: Paulist, 2011.
———. *Paul: The Pagan's Apostle*. New Haven, CT: Yale University Press, 2017.
———. *Sin: The Early History of an Idea*. Princeton: Princeton University Press, 2012.
Friedman, Maurice. *Martin Buber's Life and Work: The Later Years, 1945–1965*. New York: Dutton, 1983.
Friedman, Richard Elliott. *Commentary on the Torah*. San Francisco: HarperSanFrancisco, 2001.
Fuller, Michael E. *The Restoration of Israel: Israel's Re-gathering and the Fate of the Nations in Early Jewish Literature and Luke-Acts*. New York: de Gruyter, 2006.
Furstenberg, Yair. "Defilement Penetrating the Body: A New Understanding of Contamination in Mark 7.15." *New Testament Studies* 54 (2008) 176–200.
Goldman, Samuel. *God's Country: Christian Zionism in America*. Philadelphia: University of Pennsylvania Press, 2018.
Gregory, Andrew F., and C. Kavin Rowe, eds. *Rethinking the Unity and Reception of Luke and Acts*. Columbia, SC: University of South Carolina Press, 2010.
Halkin, Hillel. *Yehudah Halevi*. New York: Schocken. 2010.
Hamm, Dennis. "The Tamid Service in Luke-Acts: The Cultic Background behind Luke's Theology of Worship (Luke 1:5–25; 18:9–14; 24:50–53; Acts 3:1; 10:3, 30)." *Catholic Biblical Quarterly* 65.2 (2003) 216–31.

Haran, Menahem. *Temples and Temple Service in Ancient Israel.* Winona Lake, IN: Eisenbrauns, 1985.

Hart, David Bentley. *The Beauty of the Infinite: The Aesthetics of Christian Truth.* Grand Rapids: Eerdmans, 2003.

Hays, Richard B. *First Corinthians.* Louisville, KY: John Knox, 1997.

———. "'Here We Have No Lasting City': New Covenantalism in Hebrews." In *The Epistle to the Hebrews and Christian Theology*, edited by Richard Bauckham, Daniel R. Driver, Trevor A. Hart, and Nathan MacDonald, 151–73. Grand Rapids: Eerdmans, 2009.

———. *Reading Backwards: Figural Christology and the Fourfold Gospel Witness.* Waco, TX: Baylor University Press, 2014.

Hayward, C. T. R. *The Jewish Temple: A Non-Biblical Sourcebook.* London: Routledge, 1996.

Hazony, Yoram. *The Jewish State: The Struggle for Israel's Soul.* New York: Basic, 2000.

Hummel, Daniel. "The New Christian Zionism." *First Things* 274, June/July 2017, 9–11.

Jenson, Robert W. "Toward a Christian Theology of Judaism." In *Jews and Christians: People of God*, edited by Carl E. Braaten and Robert W. Jenson, 1–13. Grand Rapids: Eerdmans, 2003.

Jervell, Jacob. *Luke and the People of God: A New Look at Luke-Acts.* Minneapolis: Augsburg, 1972.

———. *The Unknown Paul: Essays on Luke-Acts and Early Christian History.* Minneapolis: Augsburg, 1984.

Johnson, Luke Timothy. *The Writings of the New Testament: An Interpretation.* Minneapolis: Fortress, 1999.

Johnson, Paul. *A History of the Jews.* New York: Harper & Row, 1987.

Juel, Donald. *Luke-Acts. The Promise of History.* Atlanta: John Knox, 1983.

Kinzer, Mark S. "Finding Our Way through Nicaea: The Deity of Jesus, Bilateral Ecclesiology, and Redemptive Encounter with the Living God," In *Searching Her Own Mystery: Nostra Aetate, the Jewish People, and the Identity of the Church*, 216–39. Eugene, OR: Cascade, 2015.

———. *Postmissionary Messianic Judaism: Redefining Christian Engagement with the Jewish People.* Grand Rapids: Brazos, 2005.

———."Sacrifice, Prayer, and the Holy Spirit: The Daily Tamid Offering in Luke-Acts." In *"Wisdom Poured Out Like Water": Essays in Honor of Gabriele Boccaccini*, edited by J. Harold Ellens, Isaac W. Oliver, Jason von Ehrenkrook, James Waddell, and Jason M. Zurawski, 463–75. Berlin: De Gruyter, 2018.

———. *Searching Her Own Mystery: Nostra Aetate, the Jewish People, and the Identity of the Church.* Eugene, OR: Cascade, 2015.

———. "Temple-Christology in the Gospel of John." In *Society of Biblical Literature 1998 Seminar Papers, Part One*, 447–64. Atlanta: Scholars, 1998.

Kister, Menahem. "Law, Morality and Rhetoric in Some Sayings of Jesus." In *Studies in Ancient Midrash*, edited by James L. Kugel, 145–54. Cambridge: Harvard University Press, 2001.

Kjaer-Hansen, Kai. *Joseph Rabinowitz and the Messianic Movement: The Herzl of Jewish Christianity.* Grand Rapids: Eerdmans, 1995.

Klawans, Jonathan. *Purity, Sacrifice, and the Temple: Symbolism and Supersessionism in the Study of Ancient Judaism.* Oxford: Oxford University Press, 2006.

Koester, Craig R. *The Dwelling of God: The Tabernacle in the Old Testament, Intertestamental Jewish Literature, and the New Testament.* Washington, DC: Catholic Biblical Association of America, 1989.

Kugel, James. *The Bible as It Was.* Cambridge: Harvard University Press, 1999.

Ladd, George Eldon. *The Revelation of John.* Grand Rapids: Eerdmans, 1972.

Levenson, Alan T. *An Introduction to Modern Jewish Thinkers: From Spinoza to Soloveitchik.* New York: Rowman & Littlefield, 2006.

Levenson, Jon D. *Creation and the Persistence of Evil: The Jewish Drama of Divine Omnipotence.* Princeton: Princeton University Press, 1988.

———. "The Jerusalem Temple in Devotional and Visionary Experience." In *Jewish Spirituality from the Bible Through the Middle Ages*, edited by Arthur Green, 32–61. New York: Crossroad, 1996.

———. *Sinai and Zion: An Entry into the Jewish Bible.* New York: Harper & Row, 1985.

Loader, William. *Jesus' Attitude towards the Law: A Study of the Gospels.* Grand Rapids: Eerdmans, 2002.

Lohfink, Norbert. *The Covenant Never Revoked.* Translated by John J. Scullion. New York: Paulist, 1991.

Maier, Johann. *The Temple Scroll: An Introduction, Translation & Commentary.* Translated by Richard T. White. Sheffield, UK: JSOT, 1985.

Marshall, I. Howard. *Acts.* Grand Rapids: Eerdmans, 1980.

———. *The Gospel of Luke.* Exeter, UK: Paternoster, 1978.

Marx, Dalia. "The Missing Temple: The Status of the Temple in Jewish Culture Following Its Destruction." In *The Presence of the Lost Temple: Report of a Jewish-Christian Dialogue*, edited by Shlomo Tucker and Michael Mulder, 83–108. Amsterdam: Amphora, 2015.

McDermott, Gerald R. "A History of Christian Zionism." In *The New Christian Zionism: Fresh Perspectives on Israel and the Land*, edited by Gerald R. McDermott, 45–75. Downers Grove, IL: IVP Academic, 2016.

Milgrom, Jacob. *Leviticus 1–16.* New York: Doubleday, 1991.

Miller, Elhanan. "Temple Mount Revival Movement Revels in Crowd-Funded Passover Sacrifice—But at What Cost?" *The Forward*, 2 May 2016. http://forward.com/news/israel/339759/temple-mount-revival-movement-revels-in-crowd-funded-passover-sacrifice-but/

Miller, John W. *How the Bible Came to Be: Exploring the Narrative and Message.* New York: Paulist, 2004.

Minear, Paul S. "Luke's Use of the Birth Stories." In *Studies in Luke-Acts*, edited by Leander E. Keck and J. Louis Martyn, 111–30. Nashville: Abingdon, 1966.

Mirsky, Yehudah. *Rav Kook: Mystic in a Time of Revolution.* New Haven, CT: Yale University Press, 2014.

Moffitt, David M. *Atonement and the Logic of Resurrection in the Epistle to the Hebrews.* Leiden: Brill, 2013.

Nanos, Mark. *The Irony of Galatians: Paul's Letter in First-Century Context.* Minneapolis: Fortress, 2002.

———. *The Mystery of Romans: The Jewish Context of Paul's Letter.* Minneapolis: Fortress, 1996.

———. "*New* or *Renewed* Covenantalism? A Response to Richard Hays." In *The Epistle to the Hebrews and Christian Theology*, edited by Richard Bauckham,

Daniel R. Driver, Trevor A. Hart, and Nathan MacDonald, 183–88. Grand Rapids: Eerdmans, 2009.

Nanos, Mark D., and Magnus Zetterholm, eds. *Paul within Judaism: Restoring the First-Century Context to the Apostle.* Minneapolis: Fortress, 2015.

Neusner, Jacob. *From Politics to Piety: The Emergence of Pharisaic Judaism.* New York: KTAV, 1979.

———. *An Introduction to Judaism: A Textbook & Reader.* Louisville: Westminster/John Knox, 1991.

———. *A Short History of Judaism: Three Meals, Three Epochs.* Minneapolis: Fortress, 1992.

Newman, Carey C., ed. *Jesus & the Restoration of Israel: A Critical Assessment of N. T. Wright's* Jesus and the Victory of God. Downers Grove: InterVarsity, 1999.

Newsom, Carol. *Songs of the Sabbath Sacrifice: A Critical Edition.* Atlanta: Scholars, 1985.

Novak, David. *Zionism and Judaism: A New Theory.* Cambridge: Cambridge University Press, 2015.

Oepke, Albrecht. "Apokathistēmi, Apokatastasis." In *Theological Dictionary of the New Testament, Vol. 1*, edited and translated by Geoffrey W. Bromiley, 387–93. Grand Rapids: Eerdmans, 1999.

Oliver, Isaac W. *Torah Praxis After 70 CE: Reading Matthew and Luke-Acts as Jewish Texts.* Tübingen: Mohr Siebeck, 2013.

Ottolenghi, Emanuele. "A National Home." In *Modern Judaism*, edited by Nicholas de Lange and Miri Freud-Kandel, 54–65. Oxford: Oxford University Press, 2005.

Parsons, Mikeal C., and Richard I. Pervo. *Rethinking the Unity of Luke and Acts.* Minneapolis: Fortress, 1993.

Pelikan, Jaroslav. *Acts.* Grand Rapids: Brazos, 2005.

Perrin, Nicholas. *Jesus the Temple.* Grand Rapids: Baker, 2010.

Pervo, Richard I. *Dating Acts: Between the Evangelists and the Apologists.* Santa Rosa, CA: Polebridge, 2006.

Pew Research Center. "Israel's Religiously Divided Society." 8 March 2016. http://www.pewforum.org/2016/03/08/israels-religiously-divided-society/.

Pitre, Brant. *Jesus, the Tribulation, and the End of the Exile: Restoration Eschatology and the Origin of the Atonement.* Grand Rapids: Baker Academic, 2005.

Puskas, Charles B. *The Conclusion of Luke-Acts: The Significance of Acts 28:16–31.* Eugene, OR: Pickwick, 2009.

Ravens, David. *Luke and the Restoration of Israel.* Sheffield, UK: Sheffied Academic Press, 1995.

Rice, Peter H. *Behold, Your House Is Left to You: The Theological and Narrative Place of the Jerusalem Temple in Luke's Gospel.* Eugene, OR: Pickwick, 2016.

Rudolph, David J. "Jesus and the Food Laws: A Reassessment of Mark 7:19b." *Evangelical Quarterly* 74.4 (2002) 291–311.

———. *A Jew to the Jews: Jewish Contours of Pauline Flexibility in 1 Corinthians 9:19–23. Second Edition.* Eugene, OR: Cascade, 2016.

———. "Messianic Judaism in Antiquity and in the Modern Era." In *Introduction to Messianic Judaism: Its Ecclesial Context and Biblical Foundations*, edited by David Rudolph and Joel Willitts, 21–36. Grand Rapids: Zondervan, 2013.

Sacks, Jonathan, ed. and trans. *Koren Siddur—Nusah Ashkenaz.* Jerusalem: Koren, 2009.

Salmeier, Michael A. *Restoring the Kingdom: The Role of God as the "Ordainer of Times and Seasons" in the Acts of the Apostles.* Eugene, OR: Pickwick, 2011.

Sanders, E. P. *The Historical Figure of Jesus.* New York: Penguin, 1993.

———. *Jesus and Judaism.* Philadelphia: Fortress, 1985.

Schiffman, Lawrence H. "The Importance of the Temple for Ancient Jews." In *Jesus and Temple: Textual and Archaeological Explorations*, edited by James H. Charlesworth, 75–93. Minneapolis: Fortress, 2014.

Scholem, Gershom. *Major Trends in Jewish Mysticism.* New York: Schocken, 1961.

———. *On Jews and Judaism in Crisis.* New York: Schocken, 1976.

Schürmann, Heinz. "Das Testament des Paulus für die Kirche." In *Traditionsgeschichtliche Untersuchungen zu den Synoptischen Evangelien*, 310–40. Düssseldorf: Patmos, 1968.

Schwartz, Seth. *Imperialism and Jewish Society 200 B.C.E. to 640 C.E.* Princeton: Princeton University Press, 2001.

Scott, James M., ed. *Exile: A Conversation with N.T. Wright.* Downers Grove, Il.: IVP Academic, 2017.

Shavit, Ari. *My Promised Land: The Triumph and Tragedy of Israel.* New York: Spiegel & Grau, 2013.

Smith, Dennis E., and Joseph B. Tyson, eds. *Acts and Christian Beginnings: The Acts Seminar Report.* Salem, OR: Polebridge, 2013.

Smith, Steve. *The Fate of the Jerusalem Temple in Luke-Acts: An Intertextual Approach to Jesus' Laments over Jerusalem and Stephen's Speech.* London: Bloomsbury T. & T. Clark, 2017.

Solovyov, Vladimir. *The Burning Bush: Writings on Jews and Judaism.* Translated by Gregory Yuri Glazov. Notre Dame, IN: University of Notre Dame Press, 2016.

Stone, Michael E., and Matthias Henze. *4 Ezra and 2 Baruch: Translations, Introductions, and Notes.* Minneapolis: Fortress, 2013.

Sulzbach, Carla. "The Fate of Jerusalem in *2 Baruch* and *4 Ezra*: From Earth to Heaven and Back?" In *Interpreting 4 Ezra and 2 Baruch*, edited by Gabriele Boccaccini and Jason M. Zurawski, 138–52. London: Bloomsbury T. & T. Clark, 2014.

Svartvik, Jesper. "Reading the Epistle to the Hebrews without Presupposing Supersessionism." In *Christ Jesus and the Jewish People Today: New Explorations of Theological Interrelationship*, edited by Philip A Cunningham, Joseph Sievers, Mary Boys, Hans Hermann Henrix, and Jesper Svartvik, 77–91. Grand Rapids: Eerdmans, 2011.

Tannehill, Robert C. *Luke.* Nashville: Abingdon, 1996.

———. *The Narrative Unity of Luke-Acts: A Literary Interpretation. Volume One: The Gospel of Luke.* Philadelphia: Fortress, 1986.

———. *The Narrative Unity of Luke-Acts: A Literary Interpretation. Volume Two: The Acts of the Apostles.* Minneapolis: Fortress, 1994.

———. *The Shape of Luke's Story.* Eugene, OR: Cascade, 2005.

Taylor, Justin. "Paul and the Jewish Leaders of Rome: Acts 28:17–31." In *Paul's Jewish Matrix*, edited by Thomas G. Casey and Justin Taylor, 311–26. Rome: Gregorian and Biblical Press, 2011.

Thiessen, Matthew. *Contesting Conversion: Genealogy, Circumcision, and Identity in Ancient Judaism and Christianity.* Oxford: Oxford University Press, 2011.

Tiede, David L. "Glory to Thy People Israel: Luke-Acts and the Jews." In *Luke-Acts and the Jewish People*, edited by Joseph B. Tyson, 21–34. Minneapolis: Augsburg, 1988.

———. *Prophecy and History in Luke-Acts.* Philadelphia: Fortress, 1980.

Tomson, Peter J. *'If this be from Heaven . . .': Jesus and the New Testament Authors in their Relationship to Judaism.* Sheffield, UK: Sheffield Academic, 2001.

———. *Paul and the Jewish Law: Halakha in the Letters of the Apostle to the Gentiles.* Minneapolis: Fortress, 1990.

Trobisch, David. *The First Edition of the New Testament.* Oxford: Oxford University Press, 2000.

Tyson, Joseph B. *Luke, Judaism, and the Scholars: Critical Approaches to Luke-Acts.* Columbia: University of South Carolina Press, 1999.

———. *Marcion and Luke-Acts: A Defining Struggle.* Columbia, SC: University of South Carolina Press, 2006.

———. "The Problem of Jewish Rejection in Acts." In *Luke-Acts and the Jewish People,* edited by Joseph B. Tyson, 124–37. Minneapolis: Augsburg, 1988.

Vall, Gregory. "'Man is the Land': The Sacramentality of the Land of Israel." In *John Paul II and the Jewish People: A Jewish-Christian Dialogue,* edited by David G. Dalin and Matthew Levering, 131–67. New York: Rowman & Littlefield, 2008.

Van Buren, Paul M. *A Theology of the Jewish-Christian Reality, Part I: Discerning the Way.* San Francisco: Harper & Row, 1980.

Wainwright, Arthur W. *Mysterious Apocalypse: Interpreting the Book of Revelation.* Nashville: Abingdon, 1993.

Walker, Peter W. L. *Jesus and the Holy City: New Testament Perspectives on Jerusalem.* Grand Rapids: Eerdmans, 1996.

Wall, Robert W. "The Acts of the Apostles." In *The New Interpreters Bible, Volume X,* 3–368. Nashville: Abingdon, 2002.

———. "A Canonical Approach to the Unity of Acts and Luke's Gospel." In *Rethinking the Unity and Reception of Luke and Acts,* edited by Andrew F. Gregory and C. Kavin Rowe, 172–91. Columbia, SC: University South Carolina Press, 2010.

Walters, Patricia. *The Assumed Authorial Unity of Luke and Acts: A Reassessment of the Evidence.* Cambridge: Cambridge University Press, 2009.

Weatherly, Jon A. *Jewish Responsibility for the Death of Jesus in Luke-Acts.* Sheffield, UK: Sheffield Academic Press, 1994.

Weinfeld, M. "Hillel and the Misunderstanding of Judaism in Modern Scholarship." In *Hillel and Jesus: Comparisons of Two Major Religious Leaders,* edited by James H. Charlesworth and Loren L. Johns, 56–70. Minneapolis: Fortress, 1997.

Wilken, Robert L. *The Land Called Holy: Palestine in Christian History and Thought.* New Haven: Yale University Press, 1992.

Williams, Jarvis J. *Maccabean Martyr Theology in Paul's Theology of Atonement: Did Martyr Theology Shape Paul's Conception of Jesus' Death?* Eugene, OR: Wipf & Stock, 2010.

Wilson, S. G. *Luke and the Law.* Cambridge: Cambridge University Press, 1983.

Witherington III, Ben. *The Acts of the Apostles: A Socio-Rhetorical Commentary.* Grand Rapids: Eerdmans, 1998.

Wright, N. T. *The Climax of the Covenant: Christ and the Law in Pauline Theology.* Minneapolis: Fortress, 1993.

———. *Jesus and the Victory of God.* Minneapolis: Fortress, 1996.

———. *The New Testament and the People of God.* London: SPCK, 1992.

———. *Paul and the Faithfulness of God.* 2 vols. London: SPCK, 2013.

———. *Paul: In Fresh Perspective.* Minneapolis: Fortress, 2005.

———. *The Resurrection of the Son of God*. London: SPCK, 2003.

———. *Surprised By Hope: Rethinking Heaven, the Resurrection, and the Mission of the Church*. New York: HarperCollins, 2008.

Wyschogrod, Michael. *Abraham's Promise: Judaism and Jewish-Christian Relations*. Edited by. R. Kendall Soulen. Grand Rapids: Eerdmans, 2004.

———. *The Body of Faith: God and the People Israel*. Northvale, NJ: Aronson, 1996.

———. "Incarnation." *Pro Ecclesia* 2 (1993) 210–17.

Yuval, Israel Jacob. *Two Nations in Your Womb: Perceptions of Jews and Christians in Late Antiquity and the Middle Ages*. Berkeley: University of California Press, 2006.

Index of Scripture and Ancient Texts

HEBREW BIBLE

NEW TESTAMENT

Luke (*continued*)

Acts (*continued*)

EARLY ECCLESIAL WRITINGS

Name Index

CPSIA information can be obtained
at www.ICGtesting.com
Printed in the USA
LVHW091342030520
654898LV00023B/415